Jane Freiman
DINNER PARTY

Also by Jane Freiman

THE ART OF FOOD PROCESSOR COOKING

Jane Freiman

DINNER PARTY

THE NEW ENTERTAINING

Photographs by Jerry Simpson

1817

HARPER & ROW, PUBLISHERS, NEW YORK

Grand Rapids, Philadelphia, St. Louis, San Francisco
London, Singapore, Sydney, Tokyo, Toronto

Material in this book has appeared in somewhat
different form in *Cuisine, Cook's, New York, The
Chicago Tribune, The Los Angeles Times, The San
Francisco Chronicle, The Seattle Post-Intelligencer,
The Toronto Star,* and *The Dallas Times-Herald.*

FIRST EDITION

DESIGNED BY JOEL AVIROM

LIBRARY OF CONGRESS CATALOG CARD NUMBER
89-45039
ISBN 0-06-016051-9

90 91 92 93 94 DT/RRD 10 9 8 7 6 5 4 3 2 1

For my mother, Harriet Ide Publicker,
who planted the seeds of this book so long ago

CONTENTS

PART ONE

The FIRST COURSE

PART TWO

DOUBLES

ACKNOWLEDGMENTS

No one writes a cookbook alone, and this book, written over the course of several years, was influenced by many people.

Culinary assistants become companions in the kitchen, and in Chicago, Brenda Newman made a significant contribution, while Lois Levine tested and retested with admirable patience and skill. In New York, Blair Verner brought her superb intellect and fine hand to many recipes, and Tracey Seaman tested accurately, skillfully, and with abundant good humor. Other friends and fine cooks, including Nancy Harris, Donna Daniels Gelb, my sister Bette Publicker, Nikki Eckert, Brooke Dojny, and Ruth Rothseid, were extremely generous with their time in offering advice, skills, and opinions. Julane Irvin-Ware deserves special thanks for giving the book its name.

I appreciate Harriet Wasserman's initial belief in this project, and thank my editor, Rick Kot, for his loyalty, diplomacy, and unwavering support. David Dolson will always deserve my gratitude for helping me create my newspaper column in which so many of these recipes originated. A special thank you also goes to Christopher Kimball, for my experience editing *Cook's* magazine, and to my attorney Jane Wald.

This book would not have materialized without the talents of photographer Jerry Simpson, designer Joel Avirom, and my stylist Marianne Rohrlich. I am enormously grateful also to Joseph Montebello for his generous support, to Rita Wolfson for her great eye and sensitivity, and to my agent Susan Lescher, for ever being the voice of reason.

Professional colleagues have been unstinting with their knowledge and time, particularly cheese expert Steve Jenkins, and the fruit and vegetable *doyenne* Elizabeth Schneider. In addition, chefs Simon Teng, Gabino

Sotelino, Gerard Rouillard, Daniel Boulud, Eberhard Müller, Brendan Walsh, Sally Darr, André Soltner, and Lidia Bastianich have generously shared their expertise and recipes.

Finally, there are friends who have been bulwarks through thick and thin: Pat Brown, Paula Wolfert, Patsy Perlman, Antoinette Castaldo, Jean and David Keh, Helene Kaye, Joan Kroll, Barry Goodman, Gael Greene, and Clark Wolf. Joe Allen deserves my gratitude for Paris and Cetona. Betsy Schultz—my friend and general partner in crime—has contributed so much time and energy to this project that it is nearly as much hers as mine. Plus a very special note of thanks to Bud, who has been my champion at every turn and whose contribution can never be Eclipsed.

Jane

Jane Freiman
New York City, April 1989

INTRODUCTION

Giving a dinner party is show business," one of my friends used to say. "You warm them up with the appetizer, keep them interested through the main course, then knock their socks off with dessert." An interesting theory, and one that certainly works for the "dinner" half of the equation.

However, defining the ingredients of a successful dinner does go beyond keeping everyone's attention focused on the food. Setting the scene, adjusting the menu to suit the occasion, and managing the myriad details that call for informed decisions about shopping, receiving guests, and expressing yourself and your taste are other very important aspects of the performance.

While the metaphor of show business may sound dramatic, it is particularly apt. When you host a dinner at home—however casual it may be —you are the principal player who can make or break the show. No matter how responsive your guests might be, they are still an audience.

For many people, having a dinner party is a natural expression of hospitality, a way of extending the family sphere. For others, it is a means of seeking approval or acceptance, a way to define personal style, or a process of finding a common point of identification with friends or acquaintances—or perhaps all of these things. But inviting someone into your home is ultimately an act of friendship, even when such an invitation may be extended for business purposes.

Personally, and in this book, I define a dinner party as a seated, or sit-down dinner. It is the way I entertain most comfortably, usually with four to ten guests, and I believe that it is the way a majority of us entertain at home on a frequent basis. A book dedicated exclusively to this subject seems overdue.

I have never been a caterer, nor have I worked as a restaurant chef. Cooking massive quantities of food and spending hours arranging platters are not skills that interest me. Large gatherings, buffets, and cocktail parties always seem to lack intimacy and specialness. I like to entertain on a smaller, less demanding scale.

During the past decade, I have given scores of dinners that I recorded in a special diary (an easy book to make using a three-ring binder; the plan is described on page 31). Leafing through those pages, it amazes me to see menus written completely in French, and appetizers such as artichoke bottoms with two mousses, chicken-liver custards with Sauce Béarnaise, or hot salmon mousse wrapped in sole fillets, sauced with sorrel-cream. Those dishes required days in the kitchen, and they were just the starters! Today, they would be served in restaurants—if at all.

I believe that we have entered a new era of home cooking that calls for simpler, but more sophisticated food, served in a straightforward manner. The best party meals are relaxed, eclectic, perhaps a little spicy, and always sensitively seasoned. Fresh ingredients, and recipes that either are relatively easy to make, or challenging and therefore worth the expense of leisure time, are key elements.

With a fast-paced life and a demanding, full-time career, my days are limited and I cannot spend as many hours in the kitchen as once seemed necessary. As a result, time-saving appliances—especially the food processor and the microwave—have become necessities, and these are integrated into my recipes.

Like so many people these days, I am health-conscious, and long ago I made a general switch from butter to olive oil for much of my cooking. I prefer grilled or barbecued foods to those that are sautéed or deep-fried, and a majority of the sauces I like to use with main courses are very light —even minimalistic. Still, foods such as savory tarts, certain vegetable dishes, and many desserts do require the luxury of butter, eggs, and cream, and these should never be banished from dinner parties, where guests often arrive in a mood to relax, splurge, and indulge.

If in the past my dinners tended to be French and formal, today they have a decidedly more casual style. I enjoy serving individual pizzas (which are fun to make) with a salad, and fresh fruit splashed with custard sauce, or a light meal based on pasta, such as Lemon-Garlic Capellini showered with colorful vegetable confetti, olive oil, and fresh basil.

When I need a substantial main course for an important dinner, I may turn to the majestic Bollito Misto—a succulent array of poached meats, poultry, and vegetables that is surprisingly full of flavor. If my guests are especially health-conscious, grilled fish with a zesty Citrus Salsa or just a thin glaze of Fresh Herb Butter is always right. Friends who love Asian food always enjoy the spice of grilled Shrimp and Scallops drizzled with a Thai-style peanut and serrano chile sauce. Each of these dishes is very different, yet they all accent an evening with dramatic culinary moments that help to make it memorable.

This book is divided into five main parts: the first course, doubles, the main course, accompaniments, and desserts. Recipes are grouped according to the role they play in a meal. If I want to serve a casual one-course meal, a heftier two courses, or even a full three-course menu, I know just where to start. The section called "doubles" is especially useful because these are recipes for pastas, pizzas, risottos, savory tarts, and hearty soups that can be served either as appetizers or light main courses.

Menus are, of course, an extremely important feature of any dinner party. My problem with set menus is that they tend to create, rather than solve, problems for me. If I find an appetizer I like, often the main course seems wrong. Sometimes the main course is appealing, but the dessert or the appetizer just won't work.

Perhaps that is why I was determined to do something different and practical, and extend the benefit of my menu-planning experience to others. On rough count, there are 165 different menus here that can be mixed and matched to accommodate a wide range of tastes and foods. I call these "flexible menus," and try to offer as many choices as possible.

Within many of the menus, there often are several different appetizer, accompaniment, and dessert suggestions. Although I do enjoy making pâtés, pasta doughs, breads, and desserts such as fruit tarts or ice creams, when I am pressed for time, I often purchase these foods, using the recipe suggestions as a guide. When I want to scale down a menu, it is easy to eliminate accompaniments, or even one course.

In this book, I also wanted to combine my experiences in—and out of—the kitchen. Virtually every chapter includes boxes that explain key cooking techniques and recipe issues, but as a food journalist, I write on many matters. It is unreasonable to expect everyone to know the difference between soy sauce and tamari, and when you are standing in a food store, trying to decide which one to buy, which goat cheese to use in a recipe, or how to tell the various chiles apart (which even some of the experts have difficulty remembering), having read information on key ingredients in advance helps to make those decisions easier.

Just as ingredients and recipes are artifacts of culture, the dynamics of any dinner party convey a great deal about what is going on in our minds, our homes, our lives, and in our world. It could be said that each occasion is like a play within a play that tells its own story about the way we want to live and eat—today.

PARTY PREPARATIONS

On My Own

Cooking and entertaining came quite naturally to me, perhaps because my mother ran a rambling house in southern California where cocktail or dinner guests were daily events.

Mother always liked to boast that *her* mother never bought a jar of mayonnaise—she always made her own. During my early years, she cooked and entertained in quite an adventuresome manner. One day after school we found live lobsters in the kitchen sink—Mother had them flown in from Maine, which my father thought was outrageous—but she was giving a dinner party. When we spotted the gold dishes on the kitchen counter, we knew that Soufflés Rothschild were not far behind (except that we hated them because they were vanilla and contained candied fruit).

I am fond of saying that I became the sous-chef at eighteen, but that is an exaggeration because by that time there was Bridgette to do the cooking, and I was most often conscripted to help Mother with the table—setting the bottom of each piece of cutlery exactly one thumb joint's distance from the edge—and arranging flowers.

I will never forget my first cooking lesson: making crepes for Mother's New Year's Eve crepes Suzette, which were always a flaming production in Nana's copper chafing dish, and which always prompted Dad to reminisce about Paris after the Liberation, when he frequented Maxim's and knew the venerable Louis Vaudable.

I suppose the seeds of this book were planted then, for when I moved from California to New York, I began giving dinners for friends. Once my repertoire was exhausted, I quite naturally turned to my cookbooks.

A colleague at the art gallery where I worked suggested trying some things from Julia Child's *Mastering the Art of French Cooking.* "If you follow the recipes exactly," she counseled, "you can't go wrong." I read the books, and decided to attempt the cheese soufflé. It flopped.

The next day, on a whim, I picked up the phone and called the late James Beard, who at the time ran the best cooking school in New York. To my surprise, Jim answered the phone himself.

"Mr. Beard," I said, "I need help. I want to take your cooking class."

In his best stage baritone, Jim replied, "I'm sorry, my dear, my classes are booked for five years."

"But I'll be too old by then," I wailed, making him roar with laughter. He let me sign up for the very next series, and when I look back on it today, I realize that those classes were a pivotal point in my life. Within a few years, I had left the art business to go into the food business.

Behind the Scenes

I share my mother's passion for fine dinnerware and beautiful flowers, and I enjoy letting menus give me cues for finding new accessories or looks for the table. But my greatest satisfaction comes from preparing something special for friends, gathering them in my home, then relaxing and enjoying their company over a good meal.

Unlike a restaurant, where each diner places his own order, guests at a dinner party are a captive audience who must eat what you serve. The challenge lies in creating a meal that suits the evening and the group, but does not make unreasonable demands on you.

My approach to menus is based on what I call "show business" logic: guests remember (1) the finale (dessert), (2) the first act (appetizer, if there is one), and then (3) the second act (main course). The exception to this rule is an unusual, spicy, or especially delicious main course such as Bollito Misto, Arizona Chicken with Corn Ragout, Veal Scallops Giardino, or Baked Curried Beef. However, I normally put my efforts into appetizers and desserts, and keep main courses relatively simple, so they appeal to everyone.

I begin planning with the main course and balance the menu around it. Try to visualize it as the center post of a seesaw, with the appetizer and desserts on each end. Then consider what is seasonally appropriate for accompaniments, and what will go best with the entrée from the standpoint of flavor and color. Starches such as potatoes, rice, pasta, or grains can anchor a particularly light meal, plus they are numerous and varied. Homemade breads are always delightful, although store-bought bread often will do. Check the first course to avoid repetitions.

Each recipe in this book is included in a menu. Complete menus appear in the doubles and main-course sections, and these can be followed or changed as necessary. Many of the menus are extensive, and may list more dishes than you wish to cook. Select what you need, and do not feel restricted—that would defeat the purpose of the book.

There is a wide range in difficulty among the menus, so it is a good idea to consult the preparation and cooking times indicated for each recipe. Often, recipe yields in the same menu will differ slightly. I never mind having an extra portion or two, particularly when I know I have invited hearty eaters. These discrepancies are not a problem. When there is a large variance in the number of servings, or if a recipe must be doubled, you will find notes regarding these adjustments.

THE MESSAGE OF THE MENU

Each menu sends a message. Cold lobsters with rice salad invoke a summer night on a screen porch, while pizzas, followed by ice cream, are informal and great for dinner in the kitchen. But whether a menu suggests a scene, has a seasonal bent, includes Oriental or Middle Eastern flavors, is classically French or Italian, or infused with an American spirit, it should demonstrate an inherent "food sense," or understanding of its roots.

Menu choices are important. Too many dishes with similar flavorings, textures, colors, or ingredients produce monotonous meals, while odd or disparate elements can blur the focus. I recall a dinner composed of all white foods: baked chicken, noodle pudding, bread and butter, and butter cookies. The hostess was terrified in the kitchen—that message came through loud and clear.

Try to vary the pacing and create highs and lows within each menu. A friend who has a dazzling personality and who has lived in France served the following meal: steamed asparagus with warm olive oil, followed by sliced lamb, a potato gratin, green salad and cheese, then flourless chocolate cake. What was the message? She is very conservative and the menu lacked pizzazz. A vinaigrette with a colorful garnish would have pepped up the asparagus. A broiled tomato half would have brightened the main course. The salad should have been omitted—in effect the asparagus served the same purpose—and a tart lemon, or other citrus dessert would have added a refreshing zing after the cheese.

On the other hand, certain ingredients can be repeated in menus. The best example is an "all fish" dinner (see page 268), which offers refinement and subtle differences in taste, as well as a sense of the unexpected.

Principles of Presentation

Serving styles have gone in and out of fashion throughout the century, but the tactical problems of getting food to the table for a sit-down dinner remain. Today, anything goes, but it is always helpful to have a definition of the various types of service in order to choose the one that suits you best.

Most Americans are familiar with family style, or *English Service.* Food is simply arranged on platters and served by the host or hostess, who passes the plates clockwise.

On the other hand, *Russian Service,* which has made a comeback, calls for a staff of one or two to pass platters, from which each guest helps himself. This became rather elaborate in days gone by, and often it is confused with *French Service,* which actually is what we now call a buffet.

Plate Service is the most modern method because it gives the cook maximum control over the way food looks when it emerges from the kitchen, and guests need not be concerned with passing or serving.

Plating also suggests a new contemporary standard—that first courses (particularly salads) and desserts, served on dinner plates, are as important as the main course. Since everyone owns ten-inch dinner plates, this is a convenient and practical way to serve at home.

There are good reasons for the shift. On salad and dessert plates, portions look smaller, and because the arrangements are often cramped, the food appears to be trivial. The very same portion seems more ample on a dinner plate, and the larger scale also helps to create a stunning effect.

A few of the one-dish meals in this book do require large platters, but unless I am putting things out on a buffet, I generally do not use them.

THE QUADRANTS OF THE PLATE

Beautiful plates, the kind that elicit immediate expressions of delight from guests, live in the eye and imagination of the cook. No one can really guarantee a lovely look, and two cooks arranging the same ingredients will often produce vastly different results.

Judgments about what looks artful or beautiful—as opposed to contrived or fussy—are always open to interpretation. Fortunately, this is an area where personal creativity and an artistic hand can take flight. The charm of plated food is its instant appeal and the effortless way it is served: people "eat" with their eyes before a morsel of food ever reaches their lips.

Most food is served on plates, or in bowls, which normally are circular or square. If you picture any plate divided into four quarters, or quadrants, you have a visual guide for arranging food. The rest is common sense plus a dash of geometry: the piece of food that occupies the greatest surface area is the most important element; move it around to find the best position. Working out combinations in the unoccupied space then becomes much easier.

For example, if a steak covers half the plate, there are two remaining quadrants in which accompaniments can be placed: balance the steak with medium-sized pieces of a colorful vegetable, and a starch. In contrast, a big baked potato would add little color, leave awkward space on the plate, or perhaps crowd the steak, making it look cumbersome.If a medium-size fish fillet and sauce occupies only a single zone, three areas are open for placement of vegetables, starch, a salad, and garnishes (or perhaps even bread).

Ladling a sauce (such as the Corn Ragout, page 192, or Bouillabaisse Sauce, page 228) over the entire surface of a plate will unify all of the elements from the standpoint of flavor and color. Often these presentations are self-contained, and accompaniments become unnecessary.

Placing round, square, triangular, or rectangular foods (timbales, slices of a terrine or sausage, fish fillets, veal scaloppine, chicken breasts, slices of cake, or scoops of ice cream) in the center of a plate automatically sets up a target or constellation arrangement—sauce and garnishes must be placed in the surrounding ring of space.

I always try to set aside a few minutes to experiment with plate setups, even if I must use raw food to help resolve questions about placement and garnish. If possible, I make a sample plate (the way restaurants do), cover it with plastic wrap, and keep it on the work surface for reference (a sketch, or Polaroids can be substituted).

Although plating suggestions are given in many of the recipes, here are some general points to consider:

■ Present main courses and accompaniments on a single plate. Separate dishes for accompaniments are burdensome to serve and clean up.

■ It is best to mix a variety of food sizes, shapes, quantities, and colors. Too many large or small pieces, too much of the same color, an overabundance of one element, or too little of another are common mistakes.

■ Be generous with portions, and try to avoid the "blank canvas" problem —most of the plate should be covered, otherwise portions look stretched. When I see two or three little baby vegetables huddled on the side of a plate, it looks like the cook ran short. Use fresh herbs, watercress, or other garnishes lavishly.

■ Symmetry equals formality. Asymmetrical or abstract arrangements will appear to be casual, even when they are carefully conceived.

Setting the Stage

For one of my entertaining articles in *New York* magazine, we featured menus composed of favorite dishes from the city's best restaurants, and decided to photograph them in settings that would complement the food.

For an American harvest lunch with a first course of Wild Mushroom Soup (see page 49), a main course of duck, and Crème Brulée (page 426) for dessert, the photography department selected a very traditional dining room in a rural New Jersey home.

Within two hours, however, the stylist had removed all the furniture (including the rug), and replaced it with antiques. Even the wall sconces had been changed. The table was set with fabulous china and crystal, and the accessories included silver stirrup cups in the shape of animal heads. The floral arrangement included fall leaves and holly, which set off the lemon-colored walls perfectly.

The food looked fabulous. Muddy-colored mushroom soup looked sumptuous in the exquisite Meissen soup bowls. The duck looked sensational, and a closeup of the Crème Brulée made my mouth water. The menu and the setting were perfectly in tune—the "look" was just right. It only required impeccable taste, unlimited access to extraordinary furniture and tableware, a sixteen-hour day, and a team of ten!

Part of the professional challenge of creating photographs that appear in magazines is bringing wonderful ideas to life. But the process is even more rewarding when I put my creativity to use on a more modest scale, and set the stage for giving a dinner at home.

Creating a "look" or style for your table will help give any dinner party a distinct mood. Even in my very urban home, I can set a tone for meals that range from country-casual, to sophisticated-modern, or traditional-formal, keeping each compatible with my basic decor and color scheme. Although well designed, a majority of the dishes and glassware I regularly use are not prohibitively expensive, and acquiring them has been a pleasurable, ongoing process.

My mother is something of an expert on tableware, and she always collected odd and old pieces. Our joint outings to antique and secondhand stores, flea markets, auctions, and house sales spurred my interest in finding lovely and unusual things, and she first made me aware of the infinite range of possibilities. When it comes to setting a table these days, there are guidelines, but no firm rules.

TABLEWARE

The old way of purchasing dinnerware was to buy two sets: "good" and "everyday" dishes, with a prescribed number of pieces. Once I realized that I rarely used cups and saucers (there are mugs or *café au lait* cups for the morning coffee, and *demitasses* for after dinner), butter plates, or rimless soup (cereal) bowls, I began to purchase groups of plates or bowls in compatible patterns and colors (beyond basic white), which boosted my ability to change the look of my table.

I still prefer to buy groups of dishes rather than sets, and rarely is the same dish color or pattern used throughout a meal. Sometimes, I set the table with dishes in alternating colors, especially pastels, which gives it a very lively look. Most often, I buy a dozen ten-inch dinner plates (although I have as few as six in some patterns). A dozen clear glass salad plates help fill in the gaps.

When it comes to glassware, I stick to basics because these items tend to break easily (the stems of wine glasses inevitably snap on the top rack of the dishwasher). Tulip-shaped white- and red-wine glasses are a good all-purpose choice, and to vary the look of the table, I have a collection of old stemware in many colors and patterns, but all of the same, elegant height (eight inches). Wine glasses should be set counterclockwise beginning at the top right of the dinner plate (just above the knife). Use a glass for each wine, plus a water glass if you like. If you plan to serve champagne or sparkling wine, it is nice to do so in tall, narrow flutes (the wide bowls of *coupe* champagne glasses, however, are lovely for presenting sorbets, granitas, and ice cream).

CUTLERY AND ACCESSORIES

Cutlery with detailing on the front and back will give you the option of setting the table American style, with silver face-up, or European style, with forks and spoons turned over. Oversize dessert and soup spoons, as well as knives with a blade, rather than a serrated cutting edge, are gracious features.

Table settings can range from a soup spoon and dessert fork for a one-dish soup meal to elaborate multicourse layouts. I regularly place forks to the left of the dinner plate, and knives (with blades turned towards the plate) and spoons to the right. However, the logic behind cutlery placement is to use it from the outside in, on each side, so that when the main course is finished, only the dessert cutlery remains.

Both a fork and knife may be set for a salad containing elements that must be cut (rather than speared). A dessert fork and spoon can be placed on the table, above the place setting (the spoon goes above the fork with the bowl facing left; the tines of the fork face right) to help avoid the clatter of cutlery falling off dessert plates.

Individual salts and peppers—shakers or grinders—go above the dessert service at each place, above the butter plate, or directly above the fork, at the left side of a place setting.

TABLE COVERINGS AND FLOWERS

For years, I scoured country antique stores for table linens of all types—cloths, mats, runners, and doilies. Lately, shawls, throws, quilts, or even an attractive piece of leather have become popular to soften a table without completely covering the surface. If the table is impervious to heat (as many are these days), it may need no covering at all. Chargers or place plates, which are put beneath dinner plates, and remain between courses, are stylish to use for formal occasions.

One hostess I know found a seamstress to sew round, welted, floor-length chintz tablecloths, with matching napkins. The flowered cloths gave her dining room the dressy (but not formal) look she liked. The same draped affect looks more formal in pale solid colors, or fabrics such as moiré, and quite casual in linen, cotton duck, or gingham. Provided the "cloth" is long enough, it can be anchored around the central table post with a length of twisted cord or rope to cover up a table if need be.

When it comes to placing napkins, virtually anything goes. They may be put on top of the empty plate, or to the left of the forks. I dislike placing them under silverware, which tends to tumble as napkins are removed, nor do I stuff them into a water or wine glass, since I like to fill glasses in advance of serving dinner.

Restaurants fold napkins in various elaborate ways, but at home I like to keep them in simple rectangles, or chevrons (take a napkin folded into a triangle, tuck two sides under, and arrange the point facing the table edge), which fit neatly on a plate.

Flowers, flowering plants, herbs, and greenery always add charm to a table, and I try to keep an eye out for inexpensive containers. In addition to baskets, small glass fish bowls make good cut-flowers vases, and stubby water glasses work for individual bouquets at each place. A series of slender laboratory beakers holding exotic flowers such as freesia or ranunculus look great in a row down the center of a long table—particularly when tied with colorful ribbons.

When I worked on the food for the Shelley Long movie *Hello Again,* the set decorator made lovely centerpieces by using a great trick: he spiked terra-cotta pots of ivy with orchid sprays that were held in place by water capsules hidden in the soil. For most of us, however, the basic trick in setting the stage is creating a style of our own.

Elements of Cheer

"The best host is not he who spends the most money to entertain his guests, but he who takes the most intelligent interest in their welfare and makes sure that they will have a good time, something good to drink, something that is both good and new, if possible," wrote the great gastronome André Simon. How wise he was.

COCKTAILS

"Something to drink?" is likely the first phrase a guest will hear from his host after the initial "hello"; indeed, it is a ritual welcome throughout the Western world. I am certain that statisticians who chart societal and historical trends could predict the future based on what people drink before dinner and how beverage preferences change over the decades.

For a time, hardly anyone asked for a mixed drink during the cocktail hour. Many of my guests preferred wine, and many still do, although there seems to be a definite resurgence in the drinking of spirits.

Good-quality dry white wine such as California chardonnay, French muscadet, and reds such as Beaujolais, California merlot, or pinot noir, are predinner staples in my home. Let me add a modest bottle of California or French champagne to that list, since a few guests are bound to prefer it to white wine.

In addition to wine, I stock a basic bar that consists of ten bottles:

- Scotch

- Vodka (I keep a small bottle on hand in the freezer for the die-hard vodka drinkers and a second at room temperature)

- Gin

- Bourbon

- Dry and sweet vermouths (in half bottles, since this does not hold very well)

- Dark rum

- Campari

- Cassis

- Dry sherry

Keep club soda, sparkling water or salt-free seltzer, tonic water, colas, and diet drinks on hand in the pantry. Orange juice, grapefruit juice, cranberry juice, lemons and limes, maraschino cherries, cocktail onions, and green olives can be added to the shopping list if they are needed for mixed drinks.

Barring a guest who requests a Pink Squirrel, a Sake Martini, or a Side Car before dinner, this bar will satisfy most cocktail demands, including a Salty Dog, Sea Breeze, or a Bourbon Manhattan, which one of my friends always requests with two maraschino cherries.

If you wish to offer cordials after dinner, stock half bottles of Kahlua, Amaretto, Frangelico, Peach Schnapps, and Grand Marnier, plus Cognac, Armagnac, Framboise or Poire Williams, and vintage port.

Since the chemistry of mixed drinks eludes me, I keep a bartender's guide as a reference. So if a guest asks for a "Kojak" (bourbon, passion-fruit juice, pineapple juice, and dark rum, stirred with a lollipop), I know better than to turn on the TV!

SERVING WINE WITH DINNER

My first sip of great red wine took place in a cooking class in the south of France, where I had gone to study with Richard Olney, the gifted cook, writer, and teacher. The wine, a 1961 Château Figeac (St. Emilion), was like velvet, and quite unlike anything I had ever tasted back home in California. I recognized at once that a fascinating new world had opened to me, and that drinking and tasting fine wine would become a lifelong pursuit. I am still learning about wine, each time I open a bottle.

The problem with pairing food and wine is that there are few real guidelines. Selections are always a matter of taste, and the sheer numbers of wines pose limitless choices. Price variations also affect one's choice of wines. Considering the large number of menus and variations included in this book, I could not hope to make specific suggestions.

When I purchase wine for a specific menu, I rely on the judgment of a knowledgeable wine seller to guide my selections. If I have wine on hand, I have a general idea of whether or not it will go with the food I am planning to prepare; when in doubt, I taste it in advance.

The old rule is, of course, that white wines are best with light foods and white meats such as fish and poultry, and that red wine is generally served with red meat. The corollary is that white wine is served before red wine. But certain menus call for a red wine to be served first, and I know any number of light reds that are delicious with fish.

When in doubt, be less concerned with what is "right" or "wrong" than with finding a wine you like. Here are some general tips for serving wine with the various foods and menus you will encounter in this book.

Soup: Fruit soups, those made from acidic vegetables such as tomatoes, or those flavored with powerful spices, are difficult to match with white wine; it may be necessary to omit wine with these appetizers. Light cream soups are good with dry white table wines, chenin blanc, or muscadet. Hearty, or slightly sweet, soups can be served with dry sherry.

Appetizer Salads: The same kind of white wines that accompany cream soups can be served successfully with composed vegetable salads and mozzarella salads, even though they include vinaigrettes. Since wine and vinegar are enemies, I do not serve wine with a tossed green salad.

Terrines: Fish and vegetable terrines are good partners for virtually any type of dry white wine, including California chardonnays and white Burgundies. Meat terrines and homemade sausage are marvelous with Beaujolais, Côtes du Rhône, or California zinfandel.

Savory Tarts, Pizzas, and Calzones: White or red table wines, or light-bodied vintage wines can accompany any of these dishes. Be guided by the ingredients used in fillings, toppings, and sauces.

Pasta and Risotto: Many of these starch-based dishes can be served with white or red table or vintage wines, although very acidic dry white wines can be difficult to drink with tomato sauces. Risottos containing fish and vegetables are best with whites, while those containing meats are better with reds.

One-Dish Meals: Beer is always a safe bet for foods based on Mexican seasonings, hot chiles, or curry. If wine is a "must," choose a very fruity Beaujolais or zinfandel. Meat dishes are excellent with full-bodied red wines (Italian brunello or Barolo), a good French Burgundy, a hearty Morgon, or a medium-bodied California cabernet sauvignon. I like California fumé blanc or beer with Oriental-flavored foods.

Grills: Unless there is a particularly assertive sauce or seasoning, grilled foods will stand up beautifully to very fine white and red wines, including full-bodied California chardonnays, some of the lesser white Burgundies, Italian red wines, a few French red Burgundies, and minor French Bordeaux wines.

Classic Main Courses: Here is the place to consider serving top-quality white Burgundies, particularly with very refined fish dishes that do not contain a great deal of acid. Poultry and meats—particularly lamb and beef—are excellent partners for great red Bordeaux wines.

Desserts: Try to avoid serving any wine (particularly Champagne) with chocolate desserts—follow these with coffee. Fruit tarts, and many of the plainer fruit desserts (but not ice creams or ices) are superb with French, American, or German dessert wines.

Choosing Cheese

I become mesmerized in cheese shops—particularly in France and Italy, where the sight and smells envelop me. When I am faced with such a dazzling array, I always have trouble deciding which cheese to buy, and often have the childish desire to take home one of each.

Like wine, a huge variety of cheese from many parts of the world is available in our markets. Remembering the myriad names and tastes is an endless process of education.

Originally, I shopped by trial and error from supermarket dairy cases, naughtily opening unfamiliar wrappers and boxes and sniffing to be sure that each cheese was sweet smelling, and not ammoniated, over the hill, or previously frozen. The telltale signs of freezing are considerable quantities of liquid left in the wrappers.

Now I am spoiled by good cheese shops where I can taste each cheese before making my selection to be sure it is in good keeping or eating condition. When I get home, I unwrap the cheeses, blot them dry with paper toweling, rewrap them in plastic, and set them aside at room temperature until serving time, so they will be in top condition.

A cheese platter can be a great menu booster, and it adds a distinctive, European note of sophistication to a menu when it is served between the main course and dessert. A grand assortment following the main course also can be accompanied by a green salad or fruit. Or, accompanied simply by fruit, cheese can stand in for dessert.

Cheeses are classified in several ways: by type of milk (cow's, goat's, sheep's, or blends), rind, curd, aroma, or texture. The selection on a cheese platter can be limited to two or three types, or aggrandized to include six to eight (see chart on page 30). Leftovers can be used in pasta sauces and for salad garnishes.

Balancing a variety of textures, flavors, and types of cheese is the key to composing a platter. I start by purchasing a soft, fresh American, French, or Italian goat cheese (see page 141). Then I add a soft-ripened cheese or one of the ultrarich double- (at least 60 percent butterfat) or triple-crème (at least 75 percent butterfat) cow's-milk cheeses (such as Camembert, Brie, Explorateur, Paglietta, or creamy Saga or Bavarian Blue).

Next I add a semisoft cheese (Port Salut, Muenster, cinder-streaked Morbier, Monterey Jack, or Taleggio) or a blue cheese (Maytag blue, Pipo Crem', or Stilton); if the platter is elaborate it can include both.

I finish by selecting a semifirm, firm, or hard (grating) cheese (Gruyère or Cantal, American raw-milk cheddar, or Parmigiano-Reggiano).

Before serving cheese, unwrap each piece and put it on a flat leaf-lined basket (leaves can be purchased from florists or picked—but be sure they are nontoxic), a serving platter, a cheese board, or another flat surface such as a marble slab. Cover the entire platter with plastic wrap, since cheese dries out quickly, and set it aside at room temperature.

I serve a separate knife with each cheese and prefer to eat it with

French or whole-wheat bread, French Dinner Rolls (page 360), or Black Pepper Brioche (page 352), rather than crackers. Great red wine is another perfect partner for cheese, particularly if there is any left over from the main course.

Playwright Clifton Fadiman gave a sensational definition of cheese when he called it "milk's leap towards immortality." Indeed, eating a piece of cheese at the peak of perfection is a sensation that can last a lifetime.

CHEESE-PLATTER GUIDE

The chart on page 30 lists cheeses commonly found in shops by texture and country of origin, so that you will find it easy to compose a platter. Since many countries make cheeses that are similar to each other in flavor or style, it should be easy to make substitutions if the cheese you wish to purchase is not available.

All cheeses listed are made from cow's milk, unless otherwise indicated. Butterfat content is listed for soft-ripened cheeses, as well as the double and triple crèmes.

	FRENCH	AMERICAN	ITALIAN	OTHER
FRESH	Brebis Frais (sheep) Chèvre Frais (goat) Fromage Frais Petit-Suisse (60–75%)	Cream Cheese (35%) Fresh Goat Cheese Fromage Blanc (Vt., Pa.) Goat Curd (N.Y.) Mozzarella Quark	Caprini (cow/goat) Mascarpone (70%) Mozzarella (40%) Mozzarella di Bufala (50%) Ricotta (30%)	
SOFT/ CREAMY	Boursault (75%) Boursin (70–75%) Brie (50%, 60%, 70%) Brillat-Savarin (75%) Camembert (45%) Caprice des Dieux (60%)	Brie Craigston Camembert	Bella Epoque Crescenza/Stracchino Paglietta/Pagliola/ Paglierina Toma Carmagnola Toma della Valcuvia	
SEMI- SOFT	Chaumes Beaumont Livarot Morbier Muenster Pont-l'Evêque Reblochon Saint-Paulin	Monterey Jack Muenster	Bel Paese Caciotta (cow/sheep) Scamorza (smoked/ white) Taleggio	Royal Tilsit (Switz.) Gouda (Holland) Havarti (Denmark) Oka (Canada) Mareosous (Belgium)
SEMI- FIRM, FIRM, OR HARD	Beaufort Cantal Comté Laguiole	Asiago Cheddar Pennsylvania Swiss	Asiago Caciocavallo Fontina d'Aosta Grana Padano Montasio Parmigiano-Reggiano Provolone Ragusano	Appenzeller (Switz.) Cheddar (Eng.) Cheshire (Eng.) Emmentaler (Switz.) Gruyère (Switz.) Raclette (Switz.)
GOAT	Banon Chabichou Crottin de Chauvignol Picodon Pouligny Sainte-Maure Selles-sur-Cher Valençay	Chenel (Cal.) Coach (N.Y.) Goat Folks (N.Y.) Brier Run (W. Va.) Kilmoyer (Mass.)	Caprella Fagottino di Capra	
SHEEP	Esbareich Laruns Ossau-Iraty/Pyrénées		Sicilian Pepato Pecorino Romano Pecorino Sardo Pecorino Toscana Incanestrato Canestrato	Feta (Bulgaria/ Greece) Kasseri (Greece) Manchego (Spain)
BLUE	Bleu d'Auvergne Bleu de Bresse Fourme d'Ambert Bleu de Gex Pipo Crem' Roquefort (Sheep)	Dietrich Goat Blue Maytag Blue Minnesota Blue Oregon Blue Saga Blue (60%)	Gorgonzola Dolce Gorgonzola Naturale Torta Zola	Blue Castello (70%, Denmark) Danablu (50%, Denmark) Stilton (Eng.)

THE DINNER PARTY DIARY

For many years, I have kept a record of my dinner party menus in a special binder that also includes an organization sheet for each party, table plans, and checklists for the bar and dining room.

This book also serves as a central filing system for often-used recipes, plus names, addresses, and telephone numbers of the markets and stores where I regularly order food. I realized that it was also a good place to store the myriad scraps of paper with household sources, notes, and warranty cards that I had previously stuffed into envelopes, secured with rubber bands, and promptly misplaced.

The dinner party diary can be used in two ways: as a recipe notebook file, and as a household organizer. The recipe-file section consists of 14 divider tabs. The organizer section consists of 4 divider tabs. I set up my book with the organizer section in front; however, you may prefer to place it after the recipes.

Once you have the binder, dividers, and plastic zipper-lock pockets (optional), a little artwork will be required to draw the twelve special pages. A sample of each page follows. The list below indicates where each page belongs in the book and how many copies are required. Plain 8½ × 11-inch paper can be used to create each page. Draw lines with a black marker, print the headings by hand, and use a copy machine to make as many as you need. If you are giving the book as a gift, however, you may want to have an "instant" printer create professional-looking pages.

If you need table templates, cut them out of index cards. Use a full 3 × 5 card for a rectangular table. Cut out a 3 × 3-inch square for a square table, and a 2½-inch round for a round table. Templates are used to trace the shape of your table on the party sheet.

It is not absolutely necessary to print recipe blanks, although I find them convenient to have.

Menu cards are available at many stationery stores. It is stylish to display a menu for an important dinner, and the cards and placecards can be stored in a plastic pouch.

ORGANIZING THE DIARY

PARTY PLANS

Party Sheet—25 copies
Seating and Notes—25 copies
Organizer—50 copies
Bar Checklist—10 copies

SERVICES

Sources—2 copies of each page
Emergency—2 copies
Repairs—2 copies

HOUSEHOLD

Inventory—2 copies of each page

MISCELLANEOUS

This is a catchall section where plastic pouches can be used to store table templates, menu cards, placecards, coupons, appliance warranty cards, and tax receipts.

RECIPE FILE

RECIPE INDEX	MEAT	VEGETABLES
HORS D'OEUVRES	PASTA	GRAINS & LEGUMES
APPETIZERS	FISH	BREADS
SOUP	POULTRY	DESSERTS
SALAD		CANDY

Recipe Index—10 copies
Recipe Blanks—50 copies

PARTY SHEET

DATE			
TIME—COCKTAILS: DINNER: LUNCH: BRUNCH: OTHER:			
GUESTS	TOTAL	PHONE	MENU AND RECIPE SOURCES
			WINES AND LIQUORS
ALLERGIES/FOOD PREFERENCES			FLOWERS AND TABLE ACCESSORIES

SEATING AND NOTES

SEATING PLAN	CATERER OR FOLLOW UP NOTES
	SPECIAL EXPENSES

HELP NAME		PHONE

ORGANIZER

DATE		
DO/CLEAN/ORDER	SHOPPING LIST	THINGS TO PURCHASE/RENT

BAR CHECKLIST

	ON HAND	REORDER	CHECK	BUY
SCOTCH				
VODKA				
GIN				
BOURBON				
CANADIAN WHISKEY				
RUM				
DRY VERMOUTH				
SWEET VERMOUTH				
CAMPARI				
TEQUILA				
CASSIS				
SHERRY				
BEER				
LIQUEURS				
WHITE WINE				
RED WINE				
CHAMPAGNE				
MINERAL WATER				
MIXERS				
JUICE				

BAR EQUIPMENT

BAR CLOTH		ICE		LEMONS	
SERVING TRAY		ICE BUCKET		ORANGES	
DOILIES		TONGS		LIMES	
CUTTING BOARD		JIGGER		CHERRIES	
OPENER		SPOON		OLIVES	
BOTTLE CAPS		PARING KNIFE		ONIONS	
COASTERS		STRAINER		NUTS	
COCKTAIL SHAKER		ZESTER			
CORKSCREW		PITCHER			
NAPKINS					

SOURCES

NAME	ADDRESS	TELEPHONE
MARKETS		
BUTCHER		
FISH		
WINES/LIQUORS		
FLORISTS		
BAKERIES		

SOURCES

NAME	ADDRESS	TELEPHONE
RENTALS		
DEPARTMENT STORES		
COOKWARE STORES		
CATERERS		
CLEANERS & LAUNDRY		
BARTENDERS		
SERVING STAFF		
OTHER		

EMERGENCY

NAME	ADDRESS	TELEPHONE
DOCTORS/DENTIST		
POLICE/FIRE DEPT./AMBULANCE		
PARAMEDICS		
HOSPITALS		
SCHOOLS		
OFFICE		
FAMILY		
UTILITIES		

REPAIRS

APPLIANCE & MODEL NO.	DEALER CONTACT	TELEPHONE

INVENTORY

ITEM	DESCRIPTION	NUMBER
DISHES		
FLATWARE		
SERVING PIECES		

INVENTORY

ITEM	DESCRIPTION	NUMBER
PLATTERS		
CASSEROLES		
GLASSWARE		
TRAYS		
TABLE LINEN		

RECIPE INDEX

NAME	SOURCE	PAGE

RECIPE BLANKS

RECIPE NAME:	
SOURCE:	
YIELD:	
OVEN TEMPERATURE:	

INGREDIENTS	PROCEDURE

PART ONE

The FIRST COURSE

SAVORY TRADITION: SOUP

FRESH STARTS: APPETIZER SALADS

TOURS DE FORCE: TERRINES

SAVORY TRADITION: SOUP

n my small collection of old cookbooks is a salmon-colored volume with a cracked spine and yellowed pages that have become brittle with age. Published by Editions Urbain-Dubois, in 1926, as a popular guide for middle-class French homemakers, the book, called *School for Cooks,* sets forth what was the wisdom of the time on the subject of soup:

"For large dinners, as well as small ones, soup should be prepared with the greatest care, for as it is served at the beginning, it automatically influences the diners' opinion of the meal it precedes. . . ."

More than half a century later, despite enormous cultural changes, the basic role of soup as a first course remains unaltered. With its universal appeal, a bowl of homemade soup begins almost any meal on a traditional note. When in doubt, I begin with soup.

THE NEW SOUPS

A surprising number of soups have remained in vogue over the past fifty years. The pages of *School for Cooks* include familiar classics—onion, sorrel, and tomato-leek, as well as asparagus, oyster, and carrot purees. Certainly the role of soup in a meal has changed very little, although some recipes have passed from fashion as a result of the decreasing availability of ingredients such as tortoise or sturgeon. Others have moved out of the modern repertoire as a result of changes in taste.

The most profound differences have occurred in the realm of soup-making methods, in the reduction in the amount of butter, flour, eggs, and cream used, and in the intensity of flavor we have come to expect.

Appliances such as the food processor have played an indisputable role in expediting preparation. The ability to chop an onion in twenty seconds, or puree a quart of vegetables and broth in less than three minutes, is an unparalleled advantage.

Overly rich soups—those thickened with a great deal of flour, egg yolks, or a superabundance of cream—are no longer considered healthful. While judicious quantities of cream or half-and-half are acceptable additions, the ratio of fat to lean flavorings has declined.

These days, no one wants to sit at a dinner party and guess whether a pale green soup is made from cucumber or artichoke. Flavor must go POW! in your mouth, which is why we are turning to soups infused with the earthiness of porcini or shiitake mushrooms, the anise perfume of fennel, the sweetness of golden squash, or the bite of curry. To be thoroughly satisfying, soup must have an intense character that is derived from primary ingredients, and be accented by supplementary flavors such as herbs, aromatic vegetables, or spices.

Despite this new set of standards, no gourmet secrets or special skills are required here. Perhaps there are a few ingredients that require a trip to a specialty store, and many cooks will want to take the time and trouble to make their own stock (page 165).

A handful of soups made from fresh ingredients and naturally thickened with fruit or vegetable purees offer maximum flavor with minimal effort; one requires no cooking. Simmering time for others is reduced by mincing, slicing, or shredding ingredients prior to cooking them in stock.

A number of these soups are enriched with half-and-half or cream. I prefer to eliminate excess fat by skipping the step of cooking the basic vegetable ingredients in butter or oil. Sautéing does moderate flavor, but the direct taste of raw ingredients is best captured by simmering them in stock, particularly if they will eventually be pureed.

While the legacy of the French *nouvelle cuisine* can be disputed, the emphasis it placed on presentation and garnishing cannot be denied. A small amount of clever garnishing with fresh herbs or vegetables, presenting two complementary soups in the same bowl, or ladling soup into bowls that help create a special look and mood are options to consider. Setting forth a savory tradition has never seemed easier.

———————

PAPAYA-MELON SOUP

———————

SCALLOP BISQUE

———————

CREAM OF WATERCRESS SOUP

———————

TOMATO SOUP WITH GARLIC AND BASIL

———————

SWEET POTATO AND APPLE BISQUE

———————

SHRIMP AND CORN CHOWDER

———————

Stock in Trade

———————

CURRIED VICHYSSOISE

———————

WILD MUSHROOM SOUP

———————

WILD AND BROWN RICE SOUP

———————

Serving Strategies

———————

TWO SOUPS IN ONE BOWL

———————

Graceful Garnishing

———————

PAPAYA-MELON SOUP

Papayas are pear-shaped tropical fruits with golden flesh, a lovely fragrance, and an exotic flavor. Their texture is similar to that of an avocado when ripe. Together with cantaloupe, they make a refreshing soup that requires absolutely no cooking. Handle a papaya as you would a cantaloupe, by peeling off the thin skin and removing the firm, black seeds with a spoon.

Chill the papayas thoroughly before beginning. If you wish to make and serve the soup immediately, the cold papayas will help chill the soup. If making ahead, chilling will help prevent the natural starch present in the fruit from causing the soup mixture to thicken to a custardlike consistency in the refrigerator. In any event, plan to serve the soup within an hour or two after making it.

FLEXIBLE MENU SUGGESTIONS

Papaya-Melon Soup is an ideal introduction to a spicy menu that continues with Curry Noodles with Scallops and Cilantro (page 146), One-Side Grilled Fish with Avocado Vinaigrette (pages 216 and 224), Grilled Ceviche (page 231), Mesquite-Grilled Cornish Hens (page 240), Yogurt and Spice-Marinated Leg of Lamb (page 252), or Curry-Rubbed Chicken (page 278). *Makes 4 servings*

PREPARATION: 15 MINUTES

½ pound ripe papaya, peeled, seeded, cubed
¾ cup chilled Chicken Stock (page 165)
¾ to 1 cup ice water
1 ripe cantaloupe (2½ pounds), halved, seeded, peeled, cubed
¼ cup plain yogurt
3 tablespoons whipping cream
2½ teaspoons lemon juice
3 to 4 tablespoons port wine
Granulated sugar (optional)

1. In a food processor fitted with the metal blade, process papaya with half the stock and water until completely pureed, about 1 minute; transfer to a bowl and refrigerate.

2. Process melon cubes, pouring remaining stock and water into the processor. Add yogurt, cream, lemon juice, and 3 tablespoons port; process until smooth.

3. Add contents of processor to mixing bowl and stir thoroughly. Adjust seasoning with an additional tablespoon of port wine and a small amount of granulated sugar if melon is bland. Serve immediately. (Can refrigerate up to 2 hours; check consistency and adjust texture with ice water before reseasoning and serving.)

SCALLOP BISQUE

At first glance you might think this recipe could not possibly work, but—quite magically—it does. The secret is that scallops cook at such a low temperature (about 125 to 130 degrees) that the addition of boiling hot stock actually cooks them in the machine.

This bisque is as delicate as the scallops, and it will vary according to their quality. On the East coast, scallop season runs from November through May. The small, ivory-colored bay scallops harvested from New England to the Carolinas give this soup the best flavor. Calico scallops from the Gulf of Mexico lack the sweetness of bay scallops, although they can be used. The large, mild-flavored sea scallops harvested from both the Atlantic and Pacific coasts often reach the market more slowly than their smaller cousins. When available later in the season, they will make a silky-textured bisque provided you trim away the remnants of fibrous membrane from the side of each scallop.

Since scallops vary, it is important to fortify the soup with a good, rich stock. Curry also plays an interesting role as a flavor enhancer without actually asserting itself.

FLEXIBLE MENU SUGGESTIONS

Serve this bisque before Four-Vegetable Tart (page 100) or Szechwan Pepper Ribeyes (page 288). *Makes 4 servings*

PREPARATION: 10 MINUTES
COOKING: 8 MINUTES

2 medium garlic cloves, peeled
4 small shallots, peeled
2 medium tomatoes, peeled, cored, seeded
2 cups fish or Chicken Stock (page 165)
½ cup dry white wine
¼ teaspoon curry powder
½ pound fresh scallops, rinsed, trimmed
1 cup whipping cream
1 tablespoon Cognac or brandy
Salt and ground white pepper
Snipped chives or dill, for garnish

1. Mince garlic and shallots and put them in a medium saucepan. In a food processor, puree tomatoes, then add them to the mixture in the pan. Stir in stock, wine, and curry powder. Cover and simmer until garlic and shallots soften, about 8 minutes.

2. Process scallops until smoothly pureed.

3. Uncover and heat stock mixture to boiling. Slowly add the cream. When the mixture boils again, immediately turn on processor and very slowly pour 2 cups (about half) of the cream mixture into the processor. (All the liquid can be added if the machine has a large capacity.)

4. If necessary, transfer half the soup from the processor to a large bowl. Continue processing, adding remaining hot cream mixture to the machine.

5. Return all of the bisque to the saucepan. Stir in Cognac; salt and pepper to taste. Reheat gently; do not allow soup to boil. Garnish with chives and serve immediately.

CREAM OF WATERCRESS SOUP

Like scallops, minced watercress or sorrel leaves are delicate enough to be "cooked" right in the food processor by the addition of boiling hot liquid. However, since the leaves lack body, potato is used as a thickener; it cooks quickly because it has been pureed into the stock.

FLEXIBLE MENU SUGGESTIONS

Cream of Watercress Soup makes a good, fast appetizer before Smoked-Salmon Pizzas (page 110). For menus based on Soy-Marinated or Herb-Rubbed Chicken (pages 238 and 278), the soup can be prepared and eaten while the chicken cooks. *Makes 4 to 6 servings*

PREPARATION: 15 MINUTES
COOKING: 15 MINUTES

4 medium scallions, trimmed, cut in 1-inch
* lengths*
1 medium potato (½ pound), peeled, cubed
1 quart Chicken Stock (page 165)
½ cup milk
1½ cups firmly packed watercress or sorrel
* leaves*
Salt and ground white pepper
Several dashes hot red pepper sauce
⅓ cup whipping cream

1. In a food processor fitted with the metal blade, coarsely chop scallions and potato. Then puree vegetables by adding 1 cup chicken stock through food chute. Transfer mixture to large saucepan with remaining stock and milk. Cover and simmer until vegetables are completely soft, about 15 minutes.

2. Process watercress (or sorrel) with ¼ teaspoon salt, ⅛ teaspoon pepper, and a dash of pepper sauce until minced.

3. Uncover and heat stock mixture to boiling. Slowly add the cream. When mixture boils again and foam begins to rise, immedi-

ately turn on processor and, with the machine running, very slowly pour 2 cups (about half) of the boiling cream mixture into the processor. (All the liquid can be added if the machine has a large capacity.)

4. If necessary, transfer half the soup from the processor to a large bowl. Continue processing, adding remaining hot cream mixture to the machine.

5. Return all the soup mixture to the saucepan. Adjust seasoning. Reheat gently and serve immediately. (Or, set aside for several hours; reheat slowly without simmering.)

TOMATO SOUP WITH GARLIC AND BASIL

Ripe plum tomatoes, minced garlic, and fresh basil leaves are elements of a soup that delivers maximum flavor with minimal calories—about 100 per serving. If you adore garlic, feel free to adjust the amount to suit your taste.

FLEXIBLE MENU SUGGESTIONS

The soup is an excellent appetizer for a light menu based on Onion and Chèvre Tart (page 104), Sausage and Artichoke Pizzas (page 108), Mushroom Pizzas on Prosciutto Crust (page 114), Pasta with Broccoli Raab (page 134), One-Side Grilled Fish with Winter Pesto (pages 216 and 227), or Herb-Rubbed Chicken (page 278). *Makes 6 to 8 servings*

PREPARATION: 10 MINUTES
COOKING: 50 MINUTES

5 pounds fresh ripe plum tomatoes
3 to 4 medium garlic cloves, peeled
2 tablespoons olive oil or Herbed Oil
  (page 73)
5 cups Chicken Stock (page 165)
Salt and ground black pepper
6 to 8 fresh basil leaves

1. Heat 3 quarts water to boiling in a 6- to 8-quart soup kettle or Dutch oven. Add tomatoes and cook on high heat until water boils again. Drain tomatoes in colander, discard water, and return kettle to stove.

2. Mince the garlic and transfer to the kettle. Stir in oil and cook over low heat for 2 to 3 minutes, without browning.

3. Puree the tomatoes in a food processor in three or four batches. Transfer puree to medium-mesh strainer set over the soup kettle. Press puree through strainer until only a dry paste composed of peel and seeds remains; discard peels and seeds.

4. Stir tomato mixture in the kettle and cook, uncovered, over medium heat for 10 minutes. Add stock. Put cover ajar and slowly simmer for 40 minutes. Adjust seasoning with ¼ teaspoon salt and ½ teaspoon pepper.

5. To serve hot, chop and swirl in basil just before serving. (Or, cool and refrigerate soup until chilled. Adjust seasoning and swirl chopped basil into cold soup.)

SWEET POTATO AND APPLE BISQUE

The term *bisque* is usually applied to classical French shellfish-and-cream soups. During the eighteenth century, bisques also were made from game or poultry, although it is not clear how or why this term came to be applied to these soups. One possible explanation is that bisques have a color identical to unglazed pottery that has just emerged from the kiln after a first, or "bisque," firing. While a vegetable bisque has little root in tradition, by virtue of its color and texture, this tangy soup merits inclusion in that category.

FLEXIBLE MENU SUGGESTIONS

The annual appearance of fresh sweet potatoes makes this a great fall soup (keep it in mind at Thanksgiving) and a wonderful foil for piquant Yogurt and Spice-Marinated Lamb (page 252), Leg of Lamb with Malay Seasoning (page 250), Chili-Rubbed Chicken (page 278), or Pork with Port Wine Sauce (page 292). It will also nicely balance the blue-cheese flavor of Saga and Watercress Tart (page 106). *Makes 6 servings*

PREPARATION: 15 MINUTES
COOKING: 50 MINUTES

1 medium garlic clove, peeled
1 medium onion, peeled
White part of 1 large leek, rinsed
2 medium tart green apples, peeled and cored
1 pound sweet potatoes or yams, peeled
1 quart Chicken Stock (page 165)
2½ cups half-and-half
1 to 2 teaspoons lemon juice, or more to taste
Salt and ground white pepper
Hot red pepper sauce
Whipping Cream
Snipped chives

1. Mince garlic. Coarsely chop the onion and leek, and transfer vegetables to a 4-quart soup kettle. Coarsely chop apples and add to the soup kettle.

2. Slice sweet potatoes and add to the kettle. Stir in the stock. Cover and simmer until vegetables are very soft, about 40 minutes.

3. In a food processor fitted with the metal blade, process 2 cups cooked soup mixture until smooth. With the motor on, slowly add ½ cup half-and-half and process until smooth; transfer mixture to a bowl.

4. Repeat step 3 with remaining soup mixture. Stir in remaining half-and-half. (Can cool, cover, and refrigerate overnight.)

5. At serving time, heat soup. Stir in lemon juice, salt, pepper, and hot pepper sauce to taste. Ladle soup into bowls and garnish by drizzling cream in an abstract pattern over surface. Sprinkle chives over cream garnish. Serve immediately.

SHRIMP AND CORN CHOWDER

A great summer soup need not be served cold. A piping hot bowl of creamy New England–style seafood chowder makes a luxurious first course for a cool evening.

One way to add depth of flavor to this very simple chowder is to swirl in a small quantity of shellfish butter made from the shrimp shells. Whole shrimp is rarely available, but if you can find it, by all means add the heads along with tail shells to the butter mixture.

A few notes on substitutions. Lobster may be substituted for the shrimp (cut the lobster shells into small pieces with heavy-duty scissors, and sauté them gently with the butter in a medium skillet). Scallops also can be used, but the soup will be extremely delicate. Substitute six tablespoons of Fresh Herb Butter (page 219) or Tomato Butter (page 220) for the Shrimp Butter in the recipe.

FLEXIBLE MENU SUGGESTIONS

Since much summer cookery takes place outdoors, you may want to complete a menu with Mesquite-Grilled Cornish Hens (page 240) accompanied by Quinoa Tabbouleh (page 330), and Ultra-Fudge Brownies (page 395) with fresh cherries.

An alternate main course would be Sage-Rubbed Veal Chops (page 242) served with a red-and-yellow tomato salad tossed with My Favorite Vinaigrette (page 72) and followed by Mixed Berry Cobbler (page 420) or fresh berries with Chocolate Madeleines (page 394).

Herb-Rubbed Chicken (page 278) cooked indoors, or outside on the grill, is a third option. Present the chicken with a green salad dressed with Lemon and Basil Vinaigrette (page 74), and consider Chocolate-Walnut Linzer Torte made with homemade peach jam (page 376) for dessert. *Makes 6 to 8 servings*

PREPARATION: 20 MINUTES
COOKING: 25 TO 30 MINUTES

SHRIMP BUTTER

Shrimp shells (below)
¼ pound unsalted butter

CHOWDER

1 medium garlic clove, peeled
1 medium onion, peeled and cubed
1 stalk celery, cut in 1-inch pieces
2 medium potatoes, peeled and halved
*   lengthwise*
3 ears fresh corn, husked and rinsed
2 cups half-and-half
2 cups milk
1¼ pounds raw shrimp, shelled, rinsed, and
*   deveined (shells reserved)*
Salt
Hot red pepper sauce

1. For the shrimp butter, put the shrimp shells in the container of a food processor fitted with the metal blade and process until chopped. Heat the butter to bubbling and slowly pour it into the machine with the motor on. Let mixture stand for 5 minutes, then strain through a fine sieve, mashing shells as firmly as possible to extract all liquid. Set the shrimp butter aside to cool (can cool, wrap, and refrigerate butter for several hours, or overnight).

2. For the chowder, mince the garlic and coarsely chop the onion and celery. Transfer vegetables to a 4-quart soup kettle or Dutch oven; set aside. Slice potatoes and add to the kettle with 4 tablespoons shrimp butter. Remove corn kernels from the cobs; add kernels to the kettle. Stir over low heat until vegetables soften slightly, about 8 minutes.

3. Add half-and-half and milk to the soup mixture. Heat to simmering, then cook over low heat until potatoes are softened, about 10 to 15 minutes. Quarter each shrimp and stir the pieces into the soup. Simmer slowly for 5 minutes. Stir in remaining shrimp butter, ¾ teaspoon salt, and several dashes hot pepper sauce. Adjust seasoning to taste and serve immediately.

STOCK IN TRADE

The very best soups are made with homemade stock (page 165), particularly one low in salt, which permits you to adjust seasoning to the perfect pitch. But, practically speaking, it may not always be possible to take the time to make stock, and not everyone has freezer space to keep it on hand. Commerical canned broth (I use the terms *broth* and *stock* interchangeably here although the two are slightly different) has been marketed in America since just after the turn of the century, and it is a viable alternative.

At least two canned stock brands—Health Valley and Pritikin—are low in sodium, and I always prefer to use these for soups, stews, and risottos.

Many other canned broths have a high sodium content; so high, in fact, that often it is unnecessary to add any salt to a finished soup. If you use canned stock, skim off any fat from the surface and dilute it as follows:

For 2 cups: add ⅓ cup cold water to each 13¾-ounce can of broth.

For 2 quarts: remove fat from one large (1 quart 14 ounces) can of broth. Add 2 cups cold water.

Unless you are using homemade or low-sodium stock or broth, cook the soup *completely* and taste it before adding any of the salt specified in the recipe.

CURRIED VICHYSSOISE

If someone were to create a set of Trivial Pursuit food questions, a very tricky one might read: "In which city was the cold leek and potato soup called *vichyssoise* first served?" Many people would guess Paris, or the town of Vichy. But they would be wrong. Although it bears a French name, vichyssoise was created in New York City by Louis Diat, the celebrated French chef of the 1930s and '40s, whose original recipe appears in *Cooking à la Ritz* (Lippincott, 1941).

This variation on his classic is enhanced by curry, which expands the possibilities for using the soup in menus. When selecting curry powder (see box, page 147), choose one that contains no salt or MSG.

FLEXIBLE MENU SUGGESTIONS

Compatible main-course choices include Shrimp and Scallops with Chile-Peanut Sauce (page 232), Grilled Ceviche (page 231), Cold Chicken-Poached Lobster (page 270), Yogurt and Spice-Marinated Leg of Lamb (page 252), or Pork with Port Wine Sauce (page 292).
Makes 8 to 10 servings

PREPARATION: 15 MINUTES
COOKING: 50 MINUTES
CHILLING: 2 TO 24 HOURS

1 medium garlic clove, peeled
1 medium onion, peeled
White part of 1 large leek, rinsed
1 quart Chicken Stock (page 165)
1 to 1½ tablespoons curry powder, depending
  on strength
1½ pounds russet potatoes, peeled
2 cups half-and-half
2 teaspoons lemon juice
Salt and ground white pepper
Hot red pepper sauce
4 teaspoons minced chives

1. Mince the garlic, onion, and leek, and transfer to a 4-quart soup kettle. Add stock and curry powder. Heat to boiling, cover, and simmer 6 to 8 minutes.

2. Shred potatoes and transfer to a large strainer or colander. Rinse shreds thoroughly with cold water to remove excess starch. Drain, then add potatoes to simmering liquid in the kettle and cook until vegetables are very soft, about 40 minutes.

3. Insert the metal blade in a food processor. Puree 2 cups hot cooked soup mixture until smooth, about 30 seconds. With motor on, pour in 1 cup half-and-half and process until smooth. Transfer mixture to large bowl.

4. Repeat step 3 until all the cooked soup ingredients are pureed and mixed with the half-and-half. Stir soup well and refrigerate until thoroughly chilled (can refrigerate overnight).

5. At serving time, season chilled soup with lemon juice, salt, pepper, and hot red pepper sauce to taste. Garnish with chives and serve chilled.

WILD MUSHROOM SOUP

The most intense mushroom flavor I know comes from boletes, those meaty wild fungi known as *cèpes* in France and *porcini* in Italy. Cèpes are also found in northern California and the Pacific Northwest. On this side of the Atlantic, these mushrooms are most commonly purchased in dried form, with the precious brittle slivers sealed in cellophane envelopes.

Dried mushrooms (available in specialty food stores) require a soak in boiling water or stock to partially reconstitute them. Since they are expensive, be sure to save the soaking liquid for use in the soup. Strain it carefully to remove the sand that always clings to the slices.

FLEXIBLE MENU SUGGESTIONS

Given its assertive flavor, this soup is best suited to menus based on substantial dishes. Follow it with Capretto with Lemon and Rosemary (page 246), Veal Scallops Giardino (page 284), Roasted Duck with Apples and Campari (page 289), Szechwan Pepper Ribeyes (page 288), or Cognac-Marinated Beef Fillet (page 298). *Makes 8 to 10 servings*

PREPARATION: 30 MINUTES
COOKING: ABOUT 1 HOUR

*1 package (2 ounces) imported dried cèpe or
  porcini mushrooms*
1 medium garlic clove, peeled
4 medium onions, peeled
2 large leeks, trimmed
¾ pound fresh mushrooms, rinsed
3½ cups Chicken Stock (page 165)
2½ cups half-and-half
Salt and ground white pepper
Chopped chives (optional)
Thin mushroom slices (optional)

1. Put dried mushrooms and 3 cups of water in a medium saucepan. Cover and simmer for 3 minutes. Uncover and remove mushrooms with a slotted spoon; reserve. Strain the liquid through a paper-towel-lined sieve. Return mushroom liquid to the saucepan and simmer until it is reduced to 1 cup. Rinse mushrooms well to remove any sand that clings, and pat them dry.

2. Mince the garlic and finely chop the onions, leeks, and fresh mushrooms. Transfer the vegetables to a 6-quart soup kettle.

3. Stir chicken stock, the dried mushrooms, and their reduced liquid into the kettle. Heat to boiling, cover, and simmer until vegetables are completely softened, about 40 minutes.

4. With the metal blade inserted in a food processor, puree 2 cups of the mushroom mixture until smooth, then add ½ cup of half-and-half. Repeat to puree all the soup mixture, then stir in remaining half-and-half. Return all the soup to the kettle and heat to boiling. Adjust seasoning with salt and pepper. Garnish with chives or mushroom slices and serve immediately. (Can cool, cover, and refrigerate soup overnight; reheat to simmering before garnishing.)

Adapted from a recipe of chef Sally Darr, La Tulipe restaurant, New York.

WILD AND BROWN RICE SOUP

The nutlike flavors of wild rice and long-grain brown rice are fully captured by this thick, sherry-laced soup, which is unusual and particularly hearty.

Wild rice is the seed of indigenous American aquatic marsh grass that is hand-gathered in the northern U.S. and southern Canada. There are two varieties: the extra-long "lakes" and the shorter "paddy" wild rice. Each is cured and parched, or toasted, after harvesting to enhance its flavor and prolong shelf life.

The lovely taupe color of long-grain brown rice comes from layers of the rice bran, which is left intact after the outer hull has been removed. (Both the hull and bran are removed from white rice.) Both grains are higher in calories, fiber, protein, and vitamins than processed white rice, and must be thoroughly cooked before pureeing for soup.

FLEXIBLE MENU SUGGESTIONS

When served as a first course, this soup does double duty since it eliminates the need for serving starch with a main course such as Yogurt and Spice-Marinated Leg of Lamb (page 252), One-Side Grilled Fish with Fresh Herb Butter (pages 216 and 219), Halibut with Warm Vinaigrette (page 268), Veal Scallops with Black Olive Gremolada (page 286), or Cognac-Marinated Beef Fillet (page 298). *Makes 8 servings*

PREPARATION: 20 MINUTES
COOKING: 1½ HOURS

White part of 1 large leek, trimmed
1½ tablespoons unsalted butter
¾ cup wild rice, rinsed, drained
½ cup brown rice, rinsed, drained
2 quarts Chicken Stock (page 165)
1 pound medium tomatoes, cored, peeled,
  seeded (or 1 cup drained, seeded canned
  Italian plum tomatoes)
1 cup half-and-half
1 cup milk
Salt and ground black pepper
1½ tablespoons dry sherry
Several dashes hot red pepper sauce

1. Coarsely chop the leek and transfer it to a 4-quart soup kettle. Add butter, wild rice, and brown rice. Stir over low heat for about 5 minutes. Add 1 quart of the stock; heat to boiling.

2. Use a food processor fitted with the metal blade to puree the tomatoes; add them to the soup kettle. Cover and simmer until rices are very soft and nearly all liquid is absorbed, about 1 to 1½ hours.

3. Combine remaining stock with half-and-half and milk. Process 1½ cups of rice mixture, while slowly adding 2 cups of the stock mixture. Process 1 minute longer. Transfer

pureed mixture to a bowl and repeat to process remaining rice and stock mixtures. The soup will have a slightly grainy texture. (Can cool, cover, and refrigerate 24 hours.)

4. Return pureed soup to the kettle and heat to simmering. Add ¾ teaspoon salt, ⅛ teaspoon pepper, sherry, and hot red pepper sauce. Adjust seasoning to taste and serve immediately.

SERVING STRATEGIES

Vibrantly colored soups, those with a variety of ingredients, or earthy purees that otherwise might seem relatively unattractive look wonderful in rimmed bowls, since the rim acts as a frame and helps to focus the eye. The wide mouths of the bowls also provide maximum surface area for garnishing. The drawback is that rimmed bowls seem dressier than rimless (cereal) bowls, which should be used if you are striving for a casual look.

A liner plate placed under each bowl allows you to serve bowls filled with hot liquid gracefully. Use a salad plate beneath rimless bowls, and a 10-inch dinner plate beneath rimmed bowls. The plate gives guests a place to put the spoon when they have finished eating, and helps to protect the table as well. Though it sounds prissy, consider placing a doily beneath each bowl for a very practical reason: to prevent it from slipping on the plate.

Don't overlook the possibility of making "natural" soup bowls from hollowed-out cabbages, pumpkins, or even sturdy loaves of bread. Setting soup at each place before guests are seated (especially in edible containers) creates a pretty scene and eliminates last-minute fussing.

If soup is to be served at table, or from a serving cart or sideboard, anything from a knockout tureen to the simplicity of a giant glass fish bowl is suitable as a container. Even an attractive kitchen pot can be used, although I like to give pots a clean kitchen-towel "necktie" to cover up drips. If you don't mind guests in the kitchen, leave a pot of soup on the stove and put bowls or mugs nearby so people can help themselves.

A note about spoons: tradition dictates that cream soups are eaten with round soup spoons, while others are sipped from oval soup spoons which, in America, measure 7½ inches in length. From a practical standpoint, these distinctions are outdated, since most standard five-piece cutlery place settings come with oval soup spoons—the round spoons must be ordered separately. Anything really goes. In fact, the most practical utensil for most soups is the European tablespoon. It has a large oval bowl, measures 8¼ inches in length, and has been adopted as the utensil of choice in many restaurants.

TWO SOUPS IN ONE BOWL

Nestling two different soups of contrasting colors and compatible flavors into one bowl is a stunning presentation reminiscent of the Chinese concept of yin-yang—the complementary pairing of moon and sun; female and male.

Here the savory fennel-leek soup sets off the sweet butternut squash puree. The two look and taste wonderful together, and each has sufficient body to maintain its own space as the soups are poured simultaneously into a single bowl.

Providing you work from light to dark, ingredients for vegetable soups, or the purees for Three-Vegetable Terrine (page 83), can be cooked and processed without rinsing out the food-processor container. Stray bits of vegetables left in the processor from the pureed fennel-leek mixture, for example, are simply absorbed by the darker squash puree. This same principle can be applied to chopping raw soup components.

FLEXIBLE MENU SUGGESTIONS

The soups yield a large number of servings, and you will have leftovers regardless of the main course in a menu. Good choices include Capretto with Lemon and Rosemary (page 246), Pork with Port Wine Sauce (page 292), Garlic-Roasted Leg of Lamb (page 295), or Cognac-Marinated Beef Fillet (page 298). Either of the soups may, of course, be served individually in menus, including Yogurt and Spice-Marinated Leg of Lamb (page 252) and Veal Scallops Giardino (page 284). *Makes 12 servings*

PREPARATION: 35 MINUTES
COOKING: 1 HOUR

FENNEL-LEEK SOUP

1 pound celery, trimmed
1 pound bulb fennel, cored, trimmed
White part of 2 medium leeks, rinsed
4 tablespoons butter
1 medium garlic clove, peeled
½ pound potatoes, peeled
1 quart Chicken Stock (page 165)
¾ cup half-and-half
1 teaspoon lemon juice
Salt and ground white pepper
Hot red pepper sauce

BUTTERNUT SQUASH SOUP

4 pounds (2 medium) butternut squash,
  halved, peeled, seeded
1 medium garlic clove, peeled
White part of 1 large leek, rinsed
1 medium onion, peeled
1 quart Chicken Stock (page 165)
½ cup half-and-half
Salt and ground white pepper
Hot red pepper sauce
Fennel fronds (optional)

1. For the fennel-leek soup, slice the celery, fennel, and leek. Melt butter in a 4- to 6-quart soup kettle. Add the vegetables and the whole garlic clove. Stir over medium heat until vegetables soften, about 15 minutes.

Slice potatoes and add to the kettle. Stir in the stock, cover, and simmer until vegetables are softened, about 40 minutes.

2. Puree the fennel soup mixture in 2-cup batches until smooth. Return puree to soup kettle and stir in half-and-half, lemon juice, ¼ teaspoon each salt and pepper, and hot red pepper sauce to taste. (Can cool, cover, and refrigerate overnight.)

3. For the squash soup, shred the squash and transfer it to a separate 4- to 6-quart soup kettle. Mince the garlic, finely chop the leek and onions, then add them to the soup kettle. Stir in the stock, cover, and simmer until vegetables are completely softened, about 40 minutes.

4. Puree the squash soup mixture in 2-cup batches until smooth. Return puree to its separate kettle and stir in half-and-half, ¼ teaspoon each salt and pepper, and hot red pepper sauce. Adjust seasoning. (Can cool, cover, and refrigerate overnight.)

5. Reheat soups to simmering. Use two measuring cups and, working from the opposite sides of each bowl, simultaneously pour ½ cup of each soup into each bowl. Do not mix soups together. Garnish with fennel fronds.

GRACEFUL GARNISHING

Thin soup can be garnished with small herb sprigs or a sprinkling of fresh-snipped or minced herbs (or dried herbs minced with parsley leaves), which will float on the surface.

Thick soups often will support a slick of cream that can be spooned decoratively on the surface. Pour it in a dot, or make an abstract pattern by holding the flat blade of a knife over the bowl and slowly pouring cream onto the blade.

Make a cream spiral (beginning at the center and working outwards), or pour it in a ring. Leave the ring plain, or create a sunburst pattern by using the tip of a paring knife to push the cream ring out toward the bowl rim at equal intervals.

A spoonful of sour cream, crème fraîche, or yogurt can be spooned or piped onto a soup that is dense enough to support its weight.

Chopped herbs, edible flowers, or slices of ingredients (cooked or raw) are other good soup garnishes.

FRESH STARTS:
APPETIZER SALADS

sing the praises of salads that were the dinner companions of my youth. I can hardly remember a meal that did not begin with greens mixed in some combination with raw vegetables, topped with a crunch of croutons, and tossed with a delicious dressing.

As a native of southern California, I always took the contents of a salad bowl for granted. Local restaurants regularly featured a garlicky Caesar salad, with crinkly ribs of romaine, and a meaty chef salad. Classic cobb salad, with its complement of chopped bacon, tomato, avocado, egg, and chicken, was practically invented in my backyard.

Today, salads have become glamorous opening acts and more refined than ever before. Even the simplest tossed salads sport mixtures of greens and herbs that create a play of texture, flavor, and color when tossed with light dressings made from European olive oil, plus vinegars infused with fruits, herbs, aromatic vegetables, or cross-cultural flavorings such as ginger, soy sauce, or sake.

In terms of ingredients, salads have become showcases for an international galaxy of lettuces, field greens, vegetables, and herbs from the gardens of France, Italy, Mexico, Central America, and Asia. Greens are grown smaller and picked younger. Novelties such as mâche (French corn salad), radicchio *rosso* (Italian red Verona chicory), peppery Japanese daikon (radish) sprouts, and exotic mushrooms are becoming popular and widely appreciated both for their visual and gustatory contributions.

For some time, restaurants have romanced appetizer salads by using them as a launching pad for new ingredients, and paid closer attention to their presentation. Now is the time to make the same shift at home, where we need to be comfortable with preparing something more than the traditional "good for you" salad.

Composed salads, which are also called "arranged" or "plated," since ingredients are arranged on the plates by the cook, add wonderful life to the beginning of a meal. Signaling the presence of an artistic hand and a keen palate, they can be occasions for indulgence with the addition of a luxurious garnish such as caviar, lustrous morsels of shellfish, a variety of colorful baby vegetables or edible flowers, or small game birds that add their precious juices to the dressing.

These appetizer salads have moved out of the perennial bowl and onto dinner plates, where they look stylish and important. The days of serving them on traditional "salad" plates, which minimize their impact, are past.

Spinach Salad with Caviar and Chives could not be easier to make and assemble, but when it is served on a dinner plate, it takes on an ineffable glamor that totally belies its simplicity. The same is true of the colorful Avocado, Grapefruit, and Seafood Salad. Even the traditional Mozzarella, Tomato, and Olive Salad can be elaborated on a dinner plate merely by purchasing large balls of mozzarella cheese and selecting big tomatoes that will produce slices to match.

As they set the stage at the beginning of a meal, salads should always be lovely to behold, substantial enough to arouse the appetite, yet not so filling that they destroy an interest in the main course. Let your imagination be your guide. This handful of recipes can provide a variety of menu options and serve as a fresh base for creative departures.

AVOCADO, GRAPEFRUIT, AND SEAFOOD SALAD

BEET-SALAD MIMOSA

SPINACH SALAD WITH CAVIAR AND CHIVES

Salad Style

CHIVE VINAIGRETTE

MOZZARELLA, TOMATO, AND OLIVE SALAD

ANCHOVY-LEMON OIL

OIL-MARINATED OLIVES

Mozzarella—Culture and Curds

HOT MOZZARELLA SALAD

MIXED LETTUCES WITH SHRIMP AND GINGER-LIME VINAIGRETTE

GINGER-LIME VINAIGRETTE

Weeds and Seeds

LETTUCE, RADICCHIO, AND FENNEL SALAD

Salads, Seriously

―――――――

MY FAVORITE VINAIGRETTE

―――――――

HERBED OIL

―――――――

LEMON-BASIL VINAIGRETTE

―――――――

Liquid Gold

―――――――

From Vinegar to Vinaigrette

―――――――

HAZELNUT VINAIGRETTE

―――――――

SHERRY-WALNUT VINAIGRETTE

―――――――

DILL DRESSING

―――――――

AVOCADO, GRAPEFRUIT, AND SEAFOOD SALAD

A pink-and-green pinwheel of avocado and grapefruit wedges, garnished with seafood, is set against an herbaceous background of Chive Vinaigrette in this colorful salad, which is simple and very light.

Plan to shop ahead for avocados, which may require three to five days of ripening from the hard-as-a-stone texture normally found in markets to a perfect, soft consistency. I also like to marinate cooked scallops (or shrimp) in vinaigrette for an hour or two.

FLEXIBLE MENU SUGGESTIONS

Follow the salad with Mesquite-Grilled Cornish Hens (page 240), Yogurt and Spice-Marinated Leg of Lamb (page 252), Chili and Garlic-Rubbed Flank Steak (page 245), Jalapeño and Jack Cheese Sausages (page 256), Leg of Lamb with Malay or Oriental Seasoning (pages 250 and 251), Chili-Rubbed Chicken (page 278), or Cognac-Marinated Beef Fillet (page 298).
Makes 6 servings

PREPARATION: 25 MINUTES
COOKING: 5 MINUTES

½ pound sea scallops (or raw peeled shrimp)
2 large pink or ruby red grapefruits, peeled
Chive Vinaigrette (page 61)
2 ripe avocados (½ pound each)

1. Put scallops or shrimp in a steamer basket (page 317). Cover and steam just until the color turns, about 3 to 4 minutes. Do not overcook. Uncover and rinse with cold water to cool. Drain on paper toweling and refrigerate until chilled. Slice each scallop crosswise into four or five "coins" (or leave shrimps whole).

2. With a sharp knife, trim grapefruit as necessary to remove all of the white outer membrane. Cut out grapefruit segments on each side of interior membranes, taking care to keep sections whole. Cover and refrigerate grapefruit sections (discard membrane).

3. Make Chive Vinaigrette and keep at room temperature.

4. Peel and halve avocados lengthwise, remove the pits, and rinse each half in cold running water. Working gently, cut avocado halves lengthwise to make twenty-four half-moon slices, each about ¼-inch thick.

5. To assemble salads, put four grapefruit segments on a dinner plate in a pinwheel pattern. Put four avocado slices between the grapefruit segments. Arrange five or six scallop slices (or whole shrimp) in the center, to cover the point where tips of grapefruit and avocado segments meet. (Can wrap and refrigerate 4 hours.)

6. Stir vinaigrette well and gently spoon 2 to 3 tablespoons into the empty spaces on each plate. Serve immediately.

Inspired by a recipe of Ambria restaurant, Chicago.

BEET-SALAD MIMOSA

The word *mimosa* refers to minced hard-cooked eggs which resemble dainty yellow flowers of the same name. The bright contrast of the crimson beets, pale yellow eggs, and light green lettuce leaves makes for a salad that is visually exciting despite its simplicity.

Like Spinach Salad with Caviar and Chives, this can be arranged in several ways. My preference is to give it a symmetrical, Art Deco look by centering the beets on each lettuce leaf and putting the egg alongside. Whatever the arrangement, spoon the dressing into the lettuce cup, around the beets, so the color of the eggs remains bright.

FLEXIBLE MENU SUGGESTIONS

The classic combination of beets and dill is great for a menu that continues with Cold Chicken-Poached Lobster (page 270) or Cognac-Marinated Beef Fillet (page 298). Alternately, serve the salad before Smoked-Salmon Pizzas (page 110), Mesquite-Grilled Cornish Hens (page 240), Sage-Rubbed Veal Chops (page 242), or Herb-Rubbed Chicken (page 278). *Makes 6 servings*

PREPARATION: 20 MINUTES
COOKING: 25 MINUTES

2 pounds fresh beets, rinsed, trimmed
Dill Dressing (page 79)
3 hard-cooked eggs, peeled
1 head Boston lettuce, rinsed and cored

1. Halve or cut beets into large pieces of roughly equal size and put them in a vegetable steamer basket (page 317). Cover and steam until beets are tender when pierced with the tip of a sharp knife, about 20 to 25 minutes (begin testing after 15 minutes, as timing varies with size). Transfer beets to paper toweling to drain; cool, peel, but do not rinse. (Can wrap in plastic and refrigerate overnight.)

2. Make Dill Dressing and set aside at room temperature.

3. Shred the beets. (Can wrap and refrigerate up to 4 hours.) Finely chop the eggs; cover and set aside for garnish.

4. Spin lettuce leaves dry. To assemble salads on dinner plates, arrange one large lettuce leaf or two small, overlapping leaves on each plate. If necessary, cut through stem-ends so that leaves lie flat. Center ½ cup shredded beets on the leaves and put 1 tablespoon chopped egg on each side of the beets. Spoon 3 to 4 tablespoons Dill Dressing over lettuce leaves, without coating the egg or beets. Serve immediately.

SPINACH SALAD WITH CAVIAR AND CHIVES

Graceful shreds of brilliant vegetables can be arranged on dinner plates in concentric rings, stripes, arcs, or other patterns to give this salad a limitless range of stunning visual effects. If refrigerator space permits, you may find it convenient to assemble, wrap, and chill the salads for several hours before adding the dressing and garnish.

FLEXIBLE MENU SUGGESTIONS

This salad has a special affinity for menus based on Shrimp and Curry Risotto (page 166) and One-Side Grilled Fish with Whole-Grain Mustard-Chive Butter or Bouillabaisse Sauce (pages 216, 277, and 228). The dominant flavors are equally harmonious before Sage-Rubbed Veal Chops (page 242), Cold Chicken-Poached Lobster (page 270), Scallop and Basil-Stuffed Sole (page 265), Garlic-Roasted Leg of Lamb (page 295), Mushroom and Prosciutto-Stuffed Chicken Breasts (page 274), or Cognac-Marinated Beef Fillet (page 298). *Makes 6 servings*

PREPARATION: 40 MINUTES
COOKING: 15 MINUTES

4 medium carrots, peeled
3 hard-cooked eggs, peeled, halved
Chive Vinaigrette (page 61)
1 jar (16 ounces) whole pickled beets,
*   drained, patted dry*
3 cups firmly packed spinach leaves, rinsed
*   (¾ pound with stems)*
½ cup sour cream or crème fraîche
2 tablespoons salmon or golden whitefish
*   caviar (page 459)*

1. Cut carrots crosswise into three pieces and put them into a steamer basket (page 317). Cover and steam until crisp-tender, about 12 to 14 minutes (or microwave carrots in a covered dish with 2 tablespoons water on high power for 4 to 8 minutes; stir once and test after 4 minutes). Rinse with cold water; chill.

2. Chop eggs finely; wrap and refrigerate. Make Chive Vinaigrette and set aside at room temperature. Shred the carrots and the beets and set each aside.

3. Arrange spinach leaves in loose stacks and use a large knife to shred the leaves by cutting crosswise. Wrap all salad ingredients separately.

4. To assemble salads in a bull's-eye pattern, arrange ingredients, just touching each other, on dinner plates as follows: put 1 tablespoon sour cream (or crème fraîche) in the center of each plate. Spoon a narrow band of egg around the cream. Spoon a ½-inch-wide ring of carrot around the egg, then follow with a ring of beet (slightly narrower than carrot ring) around the carrots. Put shredded spinach around the beets, extending it to touch inside edge of the plate rim. Be sure there are no gaps between vegetable rings so that bottom of plate does not show. (Can wrap and refrigerate up to 6 hours.)

5. At serving time, put 1 teaspoon caviar on top of each sour-cream mound. Stir vinaigrette well, and gently spoon about 2 tablespoons over each spinach ring, without disturbing other ingredients—dressing will naturally spread beneath ingredients on the plates. Serve immediately.

SALAD STYLE

Plating, or arranging salads artistically on plates in the kitchen, gives you maximum control over the way each dish looks when it is placed in front of guests.

Everyone wants to serve lovely, plentiful salads. However, their beauty will be diminished by arranging them on traditional (8½-inch) "salad" plates, which have relatively little space (barely 6 inches) for food display. Larger plates help make salads appear substantial.

Dinner plates are the best choice for appetizer salads, even if it means giving them a quick rinse between courses. Two refrigerator shelves are usually required to accommodate six or eight dinner plates, but cleaning out the fridge the day before a meal is easier than trying to arrange and serve six salads at the last minute.

CHIVE VINAIGRETTE

Chives impart a lilting flavor to this vinaigrette, but fine rings cut from the green tops of scallions can be substituted in a pinch.

FLEXIBLE MENU SUGGESTIONS

I like to use this dressing with Avocado, Grapefruit, and Seafood Salad (page 58), as an all-purpose dressing for mixed green salad (see box, page 76), on a tomato-and-avocado salad to accompany Arizona Chicken with Corn Ragout (page 192), or in menus based on One-Side Grilled Fish (page 216) with Bouillabaisse Sauce (page 228), or Shrimp and Scallops with Chile-Peanut Sauce (page 232). *Makes ¾ cup*

PREPARATION: 5 MINUTES

1 medium garlic clove, peeled
2 teaspoons Dijon mustard
Salt and ground black pepper
¼ cup white wine vinegar
½ cup Herbed Oil (page 73) or mild olive oil
1 tablespoon minced fresh chives

Mince the garlic in a food processor fitted with the metal blade. Add mustard, ¼ teaspoon salt, and ⅛ teaspoon pepper. With motor on, add vinegar in a slow stream, then drizzle in the oil. Process 5 seconds. Transfer to a bowl or jar and add chives. Cover and set vinaigrette aside at room temperature (up to 4 hours).

MOZZARELLA, TOMATO, AND OLIVE SALAD

Italians call this combination *insalata Caprese* and often serve it simply dressed with extra-virgin olive oil. The version below, sauced with Anchovy-Lemon Oil, sets off the richness of the cheese with an added punch of flavor.

I have served many variations on this theme, adding paper-thin prosciutto slices, grilled (or broiled) zucchini or eggplant slices, or roasted bell peppers to the plate. Dried tomatoes (see page 89) can be substituted for fresh tomatoes, or tomatoes can be replaced by peppers.

Small, black Niçoise olives, which are cured and packed in brine, become mild and sweet after marination in olive oil. You will need to prepare these three days before using them.

FLEXIBLE MENU SUGGESTIONS

Despite the presence of cheese and tomato, the salad can be served before Pasta with Tomato-Seafood Sauce (page 124), Pasta with Milanese Meat Sauce (page 130), or Country-Style Risotto (page 176).

It is a wonderful appetizer for a menu based on Pasta with Broccoli Raab (page 134), Milanese Asparagus Soup (page 162), or One-Side Grilled Fish with Fresh Herb or Roasted Garlic and Saffron Butter (pages 216, 219, and 222), in addition to Szechwan Pepper Ribeyes (page 288).

This salad hits the spot for Italian-inspired meals based on Sausage and Artichoke Pizzas (page 108), Sage-Rubbed Veal Chops (page 242), or Capretto with Lemon and Rosemary (page 246). Other compatible main courses are Leg of Lamb with Niçoise Seasoning (page 248) and Herb-Rubbed Chicken (page 278). *Makes 6 servings*

PREPARATION: 15 MINUTES
MARINATION: 10 TO 30 MINUTES

30 Oil-Marinated Olives (page 63), drained
1 cup Anchovy-Lemon Oil (page 63) or extra-virgin olive oil
12 ounces fresh mozzarella cheese
1 pound fresh ripe tomatoes, rinsed, cored
12 fresh basil leaves
Salt and freshly ground pepper

1. Prepare olives three days to one week in advance. Two hours before serving time, make Anchovy-Lemon Oil.

2. Cut mozzarella and tomatoes into ⅛-inch-thick slices. Arrange slightly overlapping slices of cheese and tomato in a ring on six salad plates. Scatter five olives attractively over each serving, or place them in the centers of the cheese and tomato rings. Garnish with basil.

3. Stir oil well and spoon a scant 3 tablespoons over each salad (oil will pool on plates). Sprinkle salads lightly with salt if necessary—cheese varies in saltiness—and pepper. Serve at room temperature.

ANCHOVY-LEMON OIL

~~~~~~~~~~

This oil reaches its peak, and should be used, within 1 to 2 hours.

FLEXIBLE MENU SUGGESTIONS

Unless the anchovies are in conflict with other ingredients, this recipe can be used as a substitute for Gremolada Oil (page 115), as a rub for white-fleshed fish, or as a sauce to drizzle over steamed potatoes that accompany fish. *Makes 1 cup*

PREPARATION: 10 MINUTES

1 tablespoon minced parsley leaves
½ medium shallot, peeled, minced
2 anchovies, rinsed, patted dry, minced
1 cup Herbed Oil (page 73) or mild extra-virgin olive oil
Finely zested rind of ½ small lemon
Salt and ground black pepper

Mix parsley, shallot, and anchovies in a small bowl. Stir in the oil, lemon zest, ⅛ teaspoon salt, and pepper to taste. (Can cover and set aside no longer than 4 hours.)

OIL-MARINATED OLIVES

~~~~~~~~~~

Tiny Niçoise olives are grown on the sunny hillsides of southern France and Italy, picked when they ripen to purplish-black, and cured in a mild salt brine. To enhance their flavor, drain them from the brine, transfer them to a jar with herbs, and cover them with extra-virgin olive oil. The olives can be drained and served on their own for hors d'oeuvres, and will keep indefinitely in the refrigerator. After each batch has been consumed, save the oil for use in marinades or salad dressing.

FLEXIBLE MENU SUGGESTIONS

Orso Butter (page 221), Tomato, Garlic, and Black Olive Sauce (page 89), Mediterranean Sauce (page 150), and Potato Salad Puttanesca (page 334) are other recipes that call for these olives. If you don't mind the tedious work of removing the pits, you will find they add outstanding flavor to Black Olive Bread (page 356). *Makes 1 quart*

PREPARATION: 10 MINUTES
MARINATION: 3 DAYS TO 1 WEEK

12 ounces Niçoise olives, or other small black brine-cured olives
1 sprig fresh rosemary (1 tablespoon dried)
1 bay leaf
3 cups mild or semifruity extra-virgin olive oil

Combine olives, rosemary, bay leaf, and oil in a large jar or crock. Store, covered, in cool place at least 3 days and preferably 1 week before using. Reuse oil left in jar for another batch of olives or for salad dressing.

MOZZARELLA—CULTURE AND CURDS

Fresh mozzarella cheese is an Italian specialty that has moved into the American culinary mainstream. Home cooks have discovered that the sweet, milky flavor and soft, supple texture of this fresh cheese is radically different from the rubbery, processed product most of us associate with pizza.

Mozzarella connoisseurs prefer to eat cheese that is no more than 24 hours old. Many food stores make their own mozzarella, or receive a shipment on a particular day of the week. Beware of cheeses that have a slightly acidic or sour aroma or flavor, which indicates that they may be too old to use in salads. Always refrigerate fresh mozzarella covered in its whey, or in a bowl or bag of cold water.

This cheese dates back at least to the fifteenth century, and its name may come from the Italian verb *mozzare,* which means "to cut off," or "chop up," no doubt a reference to cheese curds that were chopped by hand with a cheesemaker's wire guitar, or harp.

BUFFALO-MILK MOZZARELLA
Mozzarella di bufala is produced in Italy from the milk of the water buffalo. A cheese consortium assures its quality. When made from full-cream buffalo milk, this cheese has a fat content of about 50 percent, which accounts for its rich, creamy taste and delicate consistency. It is commonly sold in spheres the size of tennis balls, or in small *bocconcini* (little mouthfuls) the size of Ping-Pong balls. *Mozzarella di bufala* is perishable, and, despite air shipment from Italy, much of the cheese sold in this country may be older and slightly more sour than it should ideally be. Certain cheeses labeled *mozzarella di bufala* are made from a blend of buffalo and cow's milk.

COW'S-MILK MOZZARELLA
Unlike the hard, processed mozzarella we know as "pizza cheese," fresh cow's-milk mozzarella has a soft, delicate consistency, a fat content of about 40 percent, and a sweet milky flavor. The cheese may be left unsalted, or briefly immersed in salt brine. It can be used interchangeably with *bufala* and should be consumed as soon as possible after it is made, although it does not develop a sour flavor as quickly as the buffalo-milk variety.

Originally, *fior di latte,* or "flower of the milk," was the term used to describe full-cream cow's-milk mozzarella. Now the Polly-O Corporation, of Mineola, New York (best known for ricotta cheese), has taken this as a brand name for an excellent domestic fresh mozzarella that is available in supermarkets.

The Polly-O mozzarella is packed in salted water and sealed in plastic containers similar to those used for tofu. The packaging preserves its shelf life dramatically, but once opened, the cheese should be consumed within three days.

SMOKED MOZZARELLA AND SCAMORZA
Smoked buffalo- and cow's-milk mozzarellas have a wonderful smoky flavor and a yellow to golden exterior created by smoking the balls of cheese over a wood fire, sometimes stoked with leaves and straw.

Smoked mozzarella and scamorza are often confused, but there is a slight difference. Scamorza has a firmer texture than mozzarella because the curds are worked more vigorously and in slightly hotter water. Once smoked, scamorza will not mold when air-dried until it is very hard.

Despite their stronger flavor, both smoked mozzarella and scamorza can be substituted for fresh mozzarella in certain recipes.

MAKING YOUR OWN MOZZARELLA

Mozzarella is one of the simplest cheeses to learn to make at home. First, you will need to find a source for the curds, which are nothing more than milk solidified by the addition of rennet and drained. Italian restaurants that make their own mozzarella may be the best source for imported *bufala* curds, which yield the sweetest and most tender cheeses.

In many cities, you will have better luck finding cow's-milk curds in an Italian delicatessen such as Manganaro Foods, 488 Ninth Ave., New York, NY 10018, 212-563-5331. Curds must be ordered in advance; they will keep at home for up to forty-eight hours if refrigerated in plastic wrap.

The trick to making the cheeses is to work quickly. Mozzarella is called a *pasta filata,* or "pulled cheese," because the finely chopped curds are softened to the melting point in hot water (about 195–200°F), then kneaded or pulled to a taffy-like consistency before being shaped into cushions, balls, ovals, bow knots, or braids. The cheese can be eaten immediately or transferred to cool water to solidify.

At least two books offer reasonable directions and indicate sources for the specialized cheesemaking supplies that are required to make mozzarella at home from scratch. Consult Yvonne Young Tarr's *Step-by-Step Cheesemaking* (Vintage Books) or Lue Dean Flake, Jr.'s *Kitchen Cheesemaking* (Stackpole Books, Harrisburg, Pa.).

HOT MOZZARELLA SALAD

Homemade mozzarella—served while the cheese is still hot—is the sensational focus of this salad. Learning to work the soft curds quickly into sweet, milky individual cushion-shaped cheeses, keeping the cheeses hot, and then quickly assembling the salads will challenge your organizational abilities. However, cheese lovers find the sweet, buttery texture of this mozzarella to be irresistible.

Shaping cheese curds is an unfamiliar technique which actually is very easy once you overcome the fear of the hot water, or that you may do something wrong. Still, this should not be attempted for the first time under pressure of guests waiting at table.

Since the curds vary in texture and quality, I suggest a trial run to build up your confidence and speed. Be sure to read about how mozzarella is made, on page 65, before beginning.

FLEXIBLE MENU SUGGESTIONS

This salad is one of the most delicious appetizers imaginable for menus based on Sage-Rubbed Veal Chops (page 242), Capretto with Lemon and Rosemary (page 246), or Leg of Lamb with Niçoise Seasoning (page 248). *Makes 6 servings*

PREPARATION: 30 MINUTES
COOKING: 5 MINUTES

MARINADE

¼ cup firmly packed parsley leaves
1 large garlic clove, peeled
1 medium shallot, peeled
1 medium ripe tomato, peeled, seeded,
    quartered
1 teaspoon dried oregano (2 teaspoons fresh
    oregano)
Salt and ground black pepper
3 tablespoons lemon juice
1 teaspoon balsamic vinegar (see page 72)
1 cup mild extra-virgin olive oil
1½ roasted red bell peppers, seeded, peeled
    (page 315)

MOZZARELLA

4 quarts hot water
Salt
1½ pounds fresh cow's- or buffalo-milk
    mozzarella curds
12 fresh basil leaves

1. Mince parsley, garlic, and shallot; transfer to a large mixing bowl.

2. Coarsely chop and add the tomato to the bowl. Stir in oregano, ½ teaspoon salt, ¼ teaspoon black pepper, lemon juice, vinegar, and oil. Cut peppers into eighteen julienne strips and add to bowl. Cover. (Can set aside at room temperature 2 to 4 hours.)

3. Heat 4 quarts of water just to simmering. Add 1 teaspoon salt. Cut mozzarella curds into ¼-inch dice and divide curds between two large heatproof bowls.

4. Set warm serving plates nearby on work surface and have two large sheets of aluminum foil ready.

5. Add 2 quarts water to one bowl of curds. Working quickly, stir curds with a spoon until softened, 1 to 2 minutes. Test to see if curds hold together when pinched (this may be immediate or it may take 2 to 4 minutes longer).

6. Working under the water in the first bowl, immediately squeeze curds into three equal pieces. One at a time, remove each piece of cheese from the bowl with a slotted spoon or shallow strainer and quickly knead it into a smooth, cushion shape. Slip each cheese cushion carefully back into the bowl of hot water; cover bowl with foil.

7. Quickly repeat steps 5 and 6 to shape the cheeses in the second bowl. Transfer cheeses to warm plates, shaking off excess liquid. Spoon 3 to 4 tablespoons marinade over each cheese and garnish each with two basil leaves. Put three pepper strips in a pinwheel design on top of each cheese. Serve immediately.

Adapted from a recipe of Erminia Restaurant, New York.

"Cheese has always been a food that both sophisticated and simple humans love."

—M. F. K. FISHER

MIXED LETTUCES WITH SHRIMP AND GINGER-LIME VINAIGRETTE

The cross-cultural flavorings of jalapeño peppers, ginger, and Japanese tamari (wheat-free soy sauce) underscore this unique and elegant salad that is garnished with grilled shrimp (scallops may be substituted).

Finding a good assortment of lettuces—mixed baby lettuces called *mesclun* (see box, page 71) are ideal—helps make the salad beautiful and especially tasty. However, the lettuce mixture need not be as elaborate as the recipe suggests. And while black sesame seeds add dramatic color, plain sesame seeds can be substituted.

FLEXIBLE MENU SUGGESTIONS

The combination of ingredients makes a very pretty salad which is an excellent opener for menus based on Spicy Homestyle Beef Soup (page 160), Mesquite-Grilled Cornish Hens (page 240), Garlic-Rubbed Chicken (page 278), Pork with Port Wine Sauce (page 292), or Leg of Lamb with Malay or Oriental Seasoning (pages 250 and 251). *Makes 8 servings*

PREPARATION: 30 MINUTES (SALAD);
    OVERNIGHT (DRESSING)
COOKING: 10 TO 12 MINUTES

Ginger-Lime Vinaigrette (page 69)
1½ pounds medium shrimp, shelled, deveined,
    rinsed
2 teaspoons black sesame seeds
2 teaspoons white sesame seeds
4 quarts loosely packed mesclun or mixed
    lettuces (red oak, curly endive, arugula,
    Bibb, radicchio, and mâche)
½ cup fresh chives, cut in 1-inch lengths
2 cups loosely packed cilantro leaves
8 medium mushroom caps, cut in thin julienne
4 large plum tomatoes, peeled, seeded, cut in
    thin julienne

1. Make Ginger-Lime Vinaigrette; cover and refrigerate overnight.

2. Put ½ cup vinaigrette in a flat dish. Add shrimp (or scallops) and toss to coat with dressing. Heat a grill or a large skillet. Drain and discard the marinade. Grill or sauté shrimp (or scallops); set aside.

3. Adjust oven rack to middle position. Heat oven to 300 degrees. Put sesame seeds in a cake pan and bake until white seeds are lightly toasted, 3 to 5 minutes; cool.

4. Rinse lettuces, spin or pat dry, and pick them over, removing stems and tough leaves. (Can towel-wrap and refrigerate lettuce leaves in plastic bags for 6 hours.)

5. To assemble salads, tear lettuces into bite-sized pieces. Toss lettuces, chives, and cilantro with ½ cup vinaigrette just until coated. Transfer an equal amount of the mixture to eight dinner plates.

6. Garnish each plate with shrimp (or scallops) and sprinkle each salad with julienned mushrooms and tomatoes and ½ teaspoon sesame seeds. Drizzle 1 teaspoon additional

vinaigrette over each salad and serve immediately.

Adapted from a recipe of Sign of the Dove Restaurant, New York.

GINGER-LIME VINAIGRETTE

xxxxxxxxxx

While the vinaigrette needs an overnight rest, any leftover dressing will keep for 10 days in the refrigerator.

FLEXIBLE MENU
SUGGESTIONS

In addition to being the dressing for a green-salad appetizer that precedes Skewered Lamb with Curry and Fruit (page 254), this mixture can be used as a marinade for barbecued chicken, spareribs, or pork chops, provided the quantity of lime juice is reduced to 2 or 3 tablespoons. *Makes 1¾ cups*

PREPARATION: 20 MINUTES
MARINATION: OVERNIGHT

4 cubes (1 inch each) fresh ginger, peeled
1 jalapeño pepper, roasted, peeled, seeded, and halved
4 medium scallions, roots removed
½ cup fresh lime juice
¼ cup sesame oil
¼ cup tamari
¾ cup mild olive oil

Mince ginger and jalapeño. Coarsely chop the scallions. Put ginger, jalapeño, and scallions in a bowl. Stir in lime juice, sesame oil, tamari, and olive oil. Cover and set dressing aside overnight.

WEEDS AND SEEDS

To clean salad greens thoroughly, remove cores or base of stems and separate leaves. Plunge leaves into a sink or basin of cold water and gently move them around to lift off sand and grit. Drain, rinsing to remove as much grit as possible from basin or sink. Repeat the rinsing process.

Spin greens dry and transfer them to a double thickness of paper towels, or lint-free tea towels. When rolled up in towels and placed in plastic bags, greens can be refrigerated for 6 to 8 hours without losing their crispness.

To prepare lettuce for salad, tear the leaves into bite-sized pieces. Provided leaves are spun dry, greens can be placed directly in a salad bowl, covered with damp paper towels and plastic wrap, then refrigerated up to 4 hours.

Hydroponically grown herbs need not be rinsed. Garden-grown herbs should be rinsed at the last moment, gently patted dry with paper toweling, and chopped at serving time.

Seeds for many European and Asian greens and vegetables are available from gardening catalogues. Some of the best-known sources include:

Shepherd's Garden Seeds, 7389 West Zayante Rd., Felton, CA 95018, 408-335-5400.

Gardener's Eden Catalog, 100 North Point St., San Francisco, CA 94133, 415-421-4242 (published by Williams-Sonoma) is a general garden-supply catalog that also carries mesclun seeds.

Le Marché Seeds International, Box 190, Dixon, CA 95620, 916-678-9244, specializes in European and Oriental vegetables, greens, and herbs.

In addition to seeds, fresh mesclun (called Mes-A-Greens), from Paradise Farms, Box 346, Summerland, CA 93067, 805-684-9468, is sold in 6-ounce bags in many markets throughout the country.

LETTUCE, RADICCHIO, AND FENNEL SALAD

Fennel, a popular anise-flavored vegetable from the Italian kitchen, resembles a fat bunch of celery with wispy fronds and pale, whitish-green ribs. When used raw, ribs and fronds provide a delicate licorice taste.

The bright magenta color of radicchio, or red Italian chicory, makes it a popular salad ingredient; here, its bitterness works in concert with the sweetness of Boston or Bibb lettuce, the pungency of fennel, and the tang of mustard.

FLEXIBLE MENU SUGGESTIONS

This salad can precede any pasta or risotto (except those made with curry), all the pizzas and calzone, or any of the Italian-inspired main courses. *Makes 4 servings*

PREPARATION: 15 MINUTES

2 tablespoons sherry-wine vinegar
1½ teaspoons Dijon mustard
Salt and ground black pepper
2 tablespoons chopped fresh fennel fronds
1 tablespoon whipping cream
4 tablespoons mild or semifruity olive oil

SALAD GREENS

1 medium head Boston lettuce
1 small head radicchio or other red lettuce
1 small bulb fennel with fronds attached
*   (½ pound)*

1. Put vinegar, mustard, a pinch of salt and pepper, fennel fronds, and cream into a food processor fitted with the metal blade. With motor on, drizzle in the oil. Transfer dressing to a bowl or jar. (Can cover and set aside 4 hours.)

2. Core and rinse lettuce and radicchio in a sink or basin of cold water, moving leaves from side to side several times to remove sand. Drain, spin dry, and wrap leaves in a towel. Rinse fennel bulb, remove and discard the stalks, then trim off and discard the tough base. Wrap the trimmed bulb in a towel. (Can refrigerate towel-wrapped leaves in plastic bags as long as 8 hours.)

3. To assemble the salad, tear lettuce leaves into bite-sized pieces; transfer to a salad bowl. Shred radicchio by stacking and cutting the leaves crosswise; add shreds to the bowl. Cut the fennel bulb in half lengthwise, then slice it thinly across the grain and add it to the bowl.

4. At serving time, pour the dressing down the inside of the salad bowl, allowing it to fall below greens. Toss salad, pulling leaves up from bottom. Serve immediately.

SALADS, SERIOUSLY

Mixed green salad is an excellent appetizer for almost any menu, providing the salad is composed of good-quality greens, properly cleaned and dressed.

While I still retain a fondness for iceberg lettuce (particularly in a big wedge accompanied by tomatoes and slathered with blue-cheese dressing) my "serious" salads are usually based on more distinctive mixtures of Boston, Bibb, and red and green oak leaf lettuce, and romaine.

Above all, I like small, tender greens which, for many years, were harvested in my own small garden. Now, however, mâche (corn salad), mesclun (French mixed greens), or misticanza (assorted Italian greens), dandelion, arugula (also called rocket or roquette), escarole, a variety of cresses, curly endive, and frisée (sometimes called chicorée frisée), Belgian endive, radicchio, mizuna, or kyona (a slightly peppery Japanese green in the mustard family), Japanese red mustard leaves, herbs, herb flowers, and edible blossoms (particularly pansies and nasturtium flowers) are found more widely in markets and specialty greengrocers. These are a joy to eat.

It is easy to mix two or three types of greens and vary combinations according to whim, or what can be found in the market. Salads can be based on "sweet and tender" leaves (Bibb, Boston, oak leaf, or mâche) or "peppery, bitter, and crisp" greens (romaine, cress, arugula, endive, escarole, dandelion, curly endive, radicchio, mizuna, and mustard), or a balance of the two.

A green salad can be dramatically altered by a handful of fresh herbs or herb flowers. Minced chives or summer savory, shredded basil, or chopped fresh oregano leaves are wonderful to scatter over the greens moments before dressing the salad. Since the flavor of herbs will dominate, it is important to pair herbs carefully with vinaigrette.

Vegetables added to salads can help complement, or stand in contrast to, the main course. Cooked haricots verts (skinny French green beans), tender broccoli shoots, baby vegetables (which often lack real flavor but can be used for color), and grilled specialty mushrooms (shiitake, oyster, or chanterelles) all are excellent additions to salad.

Thin slices of toasted French or Italian bread brushed with Anchovy-Lemon Oil (page 63) or Gremolada Oil (page 115), or topped with warm goat or blue cheese, Italian Taleggio, or smoked or fresh mozzarella are other good garnishes.

MY FAVORITE VINAIGRETTE

Balsamic vinegar, manufactured around Modena in northern Italy, has a dark brown color, a thin syrupy consistency, and rich mellow taste that comes from aging the unfermented juice of white Trebbiano grapes in wooden casks for at least five years. As the vinegar ages, its flavor mellows and the consistency thickens. Some of these vinegars are aged as long as a hundred years or more, which makes them very concentrated and costly.

The special character of balsamic vinegar makes a dressing that I prefer above all others for salad. However, the strength and flavor of this vinegar varies slightly from brand to brand. I particularly like the Fini vinegar. Many other good balsamic vinegars are widely available in supermarkets, gourmet food shops, and department stores. After you have used this recipe as a general guide, you may wish to adjust the quantity of vinegar, depending on the brand.

FLEXIBLE MENU SUGGESTIONS

All mixed green salads go wonderfully well with this dressing. The vinaigrette is specifically included in a menu for Risotto Spinacciola with tomato salad (page 174), Bollito Misto (page 188), Capretto with Lemon and Rosemary (page 246), Leg of Lamb with Niçoise Seasoning (page 248), and Garlic- or Herb-Rubbed Chicken (page 278). *Makes ¾ cup*

PREPARATION: 5 MINUTES
STANDING TIME: 30 MINUTES TO 5 DAYS

1 medium garlic clove, peeled, crushed
3 tablespoons balsamic vinegar
Salt
½ cup mild extra-virgin olive oil

Combine garlic, vinegar, a pinch of salt, and the oil in a dish, or in a jar with a tight-fitting cover. Cover and set aside at room temperature for 30 minutes or as long as 5 days. Shake well before using. (Can add garlic cloves and replace oil and vinegar as dressing is used.)

HERBED OIL

Olive oil flavored with garlic, shallots, and herbs is one of my kitchen staples. This combination is extremely beautiful, and my friend Pari Dulac, who taught me how to make it, puts the mixture into attractive liquor bottles that she recycles from the bar of her restaurant. The clear bottles are practical containers because the tops close tightly, and the oil also makes a great gift.

Herbed Oil is best made from fresh herbs, although strong dried herbs will give it a delicate flavor. The herbs are inserted into the empty bottle. If grown hydroponically, herbs can be used without washing, since they are unlikely to have dirt or grit clinging to leaves. Otherwise, rinse them briefly in cold water and pat dry with paper toweling. Then, add enough oil to cover the herbs completely. Mild or semifruity extra-virgin olive oil will have the best flavor; pure-grade oil will provide a more neutral taste (consult page 74 for further information about olive oil).

One to four weeks of marination are required to bring the oil to its peak, and the mixture keeps indefinitely, provided the herbs are kept covered by oil. Store the bottle in a cool, dark place.

FLEXIBLE MENU SUGGESTIONS

I use this instead of olive oil to give extra flavor to salad dressing or pasta sauce, to marinate fish fillets prior to grilling, to drizzle over a pizza for extra zest, or in place of butter on vegetables. It is used in numerous recipes throughout this book.

Herbed Oil is good with lean, white-fleshed fish, which can be grilled (see page 216) and served hot or cold. To use it as a sauce, top each portion of grilled fish or chicken with 1 to 1½ tablespoons of the oil and garnish with a sprinkling of the predominating minced fresh herb. *Makes 3 to 4 cups*

PREPARATION: 15 MINUTES
MARINATION: 1 TO 4 WEEKS

6 medium garlic cloves, peeled and quartered
4 to 5 cups mild or semifruity extra-virgin olive oil
4 medium shallots, peeled and quartered
3 to 5 fresh red chiles or 2 to 3 dried red chiles (optional)
5 to 6 sprigs fresh thyme (2 tablespoons dried thyme)
4 imported bay leaves
10 to 15 sprigs fresh herbs (depending on size of herbs and bottle) including basil, rosemary, savory, or sage

1. Put the garlic and the oil in a bowl. Cover and set aside for 4 hours.

2. Put the shallots and whole (optional) chiles in an empty bottle. Add sprigs of thyme. Using a chopstick if necessary, gently push fresh herb sprigs into the bottle, packing it tightly. If this becomes difficult, add a small amount of the oil to the bottom of the bottle so that the herbs begin to float.

3. Continue adding herbs. When bottle looks full, strain enough oil into the bottle to cover the herbs completely and reach halfway up the neck of the bottle. Discard the garlic.

4. Cover tightly and let stand in a very cool place for 1 week. If herbs are strongly flavored, it may be possible to use oil after 1 week; taste to be sure. As oil is used, replenish it, covering the herb mixture in the bottle at all times.

LEMON-BASIL VINAIGRETTE

Strictly speaking this is not a vinaigrette—it contains lemon juice rather than vinegar. I have tucked it in here because I find that lemon-based salad dressings are slightly kinder to wine than vinegar-based mixtures.

FLEXIBLE MENU SUGGESTIONS

Dressings such as this are particularly useful for salads that contain cheese or meat, when you want to serve such a salad with wine. It also is delicious on boiled new potatoes.

This dressing is included in menus based on Pasta with Four Cheeses (page 132), Curry Noodles with Scallops and Cilantro (page 146), One-Side Grilled Fish (page 216) with Orso Butter (page 221), Leg of Lamb with Niçoise Seasoning (page 248), and Chili- or Garlic-Rubbed Chicken (page 278). *Makes ⅔ cup*

PREPARATION: 5 MINUTES

1 medium lemon
1 medium garlic clove, peeled
1 cup loosely packed fresh basil leaves
⅛ teaspoon salt
½ cup extra-virgin olive oil

1. Strip off half the lemon rind with a zester, or grate it into a food processor fitted with the metal blade. With the motor on, add the garlic clove and process until minced. Add basil and salt and process until basil is coarsely chopped.

2. Add 2 tablespoons lemon juice to the processor. With the motor on, slowly drizzle in the oil. Process until vinaigrette has thickened slightly and basil and lemon are finely chopped. (Can use dressing immediately or cover and set aside up to 6 hours.)

LIQUID GOLD

Olive oil is as fascinating as wine, and the wide diversity of its flavor opens up wonderful possibilities for experimentation with the refinement it can bring to foods.

Olive oil contains no cholesterol, and some experts believe its monounsaturated fat actually may help reduce cholesterol levels. It is roughly equivalent in calories to butter—about 120 per tablespoon. I use it frequently in recipes, often instead of butter.

The nuances of olive oil, like those of wine, depend on a number of factors: the country of origin, the quality and variety of the olive, the climate and soil in which the tree was cultivated, the care with which the olive was picked, the methods by which the oil was extracted, and the storage conditions.

The only sure way to determine your preference is by sampling oils. It also is helpful to know how olive oils are graded, and to have some general guidelines for matching oils to each culinary purpose.

Purchasing olive oil can be tricky. Price is not a good guide and labeling is not regulated.

Connoisseurs generally agree that the finest oils are made in small country mills in Italy, France, and Spain, where, after grinding olives into a rough paste, the oil is extracted in a hydraulic press. Oil and water are allowed to separate naturally or through centrifugal force, and the oil is clarified by filtering through cheesecloth. (Cloudiness in olive oil, or a small amount of residue at the bottom of the bottle, often result from this method of pressing and are quite acceptable.) Made in this manner, it is labeled "first cold-pressed oil."

Oil is graded according to the level of acidity it contains (which is perceived as sharpness at the back of the mouth). Extra-virgin oil has a maximum of 1 percent acidity; virgin oil has a maximum of 3 percent acidity.

Among the most commonly available oils are those designated as "pure," which is a misnomer, since pure oils are chemically refined from the residual pits, skins, and pulp of first cold pressings. Solvents are used to dissolve the oil from the residue before it is removed by distillation. The results must be blended with virgin oil to give it a neutral flavor and color.

Pure oil is good for general cooking, especially sautéing, because refining raises its smoking point to about 400 degrees. Cold-pressed oils have a smoking point of less than 300 degrees, and should not be used for high-heat cooking.

Within all grades there is a range of flavor that I specify in recipes as mild (delicate, light), semifruity (stronger, with more taste of the olive), and fruity (oil with a full-blown olive flavor).

I use mild olive oil in a majority of my recipes since it is ideal for salad dressing and mayonnaise, and it goes best with delicate foods like fish or soup. Mild oil has an affinity for herbs like tarragon, chervil,

or chives. I use it in bread, pizza, and savory pastries. On pasta, salad, and in vinaigrette, I prefer a mild extra-virgin oil; for cooking, I use mild pure oil.

Semifruity olive oil is well paired with poultry, red meat, and fresh tomatoes (particularly in combination with pasta). Robust vegetable dishes that are heavy with garlic, or with assertive herbs such as rosemary, savory, oregano, sage, and thyme, stand up to semifruity oil.

Fruity oil is best used as a condiment for soft cheeses such as mozzarella or stracchino, on sliced tomatoes or roasted peppers rolled with anchovy fillets, on grilled or baked vegetables, or over sautéed eggplant.

Buying oil in small sizes, or splitting larger bottles with friends, is a practical way to sample a range of brands. I usually have several types of oil on hand—including a mild extra-virgin oil such as Ranieri (for all cold foods), a fruity extra-virgin oil from Mancianti or Cipollini (Umbria), specifically for use on mozzarella cheese and grilled or raw vegetables, and a mild pure oil such as Bertolli for cooking.

Store olive oil in a cool, dark place. Be sure bottles are tightly sealed. Never store oil in plastic bottles or in the refrigerator, which causes it to congeal, producing funny-looking fatty solids. Many people mistakenly think refrigerated oil is spoiled, but leaving it at room temperature will restore proper consistency. If properly stored, open bottles of oil will last about a year.

NOTE: Beware of labels marked with poor English translations. Grades such as "Pure extra virgin" or "Virgin Pure" are nonsense. Also, watch for phrases like "selected for" or "packed by," which indicate the oil may have an origin different from the place it was bottled (this has become increasingly true of costly Tuscan oils since the freeze in 1985 that destroyed a major portion of the Tuscan olive trees).

FROM VINEGAR TO VINAIGRETTE

For several years, I indulged the romantic notion of making, and exclusively using, my own vinegars. I kept a *vinaigrier,* or vinegar crock, in my basement. Assorted batches of red wine were added to the crock, and each fall the vinegar was filtered and transferred to bottles for aging and use as Christmas gifts.

One year, on a subzero day, I decided to make raspberry vinegar from the leftovers of a Bordeaux wine tasting. The procedure required simmering vinegar with raspberry puree. My house was promptly filled with suffocating fumes that forced me to keep the kitchen door open to the frigid air for nearly an hour! I immediately closed my private vinegar factory and turned to the more practical solution of purchasing flavored wine vinegars.

Check the shelves of any specialty food store and you will find a profusion of white and red or wine vinegars flavored by a wide assortment of fruits such as raspberries and strawberries, aromatic vegetables like garlic and shallots, and such herbs as tarragon, basil, thyme, and sage. Vinegar can be infused with honey, or made from a particular wine such as champagne, Spanish sherry, zinfandel, or even vintage cabernet sauvignon.

Good wine vinegar is fermented in wooden casks or vats for one to three months, or until it reaches an acidity level of 4 to 7 percent. Some is aged for several years, since long maturation yields higher acidity, deeper color, and better quality. Flavorings such as fruit or herbs also can affect the color and taste.

Fruit vinegars frequently are sharper than standardized, supermarket vinegar brands. Therefore, my vinaigrette recipes are based on a 3-to-1 oil-to-vinegar proportion, rather than the usual 2-to-1 proportion. This equation is not inviolate—adjust it according to the strength of each vinegar, which can be tasted on a sugar cube or a dry leaf of lettuce.

I regularly keep a variety of vinegars—including honey, raspberry, sherry, and balsamic—on hand and mix them with top-quality olive oil, or combinations of olive oil and cold-pressed walnut or hazelnut oils.

The nut oils make wonderfully fragrant dressings that enhance tossed green salads as well as those containing fruit, poultry, game, lamb, or fresh goat cheese. Walnut and hazelnut oils are costly and perishable once the bottles or tins are opened. For best results, transfer these oils to two smaller bottles that seal tightly, and use one at a time. Since nut oils have very intense flavors, a few tablespoons are usually sufficient in vinaigrettes.

Making vinaigrette in the food processor will help keep it emulsified, usually two hours or longer. A clove of garlic, a shallot, mustard, or cream acts as a binder when the oil is slowly processed into the mixture.

When properly tossed with greens, no excess vinaigrette should appear on the bottom of a salad bowl or plates. A green salad for four will require about ½ cup of dressing. As soon as your salad is mixed, taste a leaf to see if there is sufficient dressing. If not, drizzle vinaigrette over the salad a tablespoon at a time, then toss and taste again. Adjust the seasoning and serve the salad immediately.

HAZELNUT VINAIGRETTE

Several tablespoons of pungent hazelnut oil infuse this vinaigrette with a heady flavor, which can be reinforced by adding a tablespoon or two of chopped hazelnuts.

FLEXIBLE MENU SUGGESTIONS

In combination with raspberry (or other fruit) vinegar, hazelnut oil makes a superb dressing for plain salads or those that include duck, game (quail or pigeon), pork, lamb, or goat cheese, since slightly fatty foods help to balance the acidity of fruit and the delicacy of the nuts.

In contrast, the union of honey vinegar and hazelnut oil produces a sweet dressing that is well suited to chicken salads, mixtures that include blue cheese, roasted garlic or shallots, or roasted bell peppers.

This dressing is used for a salad to accompany Sausages and Sauerkraut (page 186) and in a menu based on Chili-Rubbed Chicken (page 278). *Makes ¾ cup*

PREPARATION: 6 MINUTES

1 small garlic clove, peeled
Salt
½ teaspoon Dijon mustard
¼ cup honey or raspberry vinegar
3 tablespoons hazelnut oil
½ cup mild olive oil

Mince garlic in a food processor fitted with the metal blade. Add ⅛ teaspoon salt and mustard. Process, drizzling in vinegar and the oils. Adjust seasoning to taste. (Store in covered jar at room temperature 48 hours or refrigerate 1 week. Use at room temperature and shake well.)

SHERRY-WALNUT VINAIGRETTE

I first tasted Spanish sherry-wine vinegar in the kitchen of the late James Beard, during one of the many classes that I attended there over the years. As I recall, the vinegar was blended into a dressing for boiled potatoes, which quickly took on the winey, oakey vinegar flavor.

Sherry vinegar is made in and around Jerez, from Spanish sherry, a fortified wine pressed from the Palomino grape. By law, Jerez vinegar must have more than 5 percent acidity and be aged by a special method, often as long as six years.

The process of making sherry vinegar involves a series of 516 one-litre oak barrels, each containing vinegar of a different age. The barrel containing the oldest vinegar is called the *solera*. When vinegar is removed from the *solera* for bottling, it is replaced, round-robin style, by the youngest vinegar, which in turn is replaced by vinegar from a cask of moderate age. The point is to produce vinegar of uniform quality.

FLEXIBLE MENU SUGGESTIONS

Sherry vinegar and walnut oil are often used in tandem for a wide variety of salads, but particularly those that include poultry, game birds, cheese, and fruit. Sherry vinegar gives this dressing a complex flavor that is similar to balsamic vinegar, but less sweet.

This dressing is included in menus based on Chilaquiles (page 195) and Cognac-Marinated Beef Fillet (page 298). *Makes ¾ cup*

PREPARATION: 6 MINUTES

1 medium shallot, peeled
Salt
1 teaspoon Dijon mustard
3 tablespoons sherry-wine vinegar
1 tablespoon cream
3 tablespoons walnut oil
½ cup mild olive oil

Mince shallot in a food processor fitted with the metal blade. Add ⅛ teaspoon salt, mustard, vinegar, and cream; process 15 seconds. With motor on, slowly drizzle in walnut and olive oils. Adjust seasoning to taste. (Can store in covered jar at room temperature 48 hours or refrigerate 1 week. Use at room temperature.)

DILL DRESSING

The relatively large quantity of Dijon mustard called for in the dressing eliminates the need to add any salt.

FLEXIBLE MENU SUGGESTIONS

While this dressing is slightly too thick and sweet to be used on green salads, it would make an excellent sauce for cold poached salmon or One-Side Grilled Fish (page 216). *Makes about 2 cups*

PREPARATION: 10 MINUTES

½ cup snipped fresh dill
¼ cup firmly packed parsley leaves
2 tablespoons sugar
¼ cup cider vinegar
½ cup lemon juice
⅔ cup Dijon mustard
1 cup mild olive oil or vegetable oil

In a clean food processor fitted with the metal blade, mince dill and parsley by processing with sugar. Add vinegar, lemon juice, and mustard. Process; drizzle in oil in a thin stream. Transfer dressing to a jar (can set aside 4 hours).

TOURS DE FORCE:
TERRINES

When the term *tour de force* is applied to culinary performances, it brings to mind certain complex preparations for which a high level of technical skill is required. The stretching of strudel dough to transparent thinness, the decoration of a ham with aspic, the creation of a fondant icing from scratch, or the boning of a game bird for a galantine—these are most certainly *tours de force*.

The making of a terrine, or pâté, also falls into this category. It requires concentration, considerable skill with a knife, a keen sense of seasoning, and a measure of patience, since terrines contain an assemblage of ingredients to prepare and incorporate at the correct stage in the recipe. Furthermore, there is aesthetic judgment involved in perfectly balancing tastes, textures, and colors to produce something both delicious and lovely to behold.

I shall never forget my first fish terrine. The recipe called for two pounds of sole fillets to be pureed, chilled, then "mounted" (incorporated with an egg and cream). The equipment at my disposal was an ancient blender and a lightweight hand mixer. It took many separate batches to puree all the fish—which, to my horror, turned into a lumpy mess.

The instructions said to then add an egg, and gradually pour in some cream. But after the first half cup of cream had been absorbed, the mixer motor began to smoke. The fish was so stiff it had stopped the beaters! Someone was conscripted to wield a wooden spoon on the fish while I undertook the job of pouring the cream and turning the bowl. In the end, that terrine did get to the table, but the experience left me extremely wary.

Those of us who lead busy lives and find little enough time to cook these days might well ask why precious kitchen time should be invested in any recipe as challenging as the fish, vegetable, or meat terrines included here. For an ambitious cook, the reward would be the sheer pleasure of mastering a complicated cooking technique. For others, it might be a matter of scheduling: terrines can be prepared and refrigerated for several days in advance and served with virtually no fuss.

Most terrines yield nearly a dozen servings and are therefore excellent entertaining fare; leftovers often can be the base of a family meal the next day. Ready-made equivalents often sell for four to five times the cost of making terrines at home with ingredients whose quality is assured.

Over the years, I have found terrines to be the only rival to desserts in the recollections of my guests, for their combinations of flavors and textures linger in the memory long after the last slices have disappeared.

THREE-VEGETABLE TERRINE

CORAL SAUCE

Pâté Plating Pointers

Blunders and Binders

Technical Tactics

COLD SALT-COD TERRINE

TOMATO, GARLIC, AND BLACK OLIVE SAUCE

COUNTRY PORK TERRINE

Pâté Spice

HOMEMADE GARLIC SAUSAGE WITH PISTACHIOS

Season to Taste

THREE-VEGETABLE TERRINE

A beautiful vegetable rainbow is created when pureed cauliflower, broccoli, and mushrooms are layered in this terrine. I have served it both hot and cold with equal success, and it rarely fails to bring raves from my guests because the taste of each vegetable is so clear and fresh.

The pureed vegetables are sautéed to remove excess moisture, then bound with a funny little mixture that is similar to a whole-egg Hollandaise Sauce (see page 86).

Once the terrine is baked, you are hardly aware that it contains any eggs or butter at all, since the taste is very light. It is important to season each vegetable mixture very well, as indicated in steps 5 and 6, so the terrine will not be bland. Both lemon juice and hot red pepper sauce help to lift the flavor of each vegetable dramatically.

You really do need the food processor to shortcut pureeing the vegetables and making the binders. Provided you work from light to dark—processing the cauliflower, the broccoli, then the mushrooms—there is no need to rinse out the machine.

The delicate texture of the terrine demands a light hand when slicing. Or, if you wish to change the presentation, layer the vegetables into ten, buttered half-cup timbales (or dariole molds, see page 313), cover each loosely with a square of buttered wax paper, and bake them in a water bath for 20 to 25 minutes.

FLEXIBLE MENU SUGGESTIONS

Hot slices of the terrine (or individual molds) can be plated over Tomato-Basil Sauce (page 267) and served before Sage-Rubbed Veal Chops (page 242), Capretto with Lemon and Rosemary (page 246), or Leg of Lamb with Niçoise Seasoning (page 248). You will need to adjust quantities for these menus.

When served cold with Coral Sauce (page 85), follow the terrine with One-Side Grilled Fish (page 216) with Fresh Herb Butter or Winter Pesto (pages 219 and 227), Mesquite-Grilled Cornish Hens (page 240), or Szechwan Pepper Ribeyes (page 288) as main courses.

As an appetizer for a light meal based on Calzone (pages 116 and 118) or Sausage and Artichoke Pizzas (page 108), accompany the terrine with Tomato, Garlic, and Black Olive Sauce (page 89); again, because the yield is large, there will be leftovers for another meal. *Makes 12 servings*

PREPARATION: 45 MINUTES
COOKING: 1 HOUR
CHILLING: 4 TO 24 HOURS

½ pound fresh cauliflower, cored, trimmed
½ pound fresh broccoli florets
1 pound mushrooms, wiped clean
2 small shallots, peeled
4 tablespoons softened unsalted butter

3 eggs
3 egg yolks
3 teaspoons lemon juice
Salt and ground white pepper
Nutmeg
Hot red pepper sauce
½ cup hot (170 degrees) melted unsalted butter

Continued

1. Put cauliflower and broccoli (without mixing) in a vegetable steamer (see page 317). Cover and steam until very tender when pierced with sharp knife, about 12 minutes. Transfer hot vegetables to a cloth towel and set them aside to cool.

2. Shred the mushrooms; transfer to medium skillet. Mince and transfer the shallots to the skillet with 1 tablespoon softened butter. Sauté over medium heat, tossing frequently, until moisture evaporates and the mushrooms darken, about 20 minutes; set aside to cool.

3. Butter ends and bottom of a 4-cup enameled cast-iron terrine. Butter a sheet of parchment paper; put it in the terrine, buttered-side up, to line the bottom and two long sides; refrigerate. Adjust oven rack to lowest position. Heat oven to 350 degrees.

4. Puree the cauliflower. Heat 1 tablespoon softened butter in a medium skillet, add the puree, and stir over medium heat to remove excess moisture, about 5 to 6 minutes. Do not let puree color or brown.

5. Put 1 egg, 1 egg yolk, 1 teaspoon lemon juice, ½ teaspoon salt, a pinch of pepper, and a dash of nutmeg and hot red pepper sauce into the processor. With the motor on, add 2½ tablespoons of hot melted butter and process 5 seconds. Add cauliflower puree and process 30 seconds. Adjust seasoning to taste. Spoon cauliflower mixture into the terrine in an even layer; refrigerate terrine uncovered while preparing the next layer.

6. Repeat steps 4 and 5 to puree, bind, and layer the broccoli, then the mushrooms. Cover terrine with a sheet of buttered parchment paper.

7. Put terrine in a water bath (page 87) and bake 50 to 60 minutes, until the center is just set and the mixture rises slightly above the rim. Turn off the oven, open the door, and let the terrine stand in the oven for 10 minutes. Remove and cool 10 minutes before unmolding if terrine will be served hot (see step 8). Remove immediately, cool to room temperature, unmold, wrap, and refrigerate if served cold (see step 9).

8. To unmold and serve the terrine hot, prepare an unmolding surface such as a heavy cardboard rectangle cut longer and wider than the mold, and covered with aluminum foil. Oil the foil to prevent the terrine from sticking. Free the baked terrine from the mold by carefully inserting the blade of a thin knife down along one side to create an air pocket; then run the knife around the top edge of the terrine. Grasp the mold securely and invert it in a single, fluid motion. Carefully remove the mold, then the parchment paper. If the terrine breaks, simply slice around the fissure. Coat warm dinner plates with 3 to 4 tablespoons of the sauce, and center a slice of terrine over sauce.

9. To serve the terrine cold, unmold the terrine, cover with plastic wrap, and refrigerate 6 hours or overnight. Cut the terrine carefully (it squashes easily) into ½-inch-thick slices and transfer each to a plate with an oiled pancake turner. Serve 2 to 3 tablespoons of a cold sauce alongside.

CORAL SAUCE

xxxxxxxxxx

Half a roasted, peeled red bell pepper (page 315) gives this sauce a brilliant color that might cause it to be mistaken for mayonnaise flavored and colored with shellfish coral or roe. In spirit, it is an updated version of that old standby.

FLEXIBLE MENU SUGGESTIONS

Here is a great match for Three-Vegetable Terrine (page 83), or for Cold Chicken-Poached Lobster (page 270). *Makes about 1¼ cups*

PREPARATION: 15 MINUTES

½ roasted, peeled red bell pepper
1 egg
1 egg yolk
2 teaspoons Armagnac or Cognac
2 teaspoons sweet paprika
1 teaspoon lemon juice
¼ teaspoon Worcestershire sauce
Salt and ground white pepper
¾ cup mild olive oil or vegetable oil
¼ cup chilled whipping cream
Hot red pepper sauce

Insert metal blade in a dry food processor. Process pepper until chopped. Add egg, egg yolk, Armagnac, paprika, lemon juice, Worcestershire sauce, ½ teaspoon salt, and ⅛ teaspoon pepper and process 20 seconds. With motor on, slowly drizzle oil into the sauce. Process, slowly adding the cream. Taste; adjust seasoning with several dashes of hot red pepper sauce. Cover and refrigerate (up to 3 days) until serving time.

Inspired by a recipe of chef Gerard Rouillard.

PATE PLATING POINTERS

Terrines should be sliced and presented with attention to detail. Their colors, which often are earthy, should harmonize with sauces as well as the serving plates to create stunning visual effects.

It is helpful to remove the end pieces and use them to work out your presentations. Prepare a sample plate in advance, wrap it in plastic, and refrigerate until you are ready to use it as your assembly guide.

Count on one ⅜- to ¼-inch-thick slice of pâté per person for an appetizer. If a terrine will be served as a main course, you will need to serve two slices, which can be placed side by side or end to end in the center of a dinner plate. Sauce should be spooned artfully onto vacant spots on plates, rather than over slices.

An electric knife, a very sharp boning knife, or a thin, serrated knife is best for creating neat slices. Use as little pressure as possible when slicing. An oiled pancake turner is helpful for transferring slices to plates.

Remember that terrines are perishable. They should be served refrigerator-cold (or hot) and should remain refrigerated until the last possible moment, especially in hot weather. Do not permit terrines to stand at room temperature. If you are serving buffet-style, arrange slices on small platters, cover, and rotate platters in and out of the refrigerator as often as possible.

BLUNDERS AND BINDERS

Any mixture that is packed into a terrine or mold requires something to hold it together and help retain its shape. Traditionally, this is a binder such as the flour, egg, and milk mixture called a *panade,* Béchamel sauce, eggs, cream or crème fraîche, gelatin, gelatinous fish or meat glaze, or, in the case of many meat terrines, pork fat.

Several years ago, I was working on a restaurant recipe for a layered vegetable terrine similar to the one on page 83, but bound with Béchamel sauce. While adapting the recipe for home cooks, I found that the Béchamel made the pureed vegetable layers heavy, mushy, and bland.

Seeking an alternative, I found in my files a recipe for individual layered vegetable mousses bound with whole eggs and an egg yolk. In the course of testing the terrine, I accidentally added some melted butter to the egg mixture. Since the butter could not be removed, I took a chance and stirred in the vegetable puree.

The texture of the baked terrine was sensational. My mistake far surpassed either the Béchamel or the eggs alone. Repeated testing proved that my little egg-and-butter error (actually it is a funny whole-egg Hollandaise sauce) was reliable and durable enough to permit the terrine to be perfectly sliced hot or cold. Moreover, the mixture was undetectable; it really let the flavor of the vegetables shine: a breakthrough!

I later used it for the Cold Salt-Cod Terrine (page 88) on the supposition that pureed dried cod was at least as difficult to bind as cooked vegetables. It works equally well for Potato Croquettes (page 320) and Sweet Potato Flans (page 324).

You may want to try using this binder in similar recipes that need to be lightened or refined. It should be highly seasoned with lemon juice, salt, pepper, and hot pepper sauce (I use Tabasco—a great flavor booster).

The temperature of the butter added to the eggs is important. Melted butter should be hot (160 to 180 degrees on an instant-read thermometer), just at the point when the foam rises to the top. (It is especially convenient to microwave the butter in a Pyrex cup with a pouring spout.) Once the puree has been combined with the warm binder, the mixture must be baked as soon as possible to avoid any chance of spoilage.

Buy fresh meat whenever possible, as frozen raw ingredients exude moisture when cooked. Organ meats such as pork liver and fresh fatback are easily found in ethnic (Spanish, Chinese, etc.) markets, where they are relatively inexpensive. If fish or meat are not used within several hours of purchase, remove them from store wrappings and re-wrap in plastic.

Mixtures made of seafood, raw meats, or organ meats combined with raw eggs are highly perishable and must be chilled before and after cooking. Raw ingredients (including meats, fish, eggs, and any cooked vegetable garnitures) should not be left standing at room temperature during preparation time —refrigerate them before and after handling.

Before using meat, check for bits of bone, gristle, veins, and tough connective tissue. Remove these with a sharp boning or paring knife. Try not to remove visible fat (unless excessive), as it helps keep pâtés moist.

The dish in which pâtés and terrines are baked is also called a terrine. Usually this is a narrow rectangular vessel in enameled cast iron, earthenware, or porcelain. Rectangular terrines of enameled cast iron (made by Le Creuset) are particularly recommended, and have been used to test recipes in this book, both because they provide even heat for baking and because their long, elegant shape ensures good-looking slices.

Terrines of the same capacity (4 to 6 cups) in glazed earthenware or porcelain can be used, as can rectangular Pyrex loaf pans; however, cooking times may be slightly longer, and the shape of the slices will vary considerably. Do not use metal loaf pans.

If recipes call for lining a terrine with cooking parchment (available in supermarkets, cookware departments, and specialty food stores), butter only the ends and the top edges of the vessel. Do not substitute wax paper, which may shred when unmolded. Aluminum foil may be substituted, but keep it smooth, or unmolded terrines may have an unattractive appearance.

Spoon prepared mixtures into terrines as evenly as possible, taking care to eliminate air pockets. Smooth the top of each mixture with the back of a soup spoon. It can be mounded slightly in the mold.

Settle the contents by whacking the terrine firmly several times on a flat surface cushioned with a folded towel; this will remove air pockets that might cause spoilage or uneven texture.

When baking, cover mixtures as recipes specify; often the lid of a terrine is not used.

Terrines need to be placed in a water bath as insulation against oven heat. Use a roasting pan that will hold enough hot tap water to reach about one-half to two-thirds of the way up the outside of the terrine. Do not allow any terrine to float in water, as it may overturn.

Mixtures will cook most evenly if a cloth towel is placed in the larger pan and the terrine set on the towel. Arrange the pan, towel, and terrine in your oven, then carefully pour water into the pan. During cooking, check to be sure the water in the pan does not boil; add cold water, if necessary, to stop boiling.

Generally, the center of each mixture will remain slightly soft until the terrine is thoroughly cooked—test for doneness about 10 minutes before the end of the cooking time indicated in the recipe.

When baked, follow recipe directions for cooling. Carefully remove terrine from water bath, leaving pan with hot water in oven to cool. Transfer terrines to a cake rack to cool to room temperature.

COLD SALT-COD TERRINE

I adore salt cod (dried, salted codfish), although many people consider it to be an acquired taste. Salt-cod dishes are found throughout the Mediterranean, frequently seasoned with garlic and onions, and often ground to the consistency of mashed potatoes.

Lightly cured cod (with about 18 percent salt content), sold in many fish stores and ethnic markets, is best for the terrine, but plan ahead: it requires an overnight soak. Air-dried cod, which is similar, may be substituted.

If you have never tasted or enjoyed salt cod, this is a good recipe to consider. The texture is rather smooth, and the robust sauce makes the terrine surprisingly good.

FLEXIBLE MENU SUGGESTIONS

A Mediterranean-inspired meal can be completed by accompanying this terrine with Tomato, Garlic, and Black Olive Sauce (page 89) and following with Leg of Lamb with Niçoise Seasoning (page 248) or Garlic-Roasted Leg of Lamb (page 295). *Makes 10 servings*

PREPARATION: 40 MINUTES
BAKING: 1 HOUR
CHILLING: 12 TO 36 HOURS

1¾ pounds salt cod (not previously frozen)
3 medium shallots, peeled, sliced
3 medium garlic cloves, peeled, crushed
½ teaspoon crushed dried thyme leaves
⅓ cup milk
2 tablespoons softened unsalted butter
3 eggs
3 egg yolks
1½ tablespoons lemon juice
Several dashes hot red pepper sauce
2 tablespoons whipping cream
½ cup hot (170 degrees) melted unsalted butter
Salt and ground white pepper
Tomato, Garlic, and Black Olive Sauce (page 89)

1. One day in advance, put salt cod in a large bowl, cover with cold water, and refrigerate for 12 hours, changing water several times. Rinse cod and cut into 2-inch chunks, stripping off the tough membrane. Remove any visible bones with a tweezer.

2. Combine shallots, garlic, thyme, milk, and 2 cups water in a 4-quart saucepan. Heat to boiling; simmer 10 minutes. Off heat, add the cod pieces. Return the pan to low heat and poach the cod for 5 minutes just below the simmering point; otherwise it can toughen. Remove cod and shallot pieces with slotted spoon; set aside to cool. Discard the poaching liquid.

3. Cut a sheet of parchment paper large enough to line bottom and long sides of a 4-cup enameled cast-iron terrine. Use 1½ tablespoons softened butter to coat ends of terrine and the parchment. Put parchment in the terrine, buttered side up; refrigerate. Adjust oven rack to lowest position. Heat oven to 350 degrees.

4. Insert metal blade in a food processor. Puree warm cod and shallots in two batches; set aside. Combine eggs, egg yolks, lemon juice, hot pepper sauce, and cream in processor container. With motor on, very slowly add hot melted butter to the egg mixture. Add fish in two batches, processing each until mixed. Season to taste slightly salty and peppery.

5. Transfer cod mixture to the terrine. Tap terrine on a counter to settle the mixture. Use remaining softened butter to coat a sheet of aluminum foil. Cover terrine with foil but do not bend down edges. Bake in water bath 1 hour, or until center is springy to touch. Transfer terrine to a cake rack; cool.

6. To unmold terrine, prepare an unmolding surface such as a heavy cardboard rectangle cut longer and wider than the mold and covered with aluminum foil. Oil the foil to prevent mixture from sticking. Free the baked mixture from the terrine by carefully inserting the blade of a thin knife down along one side to create an air pocket; then run the knife around the top edge of the mixture. Grasp terrine securely and invert it in a single, fluid motion. Remove the parchment paper carefully. Refrigerate the terrine for 1 hour, then cover it completely with plastic wrap and refrigerate overnight (or up to 36 hours) before serving.

7. Two to eight hours before serving, make the Tomato, Garlic, and Black Olive Sauce.

8. To serve the terrine, cut it carefully into ½-inch-thick slices and transfer each to a plate with an oiled pancake turner. Spoon ¼ cup sauce around each slice. Serve immediately.

TOMATO, GARLIC, AND BLACK OLIVE SAUCE

Tomatoes, garlic, and black Niçoise olives sparkle in a sauce based on Herbed Oil.

FLEXIBLE MENU SUGGESTIONS

Oil-Marinated Olives (page 63) are the best to use in this recipe. The sauce can be served with Cold Salt-Cod Terrine (page 88), chilled slices of Three-Vegetable Terrine (page 83), or with One-Side Grilled Fish (page 216). *Makes 10 servings*

PREPARATION: 10 MINUTES
MARINATION: 2 TO 8 HOURS

2 medium garlic cloves, peeled, crushed
3 tablespoons red-wine vinegar
6 tablespoons mild extra-virgin olive oil (see page 75) or Herbed Oil (page 73)
¼ cup coarsely chopped pitted Niçoise olives
½ pound ripe tomatoes, peeled, seeded, diced (or 1 cup drained, seeded, diced canned plum tomatoes)
⅛ teaspoon ground Mixed Herbs (page 105) or 2 teaspoons (combined) fresh thyme, savory, sage, and basil
1½ tablespoons snipped fresh fennel fronds, or dried fennel to taste
Salt (depending on saltiness of olives)
Ground black pepper

1. Put garlic, vinegar, olive oil, olives, and tomatoes in a bowl. Cover and set aside at room temperature for 2 to 8 hours. Add mixed herbs and fennel. Adjust seasoning, adding salt and pepper as necessary.

2. At serving time, remove garlic cloves with a fork and discard. Stir sauce well; serve at room temperature.

COUNTRY PORK TERRINE

Don't be put off by ingredients such as pork liver or fresh (unsalted) fatback—this is a classic, and a truly delicious terrine that can be made up to five days in advance. The liver is barely discernible, and the thin wrapping of fat (have the butcher slice it paper thin) is not eaten. Though the recipe comes from the French kitchen, most ethnic meat markets (French, Italian, Latin, German, or Caribbean) carry the pork products you will need.

FLEXIBLE MENU SUGGESTIONS

The terrine should be served refrigerator-cold as an appetizer before One-Side Grilled Fish (page 216) with Anchovy-Lemon Oil (page 63) or Whole-Grain Mustard-Chive Butter (page 277), Herb-Rubbed Chicken (page 278), or Scallop and Basil-Stuffed Sole (page 265).

It also can be used as a light main course, garnished with cornichon (sour gherkin) fans, tiny pickled onions, assorted mustards (Pommery, classic Dijon, green or red pepper), or one of the chutneys (page 337 or 338.)

Accompaniments might include French Dinner Rolls (page 360) or Black Pepper Brioche (page 352), and French Potato Salad (page 332), Rosemary-Roasted Potato Salad (page 333), Zucchini Rice Salad (page 331), or Shoestring Vegetables with Whole-Grain Mustard (page 335). For dessert, consider Mixed Berry Cobbler (page 420) or Almond and Lemon-Stuffed Pears (page 431). *Makes 10 to 12 servings*

PREPARATION: 1 HOUR
BAKING: 2 HOURS
CHILLING: OVERNIGHT TO 5 DAYS

3 medium garlic cloves, peeled
1 medium onion, peeled
2 tablespoons butter
Salt
½ teaspoon dried thyme leaves
1¼ pounds boneless pork shoulder, trimmed, cubed, chilled
1½ pounds fresh (unsalted) pork fatback, trimmed, cubed, chilled
Ground white pepper
Pâté Spice (page 91)
1½ pounds pork liver, rinsed, trimmed, cubed, chilled
3 tablespoons Cognac or brandy
3 tablespoons port wine
¼ cup flour

½ pound chilled fresh (unsalted) pork fatback, sliced into paper-thin sheets
1 egg

ADDITIONAL SEASONINGS

6 bay leaves
2 tablespoons whole black peppercorns
2 teaspoons dried thyme leaves

1. Mince the garlic. Coarsely chop the onion. Heat the butter in a medium skillet. Add onion, garlic, a pinch of salt, and ½ teaspoon thyme. Stir over low heat until onion is soft but not brown, about 8 minutes. Spread on foil and refrigerate to chill thoroughly.

2. Mix pork shoulder and fatback cubes in a large, nonreactive baking dish. Sprinkle

with 1½ teaspoons salt, ½ teaspoon pepper, and a generous ⅛ teaspoon Pâté Spice. Toss to coat the meat thoroughly with spices. Use the food processor metal blade to grind the pork mixture in 1½-cup batches to coarse-hamburger consistency; return ground meat to dish. Combine liver with the chilled onions and grind the mixture coarsely, then stir it into the ground meat in the dish.

3. Add Cognac, port, and flour to the ground meat. Mix thoroughly and refrigerate 1 hour. Fry 2 tablespoons meat mixture in small skillet until juices run clear (never taste uncooked pork). Adjust seasoning of remaining pork mixture to taste salty and peppery, cooking 2 tablespoons again if needed.

4. Line a 6- to 7-cup enameled cast-iron terrine with a single layer of fatback. Beat the egg lightly and mix it thoroughly into the ground meat. Transfer the ground meat to the terrine and cover with a layer of fatback. Gently press bay leaves, peppercorns, and thyme on top of fatback. Cover terrine tightly with aluminum foil.

5. Adjust oven rack to lowest position. Heat oven to 325 degrees. With a sharp knife, make three slits through foil into the top of the terrine. Put terrine into a water bath and bake until the center registers 160 degrees on an instant-read thermometer, about 2 hours. Remove terrine from water bath; cool to room temperature. Clean bottom and sides of terrine with a hot towel. Wrap the terrine airtight in aluminum foil, and refrigerate 2 to 4 days before serving.

6. To slice and serve the terrine, free the baked mixture from the mold by inserting the blade of a sharp knife down along one side to create an air pocket; then run the knife around the top edge of the mixture. Use a serrated knife to cut the meat and fat crosswise into neat, ¼-inch-thick slices. Remove and discard spices on top. Remove the end, then use a pancake turner or metal spatula to remove each slice carefully, keeping the fat intact. Transfer one or two slices to each serving plate. Slices will be more attractive if fat is left intact, but it can be removed. Garnish as desired and serve chilled.

PATE SPICE

1½ teaspoons ground cloves
1½ teaspoons ground cardamom
1½ teaspoons cayenne pepper
1 teaspoon cinnamon

Mix together; store in airtight jar.

HOMEMADE GARLIC SAUSAGE WITH PISTACHIOS

Garlic lovers will adore this sausage, which, thanks to heatproof plastic wrap, is literally cooked in its own juices so there is no flavor loss. The plastic wrap forms an airtight sausage casing that withstands poaching in hot water, cooling, refrigerating, and ripening.

To remove the skins from pistachios, drop them into boiling water to blanch for about one minute, then rub them vigorously in a cloth towel to loosen the skins before picking out the pale green nutmeats.

FLEXIBLE MENU SUGGESTIONS

The sausage makes an appetizer that can be simply or elaborately garnished with the same array of condiments, breads, and salads suggested for Country Pork Terrine (page 90). Menu ideas are identical to those suggested for the terrine, but the sausage also could be served before Milanese Asparagus Soup (page 162) or Cold Chicken-Poached Lobster (page 270). Italian Baked Vegetables (page 306) served at room temperature and Shoestring Vegetables with Whole-Grain Mustard (page 335) are other main-course accompaniments to consider. Compatible desserts include Classic Fruit Tart or Milanese Fruit Tart (page 416 or 408) topped with summer fruit, or slices of Peach Turnover (page 418). *Makes a 2-pound sausage*

PREPARATION: 40 MINUTES
COOKING: 50 MINUTES
CHILLING: 36 TO 48 HOURS

1½ pounds boneless pork shoulder, cubed
½ pound fresh (unsalted) pork fatback, cubed and partially frozen
4 medium garlic cloves, peeled
3 medium shallots, peeled
1 slice fresh white bread
Salt and ground black pepper
1½ teaspoons Pâté Spice (page 91)
1 tablespoon Cognac or brandy
2 tablespoons milk
½ cup (3 ounces) shelled white pistachios, blanched, skinned

1. Combine pork and fatback in a large baking dish. Insert metal blade in the food processor. Mince the garlic and shallots, then sprinkle them over the meat cubes. Tear bread and process to fine crumbs; sprinkle ⅓ cup bread crumbs over meat (discard or reserve remaining crumbs).

2. Sprinkle ¾ teaspoon salt, ¾ teaspoon pepper, and the Pâté Spice evenly over the meat. Use the metal blade to process 1½ cups meat cubes to coarse-hamburger consistency; set ground mixture aside. Repeat to grind all the meat mixture.

3. Mix Cognac with the milk and sprinkle the liquid over the ground meat. Thoroughly mix in the pistachios. Fry 1 tablespoon of the meat mixture until juices run clear (never taste uncooked pork). Adjust seasoning of remaining pork mixture to taste slightly salty and peppery, cooking 1 tablespoon again if needed.

4. Put two 19-inch-long sheets of heatproof plastic wrap on a work surface, with long edges overlapping by 4 inches, to form a large sheet of plastic. Center all the meat mixture on the wrap in a 12 × 2-inch salami-shape mound. Fold one long edge of plastic over the meat and roll up the plastic lengthwise. Tie one end securely with string. Twist the open end until the meat mixture is snug in the wrap and use the twisting pressure to help shape the package like a salami; tie the end securely.

5. Cut another 19-inch sheet of wrap. Put sausage seam-side down on plastic. Wrap as before but do not tie ends. Repeat seam-side-down wrapping four more times. Twist, then tie both ends securely with string. Bend ends upwards, and tie again, in a double thickness, to make a watertight package. Put sausage on coldest refrigerator shelf for 12 hours, or overnight, before cooking.

6. To cook, pour 3 inches of water into a deep skillet or roasting pan large enough to contain the package. Heat water to simmering. Add the package (which will float). Put a cover slightly ajar (or make a foil cover) and poach the sausage at a slow simmer for 25 minutes. Turn package over and poach 25 minutes longer. Carefully lift hot package from water. Cool to room temperature in wrapper.

7. Without opening, wrap package in aluminum foil. Refrigerate 24 hours to 5 days. Unwrap and cut diagonally into ¼-inch-thick slices. Serve chilled.

SEASON TO TASTE

Recipes for the cold pâtés (and also for a number of pasta sauces) call for adjusting the seasoning of various mixtures to taste slightly salty and peppery.

In the case of the Country Pork Terrine and Homemade Garlic Sausage with Pistachios (pages 90 and 92), the meat mixtures cannot be tasted raw—it is necessary to cook a small amount and taste it for seasoning. Bear in mind that heat accentuates the effect of seasoning, whereas cold dulls flavors. Therefore, pâté mixtures that do taste salty and peppery (i.e., overseasoned) when they are hot will probably be just right when they are served cold.

The same principle applies to pasta salads, potato or rice salads, and pasta sauces which, when tossed with pasta or starchy vegetables or grains, tend to become slightly bland. For best results, always taste such mixtures shortly before serving and adjust the seasoning as required.

PART TWO

DOUBLES

CHARMED CIRCLES:
SAVORY TARTS, PIZZAS, AND CALZONES

TALES OF DOUGH:
PASTA AND SAUCE

TAKING STOCK:
HEARTY SOUPS AND RISOTTOS

CHARMED CIRCLES:
SAVORY TARTS, PIZZAS, AND CALZONES

Among my favorite foods are charmed doughy circles of French and Italian origin—savory tarts, pizzas, and calzone. I always enjoy their bracing aromas, the tang of melted cheese, the surprise of hidden treasures nestled within a filling, or the lovely color and pattern of foods that adorn them. While each is good as an appetizer, each also can have a second or "double" use as the light main course of a casual menu.

Although making tarts, pizzas, and calzone is less complex than mastering a terrine, procuring special ingredients or tackling an unfamiliar pastry technique is undoubtedly more difficult than making soup or assembling a salad. Still, there are ample rewards when these enticing foods are served, whether as a first course or, with the addition of a green salad and dessert, as the mainstay of a complete meal.

Most savory tarts are sophisticated cousins of the French quiche, assemblages of ingredients bound with eggs and cream. However, each tart in this chapter has a twist—be it an interesting cheese, a refined crust, some distinctive spice, or special visual effect—that sets it apart.

Think of calzone as pizzas gone wrong—folded-over circles that enclose a meltingly delicious mess. Like most turnovers, calzone are initially flat, but steam trapped inside the pocket makes each one puff dramatically. The intense oven heat also creates a wonderfully chewy exterior crust.

Growing up in California, I always ate "street pies," thin, large-scale pizzas with the predictable cheese-and-tomato topping. But after a trip to the Italian Riviera, I discovered small pizzas, which one of my friends calls "art pies," with toppings that often excluded cheese.

My notes from that trip record my conversations with a superb pizza baker on the subject of his wonderful chewy pizzas, baked in a wood-burning oven. His menu at the Pizzeria Alfonso included *pizza bianca* (white pizza with cheese but no tomato sauce), *frutti di mare* (seafood, including rings of squid), *quattro stagione* (the four seasons represented by prosciutto, mushrooms, cheese, and artichokes), mushroom pizzas, and pizzas topped with green olives. Sadly, his name is lost, but his pizzas are my inspiration here.

To replicate those crusts, I began using a stone liner in my electric oven, which produced delicious results. Practically speaking, it may be easier to bake pizzas and calzone on metal cookie sheets.

Paddling of pizzas in and out of the oven is quite a stylish maneuver when guests are around, and transferring them from the baker's peel to each plate injects a casual, yet quite sensational, note of theater into an evening. Invariably, I find that guests want to get in on the act—particularly friends who have fantasies of owning or working in restaurants (as so many people do these days). Now, that's entertaining.

FOUR-VEGETABLE TART

Pastry in a Flash

The Power of Flour

ONION AND CHEVRE TART

Mixed Herbs

SAGA AND WATERCRESS TART

SAUSAGE AND ARTICHOKE PIZZAS

The Refrigerated Rise

SMOKED-SALMON PIZZAS

The Pizza Process

PROSCIUTTO AND LEEK PIZZAS ON OREGANO CRUST

Romancing the Stone

MUSHROOM PIZZAS ON PROSCIUTTO CRUST

GREMOLADA OIL

CALZONE WITH PROSCIUTTO AND BRIE

CALZONE WITH SAUSAGE AND PUMATE

Table Manners

FOUR-VEGETABLE TART

Fresh vegetables retain their individuality in this dramatic and colorful tart, which is topped with roasted red bell peppers. Broccoli florets are arranged like a green fringe in a ring around the outer edge, so the bright red-pepper center shows through.

Because small amounts of cheese (Jack, Gruyère, or Munster) rather than custard hold the layers together, the type and quality of the cheese used is very important. It should have a nutty, mild taste rather than an assertive or sour flavor.

To mold the crust, you will need a 9-inch tart pan (with removable bottom and preferably with a black finish), or a 9-inch × ¾-inch flan ring placed on a baking sheet.

FLEXIBLE MENU SUGGESTIONS

If the tart is served as an appetizer, round out the menu with One-Side Grilled Fish (page 216) and Anchovy-Lemon Oil (page 63) or Tomato Butter (page 220). Good alternatives to the fish are Leg of Lamb with Niçoise Seasoning (page 248) or Mushroom and Prosciutto-Stuffed Chicken Breasts (page 274).

In menus that feature the tart as a main course, begin with Scallop Bisque (page 40), Chicken Saté with a Taste of Tokyo (page 455), or Smoked Fish Rillettes (page 454) with crackers or French Dinner Rolls (page 360). For dessert, any of the ices (pages 434 to 437) with Mixed Nut Sablés (page 442) or Coconut-Lime Tuiles (page 440) would be good if the menu includes the bisque or rillettes. Double Chocolate Ice Cream (page 399) or Espresso-Brownie Chunk Ice Cream (page 397) would nicely complete a menu that begins with the skewered chicken. *Makes 6 to 8 servings*

PREPARATION: 1 HOUR
BAKING: 45 MINUTES

CRUST

1 cup unbleached all-purpose flour, plus
    additional flour
Salt
¼ pound frozen unsalted butter, cut in
    8 pieces
¼ to ⅓ cup ice water
1 tablespoon Dijon mustard

FILLING

2 large red bell peppers
1¼ pounds broccoli, rinsed
½ pound Monterey Jack, imported Gruyère,
    or Munster cheese, chilled, cubed

1 large onion (6 ounces), peeled
¾ pound small zucchini
3½ tablespoons olive or vegetable oil
½ tablespoon butter

1. For the crust, insert the metal blade in a food processor. Add 1 cup flour, ¼ teaspoon salt, and butter. Process until butter disappears. With the machine running, pour, ¼ cup ice water and process until dough begins to clump. (Or pulse in remaining water until dough clumps.)

2. Sprinkle 1 tablespoon flour on work surface. Remove dough from processor, handling as little as possible, and press together

into a smooth disk. Flour top of dough lightly and roll to a 13-inch circle. Transfer dough to a 9-inch fluted tart pan with removable bottom. Gently press it into the pan, fitting it snugly around the bottom edge and against the side of the pan. Trim excess from the top and sides of the pan, cover it loosely, and freeze 10 minutes.

3. Adjust oven rack to lowest position. Heat oven to 375 degrees. With skewer, pierce dough at 2-inch intervals. Put a sheet of aluminum foil snugly over the bottom and sides. Fill foil with pie weights, beans, or rice. Bake 35 minutes.

4. Cool crust 5 minutes. Carefully remove weights and foil. Return it to the oven for 3 to 7 minutes, or until crust is thoroughly cooked and lightly browned. Immediately brush mustard over inside of crust; cool.

5. For the filling, roast peppers on gas stove burner or under broiler, turning until their skins blacken. Transfer peppers to a plastic bag, twist bag closed, and set aside 10 minutes.

6. Remove broccoli florets, saving stems for another use. Put florets in a vegetable steamer basket (page 317). Cover and steam until crisp-tender, about 5 minutes. Rinse with cold water, then drain florets thoroughly on cloth towels.

7. Shred and set the cheese aside. Slice and transfer the onion to a large skillet. Slice the zucchini.

8. Add half the oil to the skillet with the onion and toss over medium heat until softened, about 6 minutes; set aside. With remaining oil, toss zucchini over medium heat until tender, about 7 minutes; set aside.

9. To assemble the tart, sprinkle ½ cup grated cheese on bottom of tart crust. Drain and pat zucchini dry (discard any liquid), then arrange it in an even layer in tart. Cover with ⅓ cup cheese. Spread onions in an even layer and top them with ½ cup cheese.

10. Scrape off pepper skins and split each pepper lengthwise. Open peppers flat, removing the seeds and cores. Pat peppers dry and put them in an even layer covering the cheese. Sprinkle remaining cheese along the outer edge of the tart, leaving a 2-inch-diameter circle of red pepper showing at the center. Arrange broccoli florets in a circle over the cheese. (Can keep at room temperature 2 hours.)

11. Heat oven to 375 degrees. Butter a sheet of aluminum foil and use it to cover the tart loosely. Bake 25 to 30 minutes, until cheese is thoroughly melted and vegetables are hot. Serve immediately.

PASTRY IN A FLASH

I know of no faster, easier, or more foolproof method for making pastry dough than the food-processor "frozen-butter method" used for recipes in this chapter. These doughs can be mixed and rolled out immediately, eliminating delays while you wait for the pastry to chill.

The key is to use firmly frozen butter, which keeps the dough exceptionally cold during processing. Other ingredients such as ice water, chilled wine, refrigerator-cold eggs, or cold milk help the butter act effectively as a coolant.

Two pastry problems—dough that is too soft to roll and dough that becomes elastic and will not stretch properly—are eliminated when this method is used for tart or pie doughs. The ice-cold temperature of processed dough permits it to be rolled out immediately since the development of gluten, which causes elasticity in doughs (and toughness when pastry is baked), is kept to a minimum.

Gluten is the protein structure formed in dough when wheat flour is mixed with liquid. By processing the cold butter thoroughly into the flour, particles of fat actually "waterproof" the flour, helping to prevent development of gluten that would cause the dough to become elastic and the resulting pastry to toughen. Care must be taken not to overwork the dough in the processor after liquid is added. Shaping dough into a flat disk (rather than forming it into a ball) helps to prevent overworking dough during rolling.

Most of these recipes call for ¼ pound (1 stick) of frozen, unsalted butter, which is a handy measurement since butter is so often stored by the stick in the freezer. To prepare butter for processing, slice the stick into 8 pieces (each equivalent to 1 tablespoon). A large knife or cleaver is recommended, since the natural heft of the utensil helps to exert pressure on the butter without causing it to soften.

This frozen-butter method can be applied to any tart or pie-crust recipe, to rough puff pastry, and to croissant dough, with no loss of quality.

Depending on the dough called for in a recipe, butter is processed into flour in a certain sequence. For classic doughs that contain flour, butter, salt, and liquid—but no egg—process the butter into the flour until it completely disappears and the mixture takes on a sandy texture.

Doughs that call for an egg or egg yolk are processed in two or three stages. First, the frozen butter may be coarsely chopped. Then, the egg and some, or all, of the liquid required in the recipe is pulsed into the butter. Flour is then pulsed in until the dough begins to clump.

For rough puff pastry or croissant dough, butter can be processed to a beadlike or pealike consistency so that the granules of fat help promote the expansion of those doughs during baking.

For best results, follow the processing sequence precisely. Again, be sure the butter is freezer-cold at the moment it is added to the processor.

THE POWER OF FLOUR

Combining two different types of flour creates doughs that are especially workable, with excellent baked results. A majority of the doughs for savory tarts in this chapter are made with a blend of unbleached flour and plain (*not* self-rising) cake flour to produce very tender crusts.

For pizzas and calzone, a mixture of bread flour and plain cake flour is usually best, since bread flour has a high protein content that promotes the development of gluten (see page 345) and the elasticity needed for stretching dough into circles, while cake flour helps to give the baked dough a fine crumb.

It has become standard practice for me to keep three types of flour on hand in my kitchen: bread flour (for breads, pizzas, and pasta), unbleached all-purpose flour (for most pastry and general use), and plain cake flour (for cakes, and blending into pastry and yeasted doughs).

Storing this much flour can be a nuisance. Therefore, feel free to substitute unbleached all-purpose flour for the total amount of a bread- and cake-flour combination, or for the total amount of an unbleached-flour and cake-flour mixture in any of these recipes.

How will the results differ with substitutions? That depends on the area of the country where the unbleached all-purpose flour is purchased. In the southern half of the U.S. and in the west, unbleached flour is generally softer (less absorptive and lower in protein, hence gluten) than the same type of flour sold in the midwest, northwest, and northeast.

The side panel of every flour bag gives you an average number of grams of protein per cup (4 ounces). All-purpose flour with an average protein content of 10 to 12 grams per cup is the best substitute to use for flour blends.

If you are going to the trouble of blending flours, as indicated in the recipes, consult the chart on page 131 to be sure you begin with flours that match the protein content of the ones I use in recipes.

Because of the wide variations in flour, the amount you may need can vary from the minimum specified in a recipe to as much as $\frac{1}{4}$ to $\frac{1}{2}$ cup more than the maximum amount indicated. It is best to begin with the smallest amount specified in recipes and to add flour gradually (2 tablespoons at a time) rather than try to salvage a dry, unworkable dough.

ONION AND CHEVRE TART

Over the years, my family had a running joke about what my mother had planned for dinner. "I haven't decided yet," was her usual reply. "But chop two onions and then I'll figure it out." Little wonder I developed such a fondness for these odoriferous members of the lily clan.

In this savory tart, four different onions—shallots, Spanish onions, scallions (green onions), and chives—are combined in the filling. To downplay their sweetness when cooked, acidic fresh goat cheese (page 141) is processed into the custard. A final dusting of grated Parmesan gives the tart a beautiful bronzed finish.

FLEXIBLE MENU SUGGESTIONS

The tart is a delicious first course for menus based on Scampi alla Busara (page 272), One-Side Grilled Fish (page 216) with Tomato Butter (page 220), Sage-Rubbed Veal Chops (page 242), Leg of Lamb with Niçoise Seasoning (page 248), or Herb-Rubbed Chicken (page 278).

As a main course it can be preceded by Tomato Soup with Garlic and Basil (page 44) and followed by Almond and Lemon-Stuffed Pears (page 431) or Black Plum Sorbet (page 437) and Mixed Nut Sablés (page 442). *Makes 8 servings*

PREPARATION: 30 MINUTES
BAKING: 55 MINUTES

CRUST

¼ pound frozen unsalted butter, cut in 8
    pieces
Salt
4 tablespoons chilled dry white wine
1 egg yolk
1½ to 1¾ cups unbleached all-purpose flour

FILLING

1 ounce Parmesan cheese (two 1-inch cubes)
4 medium shallots, peeled
2 medium onions, peeled, halved
2 tablespoons olive oil
1 large bunch scallions, trimmed
¼ pound (½ cup packed) fresh goat cheese
3 eggs
Salt and ground black pepper
Ground nutmeg

Hot red pepper sauce
½ cup half-and-half
1 cup whipping cream
1 tablespoon Dijon mustard
2 tablespoons snipped fresh chives

1. For the crust, put the butter in a food processor fitted with the metal blade. Pulse to chop it to the consistency of small beads. Pulse in ¼ teaspoon salt, the wine, and egg yolk. Add 1½ cups flour and process by pulsing until dough begins to clump. (Pulse in 2 tablespoons more flour if dough is sticky.)

2. Gather dough into a flat disk and roll it, on a generously floured surface, into a 14-inch circle. Transfer the circle of dough to an 11-inch fluted tart pan with removable bottom. Ease dough into pan and fit it snugly around the bottom edge and against

the side. Trim to form a raised edge that is parallel to, and about ⅛ inch higher than, the side of the pan. Freeze the dough for 10 minutes. Pierce it at 1-inch intervals with the point of a skewer. (Can wrap and freeze overnight.)

3. Adjust oven rack to lowest position. Heat oven to 375 degrees. Line the dough with aluminum foil and add pie weights or rice. Bake 20 minutes (25 minutes if frozen overnight). Remove foil and weights; set the crust aside to cool.

4. For the filling, grate the Parmesan cheese by processing until it is powdery; set aside. Mince the shallots and coarsely chop the onion. Heat the olive oil in a skillet and cook onion mixture over medium heat until lightly colored, stirring frequently, about 15 minutes; cool. Slice the scallions into thin rings; set aside.

5. If necessary, remove and discard goat-cheese rind or coating. Using the metal processor blade, pulse together the goat cheese, eggs, ¼ teaspoon salt, ½ teaspoon ground black pepper, and several dashes each of nutmeg and hot red pepper sauce. Add half-and-half and process until smooth, then add cream and process just until mixed. Taste and adjust the seasoning.

6. Brush the inside of the cooled crust with mustard. Scatter the cooked onion mixture, scallions, and chives evenly in the crust. Add the egg mixture, and sprinkle the top with the Parmesan cheese. Bake until the center of the tart is just set, about 35 minutes. (Can bake 4 to 6 hours ahead and rewarm in 300-degree oven.) Serve lukewarm.

MIXED HERBS

Spending a month in Provence indelibly influenced my recipe for Mixed Herbs, which is similar to *herbes de Provence,* and is one of my flavoring basics.

Even in my apartment kitchen I am able to grow pots of fresh herbs in a sunny window so I always have thyme, sage, rosemary, and chives on hand, and during the summer, basil does very well. I regularly snip the herbs, dry them on strings in my kitchen, and strip the dried leaves off the stems for this mixture, since home-dried herbs usually are fresh and potent in flavor.

The mixture can also be made from commercially packed dried herbs, and transferred to a small jar. This recipe should provide a six-month supply. Try not to keep dried herbs longer than six months, and certainly no more than one year. A good way to keep track of their age is to mark the top of each bottle with the date of purchase or bottling. Dating helps ensure that the flavor of herbs used in recipes is optimal.

This same mixture can be made of minced fresh herbs, which should be used moments after chopping and combining. *Makes about ¼ cup*

PREPARATION: 5 MINUTES

1 tablespoon dried basil
1 tablespoon dried summer savory
1 tablespoon dried oregano
1½ teaspoons dried thyme
1½ teaspoons dried sage leaves

Mix herbs together and transfer to an airtight jar.

SAGA AND WATERCRESS TART

Saga is a luscious triple-crème Danish blue cheese that made its American debut in 1978. Think of it as a blue Brie, and it won't be difficult to understand how it flavors this tart so superbly. You can substitute Danablu or imported *Gorgonzola dolce,* but be sure that these cheeses are fresh tasting and smelling, without any hint of ammonia. If you absolutely cannot find one of the double- or triple-crème cow's-milk blues or the Italian Gorgonzola, then it may be better to choose another recipe. Sheep's-milk blues (see the cheese chart on page 30) are too assertive to use here.

Whole-wheat pastry is a natural partner for the cheese, and an astringent watercress custard, spiraled into the tart, cuts the richness with a stunning effect.

FLEXIBLE MENU SUGGESTIONS

A French Sauternes, German Riesling, or California chenin blanc would be wonderfully compatible with the tart, and you can continue serving these wines with a main course of Sausages and Sauerkraut (page 186). Garlic-Roasted Leg of Lamb (page 295) can also follow the tart, but will require a red wine.

If the tart is to be a main course, begin with Sweet Potato and Apple Bisque (page 43), and serve Ultra-Fudge Brownies (page 395) or Chocolate Madeleines (page 394) and fresh raspberries or strawberries for dessert. *Makes 6 to 8 servings*

PREPARATION: 30 MINUTES
BAKING: 45 MINUTES

CRUST

¼ pound frozen unsalted butter, cut in 8 pieces
1 egg
Salt
¼ cup plain cake flour
½ to ¾ cup whole-wheat flour

FILLING

4 ounces Saga Blue or other creamy blue cheese)
2 ounces cream cheese
1⅓ cups whipping cream
1 egg yolk

4 eggs
Ground black pepper
Hot red pepper sauce
1 teaspoon sugar
1 medium bunch watercress, stemmed
Nutmeg

1. For the pastry, insert the metal blade in a dry food processor. Add butter, egg, and ⅛ teaspoon salt, and pulse until the mixture has the texture of small beads. Add cake flour and ½ cup whole-wheat flour. Process by pulsing until the dough begins to clump. (Can pulse in remaining whole-wheat flour if dough is very sticky.)

2. Adjust oven rack to lowest position. Heat oven to 375 degrees. Press dough into a flat disk, place it between overlapping sheets of wax paper, and roll to a 13-inch circle; transfer to a baking sheet and freeze 5 minutes.

3. Remove wax paper from the top and invert dough over a 9-inch fluted tart pan with removable bottom. Remove the remaining paper and gently press dough into pan, fitting it snugly around the bottom edge and against the side of the pan. Trim off excess dough and freeze 15 minutes. Line the dough with aluminum foil and add pie weights or rice. Bake 15 minutes. Remove foil and set crust aside to cool.

4. For the filling, put the cheeses in a processor fitted with the metal blade; process until smooth. Process in all but 2 tablespoons of the cream. Mix in egg yolk, 3 eggs, a pinch of pepper, several dashes of hot red pepper sauce, and sugar—do not overprocess. Transfer the mixture to a measuring cup.

5. Heat 2 quarts water to boiling in a large saucepan. Stir in watercress and cook until water boils again. Drain, rinse with cold tap water, then twist watercress dry in a cloth towel. Chop the watercress coarsely and mix it with the remaining egg, 2 tablespoons cream, and several dashes of nutmeg.

6. Pour the cheese mixture into the tart crust. Working carefully, pour the watercress mixture in a spiral design from inside edge to center of tart (it may displace the cheese mixture slightly). Bake at 375 degrees for 25 to 30 minutes, or until center is just set. Serve warm.

Recipe developed by Blair Verner.

SAUSAGE AND ARTICHOKE PIZZAS

Is a pizza a pizza without tomato sauce and mozzarella cheese? Absolutely, and pizzas topped with mixtures of vegetables, meat, and cheeses that I first tasted in Italy are my inspiration here.

Artichokes, imported Italian Fontina and Provolone cheeses, and air-dried sausage make an interesting, different, and delicious quartet. But the pizzas will only be as good as the basic ingredients. Air-dried sausage is available in Italian food stores (a good brand has been made by Alps in Astoria, N.Y., since 1929) and many supermarkets.

Since both the sausage and Provolone tend to be salty, there is neither salt nor pepper in the recipe—but be sure to taste the cheeses and sausage and let the flavor of the ingredients be your guide to seasoning.

FLEXIBLE MENU SUGGESTIONS

Pizza is a natural appetizer before Scampi alla Busara (page 272), One-Side Grilled Fish (page 216) with Orso Butter (page 221), or Herb-Rubbed Chicken (page 278).

Double the recipe to serve this as a main course for four (it does not work easily for six). Begin with Tomato Soup with Garlic and Basil (page 44), Mozzarella, Tomato, and Olive Salad (page 62), Lettuce, Radicchio, and Fennel Salad (page 70), or Milanese Asparagus Soup (page 162). End on a casual note with Double Chocolate Ice Cream and Bittersweet Chocolate Sauce (pages 399 and 400), Espresso-Brownie Chunk Ice Cream (page 397), or Baked Stuffed Apples (page 425). *Makes 2 pizzas (9 inches each)*

PREPARATION: 20 MINUTES
RISING: 4 HOURS OR OVERNIGHT
BAKING: 10 MINUTES

SPONGE

¾ teaspoon dry active yeast
⅓ cup warm (110 degrees) water
½ cup bread flour or unbleached all-purpose flour

DOUGH

1¼ to 1⅓ cups bread flour or unbleached all-purpose flour
Salt
⅓ cup warm (110 degrees) water

TOPPING

1 medium clove garlic, peeled
2 tablespoons mild olive oil or Herbed Oil (page 73)
6 ounces Fontina cheese, chilled (1½ cups shredded)
2 ounces Provolone cheese, chilled (½ cup shredded)
12 thin slices air-dried Italian sausage, or 2 ounces cooked, crumbled fresh Italian sausage
2 to 3 marinated artichoke hearts, quartered and drained
1 teaspoon Mixed Herbs (page 105)

1. For the sponge, combine yeast and warm water in a mixing bowl or 1-quart airtight container. Stir well. Stir in flour to form a thick paste. Cover tightly and set aside until double in volume, about 2 hours. (Can cover and refrigerate 2 days.)

2. For the dough, insert the metal blade in a food processor. Add 1¼ cups flour, ¾ teaspoon salt, water, and the sponge. Process until dough forms a soft, moist (but not sticky) ball, about 40 seconds. Proceed with step 3 if dough will rise in a bowl. Omit step 3 and continue with step 4 if you are using a refrigerated rise (see page 109).

3. Rinse a large mixing bowl with warm water. Without drying the bowl, add dough and cover tightly with plastic wrap. Set aside at room temperature until dough triples in volume, about 2 to 3 hours. Remove dough from the bowl and cut it in half. Knead each piece into a 4-inch diameter cushion; cover and refrigerate for 30 minutes.

4. Or, remove dough from food processor, cut it in half and shape it into cushions. Transfer each dough cushion to a zipper-lock plastic bag and refrigerate overnight, or up to 3 days; dough is ready to stretch.

5. Mince and mix the garlic with the oil; set aside. Shred the cheeses and set aside.

6. Adjust oven rack to lowest position (add optional oven stone). Heat oven to 450 degrees. Lightly flour work surface. Roll or stretch each cushion of chilled dough to a 9-inch circle, rotating and stretching as you work. Transfer dough circles to a baking sheet, or assemble each one separately on a floured baker's peel.

7. Brush each dough circle generously with garlic oil. Leaving a ½-inch border at the edge, cover each with ¾ cup of shredded Fontina. Top each pizza with six sausage slices (or half the cooked crumbled sausage), four pieces of artichoke (cut up if large), half the Provolone, and half the herbs. Drizzle 1 teaspoon oil over each pizza.

8. Bake pizzas (or slide them one at a time onto the hot oven stone) for 8 to 10 minutes, or until cheese bubbles and crust is lightly browned. Serve immediately.

THE REFRIGERATED RISE

Once pizza or calzone dough is mixed and thoroughly kneaded, it can be set aside to rise by one of two different methods.

The conventional technique is to place the dough in a warm, wet mixing bowl (or in an oiled bowl, if you prefer) and cover the bowl tightly with plastic wrap. When set aside at a room temperature of about 75 to 80 degrees, dough will double or triple in volume within 2 to 3 hours. Dough that has risen at room temperature is then ready to be divided into portions, worked into flat disks or cushion shapes, and refrigerated. Chilling the dough at this point makes it easier to stretch.

Another method is to mix the dough, cut it into serving portions, and shape it into cushions. Each piece then can be placed in a rinsed-out zipper-lock plastic bag and refrigerated overnight. This "refrigerated rise" actually *replaces* the room temperature rise in a bowl. Dough is now ready to use, or leave in the refrigerator until cooking time, up to 2 days longer, if desired.

Note that this same technique is used for making bread doughs (see box, page 347).

SMOKED-SALMON PIZZAS

The flavor of smoked salmon can be wonderfully enhanced by placing it on the surface of a hot baked circle of pizza dough spread with chive-laced sour cream. The heat of the dough warms both the salmon and the cream slightly, making this a knockout replacement for a traditional smoked-salmon appetizer.

Top-quality smoked salmon, sliced paper thin, works best for these pizzas. Provided they are cut from the center of a salmon fillet, 1 to 1½ slices should amply cover the surface of each pie.

FLEXIBLE MENU SUGGESTIONS

As an appetizer, allow half a pizza (two quarters) per person, or make the pizzas in miniature (4½-inch rounds). To complete the menu, serve Roasted Duck with Apples and Campari (page 289) or Mushroom and Prosciutto-Stuffed Chicken Breasts with Whole-Grain Mustard-Chive Butter (page 274).

It will be necessary to double the recipe to serve four as a main course for a casual dinner. Begin then, with Cream of Watercress Soup (page 43), Beet-Salad Mimosa (page 59), or the ever-useful Lettuce, Radicchio, and Fennel Salad (page 70)—each is compatible with the salmon. Apple Crisp (page 424) or any of the ices (pages 434 to 437) are desserts that complement the pizzas. *Makes 2 pizzas (9 inches each)*

PREPARATION: 20 MINUTES
RISING: 4 HOURS OR OVERNIGHT
BAKING: 10 MINUTES

SPONGE

¾ teaspoon dry active yeast
⅓ cup warm (110 degrees) water
½ cup bread flour or unbleached all-purpose flour

DOUGH

1¼ to 1⅓ cups bread flour or unbleached all-purpose flour
Salt
⅓ cup warm (110 degrees) water

TOPPING

Olive oil
Ground black pepper
3 tablespoons minced chives
6 tablespoons sour cream or crème fraîche
6 ounces thinly sliced smoked salmon

1. For the sponge, combine yeast and warm water in a mixing bowl or 1-quart airtight container; stir well. Stir in flour to form a thick paste. Cover tightly and set aside until double in volume, about 2 hours. (Can cover and refrigerate 2 days.)

2. For the dough, insert metal blade in a food processor. Add 1¼ cups flour, ¾ teaspoon salt, water, and the sponge. Process until dough forms a soft, moist (but not

sticky) ball, about 40 seconds. Proceed with step 3 if dough will rise in a bowl. Omit step 3 and continue with step 4 if you are using a refrigerated rise (see page 109).

3. Rinse a large mixing bowl with warm water. Without drying bowl, add dough, cover the bowl tightly with plastic wrap, and set aside at room temperature until dough triples in volume, about 2 to 3 hours. Remove dough from bowl and cut it in half. Knead each piece into a small cushion shape. Cover and refrigerate for 30 minutes; dough is ready to stretch.

4. Or, remove dough from the food processor, cut it in half, and shape it into cushions. Transfer dough cushions to a zipper-lock plastic bag and refrigerate overnight, or as long as 3 days; dough is ready to stretch.

5. Adjust oven rack to lowest position (insert optional oven stone). Heat oven to 450 degrees. Lightly flour work surface. Roll or stretch each piece of dough to a 9-inch circle, rotating and stretching as you work. Transfer dough circles to a baking sheet or, working individually, to a floured baker's peel.

6. Brush each dough circle generously with oil; sprinkle with pepper. Bake on sheets (or slide pizzas onto hot oven stone) for 8 to 10 minutes, until bottom of crust is lightly browned. Meanwhile, mix chives into sour cream. When pizzas are baked, immediately spread 3 tablespoons sour cream on each hot dough circle. Top with smoked salmon. Serve immediately.

THE PIZZA PROCESS

Thin-crusted individual pizzas are simple to prepare in advance, refrigerate until serving time, roll, and top with a variety of cheeses, meats, vegetables, and herbs.

The fastest way to make pizza (or calzone) dough is to mix it in a processor. I calculate that 20 to 30 seconds of processing with the metal blade is equivalent to 6 to 8 minutes of hand kneading. Double batches of dough may require up to 1 minute of processing. Dough is completely kneaded when the texture is uniform and no firm areas remain in the center. (Of course, pizza doughs may be kneaded by hand.)

Following a 2- to 2½-hour rise at room temperature, or prior to a refrigerated rise overnight in a plastic bag (the two are interchangeable in these recipes), divide the dough and fashion it into flat, cushion-shaped disks. Chilled disks of dough can be used immediately, or left in a zipper-lock plastic bag for as long as 3 days (including the overnight rise). Aging pizza dough longer than 12 hours helps to develop acids that create a good flavor and superior crusts. It is best not to freeze pizza dough.

Slightly chilled cushions of dough stretch into perfect rounds for pizza or calzone. Do *not* knead the shaped dough or it will become elastic and will not stretch properly.

For best results, use the type of flour specified in the recipes (see page 131 if you wish to make substitutions) since different flour combinations help to produce nuances of flavor and texture in crusts.

PROSCIUTTO AND LEEK PIZZAS ON OREGANO CRUST

Flecks of oregano in the pizza dough complement the toppings and boost the flavor of the thin, crackly-crisp crust. Here, the dough is garnished—rather than blanketed—with leek, prosciutto, and Fontina cheese, making these pizzas delicate rather than hearty. If you prefer rosemary to oregano, substitute the dough from the recipe for Rosemary Breadsticks (page 343), but you may need to adjust the menus so that herbs do not clash.

FLEXIBLE MENU SUGGESTIONS

In a menu for four, serve the pizzas before Veal Scallops Giardino (page 284). Follow additional serving suggestions for Sausage and Artichoke Pizzas (page 108). However, since this is such a very light main course, a substantial appetizer and dessert is needed.

Makes 4 pizzas (6 inches each)

PREPARATION: 30 MINUTES
RISING: 4 HOURS OR OVERNIGHT
BAKING: 7 TO 10 MINUTES

SPONGE

¾ teaspoon dry active yeast
⅓ cup warm (110 degrees) water
⅓ cup bread flour or unbleached all-purpose flour

DOUGH

½ to ⅔ cup bread flour or unbleached all-purpose flour
½ cup plain cake flour
Salt
1 tablespoon dried oregano leaves
2 tablespoons warm (110 degrees) water
2 tablespoons olive or vegetable oil

TOPPING

2 medium garlic cloves, peeled
6 tablespoons olive oil or Herbed Oil (page 73)
2 tablespoons tomato paste

1½ cups julienned leek (white part only)
Salt and ground black pepper
4 paper-thin prosciutto slices
6 ounces Fontina cheese
Additional flour for rolling dough

1. For the sponge, combine yeast and warm water in a mixing bowl or 1-quart airtight container; stir well. Stir in flour to form a thick paste. Cover tightly and set aside until doubled, about 2 hours. (Can cover tightly and refrigerate 2 days.)

2. In a processor fitted with the metal blade, combine ½ cup bread flour with cake flour, ½ teaspoon salt, oregano, water, and oil. Process 10 seconds. Add the sponge and process until dough forms a smooth, silky ball (add remaining flour or additional water by tablespoons, if necessary). Proceed with step 3 if dough will rise in a bowl. Omit step 3 and continue with step 4 if you are using a refrigerated rise (see page 109).

3. Put dough in a warm wet bowl, cover tightly with plastic wrap, and set aside at room temperature until tripled, about 2 to 2½ hours. Remove dough from bowl and cut it into four pieces. Knead each piece into a small cushion shape. Cover and refrigerate for 30 minutes; dough is ready to stretch.

4. Or, remove dough from food processor, cut it in four pieces, and shape it into cushions. Transfer dough cushions to a zipperlock plastic bag and refrigerate overnight, or as long as 3 days; dough is ready to stretch.

5. For the topping, mince the garlic. Transfer it to a bowl and stir in 3 tablespoons oil and the tomato paste; set mixture aside.

6. Put leek and remaining oil in a medium skillet and toss over medium heat until soft, about 8 minutes. Sprinkle lightly with salt and pepper; set aside.

7. Adjust oven rack to lowest position (insert optional oven stone). Heat oven to 450 degrees. Remove dough cushions from bag; do not knead. On a floured surface, stretch or roll each piece of dough to a 7-inch circle and transfer each to a baking sheet, two circles to a sheet. (Or, put each dough circle one by one on a floured baker's peel.)

8. Spread each dough circle with 1 scant tablespoon tomato mixture. Tear up and scatter one prosciutto slice on each piece of dough and top each with one quarter of the leeks. Slice the Fontina into 1½ × 2-inch paper-thin rectangles; put three or four Fontina slices on each pizza.

9. Bake pizzas on sheets (or use the peel to slide each pizza onto the oven stone as oven space permits) until dough is crisp, about 7 to 10 minutes. Serve immediately.

ROMANCING THE STONE

While excellent pizzas can be made on metal baking sheets, baking on an oven stone yields a crust of superior texture. My oven stone is more than ten years old, and I automatically count on using it for pizza and calzone. I am also accustomed to assembling pizzas on a flour-rubbed peel or paddle, and shimmying them off onto the stone (a long metal spatula can be used to help loosen doughs, if necessary).

I began baking pizzas on an oven stone set on a rack over a wood fire in a Weber kettle. Indoors, I transferred the stone to the lowest rack of my oven. After heating the stone for 30 minutes on the highest oven setting, I was able to simulate the effect of the special pizza ovens that create such wonderful crusts.

Oven stones absorb and radiate heat during cooking, significantly raising the temperature of the surface on which pizzas and calzones are baked, which promotes even cooking and browning. Some stones are large enough to handle two pizzas (8 to 9 inches each) at a time.

Cookware stores offer kits that contain both baking stones and the peels. Buy a stone with a porous (unglazed) surface in the largest size available.

There are two notes of caution. Oven stones remain hot long after the oven has cooled. Do not attempt to touch them or remove them from the oven until they are completely cool. If it is essential to remove a warm stone from the oven, protect your hands and place the stone out of the reach of children. Follow manufacturer's directions for cleaning and maintaining your stone.

If you have an electric oven, you should be aware that oven stones radiate heat that may adversely affect the oven thermostat with prolonged use. However, they work perfectly in gas ovens.

MUSHROOM PIZZAS ON PROSCIUTTO CRUST

Prosciutto dough makes a fabulous crust for pizzas topped (rather than baked) with strips and slices of cooked vegetables and nearly transparent slices of shaved Parmesan cheese. A drizzle of lemon- and garlic-scented Gremolada Oil moistens the assemblage and punches up the flavor of the vegetables.

Please organize your ingredients ahead of time! Since all the toppings are added at the last minute, they must be ready when the plain, baked disks of dough emerge from the oven. Otherwise the pizzas cannot be put together quickly enough to bring them to the table hot.

FLEXIBLE MENU SUGGESTIONS

Quarter the pizzas (allow two wedges per person) and serve them before Sage-Rubbed Veal Chops (page 242), One-Side Grilled Fish (page 216) with Tomato Butter (page 220), or Herb-Rubbed Chicken (page 278).

The recipe can be doubled as a main course for four. Begin with Tomato Soup with Garlic and Basil (page 44) or Milanese Asparagus Soup (page 162), and follow with a knockout dessert like Gianduia Cheesecake (page 384) or Ultra-Fudge Brownies (page 395) topped with ice cream and Instant Hot Fudge Sauce (page 401). *Makes 2 pizzas (9 inches each)*

PREPARATION: 35 MINUTES
RISING: 2½ TO 3 HOURS OR OVERNIGHT
BAKING: 7 TO 10 MINUTES

DOUGH

1 teaspoon dry active yeast
½ teaspoon sugar
½ cup warm (110 degrees) water
1⅓ to 1½ cups bread flour or unbleached all-purpose flour
Salt and coarsely ground black pepper
Olive oil
2-ounce chunk prosciutto, cut in ½-inch cubes

TOPPING

3 medium shallots, peeled
Olive oil
½ pound mushrooms, rinsed
Salt and ground black pepper

½ roasted, peeled, julienned red or yellow bell pepper (see page 339)
2-ounce (or larger) chunk Parmesan cheese
Additional flour for work surface
Gremolada Oil (page 115)

1. Dissolve yeast and sugar in warm water. Cover and set aside for 10 minutes.

2. Insert the metal blade in a food processor. Add 1⅓ cups flour, a pinch of salt, ½ teaspoon pepper, and 3 tablespoons of olive oil. With motor on, add yeast mixture to dry ingredients in a thin stream. Process 30 seconds longer. (If dough is very sticky, process in remaining flour.) Add prosciutto and process until dough is thoroughly kneaded and prosciutto is finely chopped. Proceed with step 3 if dough will rise in a bowl. Omit step

3 and continue with step 4 if you are using a refrigerated rise (see page 109).

3. Put dough in a warm, wet bowl, cover tightly with plastic wrap, and set aside until doubled, about 2 to 2½ hours. Remove dough from bowl and cut it in half. Knead each piece into a small cushion shape. Cover and refrigerate for 30 minutes; dough is ready to stretch.

4. Or, remove dough from food processor, cut it in half, and shape it into cushions. Transfer dough to a zipper-lock plastic bag, seal the bag, and refrigerate overnight, or as long as 3 days; dough is ready to stretch.

5. For the topping, mince and transfer the shallots to a medium skillet with 2 tablespoons oil. Slice the mushrooms. Sauté over medium heat until mushrooms give up their juices and darken, about 10 to 12 minutes. Salt and pepper mushrooms lightly; set aside in the skillet. Bring the red pepper to room temperature, if necessary. Use a vegetable peeler or a very sharp cleaver to shave the Parmesan cheese into paper-thin slices; set slices aside.

6. Adjust oven rack to lowest position (add optional oven stone). Heat oven to 550 degrees or highest oven setting. Stretch each piece of dough into a 9-inch circle, or roll into circles on lightly floured work surface. Transfer circles of dough to a baking sheet or baker's peel. Drizzle each circle with 1 teaspoon olive oil and sprinkle it lightly with pepper. Bake on sheets (or slide dough onto oven stone) for 7 to 10 minutes. Heat and keep the mushrooms hot.

7. Transfer dough disks from oven to dinner plates. Working quickly, drizzle 1 tablespoon Gremolada Oil over each dough circle and add half the mushrooms. Top each circle with julienned peppers and 3 more tablespoons Gremolada Oil. Scatter shaved Parmesan over pizzas. Serve immediately.

GREMOLADA OIL
~~~~~~~~~~~

Garlic, lemon, and parsley are the ingredients used in Gremolada, the Italian seasoning paste for *osso buco*. Here, the minced bits of lemon, garlic, and parsley perfume olive oil, adding a final fillip of flavor to vegetable pizzas.

If you have a small food processor, you can strip off the lemon zest with a vegetable peeler and process it together with the garlic and parsley until the mixture is minced.

FLEXIBLE MENU SUGGESTIONS

This recipe is similar to Anchovy-Lemon Oil (page 63), and in some cases the two are interchangeable. However, the presence of garlic gives this oil a strong flavor that tends to dominate delicate foods such as cheese. Try this as a marinade or rub for chicken, fish, veal, or lamb. *Makes ½ cup*

PREPARATION: 10 MINUTES

1 medium lemon
1 small garlic clove, peeled
¼ cup firmly packed parsley leaves
½ cup olive oil or Herbed Oil (page 73)

Grate the lemon zest into a bowl (reserve the lemon for another use). Mince and add the garlic and parsley. Stir in the oil. Cover and set aside for 1 hour (but no longer than 12 hours).

CALZONE WITH PROSCIUTTO AND BRIE

Unlike pizza, calzones offer an element of surprise since their fillings remain a mystery until the first bite. When served hot from the oven they are crisp and chewy, chock-full of mushrooms and prosciutto, and oozy with cheese.

These turnovers are simply rounds of pizza dough folded in half and sealed. They can be made, filled, and frozen for as long as six to eight weeks. If defrosted in the refrigerator, they will bake perfectly.

If you are not accustomed to handling pizza dough, you may wish to assemble each calzone (steps 7 and 8) on a separate sheet of heavy-duty aluminum foil, which makes them quite easy to move from the work surface to the refrigerator. It is important to avoid tearing the dough, or turnovers will not bake evenly or puff. If tears occur, moisten the dough with water and pinch it together. Irregularities in the top add charm to the look of the baked calzone, but the real danger lies in the bottom of the dough sticking to the work surface, since it is weighted down by the filling. Once the filled turnovers are refrigerated for an hour or longer (step 8), the dough is more resistant to tearing and sticking, and it should be relatively easy to transfer the calzone to the cornmeal-coated baking sheets (or a floured baker's peel if you are using an oven stone) without incident.

FLEXIBLE MENU SUGGESTIONS

Calzones are a bit too large to serve whole as a first course. You can cut each one in half to make four appetizer servings, slice each crosswise into one-inch-wide strips and serve them as a combination hors d'oeuvre and first course, or make four miniature turnovers from this recipe.

I prefer to serve calzones as a main course for four or six, and the recipe doubles or triples easily. Bear in mind that it will take about one minute to knead a double batch of the dough thoroughly. Follow serving suggestions for Sausage and Artichoke Pizzas (page 108). *Makes 2 large turnovers*

PREPARATION: 45 MINUTES
RISING: 4½ TO 5 HOURS OR OVERNIGHT
BAKING: 35 MINUTES

SPONGE

¾ teaspoon dry active yeast
⅓ cup warm (110 degrees) water
⅓ cup bread flour or unbleached all-purpose flour

DOUGH

1½ to 1¾ cups bread flour or unbleached all-purpose flour
½ cup plain cake flour
Salt
⅔ cup warm (110 degrees) water

FILLING

3 large mushrooms, wiped clean
¼ pound mozzarella cheese, chilled
1 ounce Parmesan cheese, rind removed (two
*   1-inch cubes)*
¼ pound Fontina cheese, rind removed, cubed
⅓ cup firmly packed parsley leaves
1 large garlic clove, peeled
1 teaspoon dried oregano
2 tablespoons olive or vegetable oil
4 to 6 paper-thin prosciutto slices (about 2
*   ounces)*
1 ounce Brie, rind removed (a 1½-inch
*   square), cut into ⅛-inch dice*
1 tablespoon cornmeal

1. For the sponge, combine yeast and water in a mixing bowl or in a 1-quart airtight container; stir well. Stir in flour to form a thick paste. Cover tightly and set aside until mixture doubles in volume, about 2 hours. (Can cover tightly and refrigerate 2 days.)

2. For the dough, put 1½ cups bread flour, the cake flour, and ¾ teaspoon salt in the container of a food processor fitted with the metal blade. Process, quickly adding water to the machine. Add the sponge and process until dough is soft and slightly sticky, about 30 to 45 seconds. Proceed with step 3 if dough will rise in a bowl. Omit step 3 and continue with step 4 if you are using a refrigerated rise (see page 109).

3. Transfer dough to a large, wet bowl. Cover the bowl tightly with plastic wrap and set it aside at room temperature until the dough triples in volume, about 2½ to 3 hours. Remove dough from the bowl and cut it in half. Knead each piece into a small cushion shape. Cover and refrigerate for 30 minutes; dough is ready to stretch.

4. Or, remove dough from food processor, cut it in half, and shape it into cushions.

Transfer dough cushions to a zipper-lock plastic bag and refrigerate overnight, or as long as 3 days; dough is ready to stretch.

5. For the filling, slice the mushrooms; set aside. Shred the mozzarella; set aside in a mixing bowl. Grate the Parmesan cheese, then add it to the bowl. Coarsely chop or shred the Fontina; add it to the bowl.

6. Mince the parsley together with the garlic and oregano. Transfer the mixture to a small bowl and stir in the oil; set aside.

7. Lightly flour a work surface. Remove chilled dough from the bag without kneading. Stretch or roll each piece of dough to a 10-inch circle. Leaving a 1-inch border at the edge, spread each dough circle with half the parsley-oil. Layer one side (one half) of each dough circle with two or three prosciutto slices, half the mushrooms, half the grated cheeses, and half the Brie.

8. With a finger dipped in water, moisten the unoiled border of the dough. Fold the dough circle in half to enclose the filling in a half-moon shape. Press tightly to seal and thin out the edge of the dough. Roll about ¼ to ½ inch of the dough back up and onto itself, and press down to form a tightly crimped, raised edge. Refrigerate for 1 hour (can wrap in plastic and freeze).

9. Sprinkle cornmeal evenly over a baking sheet. Gently transfer chilled turnovers to the baking sheet.

10. Adjust oven rack to lowest position. Heat oven to 550 degrees (or highest oven setting). Put baking sheet in oven and immediately spray turnovers with water. Bake 30 to 35 minutes, until lightly brown, spraying again halfway through baking. Serve immediately, taking care to let steam escape as turnovers are cut.

CALZONE WITH SAUSAGE AND PUMATE

Pumate are tomatoes from Italy that travelers often see drying on straw mats in the sun. These sun-dried tomatoes have a concentrated flavor and a texture that ranges from leathery to plummy soft. Look for those packed in olive oil; thus preserved they remain supple and ready to eat. The oil will be tinted red and infused with their pungent aroma—save it for use in salad dressings. The tomatoes and their oil also are used in Tomato Flatbread with Two Herbs (page 346).   •

You can now choose between imported or domestic dried tomatoes; both are often found in specialty stores and supermarkets. Be sure to read the introduction to the Calzone with Prosciutto and Brie (page 116) for information on handling the assembled turnovers.

FLEXIBLE MENU SUGGESTIONS

Because the calzones contain *pumate*, omit tomato soup from the list of menu possibilities. Otherwise, follow suggestions for Sausage and Artichoke Pizzas (page 108).
Makes 2 to 4 servings

PREPARATION: 45 MINUTES
RISING: 4½ TO 5 HOURS OR OVERNIGHT
BAKING: 35 MINUTES

SPONGE

¾ teaspoon dry active yeast
⅓ cup warm (110 degrees) water
⅓ cup bread flour or unbleached all-purpose flour

DOUGH

1½ to 1¾ cups bread flour or unbleached all-purpose flour
½ cup plain cake flour
Salt
⅔ cup warm (110 degrees) water

FILLING

1 ounce (two 1-inch chunks) Parmesan cheese, rind removed
⅓ cup firmly packed parsley leaves
6 large fresh sage leaves or ½ teaspoon dried sage
1 medium shallot, peeled
2 tablespoons olive oil, or pumate oil
¼ pound semisoft Italian cheese (Fontina, Bel Paese, or caciotta), rind removed, chilled
¼ pound fresh mozzarella, chilled
½ pound sweet Italian sausage, cooked and chopped (casing removed)
⅓ cup firmly packed pumate, drained and thinly sliced
1 tablespoon cornmeal

1. For the sponge, combine yeast and water in a mixing bowl or in a 1-quart airtight container; stir well. Stir in flour to form a thick paste. Cover tightly and set aside until mixture doubles in volume, about 2 hours. (Can cover tightly and refrigerate 2 days.)

2. For the dough, put 1½ cups bread flour, the cake flour, and ¾ teaspoon salt in the container of a food processor fitted with the metal blade. Process, quickly adding water. Add the sponge and process until dough is soft and slightly sticky, about 30 to 45 seconds. Proceed with step 3 if dough will rise in a bowl. Omit step 3 and continue with step 4 if you are using a refrigerated rise (see page 109).

3. Transfer dough to a large warm, wet bowl. Cover tightly with plastic wrap and set aside at room temperature until dough triples in volume, about 2½ to 3 hours. Remove dough from the bowl and cut it in half. Knead each piece into a small cushion shape. Cover and refrigerate dough for 30 minutes; dough is ready to stretch.

4. Or, remove dough from food processor, cut it in half, and shape it into cushions. Transfer dough cushions to a zipper-lock plastic bag and refrigerate overnight, or as long as 3 days; dough is ready to stretch.

5. For the filling, grate the Parmesan by processing it to a powder; set aside. Mince the parsley, sage, and shallot, transfer to a small bowl, and stir in the oil; cover and set aside. Coarsely chop the semisoft cheese by pulsing in the processor (or shred the cheese). Cut the mozzarella into ¼-inch dice. Set cheeses aside with the Parmesan.

6. Lightly flour a work surface. Remove chilled dough cushions from the bag without kneading. Stretch or roll each piece to a 10-inch circle. Leaving a 1-inch border at the edge, spread each dough round with half the parsley oil. Layer one side (one half) of each dough circle with half the crumbled sausage, half the cheeses, and half the dried tomato slices.

7. With a finger or brush dipped in water, moisten the unoiled border of dough. Fold the dough circle in half to enclose the filling in a half-moon shape. Press tightly to seal, and thin out the edge of the dough. Roll about ¼ to ½ inch of the dough back onto itself, and press down to form a tightly crimped, raised edge. Refrigerate for 1 hour before baking (can wrap in plastic and freeze 8 weeks).

8. Sprinkle cornmeal evenly over a baking sheet. Gently transfer chilled turnovers to the baking sheet.

9. Adjust oven rack to lowest position. Heat oven to 550 degrees (or highest oven setting). Put baking sheet in oven and immediately spray turnovers with water. Bake 30 to 35 minutes, until lightly brown, spraying once more halfway through baking. Serve immediately, taking care to let steam escape as turnovers are cut.

TABLE MANNERS

If individual pizzas and calzone are to be served whole (not sliced, halved, or quartered in the kitchen), I would not hesitate to serve them with steak knives, which will help diners get through the crust. Count on plunking them down on your biggest dinner plates. Oversized buffet plates or small cutting boards also would provide an ample surface and a great look.

TALES OF DOUGH:
PASTA AND SAUCE

Behind every dish of pasta is the potential for a story, be it the provenance of a sauce, a woeful personal tale of farinaceous disaster, or the seduction of that first encounter with an ethereal plate of spaghetti.

In his *Decameron,* Boccaccio writes of "a whole mountain of grated Parmesan cheese, upon which people did nothing else but macaroni and ravioli and cook them in chicken broth: then they threw them down the hillside and the more the people caught, the more they had." What a wonderful image of abundance and sensuality—qualities that the making, cooking, and eating of pasta continue to evoke after nearly half a millennium.

Although it came to America as an Italian import, pasta is so thoroughly integrated into the culinary mainstream that we no longer even pause to consider its origin. But we have traveled a great distance from the old-fashioned spaghetti-and-meat-sauce aesthetic. Today, pasta is synonymous with fresh, adventuresome eating, nutritional value, and quick preparation.

Do you know *anyone* who dislikes pasta? In all my years as a food writer, I have only encountered one person who does. Most people adore it, particularly when the noodles are homemade—an exceptional treat. Pasta is an ideal menu "double," because it is so successful either as an appetizer or a light main course.

Among the handful of recipes in this chapter are relatively hearty pastas with traditional sauces that I acquired, or tasted, during my travels in Italy. Italians serve these to begin a meal, as you may wish to do, but their heft and richness also make them excellent main courses. The usual practice in Italian kitchens—to marry pasta and a hot sauce by briefly tossing them together over low heat until the sauce gently hugs each tender morsel of dough—gives each dish a built-in air of informality and immediacy. Guests need only add a gentle dusting of grated Parmesan cheese (unless the sauce contains fish or seafood) to bring each pasta to perfection.

American and French chefs take a less orthodox approach to serving pasta than do Italians, often giving vividly colored noodles a dramatic placement by nesting them over the center of the sauce. I have found this presentation to be especially good for a first course because it begins the meal with a message: this course, and this dinner, is important and special. Sauces that are served on top of pasta, and then stirred in, strike a balance between the two approaches.

The way in which pasta is served does make an important statement about style. However, the integrity of each dish can only be guaranteed by carefully selected, fresh ingredients: ripe tomatoes, small zucchini, and fresh herbs, whether we grow them ourselves or pluck them from the supermarket shelves. Cultivating a taste for exquisite olive oils and cheeses at the peak of perfection is a pleasurable task that will increase your understanding of the vital role these two ingredients can play.

Many of these sauces can, of course, be served with store-bought pastas, as there are many flavors and colors available. Still, homemade doughs that can be made so quickly and easily with fresh ingredients and pungent spices help to give each pasta dish an extra dimension of flavor once the noodles emerge hot and tender from the chaos of the pasta pot —giving any tale of dough a happy ending.

PASTA WITH TOMATO-SEAFOOD SAUCE

MY FAVORITE TOMATO SAUCE

Pasta Pointers

TOMATO PASTA DOUGH

Rolling Your Own

PASTA WITH MILANESE MEAT SAUCE

Flour Facts

PASTA WITH FOUR CHEESES

PASTA WITH BROCCOLI RAAB

Homemade Versus Store-Bought Pasta

SPINACH AND HERB PASTA WITH GOAT-CHEESE SAUCE

Three Stories on Style

SPINACH AND FRESH HERB PASTA DOUGH

SCALLION AND BLACK PEPPER PASTA DOUGH

The Chameleon Chèvre

SCALLION AND GOAT-CHEESE AGNOLOTTI

SCALLION AND BLACK PEPPER LASAGNE WITH BLACK OLIVE PESTO

CURRY NOODLES WITH SCALLOPS AND CILANTRO

Indian Sun

CURRY PASTA DOUGH

LEMON-GARLIC PASTA DOUGH

LEMON-GARLIC CAPELLINI WITH MEDITERRANEAN SAUCE

PASTA WITH TOMATO-SEAFOOD SAUCE

I am always happy when I taste a dish of pasta that brings back memories of Italy, particularly one pasta I cooked often during a summer sojourn with friends at a glorious villa in the small Tuscan town of Cetona. The villa's garden supplied an abundant quantity of fresh herbs, and the extremely meaty fresh Italian plum tomatoes from the market enabled me to make My Favorite Tomato Sauce (page 126) without tomato paste. Local sausages, which my host purchased on early-morning forays to the butcher, replaced the seafood suggested here—with exquisite results.

Even with boxed pasta and a sauce fortified by tomato paste, this is a great double. Tomato or Spinach and Fresh Herb Pasta (pages 128 and 139) elevate the sauce to delectable heights.

Cooked vegetables, leftover boneless chicken or duck, or chunks of cooked sausage (use sausage pan drippings in addition to oil to sauté garlic) can be substituted for the shellfish in the sauce. At the last moment, I also like to stir in fresh chopped herbs (basil, or summer savory when I can get it). If poultry or meat is substituted for fish, then I pass a generous bowl of grated Parmigiano-Reggiano cheese so that guests can help themselves.

FLEXIBLE MENU SUGGESTIONS

As an appetizer, this pasta can precede a number of different main dishes. Menus based on Sage-Rubbed Veal Chops (page 242), Capretto with Lemon and Rosemary (page 246), Leg of Lamb with Niçoise Seasoning (page 248), Garlic- or Herb-Rubbed Chicken (page 278), or Szechwan Pepper Ribeyes (page 288) are excellent choices. For an all-fish menu, follow the pasta with One-Side Grilled Fish (page 216) with Winter Pesto (page 227) or Roasted Garlic and Saffron Butter (page 222). A first course of pasta eliminates the need to serve rice or potatoes with the main course, but you may wish to add a julienne of roasted peppers preserved in oil (page 339), a green salad (page 71), and homemade bread (page 340), as appropriate, or even try serving the main course Italian style—without accompaniments—which I tend to do because it is so simple and easy. Menu notes that accompany the main-course recipes listed above will help guide your choices.

This pasta is also good as a light main course for two to four. Lettuce, Radicchio and Fennel Salad (page 70) makes a good appetizer, as do little sandwiches made of Black Pepper Brioche or Umbrian Cheese Bread (see suggestions page 352 or 350). Follow the pasta with Espresso-Brownie Chunk Ice Cream (page 397) during the summer. Otherwise, Almond and Lemon-Stuffed Pears (page 431) are a delicious finale. *Makes 4 servings*

PREPARATION: 25 MINUTES
COOKING: 30 MINUTES

Tomato or Spinach and Fresh Herb Pasta
  Dough (pages 128 or 136), or ½ pound
  spaghetti or other dried pasta
My Favorite Tomato Sauce (page 126)
½ pound sea or bay scallops, shelled shrimp,
  or shelled cooked mussels (mussel liquid
  reserved)
½ teaspoon salt

1. Make and roll pasta dough to second thinnest setting on the pasta machine, following procedures on page 129. When dough strips are partially dried, cut them into capellini, using the narrow pasta-machine cutter. Transfer noodles to a cloth towel until serving time. (Can cover with a towel and set aside at room temperature up to 6 hours.)

2. Make the tomato sauce through Step 1. Rinse scallops or shrimp in strainer under cold water to remove sand and shell fragments; drain and pat dry with paper towels. Leave shellfish pieces whole if they are small; otherwise, cut them into ¼-inch dice; refrigerate until serving time. (Cooked mussels are ready to use whole; do not rinse.)

3. Continue with Step 2 of the sauce and, after cooking the garlic, add scallops or shrimp and toss over low heat until opaque, about 2 minutes; remove to plate with a slotted spoon (can wrap and refrigerate until serving time). Finish the sauce (can substitute mussel-steaming liquid for chicken stock), adding any fish juices that accumulate on the plate. (Can cool, cover, and refrigerate sauce and seafood separately, as long as overnight.)

4. At serving time, heat 4 quarts of water to boiling; add salt. Stir in noodles and boil until tender, about 1 to 2 minutes for fresh pasta or 6 to 8 minutes for dried pasta. Drain very well in a colander.

5. Heat cooked seafood with tomato sauce in a large skillet. Add the cooked, drained pasta to the sauce. Gently toss over lowest heat until pasta is just coated with sauce. With tongs, transfer noodles to warm serving dishes. Spoon a heaping tablespoon of the sauce and shellfish that remains in the skillet over each portion. Serve immediately.

MY FAVORITE TOMATO SAUCE

One year, after returning from a trip to Italy, I began making fresh tomato sauces in an attempt to re-create the flavor of a sauce I had tasted there. After several unsatisfactory tries, I added a small amount of tomato paste—an ingredient used in many parts of Italy but one that purists here shun—to bolster the texture of the tomatoes, with great success.

Using tomato paste with one single ingredient—tomatoes—listed on the tin or tube is important. Pastes made with additives seem bitter, and this makes a great difference in the taste of the finished sauce.

Ripe tomatoes also are critical. While fresh, homegrown plum tomatoes are my first choice, round tomatoes are fine. Underripe tomatoes often can be improved if left to ripen without refrigeration for a few days, even in winter.

The quantity of olive oil called for may be a surprise, but do not reduce the amount (olive oil never tastes greasy unless it is of bad quality).

At serving time, transfer the sauce to a large skillet. Add the pasta and toss it with the sauce over very low heat, using wooden spatulas or spoons (rather than tongs) to prevent breakage.

FLEXIBLE MENU SUGGESTIONS

Consider this an all-purpose sauce for any of the homemade pastas, or dried, boxed noodles. It is also used in Pasta with Tomato-Seafood Sauce (page 124) and Scallion and Goat-Cheese Agnolotti (page 142). A small amount of this sauce is needed for Risotto Primavera (page 172). *Makes 4 servings (2 cups)*

PREPARATION: 20 MINUTES
COOKING: 30 MINUTES

¼ cup firmly packed parsley leaves
3 medium garlic cloves, peeled
1 pound ripe tomatoes, peeled and seeded
⅓ cup mild olive oil or Herbed Oil (page 73)
1½ cups Chicken Stock (page 165)
4 tablespoons tomato paste
1½ teaspoons dried Mixed Herbs (page 105)
    or 2 tablespoons fresh minced herbs
Salt and ground black pepper

1. Mince the parsley; set aside. Mince garlic and transfer to medium nonreactive skillet. Coarsely chop the tomatoes.

2. Add oil to the skillet and cook garlic over low heat until fragrant, about 1 minute. Stir in tomatoes, stock, and tomato paste. Simmer rapidly, stirring frequently, until mixture reduces by half and sauce measures 2 cups.

3. Stir parsley, herbs, salt, and pepper into the sauce. Adjust seasoning to taste slightly salty and peppery. (Can cool and set sauce aside, or cover and refrigerate 48 hours.) Sauce is ready to reheat and serve.

PASTA POINTERS

It is fascinating to watch an Italian cook make pasta dough by hand in the traditional manner, first mounding flour on a work surface, making a well in the middle, carefully adding the beaten eggs and flavorings to the center, and gradually incorporating them into the flour (usually with two fingers or a fork). During my Tuscan summer, I would often watch Marcella, the housekeeper, perform this ballet of patience and skill, kneading a lumpen mass of dough in her strong hands until it was smooth and elastic enough to produce her feather-light, silky noodles. "Signora," she would instruct me, "this is the way you make the *real* pasta."

I often think of those lazy afternoons while I am whipping up pasta dough in the food processor in four seconds flat. I'm certain Marcella would be horrified (or perhaps fascinated), but using the processor is so quick and simple.

Begin with flavorings and large eggs, into which you quickly pulse the flour. Since it is important not to overprocess these delicate doughs, use one-second pulses (measure one second by slowly counting one-thousand-one) until small beads form.

Doughs will vary in texture with the size of eggs, the moisture of ingredients, and variations in flour. If a beadlike texture is not obvious after four to six pulses, test the dough as follows: put about 1 tablespoon of the mixture in the palm of your hand and squeeze firmly. If the mixture holds together, dough has the correct consistency and a sufficient quantity of flour. The dough will then need a 20- to 30-minute rest in plastic wrap before rolling.

Dough that contains too little flour will be soft or sticky, or may mass together like pastry dough. Add 2 tablespoons of flour at a time, and pulse it in without overprocessing.

When pasta dough is too dry, the mixture crumbles in your hand and will not hold together. A good remedy is to beat a whole egg in a cup (as for scrambled eggs), drizzle half the egg over the top of the dry mixture, and then process with half-second pulses until beads form.

As you add flour or beaten egg to adjust the consistency of pasta dough, do not let the processor run continuously or dough can toughen.

Perfect dough will have a soft, even texture after resting. If dough sticks to the plastic wrap, it will need to be dusted with a generous amount of flour as it is passed through the pasta machine so that it is strong enough to withstand the final stretching. Dry doughs that break apart after a rest in plastic wrap should hold together after a few turns through the pasta-machine rollers.

TOMATO PASTA DOUGH

The concentrated flavor of tomato paste gives these noodles a light taste and lovely orange color. Cut the noodles very thin.

FLEXIBLE MENU SUGGESTIONS

Toss tomato noodles with Tomato-Seafood Sauce (page 124), use them in Pasta with Four Cheeses (page 132), or as an accompaniment to main courses such as Sage-Rubbed Veal Chops (page 242), Mushroom and Prosciutto-Stuffed Chicken Breasts (page 274), or Garlic-Rubbed Chicken (page 278). *Makes 10 ounces of dough*

PREPARATION: 5 MINUTES

1 large egg
1 large egg yolk
4 tablespoons tomato paste
Salt
Hot red pepper sauce
1¼ to 1½ cups bread flour or unbleached all-
*   purpose flour*
Flour for rolling dough

1. Insert the metal blade in a dry food-processor container. Process the egg, egg yolk, tomato paste, and ½ teaspoon salt with several dashes of hot red pepper sauce until the mixture is foamy, about 30 seconds.

2. Add 1¼ cups flour and process with 1-second pulses until the mixture has the consistency of small beads. Do not overprocess or let machine run. If dough is too wet for beads to form, process in additional flour by tablespoons, using 1-second pulses, until dough forms beads that hold together when pinched.

3. Wrap dough in plastic, press it into a flat disk, and set it aside for 20 minutes. (Can refrigerate 24 hours.) If dough glues itself to plastic wrap, a generous quantity of additional flour should be worked into the dough strips during rolling. Otherwise, rub a moderate amount of flour onto dough strips while stretching them according to directions on page 129.

A hand-cranked pasta machine is standard equipment for anyone interested in making pasta at home. Most machines have six or seven thickness settings, and are at least six inches wide. Once the pasta dough has been made and set aside to rest as the recipe directs, it is ready to roll according to the following directions.

1. Unwrap and cut the dough into three pieces. If dough sticks to the plastic wrap, sprinkle the work surface with 2 to 3 tablespoons of flour; use 1 to 2 tablespoons of flour on the work surface if wrap does not adhere to the dough. Work one piece of dough at a time; keep remainder wrapped.

2. Open the rollers to the widest setting. Dip each side of the piece of dough in flour and flatten it slightly. Quickly roll the dough through machine. Do not stop or reverse rollers. You will get a flattened, elongated dough strip.

3. Lightly flour both sides of the dough strip, and fold it in half, crosswise. Gently press the folded edge to flatten it slightly. Roll the strip of dough, folded edge first, through the machine. If the dough strip is smooth, repeat flouring, folding, and rolling through the machine once more. If the dough is very sticky, it should be floured, folded, and rolled through the machine twice more. (If dough shreds, it may need as many as four turns to create a smooth, elastic consistency for stretching.)

NOTE: From this point on, dough strips are rolled through successively narrower openings of the pasta machine *without folding*. Dough may be rolled to the second-to-the-thinnest setting, or as thin as your machine will go. Wide noodles, or filled pastas, usually require dough strips that are thinner than those used for cutting into noodles (consult each recipe for instructions). Keep in mind that all noodles swell and increase in size and thickness during cooking.

4. To finish stretching the dough strip, dust each side with flour, and roll it through the machine, allowing it to pass over the top like laundry through a wringer. Remove it from beneath the machine, and put it flat on the work surface. Flour the strip again lightly and repeat rolling it through, adjusting the machine to a narrower setting each time. (If dough strip becomes unwieldy and long, cut it in half crosswise before the final pass through the rollers. The optimum length for noodles is 15 inches.)

5. Transfer dough strips to a cloth towel after the final stretch. Let them dry to a supple, but leathery, consistency (if too dry, strips will shatter when cut), turning them several times. While strips dry, begin again at step 2, and roll out the remaining dough pieces. When you are finished, the first strips should be dry enough to cut. If you are making wide or filled noodles, you may now wish to cut dough strips to the desired size.

6. To use the noodle cutter, insert the crank handle into the desired cutting head. Press one end of a dough strip onto cutter head and quickly roll it through. You can hang noodles on a pasta-drying rack, over a broom handle suspended between two chairs, or simply remove them from beneath the pasta cutter, twirl them into loose, little nests, and set them aside on cloth towels (spread towels on baking sheets if you are short of space) until serving time.

PASTA WITH MILANESE MEAT SAUCE

Milan is one of my favorite cities in Italy, as much for food as for fashion. After my first visit some years ago, I was captivated by Milanese style and determined to learn more about it by writing a travel article. The story gave me access to prominent Milanese restaurant kitchens, including that of Bagutta, a lively and popular *trattoria* in the heart of the shopping district. Among the restaurant's signature dishes is a subtle sauce for rigatoni that features five different meats, peas, and a splash of cream. The mixture is cooked very slowly so that the ground meat retains its juiciness. The sauce must be seasoned carefully, otherwise it can be bland.

FLEXIBLE MENU SUGGESTIONS

If ingredients such as two chicken livers are difficult to purchase, plan to serve this pasta before Garlic- or Herb-Rubbed Chicken (page 278). It also can precede One-Side Grilled Fish (page 216) with Fresh Herb Butter (page 219), Orso Butter (page 221), Roasted Garlic and Saffron Butter (page 222).

This makes a wonderful main course. Begin with Lettuce, Radicchio, and Fennel Salad plus Parmesan and Black Pepper Brioche or Umbrian Cheese Bread (page 70, 348, 350), or the Mozzarella, Tomato, and Olive Salad (page 62). A rather plain dessert, such as Almond and Lemon-Stuffed Pears (page 431)or fresh fruit with Quick Custard Sauce (page 443) might follow the pasta. For a spirited Italian ending, take the time to bake the luscious Dome Cake (page 388). *Makes 4 to 6 servings*

PREPARATION: 35 MINUTES
COOKING: 40 MINUTES

SAUCE

2 medium onions (1½ pounds), peeled, cubed
¼ cup plus 1 tablespoon mild olive oil
¼ pound boneless veal, cubed
¼ pound boneless pork shoulder, cubed
2 ounces boneless beef chuck, cubed
¼ pound boned skinned chicken breast, or
   veal sweetbreads, cut in ¼-inch dice
¼ cup dry Marsala wine
¼ cup dry red wine
1 cup fresh or thawed frozen peas
⅓ cup beef broth
⅓ cup tomato paste
½ teaspoon dried sage leaves, crumbled
¼ teaspoon dried rosemary leaves, crumbled

2 chicken livers, trimmed
¼ cup whipping cream
Salt and ground black pepper

FINISHING AND GARNISH

10 ounces homemade fresh pasta (Tomato, or
   Spinach and Fresh Herb, page 128 or 139)
   or ¾ pound fresh pasta, dried rigatoni,
   penne, or spaghetti
3 tablespoons mild olive oil, or Herbed Oil
   (page 73)
Minced parsley
Grated Parmesan cheese

1. Mince onions and put into a 10- to 12-inch heavy, nonreactive skillet. Add ¼ cup olive oil and stir over medium heat until onions soften, about 5 minutes.

2. In a food processor fitted with the metal blade, chop veal, pork, and beef to medium hamburger consistency with three to four 2-second pulses; add ground meat to the skillet. Add chicken (or sweetbreads); toss until meat turns pale, about 5 minutes. Add Marsala and red wine and stir over low heat, uncovered, until liquid evaporates, about 25 minutes.

3. While meat cooks, blanch fresh peas in small saucepan of boiling water until crisp-tender, about 4 minutes (or defrost and rinse frozen peas). Drain peas; set aside.

4. Stir beef broth into tomato paste until smooth, and add the mixture to the skillet. Stir in sage and rosemary, and simmer until sauce thickens slightly, about 8 minutes.

5. Heat 1 tablespoon oil in separate, small skillet. Add chicken livers and toss until seared, about 1½ minutes. Transfer the livers to a strainer, drain them for 3 minutes, then cut them into ¼-inch dice. Stir livers, peas, and cream into the sauce. Season sauce to taste salty and peppery, as it becomes bland when mixed with pasta. (Can cover and set sauce aside up to 6 hours.)

6. Heat 4 quarts water to boiling in a large soup kettle. Stir in 1 teaspoon salt and the pasta. Boil until pasta is tender, 2 to 9 minutes, depending on the type of pasta used.

7. Drain the pasta, then return it to the kettle with 3 tablespoons oil. Toss over low heat until water evaporates and oil coats the pasta. Transfer pasta to warm serving bowls or plates. Spoon meat sauce over each portion and garnish with minced parsley. Serve immediately, and pass grated Parmesan separately.

FLOUR FACTS

Teaching cooking classes in different parts of this country and Canada has taught me firsthand that flour varies regionally and seasonally, which is why I pay attention to the type of flour I use in doughs for pasta, pizza, and breads, and give a range in flour measurements. Over the years, I have had consistently good results using bread flour for pasta doughs made in the food processor. Bread flour (notably Pillsbury's) is available in many grocery stores. The best substitute is unbleached all-purpose flour.

The strength, or absorption power, of flour is dependent on the wheat from which the flour was milled. The harder the wheat, the higher the protein content, the stronger the flour, and the less you need. The average protein content, which distinguishes one flour from another, is listed in grams per cup (4 ounces) on the side panel of every flour bag. The chart below defines the flours used in recipes— for best results match the flour you purchase to the following standards:

TYPE OF FLOUR	AVERAGE PROTEIN PER CUP
Bread flour	14 grams
All-purpose unbleached flour	11 to 12 grams
Bleached all-purpose flour	10 grams
Plain (bleached) cake flour	8 grams

NOTE: Self-rising cake flour (which contains baking powder) *cannot* be substituted for plain cake flour.

PASTA WITH FOUR CHEESES

Pinpointing the origin of this sauce would be a fascinating task, since several Italian authorities state that the source of this recipe is unknown. Logic suggests that because it is composed of four cheeses, the sauce was devised as a solution to using up leftovers—at home or in a restaurant—and it is difficult to envision a more delicious way of doing so.

Fontina, Provolone, and Parmigiano-Reggiano are nicely balanced by cream cheese, which I use here as a thickener because it contains less fat than butter. A considerable variety of cheeses can be used, however. Imported Gruyère or Taleggio could replace the Fontina; Romano could stand in for the Parmigiano or Provolone; and an acidic fresh goat cheese (see page 141) could be substituted for cream cheese. You can add a fifth cheese to this sauce, but avoid using two very salty cheeses (such as Provolone and Romano) together.

The critical step in this receipe, the final tossing of pasta with sauce, must be done very quickly so that the cheese does not turn to glue as the pasta cools. Heated serving bowls or plates help keep the pasta warm, or it may be left in the skillet during the journey from stovetop to table.

FLEXIBLE MENU SUGGESTIONS

This is a marvelously rich prelude to Sage-Rubbed Veal Chops (page 242), Capretto with Lemon and Rosemary (page 246), Scampi alla Busara (page 171), or Garlic- or Herb-Rubbed Chicken (page 278).

As a main course, the pasta could be introduced by Lettuce, Radicchio, and Fennel Salad (page 70) or a green salad dressed with Lemon-Basil Vinaigrette (page 74); add Prosciutto Bread (page 354), Tomato Flatbread with Two Herbs (page 346), or Rosemary Breadsticks (page 343) to round out the first course. Apple Crisp (page 424) and Chocolate-Walnut Linzer Torte (page 376) deviate from the Italian aesthetic, but I would not hesitate to serve either for dessert (peach or apricot jam is best for the torte filling). *Makes 4 servings*

PREPARATION: 30 MINUTES
COOKING: 10 MINUTES

2 ounces (four 1-inch cubes) imported Provolone cheese, chilled
1 ounce (two 1-inch cubes) Parmesan cheese
2 ounces (four 1-inch cubes) imported Fontina cheese, chilled, rind removed
2 ounces cream cheese, room temperature
1 cup whipping cream
¼ cup firmly packed parsley leaves
1 medium garlic clove, peeled

Salt and ground black pepper
10 ounces homemade fresh pasta (Tomato, or Spinach and Fresh Herb, page 128 or 139), or ½ pound spaghetti or linguine

1. In a food processor fitted with the metal blade, process the Provolone until minced; set aside in a bowl. Add the Parmesan and process until powdery; add to bowl. Chop the Fontina to the consistency of small peb-

bles; add it to the bowl. Process cream cheese with ½ cup whipping cream until smooth.

2. Mince the parsley and set aside. Mince the garlic and transfer it to a large skillet. Add the cream-cheese mixture, remaining cream, ¼ teaspoon salt, and ¼ teaspoon pepper. Set mixture aside in the skillet until serving time. (Can assemble garlic-cream in a bowl, cover, and refrigerate up to 6 hours. Can cover and refrigerate chopped cheeses.)

3. Heat 4 quarts of water to boiling in a large soup kettle. Stir in ½ teaspoon salt and the pasta. Boil until pasta is tender, about 2 to 9 minutes, depending on the type of pasta used. Drain pasta thoroughly in a colander.

4. Heat the garlic-cream to simmering. Add the cheeses and cook over low heat, stirring until the cheeses melt. Taste the sauce, which may not require salt, then adjust seasoning so that sauce is slightly salty and peppery. Immediately add drained pasta to the skillet. Gently toss pasta with sauce over very low heat until noodles are just coated. Garnish with reserved parsley and serve immediately.

PASTA WITH BROCCOLI RAAB

Until recently, broccoli raab was a vegetable little known outside Italian or Chinese neighborhoods. Also called *broccoletti di rape, choy sum,* Chinese broccoli, or bitter broccoli, it has skinnier stalks, small shaggier florets, and larger leaves than its garden-variety cousin.

The surprise is in its bitterness, which can be overpowering when this vegetable is served alone. However, the bite of broccoli raab is pleasantly muted by pairing it with pasta, garlic, hot red pepper, and grated Parmesan cheese. It may be necessary to order broccoli raab from a specialty produce store, where it should be available during winter months. Otherwise, substitute regular broccoli.

This recipe, created by Italian restaurateur Lidia Bastianich of Felidia restaurant in New York, was my introduction to broccoli raab. The dish was scheduled for a magazine article, but at the last moment, there was no space for it. However, this pasta is very unusual (there is not a great deal of sauce), and I like it so much, I am pleased to include it here.

FLEXIBLE MENU SUGGESTIONS

Serving a pasta first course that includes a green vegetable but contains no tomato creates interesting menu choices. Try this with penne or ziti before One-Side Grilled Fish (page 216) with Orso Butter (page 221), Sage-Rubbed Veal Chops (page 242), Capretto with Lemon and Rosemary (page 246), Leg of Lamb with Niçoise Seasoning (page 248), Scampi alla Busara (page 272), Herb-Rubbed Chicken (page 278), or Garlic-Roasted Leg of Lamb (page 295). Keep in mind that the presence of pasta and broccoli eliminates the need for starch or green-vegetable accompaniments with the main course.

Pasta with Broccoli Raab makes a terrific main course. I heartily recommend adding half a pound of sweet Italian sausage that has been lightly browned before sautéing the garlic and pepper in step 2, then is braised with the broccoli raab and chicken stock (you can eliminate the butter) in step 3. The sausages (cooked meat, poultry, or even shrimp could be substituted) should be cut into small pieces before tossing with the pasta. Begin a menu with Mozzarella, Tomato, and Olive Salad (page 62), or Tomato Soup with Garlic and Basil (page 44). Then serve Almond and Lemon-Stuffed Pears (page 431) or Lemon Tirami Su (page 429) for dessert. *Makes 6 to 8 servings*

PREPARATION: 25 MINUTES
COOKING: ABOUT 35 MINUTES

1½ pounds broccoli raab (or broccoli) rinsed
4 large garlic cloves, peeled
1 small hot red chile (seeded, cored) or ¼
  teaspoon red pepper flakes
⅓ cup olive oil or Herbed Oil (page 73)

2 tablespoons butter
1½ cups Chicken Stock (page 165)
Salt
1½ pounds ziti or other dried pasta,
  preferably imported
¼ pound Parmesan cheese (preferably
  Parmigiano-Reggiano), grated

1. Pick over broccoli raab (or broccoli), discarding large tough leaves (approximately one-third). Cut off florets and set aside. Cut broccoli raab stems into 1-inch pieces; set aside. (Or, peel and slice broccoli stems about ¼ inch thick; set pieces aside).

2. Mince the garlic and red chile and transfer the mixture to a large skillet. Add olive oil and cook over low heat until garlic begins to color, about 3 minutes.

3. Add all the broccoli raab or broccoli. Cover and cook over medium heat for 5 minutes, stirring occasionally. Add butter and chicken stock. Simmer, uncovered, until florets are tender and liquid reduces by half, about 10 minutes longer. (Can transfer to a bowl, cover, and set sauce aside at room temperature up to 6 hours.)

4. Heat 4 quarts of water to boiling in a large stockpot. Add ¼ teaspoon salt and the ziti; stir well. Boil uncovered until pasta is tender, about 8 to 9 minutes; drain.

5. Return the pot to the stove and add the drained pasta. Add the sauce mixture and stir over low heat until sauce is mostly absorbed, about 3 minutes. Stir in ½ cup grated cheese. Adjust seasoning to taste with salt, if needed. Serve pasta immediately, with remaining cheese for garnish.

HOMEMADE VERSUS STORE-BOUGHT PASTA

The popularity of pasta has made it mandatory for specialty food stores and supermarkets to sell a variety of plain and flavored noodles as well as uncut fresh pasta sheets. With such top-notch pasta available and frequently packaged to keep up to a week in the refrigerator, why bother to make it at home?

If time is at a premium, or you do not own a pasta machine, or if making pasta seems too messy (and it can be), there is no need ever to make it at home. But let me tell you why I often do.

Noodles that contain vegetables, herbs, or spices have a far more distinctive taste than most commercially made pastas. Even though the dough is tempered by boiling, the Curry, or Spinach and Fresh Herb pastas (pages 148 and 136) are surprisingly full of flavor. Homemade doughs also can be customized. While the Mediterranean Sauce (page 150) would be delicious with many different pastas, serving it over noodles made with Lemon-Garlic Pasta Dough (page 149) allows you to produce a subtle play between the flavors of the pasta and sauce—a fine-tuning that offers something special, and different, to your guests.

SPINACH AND HERB PASTA WITH GOAT-CHEESE SAUCE

Alfredo Sauce is a classic, but I like to give it a gentle infusion of garlic, and put a spin on tradition by pureeing fresh goat cheese into the garlicky cream. While the result is wildly rich, the slight acidity of the cheese helps to create a beautifully balanced sauce. Since a nest of vivid green, herbed noodles is placed over (rather than tossed with) the ivory sauce, this dish has a composed, formal look that belies the ease with which both the pasta and sauce are made.

Commercial fresh pasta can be substituted for homemade. However, you may wish to toss the noodles with chopped fresh basil or sage in step 6, so that the herbal flavor is not missing from the dish.

FLEXIBLE MENU SUGGESTIONS

Follow appetizer and main-course guidelines for Pasta with Four Cheeses (page 132).
Makes 4 to 6 servings

PREPARATION: 35 MINUTES
COOKING: 20 MINUTES

Spinach and Fresh Herb Pasta Dough
  (page 139)

SAUCE

2 small garlic cloves, peeled
6 tablespoons unsalted butter
2 cups whipping cream
Salt and ground black pepper
Nutmeg
6 ounces fresh goat cheese (page 141)
Hot red pepper sauce
1 roasted skinned red bell pepper, or Red or
  Yellow Peppers Preserved in Oil (page
  339), cut into thin julienne strips

1. Make the pasta dough and roll it to the second thinnest setting of a pasta machine, following procedures on page 129. Cut the partially dried dough strips into thin noodles by rolling them through the thinnest pasta-machine cutter. Transfer noodles to cloth towel until serving time. (Can cover and set aside on towel up to 6 hours.)

2. For the sauce, put garlic, 4 tablespoons butter, and cream in a large skillet. Simmer until cream reduces to 1⅔ cups. Strain and discard garlic. Add ⅛ teaspoon salt, ⅛ teaspoon pepper, and several dashes of nutmeg.

3. Insert the metal blade in the container of a food processor and process goat cheese until smooth. With the motor on, slowly pour the hot cream mixture into the cheese. If the container becomes too full, pour half the mixture into a medium saucepan and continue processing. Transfer all the sauce to a saucepan. Adjust seasoning to taste with salt, pepper, nutmeg, and several dashes of hot red pepper sauce. (Can cover sauce with plastic wrap directly touching its surface and set aside up to 6 hours.)

4. At serving time, heat 4 quarts of water to boiling in a large soup kettle. Stir in ½ teaspoon salt and the noodles. Boil until noodles are tender, about 2 minutes. Drain noodles well in a colander.

5. Reheat sauce by whisking over low heat, but do not let sauce simmer.

6. Melt remaining 2 tablespoons butter in a large skillet. Add drained noodles, sprinkle with salt and pepper, and toss gently over very low heat until they are sealed.

7. Stir sauce well and ladle ¼ cup onto each warm dinner plate—cover each plate completely with sauce. Put a portion of noodles in the center of each plate, leaving a 1- to 1½-inch border of sauce. Garnish with red pepper strips and serve immediately.

"Despite Popeye, spinach is not remarkably rich in iron, though it is a good source of vitamin A."

—HAROLD McGEE

THREE STORIES ON STYLE

THE ITALIAN LOOK

In Italian kitchens it is standard procedure to toss cooked pasta lightly in its sauce, over low heat, so that the noodles become evenly coated with the sauce, yet individual strands or rounds of pasta remain separate.

Combining pasta and sauce in this manner also helps distribute flavor throughout the noodles, keeps the pasta very hot, eliminates messy tossing at table, and guarantees that a watery puddle of boiling water (which can totally dilute a sauce) will never collect in the bottom of your bowl.

For best results, heat the sauce in a large skillet. Drain pasta in a colander, shaking it well to remove all excess liquid. Add pasta to the skillet, and use two wooden spoons or spatulas to lift and coat the noodles with sauce without breaking the long strands. Once tossed, the pasta can easily be transferred from the skillet to rimmed soup bowls with a pair of tongs. It should be served immediately. Garnishes can include grated or shaved Parmesan cheese, and fresh herbs.

PASTA OVER SAUCE

One of the most beautiful ways to present pasta is to serve it on a standard (10-inch) dinner plate on top of the sauce. This works best when there is a strong visual contrast between the colors of the pasta and sauce, and with thin noodles rather than other shapes.

Plating pasta in this manner requires two extra steps: sautéing the noodles briefly in olive oil or butter to remove excess moisture, then keeping noodles hot while sauce is ladled (most efficiently with a ¼-cup dry measure) onto warm plates.

This presentation is very good for first courses, when portion sizes are relatively small, or when sauces are very rich. With few exceptions, let brightly colored noodles act as their own garnish, and place additional elements of garniture (such as herb sprigs) on the sauce. If you want to serve plain noodles in this way, or over a particularly pale sauce, the pasta can be enlivened by adding minced parsley or fresh herbs to the oil or butter when the pasta is briefly sautéed. Toss the noodles well to distribute the flecks of green throughout.

Tongs are the preferred utensils for transferring noodles from the skillet to plates. If you are rushed, just plop the noodles over the center of the sauce as best you can, and try to leave at least a 1-inch border of sauce around the noodle nest. For a more elegant presentation, swirl a portion of noodles around the tongs or a meat fork to make a "hive" shape, which looks particularly graceful and delectable floating atop a sauce.

SAUCE OVER PASTA

When cold sauces are served with hot pasta they should be added at the last possible moment so that each component of the dish can retain its integrity. Therefore, it is best to present them in the same manner as a garnish—on top of pasta. Black Olive Pesto (as well as traditional pesto) and the Mediterranean Sauce (pages 144 and 150) are excellent examples, which also add dramatic color to the dish. In addition, a chunky, colorful sauce such as the mixture of scallops and cilantro that graces curry noodles, can be effectively presented in this way.

SPINACH AND FRESH HERB
PASTA DOUGH

Tender spinach and fresh herb leaves puree beautifully into this pasta dough, to give the cooked noodles a bright green color and a delicate herb flavor.

Of the ½ cup spinach-and-herb mixture called for in the recipe, ¼ cup spinach and ¼ cup basil leaves is an ideal proportion, although ½ cup packed basil leaves alone would be fine. Herbs that are very strong or can turn bitter—such as sage, oregano, and marjoram—are best when used in smaller quantities. I usually mix twelve to twenty sage leaves or ⅛ cup fresh oregano or marjoram with the spinach. Ratios can change according to your taste and the herbs you have on hand.

FLEXIBLE MENU SUGGESTIONS

This dough is wonderful with the Goat-Cheese Sauce (page 136), and it may be used interchangeably with Tomato Pasta Dough (page 128). These noodles make a good accompaniment to Mushroom and Prosciutto-Stuffed Chicken Breasts (page 274) and Cognac-Marinated Beef Fillet (page 298). *Makes 10 ounces of dough*

PREPARATION: 8 MINUTES

½ cup firmly packed stemmed spinach and
fresh herb leaves (basil, sage, oregano, or
marjoram)
Salt
1 large egg
1 large egg yolk
1¼ to 1½ cups bread flour or unbleached all-
purpose flour
Flour for rolling dough

1. Insert the metal blade in a dry food-processor container. Process spinach and herbs until chopped. Add ½ teaspoon salt, egg, and egg yolk. Process until mixture is pale green and foamy, about 30 seconds.

2. Add 1¼ cups flour. Process with 1-second pulses until the mixture has the consistency of small beads. Do not overprocess or let machine run. If dough is too wet for beads to form, process in additional flour by tablespoons, using 1-second pulses, until dough forms beads that hold together when pinched.

3. Wrap dough in plastic, press it into a flat disk, and set it aside for 20 minutes. (Can refrigerate 24 hours.) If dough glues itself to plastic wrap, a generous quantity of additional flour should be worked into the dough strips during rolling. Otherwise, rub a moderate amount of flour onto dough strips while stretching them according to directions on page 129.

SCALLION AND BLACK PEPPER PASTA DOUGH

Coarsely ground black pepper gives these noodles a jolt of flavor as well as lively flecks of color, while scallions puree easily into the egg mixture to tint the dough lightly.

FLEXIBLE MENU SUGGESTIONS

When rolled and cut thinly, this recipe makes enough noodles to serve eight as an accompaniment in a menu based on Sage-Rubbed Veal Chops (page 242), Chili-Rubbed Chicken (page 278), or Mushroom and Prosciutto-Stuffed Chicken Breasts (page 274). However, for a filled pasta such as the agnolotti on page 142, the yield is four servings, and it expands to six portions when the noodles are used for the lasagne on page 144. *Makes about 1 pound of dough*

PREPARATION: 15 MINUTES

4 large scallions, trimmed, cut into 1-inch
lengths
2 large eggs
1 large egg yolk
Salt and finely ground black pepper
1⅔ to 1¾ cups bread flour or unbleached
all-purpose flour
Flour for rolling dough

1. Insert the metal blade in a dry food-processor container. Pulse to chop the scallions, then add the eggs, egg yolk, ¾ teaspoon salt, and 1¼ teaspoons pepper. Process until mixture is pale green and foamy, about 1 minute.

2. Add 1⅔ cups flour. Process with 1-second pulses until the mixture has the consistency of small beads. Do not overprocess or let machine run. If dough is too wet for beads to form, pulse in additional flour by tablespoons, using 1-second pulses, until dough forms small beads that hold together when pinched.

3. Wrap dough in plastic, press it into a flat disk, and set aside for 20 minutes. (Can refrigerate 24 hours.) If dough glues itself to plastic wrap, a generous quantity of additional flour should be worked into the dough strips during rolling. Otherwise, rub a moderate amount of flour onto dough strips while stretching them according to directions on page 129.

THE CHAMELEON CHEVRE

Goat cheese is one of the brightest stars in the galaxy of ingredients that crossed the Atlantic during the gourmet-food boom of the 1970s. It can be served in a variety of ways —in appetizers, salads, sauces, entrées, savory tarts—and is often used as a filling for pasta. The best cheeses are made from fresh goat's milk. Even today, much of the cheese-making is done by hand, and chèvres comes in a dazzling array of shapes and sizes, adding to their considerable charm.

When very fresh, these cheeses have a sweet, nutty flavor and a moist surface (with no rind), although some may be coated with ash, fresh or dried herbs, or spices such as ground black pepper. Fresh cheeses have a spreadable consistency and melt easily, making them suitable for fillings. Smaller fresh cheeses can be rolled in herbs or spices and presented whole.

A few goat cheeses are covered by a soft white rind. These ripen from the outside in, and sometimes have a more pronounced flavor and creamier interior than fresh varieties —a few become as creamy as Brie. When thinly sliced, this type of chèvre makes a wonderful garnish for salads and appetizers. Often it is coated with ground bread crumbs or nuts and sautéed, or served hot and grilled on toast.

Aged chèvre develops a crumbly interior, a dry, firm rind, and a piquant flavor much prized by connoisseurs. These are generally reserved for cheese platters; occasionally they are softened in olive oil.

Fresh goat cheeses should have a snow-white exterior free of hard spots; however, mold is not harmful. Many come wrapped in paper (which may be wet or dry). If possible, always check the condition of the cheese under the wrapper. Be especially wary of cheeses that are sealed in plastic wrap, since excess moisture can accumulate inside during refrigeration.

Older cheeses are generally left unrefrigerated to ripen naturally, and their textures and the condition of the rind will vary accordingly. Soft white rinds tend to yellow or become slightly gray with age.

Traditionally, chèvres have been known by their French names, although with the rise of domestic production many names have English equivalents:

bouchon: cork	crottin: button
bûche: log	lingot: brick
coeur: heart	pyramide: pyramid
clochette: little bell	rond: disk or puck
	taupinière: dome

Whether chèvre is imported from France or Italy or made domestically, it should never be overly salty or strongly goaty. Try to avoid purchasing bland, factory-produced goat cheeses made from frozen curd and powdered milk, extruded from a machine. Bucheron, Montrachet, Lezay, and any cheese sealed in a cry-o-vac package fall into this category.

SCALLION AND GOAT-CHEESE AGNOLOTTI

Agnolotti are relatively easy to make, and guests never fail to remark on how lovely they look or how good they taste.

Goat cheese provides a tangy filling for pasta, and since it is drier than ricotta, it causes fewer problems with agnolotti sticking or opening. A busy cheese shop with good turnover is the best source for most goat cheese (see page 141). Choose from among the mild, fresh varieties or the slightly more assertive, creamier chèvres with tender white rinds. Do not use aged chèvre or feta.

FLEXIBLE MENU SUGGESTIONS

Although this dish contains no fish, it can be substituted in menus for Pasta with Tomato-Seafood Sauce (page 124). Agnolotti can also precede One-Side Grilled Fish (page 216) with Orso Butter (page 221), and they are included in menus based on Garlic-Rubbed Chicken (page 278), Szechwan Pepper Ribeyes (page 288), Garlic-Roasted Leg of Lamb (page 295), and Cognac-Marinated Beef Fillet (page 298). *Makes 4 servings*

PREPARATION: 1 HOUR
COOKING: 10 MINUTES

My Favorite Tomato Sauce (page 126)
6 tablespoons grated Parmesan cheese

FILLING

½ pound fresh goat cheese
1 egg yolk
Salt and ground white pepper
1 tablespoon shredded basil leaves (or ¼ teaspoon dried basil)
1 tablespoon minced chives, or scallion green
Scallion and Black Pepper Pasta Dough (page 140) or 1 pound fresh spinach sheet pasta
Fresh basil sprigs or minced chives

1. Make the tomato sauce. (Can cool, cover, and refrigerate sauce up to 48 hours.) Measure 2 tablespoons grated Parmesan for the filling; set remainder aside for garnish.

2. For the filling, remove rind or coating from the goat cheese, if necessary. In a food processor fitted with the metal blade, pulse to mix the goat cheese, 2 tablespoons Parmesan, and the egg yolk. Taste, add salt if needed, and ⅛ teaspoon ground pepper. Pulse in the basil and chives. Adjust seasoning. Cover and refrigerate until ready to fill the pasta (can refrigerate up to 8 hours).

3. Make the pasta dough and divide it into three pieces. Roll each piece to the second thinnest setting of a pasta machine, keeping strips as wide as possible. (Omit this step if using store-bought sheet pasta.)

4. Flour dough very lightly and use a plain, circular cookie cutter to cut out twenty-four to thirty 3½-inch circles of dough. Wrap circles loosely in plastic; set aside.

5. To fill and shape agnolotti, use a dry work surface or cloth towel and work on one dough circle at a time. Moisten one side of the dough lightly with a damp pastry brush. Put a rounded 1½ teaspoons of filling in the center. Fold the circle of dough in half to enclose the cheese, and press edges together tightly to eliminate excess air. Seal by trimming each semicircle with the fluted wheel of a ravioli cutter. Repeat to fill all the dough circles, transferring each finished agnolotto to a towel-lined baking sheet. Cover with a cloth towel and loosely with plastic wrap and refrigerate until serving time. (Can refrigerate up to 6 hours.)

6. At serving time, reheat the tomato sauce in a large skillet and season sauce highly with salt and pepper; keep sauce warm.

7. To cook the agnolotti, heat 6 quarts of water to boiling in a large soup kettle. Add ½ teaspoon salt and the pasta. Cook until the curved double edges of the agnolotti are tender, about 2 to 3 minutes after the water returns to a rapid boil. Drain well in a colander.

8. Transfer drained agnolotti to the skillet. Gently toss over low heat until they are thoroughly coated with sauce, about 1 to 2 minutes. Transfer them to warm serving bowls with a slotted spoon. Top each portion with a heaping tablespoon of remaining sauce and with the remaining grated Parmesan cheese. Garnish with a sprig of basil or a sprinkling of chives and serve immediately.

I am taking enormous liberties by shaping pasta into half-moons, or *mezzalune,* and calling it *agnolotti,* and I can see authorities on Italian cooking shaking their heads in exasperation. Technically, half-moons are a type of *tortelli,* which is another name for ravioli.

Strictly speaking, *agnolotti* are ring-shaped envelopes of dough from the Piedmont, and to make matters worse, they are most frequently filled with vegetables or meat and sauced with butter and cheese. Here I stuff them with goat cheese of all things, and toss them in tomato sauce; however, no guest has ever complained or corrected the error of my ways.

SCALLION AND BLACK PEPPER LASAGNE WITH BLACK OLIVE PESTO

Scallion and black pepper noodles, daubed with a pungent impasto of black olives, offer a minimalist's approach to vegetable lasagne that I first encountered in a restaurant on the Italian Riviera. Having ordered "lasagna," I naturally expected a layered, baked dish. Imagine my surprise when a single, broad, sauce-smeared noodle arrived at my place. I asked the waiter whether this could be the wrong dish. "Oh," he replied, "you expected *lasagne al forno,*" [baked, layered lasagne]. "*This* is *lasagna.*"

The idea took hold. A single, broad noodle square offers an exciting background for a dramatic and colorful sauce, such as this inky pesto. Because the pasta squares swell dramatically during cooking, serve this on a warm dinner plate. Feel free to push the noodles around to make them fit on the plate—they will undulate, wavelike, in sections, and as you eat you may find some sauce has worked its way under some of the little folds in the dough. Since the large surface of the noodles causes them to cool down quickly, have the plates warm and the sauce made and ready to go before cooking the pasta—it is important to get this on the table as rapidly as possible.

FLEXIBLE MENU SUGGESTIONS

In a menu created for an entertaining issue of *Cook's* magazine, I suggested serving the lasagne as a first course for an early fall dinner, followed by One-Side Grilled Fish (page 216) with Bouillabaisse Sauce (page 228), Rosemary Breadsticks (page 343), green salad with Chive Vinaigrette (page 61), and Lemon Tart Brulée (page 406). It is a lovely meal. However, this pasta also would be delicious before other main courses, including Sage-Rubbed Veal Chops (page 242), Capretto with Lemon and Rosemary (page 246), Leg of Lamb with Niçoise Seasoning (page 248), Herb-Rubbed Chicken (page 278), or Garlic-Roasted Leg of Lamb (page 295).

If you wish to serve the lasagne as a main course, begin with an antipasto of mixed Italian meats such as prosciutto, salami, and paper-thin slices of mortadella, accompanied by Umbrian Cheese Bread (page 350). Serve Gianduia Cheesecake (page 384), the Almond Soufflé Tart (page 414), or Lemon Tirami Su (page 429) for dessert.

The sauce also can be used as a garnish for Stuffed Tomatoes (page 312). *Makes 6 servings*

BLACK OLIVE PESTO

1 can large, pitted black olives (9 ounces)
2 small garlic cloves, peeled
2 small shallots, peeled
1 fresh, hot red chile (2 inches long)
2 tablespoons minced parsley leaves
¾ teaspoon minced thyme leaves
¾ teaspoon red wine vinegar
Salt
½ cup extra-virgin olive oil, or Herbed Oil
    (page 73)
1 lemon
1 small bunch fresh chives

Scallion and Black Pepper Pasta Dough
    (page 140)
Flour

1. To make the sauce, rinse, drain, and pat the olives dry. Put them in a food processor fitted with the metal blade and process until chopped; transfer to a bowl. Mince the garlic and shallots, then stem, seed, and mince the chile; transfer to the bowl. Stir in the parsley, thyme, vinegar, ¼ teaspoon salt, and the olive oil. Adjust seasoning to taste. (Can cover and refrigerate sauce overnight.)

2. Make the pasta dough and divide it into three pieces. Roll each piece to the thinnest setting of a pasta machine, keeping strips as wide as possible. Cut dough into 5-inch squares and rub each lightly with flour. Put cut pasta squares in single layers on wax paper. (Can put paper on a baking sheet, cover loosely with plastic wrap, and set aside at room temperature up to 6 hours.)

3. Shortly before serving time, bring sauce to room temperature, if refrigerated. Use a zester to make fine julienne strips of lemon zest, or cut the zest into strips with a knife. (Reserve lemon for other uses.) Snip chives into 1-inch lengths; set garnish aside.

4. Bring 8 quarts of water to a boil in a large soup kettle. Add 2 teaspoons salt. Add pasta squares one at a time and cook until tender, about 3 minutes. Drain, then quickly blot squares dry with a cloth towel.

5. Working quickly, put one pasta square on each warm dinner plate. Top with 3 to 4 tablespoons sauce, spreading the sauce over two-thirds of the noodle. Garnish each portion with lemon zest and chives. Serve immediately.

CURRY NOODLES WITH SCALLOPS AND CILANTRO

Seafood, hot chiles, and fresh cilantro are age-old partners in cooked curries, and here they are redefined with pasta in a symphony of seafood and spice (the recipe is pictured in the color section). Curry powder tints the skinny golden noodles, which are cooked and then swirled into a hive on the center of a warm dinner plate. The sauce, a straightforward sauté of scallops, spiked with serrano peppers (see page 199), is poured over the pasta, leaving the plate adorned with what a friend of mine calls "cubitos" of flavor and color.

FLEXIBLE MENU SUGGESTIONS

The distinctive spicing does restrict the range of this pasta in menus, but the ensemble makes an excellent opener for meals based on Soy-Marinated Chicken (page 238) or Yogurt and Spice-Marinated Leg of Lamb (page 252).

To serve the pasta as a light main course, start with Papaya Melon Soup (page 41). I would offer a mixed green salad with Lemon-Basil Vinaigrette (page 74), blue cheese, and French Dinner Rolls (page 360) after the pasta to add weight to the menu (or serve the salad first, instead of soup), then add individual Almond Soufflé Tarts (page 414). *Makes 4 servings*

PREPARATION: 30 MINUTES
COOKING: 15 MINUTES

Curry Pasta Dough (page 148)

SAUCE

1 medium garlic clove, peeled
6 medium shallots, peeled (1½ ounces)
2 serrano peppers (or 1 small jalapeño), stemmed, seeded, quartered
1 tablespoon olive oil
¾ pound small bay scallops (or sea scallops or raw shelled and deveined shrimp, cut in ½-inch dice), rinsed, patted dry
⅓ cup dry white wine
1¼ cups Chicken Stock (page 165)
Salt
¼ cup firmly packed fresh cilantro leaves
3 tablespoons olive oil
1 small tomato, peeled, seeded, diced
4 tablespoons softened butter
Ground black pepper

1. Make the Curry Pasta Dough.

2. Divide pasta dough in half and roll out each piece to the thinnest setting on a pasta machine, following the method on page 129. Then roll the partially dried strips through the thinnest machine cutter. Transfer noodles to cloth towel until serving time. (Can cover and set aside up to 6 hours.)

3. For the sauce, mince the garlic, shallots, and serranos. Heat 1 tablespoon oil in a 10-inch skillet. Add the garlic mixture and cook over low heat about 2 minutes.

4. Add scallops and toss just until opaque, about 2 minutes; use a slotted spoon to set seafood mixture aside. Add wine and Chicken Stock to the skillet and reduce by

simmering until mixture measures ⅔ cup; set aside in the skillet. (Can cover and refrigerate sauce ingredients up to 6 hours.)

5. At serving time, heat 4 quarts of water to boiling in large soup kettle. Stir in ½ teaspoon salt and the pasta. Cook until pasta is tender, about 1 minute after water boils again. Drain pasta in a colander. Mince the cilantro.

6. Add olive oil to the empty kettle. Toss pasta gently in oil to remove excess water and coat noodles; cover and keep pasta warm.

7. Heat tomato in the sauce mixture. Add scallops and simmer gently until hot. Whisk in the butter and season with ¼ teaspoon salt, and pepper to taste. Adjust seasoning and stir in the cilantro.

8. Use tongs or a large fork to make a hive-shaped portion of hot noodles on four warm dinner plates. Spoon hot scallop mixture and sauce over noodles. Serve immediately.

INDIAN SUN

What we know as curry powder actually is a south Indian *masala,* or spice blend, that can have an infinite range of regional and personal variations. Authentic Indian cooks always prefer to select and roast their own spices and mix them to taste, especially since spices lose their pungency with age.

Curry powder comes in many different blends, and can include ginger, coriander, turmeric, fenugreek seed, cloves, cinnamon, cumin, powdered mustard, black and red pepper, and kari or curry leaves, all roasted and ground to a powder. Coriander, cumin, and fenugreek tend to dominate the flavor, while mustard and turmeric lend bitterness and a sunny, yellow color. Heat is added by cayenne pepper.

Depending on your taste, you can use a relatively hot curry powder such as Subadhar, available in specialty food stores, or a mild curry powder from the supermarket. Other good blends are sold in spice shops or Indian food stores, where you also can buy spices to roast, and then grind your own. A recipe for a Hot Curry Powder that can be made at home from ground spices appears on page 203. Commercially prepared curry powders that add MSG or salt should be avoided. It is a good idea to taste curry powder before buying or using it.

CURRY PASTA DOUGH

The pungent spices in curry powder help inject maximum flavor into this dough, which also takes on a bright yellow color that does not fade during cooking.

FLEXIBLE MENU SUGGESTIONS

While these unusual noodles are somewhat limited in use, they are outstanding with Scallops and Cilantro (page 146). When cut as thin as possible and tossed lightly in olive oil or butter, they will serve four to six as an accompaniment to Shrimp and Scallops with Chile-Peanut Sauce (page 232), Grilled Ceviche (page 231), Soy-Marinated Chicken (page 238), or Garlic-Rubbed Chicken (page 278). *Makes about 11 ounces of dough*

PREPARATION: 10 MINUTES

2 large eggs
1 large egg yolk
2 tablespoons curry powder
1 tablespoon olive or vegetable oil
Salt
Hot red pepper sauce
*1 to 1¼ cups bread flour or unbleached all-
    purpose flour*
Flour for rolling dough

1. Insert the metal blade in a dry food-processor container. Add the eggs, egg yolk, curry powder, oil, ¼ teaspoon salt, and several dashes of hot red pepper sauce. Process until the mixture is foamy, about 20 seconds.

2. Add 1 cup flour. Process with 1-second pulses until the mixture has the consistency of small beads. If dough is too wet for beads to form, process in additional flour by tablespoons, using 1-second pulses, until dough forms beads that hold together when pinched.

3. Wrap dough in plastic, press into a flat disk, and set it aside for 20 minutes. (Can refrigerate 24 hours.) If dough glues itself to plastic wrap, a generous quantity of additional flour should be worked into the dough strips during rolling. Otherwise, rub a moderate amount of flour onto dough strips while stretching them according to directions on page 129.

LEMON-GARLIC PASTA DOUGH

The acidity of lemon and the pungency of garlic balance each other in this pasta dough, although their flavors are tempered somewhat by boiling. This is a good dough to cut into *capellini* (little hairs). Wider noodles tend to be heavy because the dough contains solid ingredients.

Use a zester or a grater to remove the lemon rind so that the pieces are as thin and small as possible. If you have time, mince the garlic separately and soften it for several hours in 1 teaspoon olive oil before adding it to the dough (the oil also may be added, and the dough may take 2 to 3 additional tablespoons of flour).

FLEXIBLE MENU SUGGESTIONS

This is a good substitute for Scallion and Black Pepper Pasta Dough (page 140) and may be used with any of those menu suggestions. The noodles are superb with Mediterranean Sauce (page 150), and are compatible with any of the other pasta sauces. They can also accompany Veal Scallops Giardino (page 284). *Makes about 12 ounces of dough*

PREPARATION: 20 MINUTES

Zest of 2 medium lemons
4 medium garlic cloves
Salt
2 large eggs
2 large egg yolks
1¼ to 1⅓ cups bread flour or unbleached all-
*   purpose flour*
Flour for rolling dough

1. Zest the lemons, then mince the garlic with the zest and ¼ teaspoon salt. Transfer the mixture to a food processor fitted with the metal blade. Add the eggs and egg yolks and process until the mixture is foamy, about 20 seconds.

2. Add 1¼ cups flour and process with 1-second pulses until the mixture has the consistency of small beads. If dough is too wet for beads to form, process in additional flour

by tablespoons, using 1-second pulses, until dough forms beads that hold together when pinched.

3. Wrap dough in plastic, press it into a flat disk, and set it aside 20 minutes. (Can refrigerate 24 hours.) If dough glues itself to plastic wrap, a generous quantity of additional flour should be worked into the dough strips during rolling. Otherwise, rub a moderate amount of flour onto dough strips while stretching according to directions on page 129.

LEMON-GARLIC CAPELLINI WITH MEDITERRANEAN SAUCE

During the summer, I like to serve food that requires relatively little effort to make or to eat. This dish fits beautifully into that category, especially when the tomatoes, zucchini, and basil are just in from the garden. Since the taste of the sauce is also dependent on the quality of ingredients such as olives, capers, and Parmesan cheese, be sure that these are the best you can buy.

The recipe calls for cutting basil leaves into what the French call a *chiffonnade,* or julienne, to add to the sauce at the last moment. To maximize the herbal punch of basil, use a very sharp knife to cleanly cut the leaves crosswise, or on a diagonal. If properly cut, bruising (discoloration which indicates a slight flavor loss) will be minimal.

FLEXIBLE MENU SUGGESTIONS

Half of a Red Pepper Preserved in Oil (page 339) can be substituted for the roasted red bell pepper in the recipe.

Despite its simplicity, this pasta is garlicky and surprisingly rich. It is a great first course for menus based on a grilled white-fleshed fish or chicken breasts with Whole-Grain Mustard-Chive Butter (page 277), Sage-Rubbed Veal Chops (page 242), Capretto with Lemon and Rosemary (page 246), Leg of Lamb with Niçoise Seasoning (page 248), and Herb-Rubbed Chicken (page 278).

If you plan to serve this as a light main course, thinly sliced prosciutto would make an outstanding first course. For dessert, add fresh fruit with Gianduia Lace Cookies (page 386) or Chocolate-Walnut Linzer Torte (page 376), depending on whether you wish to end the meal on a light or more substantial note. *Makes 4 servings*

PREPARATION: 35 MINUTES
COOKING: 3 MINUTES

Lemon-Garlic Pasta Dough (page 149)

SAUCE

1 medium zucchini (4 ounces)
⅔ cup olive oil or Herbed Oil (page 73)
3 fresh Italian plum tomatoes
½ small red bell pepper

¼ cup thinly sliced scallions
1 tablespoon drained, rinsed capers
2 tablespoons finely chopped green olives
¼ cup coarsely chopped, pitted Oil-Marinated Olives (page 63) or pitted black olives
2 tablespoons minced parsley
Salt and ground black pepper
¼ cup basil leaves
1 chunk Parmesan cheese (about 2 ounces)

1. Make the pasta dough and roll it to the second thinnest setting on the pasta machine, following procedures on page 129. Cut thin noodles by rolling the partially dried strips through the pasta-machine cutter. Transfer noodles to a cloth towel until serving time.

2. For the sauce, remove the stem and tip from the zucchini and cut it lengthwise into six thin slices. Heat a stovetop grill or broiler. Brush the grill or broiler and zucchini slices lightly with olive oil. Grill or broil until zucchini is marked on each side. Cool and cut the slices into ¼-inch squares; transfer zucchini to a mixing bowl.

3. Roast tomatoes and bell pepper over a gas flame, or under the broiler, until the skins char. Peel, coarsely chop, and add tomatoes to the bowl. Peel and cut the pepper into ¼-inch dice; add ¼ cup to the bowl (reserve remainder for another use).

4. Stir scallions, capers, olives, parsley, and ½ cup oil into the zucchini mixture. Season with ¼ teaspoon salt and ¼ teaspoon pepper. (Can cover and set sauce aside at room temperature up to 4 hours.)

5. At serving time, stack and shred the basil leaves crosswise into very thin strips. Make eight paper-thin slices of Parmesan cheese by drawing a cheese knife or a vegetable peeler over the cheese chunk; set basil and cheese aside.

6. Bring 4 quarts of water to a boil in a soup kettle. Add ½ teaspoon salt and the pasta and cook until tender, about 3 minutes; drain. Put remaining olive oil (or 2 tablespoons) in the kettle, add the drained pasta, and toss over low heat just until excess liquid evaporates. Add shredded basil to sauce ingredients. Toss pasta with the sauce. Top each portion with two slices of shaved cheese and serve immediately.

TAKING STOCK:
HEARTY SOUPS AND RISOTTOS

Hearty soups and risottos are my reliable standbys for meals that must be substantial and down-to-earth but still unique. Like old-fashioned stews, they are nourishing and valuable assets in the menu larder because they take shape in a single pot, and they do double duty—as an appetizer or as a main course—at the table.

These uncommon doubles share two essential ingredients: stock and starch. Behind every good soup or risotto is at least a quart of homemade stock, an essential building block of flavor, and the single component that brings a diverse assemblage of ingredients into delicious, fragrant union. Starch is present in these soups in the form of rice, noodles, or a flour-based thickener. Reduce risotto to its essence and it is merely a sumptuous, soupy rice.

SOUP OF THE EVENING

There is a natural intimacy that comes from sharing a tureen of soup and good bread, which is why I often think of a soup meal as a wonderfully relaxing way to entertain close friends.

While this type of elemental, stripped-down menu may have been unacceptable in years past, today guests are likely to be relieved by the prospect of a simple dinner that does not require hours at table. Adding cheese and a salad, or perhaps just fresh fruit, can complete the menu with minimal effort. Other embellishments, such as homemade bread or a special dessert, are added bonuses.

The four soups included in this chapter differ in spirit and character from those I would serve strictly as appetizers, although each of these recipes can be a memorable first course. Like pasta or risotto, I see them as quintessential "doubles," light foods that combine protein, starch, and vegetables in a single dish, and which, by virtue of their ingredients, textures, and certain complexities of seasoning, are well positioned to stand on their own.

CREATING A STIR

Risotto could be called Italy's comfort food, which may help to explain why this unique dish of creamy short-grain rice is nipping at the heels of pasta's popularity. Despite its hearty character, risotto may be the single dish that best expresses the Italian capacity for culinary subtlety and complexity: a multitude of vegetables, fish, poultry, meats, herbs, spices, and seasonings can be painted on the otherwise blank, souplike canvas of rice, broth, butter, and cheese.

Its unique charm also can be colored by ingredients. Risotto is sometimes tinted purple by blueberries; or a stunning yellow by saffron or curry. A red, orange, or pink flush can be provided by cooking the rice with red wine, salmon, shrimp, tomatoes, strawberries, or pumpkin; green risotto can be stirred up from mixtures of herbs or spinach. Then there are the surprisingly delicious black risottos, stained by the ink of squid or cuttlefish.

There is a saying in Italy's Po Valley that for a woman to have a good chance at marriage, her hands must be marked in a way that proves she has spent years stirring risotto. Despite the hectic pace of life today, spending nearly half an hour over a pot of rice on the stove can become an enormously pleasurable and relaxing task—indeed for many cooks, it is a joy. Those who may find it a chore will want to use the microwave method (page 169).

The keys to success with risotto are purchasing imported Italian short-grain rice (see page 167), using unsalted, homemade stock (page 165), and buying the very best Parmesan cheese your budget will allow (page 163).

Purists often insist on making their own stock, and it is important to match the stock with the risotto ingredients. Chicken stock is most commonly used, but vegetable and fish stocks are other good choices.

Grated Parmesan cheese is another critical ingredient, and imported Parmigiano-Reggiano is best. Grana Padano is another good cheese, for it has a wonderful, milky richness that will never impart the sourness, or "off" flavor, of a second-rate Parmesan.

I have read that Italians will drive further to eat a fine risotto than the best ravioli. However, superb risotto can be made right at home. Its lure, and the quality that makes it worth the effort, may be found in those final moments when the steaming, porridgelike rice is ladled into serving bowls. Just watch the looks of amazement and anticipation on the faces of friends who are trying it for the first time, or the gratitude of those who already adore this dish. Risotto often inspires passion, and rarely is anyone indifferent to its seductive spell.

MILANESE MINESTRONE

DUCK AND SAUSAGE GUMBO

SPICY HOMESTYLE BEEF SOUP

MILANESE ASPARAGUS SOUP

A Parmesan Primer

CHICKEN STOCK

SHRIMP AND CURRY RISOTTO

Top-Grade Grains

The Venetian Method

The 20-Minute Microwave Risotto Method

SAFFRON RISOTTO

A Consuming Dilemma

RISOTTO PRIMAVERA

RISOTTO SPINACCIOLA

COUNTRY-STYLE RISOTTO

MILANESE MINESTRONE

Examine the vegetables in any version of minestrone, and you could draw a map of Italy by the variation in the ingredients—it is a bellwether of Italian regional cooking.

Nearly as thick as a stew, this Milanese version is distinguished by the presence of Italian short-grain rice (see page 167), a staple of Lombardy that often replaces pasta. Additional body comes from the starch present in white beans, which are rinsed and added raw to the cooking liquid.

Subtlety of taste and texture comes from ten different vegetables added in sequence to avoid overcooking. Parmesan cheese further enhances the flavor, and offers an opportunity to use those precious leftover rinds of Parmigiano-Reggiano.

FLEXIBLE MENU SUGGESTIONS

For menus that call for this soup as an appetizer, follow serving suggestions for Pasta with Broccoli Raab (page 134); add Garlic-Rubbed Chicken (page 278) to the main-course list. If you plan to serve this as a main course, consult serving notes for Milanese Asparagus Soup (page 162). *Makes 10 to 12 servings*

PREPARATION: 50 MINUTES
COOKING: ABOUT 90 MINUTES

1 medium onion, peeled
1 medium bunch scallions, trimmed
2 medium tomatoes, peeled and seeded
2 tablespoons olive or vegetable oil
4 tablespoons unsalted butter
2½ quarts Chicken Stock (page 165)
½ cup white (Great Northern) beans, rinsed
3 medium celery ribs, leaves removed
2 small zucchini, quartered lengthwise
2 medium carrots, peeled, halved lengthwise
1 large potato, peeled, quartered lengthwise
1 wedge (about ¼ pound) green cabbage, cored
1 cup short-grain Italian rice, rinsed
½ cup frozen peas, thawed
¼ pound Parmesan cheese (preferably Parmigiano-Reggiano), rind removed, cubed
2 tablespoons fresh basil, chopped (1 tablespoon dried)
1 teaspoon fresh marjoram or oregano leaves, chopped (½ teaspoon dried)
¼ cup minced parsley
Salt and ground black pepper

1. Finely chop the onion and scallions, and coarsely chop the tomatoes. Heat olive oil and butter in a 6-quart soup kettle or Dutch oven. Add the onion, scallions, and tomato and stir vegetables over low heat until softened, about 10 minutes. Add stock, 1 quart water, and white beans. Cover and simmer for 15 minutes.

2. Slice the celery, zucchini, carrots, and potato into ⅛-inch-thick pieces. Shred the cabbage by slicing it across the grain (there should be 2 cups). Add the vegetables (and add unwaxed Parmesan rind; optional) to the kettle and simmer for 30 minutes. Stir in the rice and peas, and simmer for 40 minutes longer.

3. Test the beans for tenderness by mashing with a spoon. If still firm, continue simmering the soup until white beans are soft, usually about 10 minutes longer (remove Parmesan rinds if necessary). (Can cool and refrigerate soup up to 48 hours.)

4. Use the metal blade of a dry food processor to grate the Parmesan cheese by processing until powdery; set cheese aside. At serving time, reheat soup if refrigerated. Stir in grated Parmesan, fresh herbs, and parsley. Then adjust seasoning to taste, taking care not to oversalt. Serve immediately.

DUCK AND SAUSAGE GUMBO

For me, this gumbo is the next best thing to a trip to New Orleans. Tender juicy morsels of duck and smoked sausage, the wonderful sting of cayenne, and an undercurrent of filé powder say "that's Cajun"—my way.

The requirement of cutting up a whole duck puts this soup into the realm of a "cooking adventure," but this job can be done easily by a butcher. Procuring two essential ingredients also may require some advance legwork. Filé powder, derived from the dried crushed leaves of sassafras trees found throughout the Gulf of Mexico, is an essential spice. Okra, a missile-shaped member of the cotton family filled with a sticky substance that helps to thicken the soup, also is a must.

Gumbo may be cooked through step 8, then cooled and refrigerated before adding the reserved duck and reheating the soup.

FLEXIBLE MENU SUGGESTIONS

I like to serve gumbo as an appetizer with American in Paris Biscuits (page 366). Since the soup contains poultry and sausage, One-Side Grilled Fish (page 216) with Whole-Grain Mustard-Chive Butter (page 277) is a logical second course.

To serve gumbo as a main course, begin with hors d'oeuvres such as Spiced Nuts or Chutney Toasts (pages 447 and 449). Then, accompany the soup with the biscuits (above), Soft Rolls (page 364), or Ham and Jalapeño Cornbread (page 367). Finish with Banana Ice Cream and Coconut-Lime Tuiles (pages 438 and 440), or serve the cookies with fresh fruit. If you are feeling particularly ambitious, Lemon-Praline Soufflé Glacé (page 433) would be a fabulous dessert. *Makes 8 to 10 servings*

PREPARATION: 45 MINUTES
COOKING: 4½ HOURS

1 fresh or defrosted duck (about 5 pounds)
2 quarts Chicken Stock (page 165)
3 medium garlic cloves, peeled
1 medium onion, peeled, cubed
2 medium celery stalks, leaves removed
1 medium green bell pepper, cored, seeded, cut into 8 strips
½ pound okra, stems and tips removed
1 pound Italian plum tomatoes, peeled (or a 28-ounce can, drained)
1 piece (6 ounces) kielbasa or other smoked sausage, chilled
2 teaspoons filé powder

1 bay leaf
½ teaspoon dried thyme leaves
Salt
¼ to ½ teaspoon cayenne pepper, or more to taste
⅓ cup uncooked long-grain rice
Ground black pepper

1. Adjust oven rack to lowest position. Heat oven to 425 degrees. To cut up the duck, remove the legs and second joints in one piece, leaving the parts connected. Cut away the neck skin. Remove the entire breast, leaving skin and bone intact, by holding the

tip of the duck breast and carefully cutting through each side of rib section with a poultry shears or sharp scissors. Remove and discard the skin from the back.

2. Put all duck meat and bones (including giblets but not liver) in a roasting pan, skin-side up. Pierce duck breast several times with the tip of a knife or skewer. Roast 20 minutes; remove and set breast aside to cool. Return pan to the oven for 5 minutes longer, or until thickest parts of legs are rare (130 degrees on an instant-read thermometer). Remove legs; cool. Refrigerate legs and breast.

3. Reduce oven heat to 350 degrees. Turn remaining pieces in the pan and roast 15 minutes longer, or until they are deeply browned. Transfer pieces to a 6- to 8-quart soup kettle. Strain the fat into a heatproof cup and reserve.

4. Put roasting pan on stovetop (over two burners if possible) and heat. Pour in 1½ cups cold water, and clean pan bottom with wooden spatula to remove cooked-on matter. Heat the liquid to boiling, then pour it into the soup kettle. Add 2½ cups water and the stock to the kettle. Cover and simmer 2 hours. (Can uncover, cool, and refrigerate overnight.)

5. Remove duck pieces from the stock. Strip off meat from bones, neck, wings, and giblets; set aside. Discard the bones and skin. Strain stock, which should measure 2½ to 3 quarts; reserve. (Can refrigerate stock and meat overnight.)

6. Mince the garlic, then coarsely chop the onion and celery. Clean and dry the soup kettle, and heat 2 tablespoons of the strained duck fat. Add the vegetables and stir over low heat until softened, about 5 minutes.

7. Slice the green pepper into strips. Slice okra into rings; transfer the vegetables to the kettle, and stir over low heat until okra becomes slightly sticky.

8. Slice tomatoes and add to kettle, then slice the sausage and set aside. Remove any fat from the surface of the stock. Stir in the stock, filé powder, bay, thyme, ⅛ teaspoon salt, and cayenne pepper. Cover and simmer until vegetables soften completely, about 30 to 40 minutes. Add rice and sausage. Slowly simmer until rice cooks and soup thickens, about 35 to 40 minutes. (Can cool, cover, and refrigerate 24 hours.)

9. Remove and discard skin and bones from the duck breast and legs. Split breast meat lengthwise, then slice each piece of the breast crosswise into thin strips. Slice leg meat into strips; wrap and set aside until serving time.

10. Reheat soup, if refrigerated. Adjust seasoning with salt and pepper. Stir in all the duck meat. Heat soup thoroughly, but do not allow it to boil or the duck pieces may toughen. Serve immediately.

SPICY HOMESTYLE BEEF SOUP

My trip to mainland China, in 1983, sparked an intense interest in Chinese cooking. Thanks to my friend, Chinese restaurateur David Keh, I subsequently have been able to spend time collecting recipes in two of his restaurant kitchens in New York.

One afternoon, David asked if I wanted to learn to make his favorite soup, a homestyle beef-noodle soup that was a special Taiwanese-Szechwan dish not often found in restaurants. It was only after I said "yes" that I learned the cooking lesson would take place in the middle of the night, during his mah-jongg game.

The players (all men) gathered at 11 P.M. in an apartment in Chinatown. Mrs. Yuan, our hostess, showed me how she had begun the soup a day in advance by simmering the beef with green onions, garlic, and ginger to create a light, but very flavorful, broth.

About an hour before serving the players, Mrs. Yuan deftly sliced and stir-fried the chilled meat with Szechwan garlic-chili paste, then simmered it to final tenderness in the broth. I later learned that cooking meat more than once is a common practice for soup, and that major ingredients for stir-fries are cooked twice as well.

Noodle soup is a most wonderful and varied dish, and despite the late hour of my own first encounter with this spicy version, it can be served any time of the day or night. (Notes on Chinese ingredients appear on page 208.)

FLEXIBLE MENU SUGGESTIONS

The soup makes a filling appetizer that can be followed by Soy-Marinated Chicken (page 238).

If you prefer to serve it as a main course, begin with Mixed Lettuces with Shrimp and Ginger-Lime Vinaigrette (page 68). Pink Grapefruit or Black Plum Sorbet (pages 435 or 437) and Mixed Nut Sablés (page 442) can be served for dessert, although fresh fruit will do. *Makes 6 to 8 servings*

PREPARATION: 30 MINUTES
CHILLING: 12 HOURS
COOKING: ABOUT 4 HOURS

BROTH

3 pounds boneless beef brisket
3 quarts Chicken Stock (page 165) or cold
*   water*
1 medium garlic clove, peeled
4 cubes (1 inch each) fresh ginger, peeled
4 medium scallions, trimmed
Salt

MEAT AND GARNISH

¼ cup all-purpose soy sauce
3 tablespoons garlic-chili paste
4 tablespoons vegetable oil
1 medium bunch scallions, trimmed, halved
½ cup loosely packed cilantro leaves
½ pound Chinese soup noodles (lo mein) or
*   fresh linguine*

1. For the soup, put the brisket and stock or water in a 6-quart soup kettle. Mince the garlic and ginger, and coarsely chop the scallions. Add the vegetables to the kettle with ¼ teaspoon salt. Heat to simmering. Skim off foam that rises and simmer until beef is tender, about 3 hours. Cool and refrigerate meat in the broth until it is thoroughly chilled. (Can refrigerate 48 hours.)

2. Slice beef by hand into thin strips as for beef Stroganoff and set aside.

3. Strain the broth into a clean soup kettle. Measure and mix 1 cup broth with ¼ cup soy sauce; set aside. Heat a wok, add chili paste, oil, and sliced beef. Stir-fry until coated, then add the soy-broth and simmer 3 minutes.

4. Transfer the contents of the wok to the stockpot, partially cover, and simmer 1 hour.

5. At serving time, sliver the scallions lengthwise to make ¾ cup when loosely packed; set aside. Heat 6 cups of water to boiling. Add the noodles and boil until tender; drain well. Transfer hot noodles to serving bowls and top with several scallion slivers and two or three cilantro leaves. Ladle broth and meat strips into the bowls, over the noodles. Garnish with additional cilantro and slivered scallions. Serve immediately.

"It has been said many times that rice is common in southern China, and wheat in northern China. That is generally true."

—FOOD IN CHINESE CULTURE

MILANESE ASPARAGUS SOUP

Emerald stalks of fresh asparagus, prized for their delicate flavor, make a velvety soup that is wonderful late in asparagus season when prices are low. Add a loaf of homemade bread and a simple fruit dessert for a casual soup meal.

Thickening with a *roux* gives the soup body and retains the old-fashioned charm of this recipe, inspired by Italian cookbook author Anna Gosetti della Salda. An authentic touch would be to garnish each bowl of soup with a toasted crouton. Since I normally accompany the soup with fresh homemade breads heavily flavored with cheese, I have omitted the garniture, but it may be good for certain menus. Croutons may be left plain or topped with Parmesan or Fontina cheese (broil 2 tablespoons grated Parmesan or Fontina on slices of toasted French bread until melted.)

FLEXIBLE MENU SUGGESTIONS

As an appetizer, the soup is great before Sausage and Artichoke Pizzas (page 108), Mushroom Pizzas on Prosciutto Crust (page 114), One-Side Grilled Fish (page 216) with Roasted Garlic and Saffron Butter (page 222), Grilled Ceviche (page 231), Sage-Rubbed Veal Chops (page 242), Leg of Lamb with Niçoise Seasoning (page 248), Veal Scallops with Black Olive Gremolada (page 286), Roasted Duck with Apples and Campari (page 289), or Pork with Port Wine Sauce (page 292).

For a light, informal meal based on the soup, start with an hors d'oeuvre such as Goat Cheese and Chive Gougère (page 452) or Polenta Diamonds (page 450). More substantial appetizers include Mozzarella, Tomato, and Olive Salad (page 62) or Homemade Garlic Sausage with Pistachios (page 92). Homemade breads—Umbrian Cheese, Parmesan and Black Pepper, Black Olive, or Tomato Flatbread with Two Herbs (pages 346 to 357)—are superb with the soup, and either Almond Soufflé Tart (page 414) or Almond and Lemon-Stuffed Pears (page 431) would give menus a polished ending. *Makes 6 to 8 servings*

PREPARATION: 50 MINUTES
COOKING: 40 MINUTES

1 quart milk
3 cups Chicken Stock (page 165)
3 tablespoons butter
6 tablespoons flour
2¼ pounds thin asparagus spears, rinsed
⅔ cup half-and-half
Salt and ground white pepper
Nutmeg

1. In a large saucepan combine milk, stock, and 1 cup cold water; heat to boiling, then set the milk mixture aside. Melt 3 tablespoons butter in a 6-quart soup kettle. Add flour, and stir over low heat until flour is cooked but not brown, about 2 minutes.

2. Off heat, add the hot milk mixture, whisking vigorously to prevent lumps from forming; set it aside. Remove and discard the tough bottom third of the asparagus spears.

Add the spears to the kettle, cover, and heat to simmering. Set cover ajar and simmer until spears are very soft, about 40 minutes.

3. Transfer 2 cups of the cooked asparagus mixture to a food processor fitted with the metal blade. Puree the mixture until smooth, then repeat to puree all the soup. Return pureed soup to the kettle, stir in half-and-half, and season with salt, pepper, and a dash of nutmeg. (Can cool, cover, and refrigerate 48 hours.) At serving time, heat soup and season to taste. Serve immediately.

A PARMESAN PRIMER

The quality of a cheese can easily determine the flavor of a dish, and no cheese proves to be more of a critical element than Parmesan, particularly in pasta, risotto, bread, soup, or in a savory tart.

Parmesan is a generic term used to describe a family of hard Italian cow's-milk grating cheeses made for centuries in and around the province of Emilia-Romagna, near Parma.

Parmigiano-Reggiano, a cheese generally considered to be the best-quality cheese in the Parmesan family, is easily recognized by its sweet, nutty flavor. Its name is also embossed on the side of the rind. Production of this cheese is restricted by Italian law and monitored by a consortium.

The heart of Parmigiano country stretches roughly from Bologna to Parma, where from April to October, a blend of whole and skim milk is taken from two daily milkings. In Parmesan factories, much of the work of making the 72-pound cheese wheels is still done by hand.

The cheesemaking process begins when heated milk is combined with some whey (a cloudy yellowish liquid) taken from a previous batch of cheese, and rennet (an animal enzyme that makes milk coagulate). When the warm milk sets to a flanlike consistency, it is cut with a metal harp, which releases the whey.

After a round of heating, cooling, and draining, the curds, or solids, are transferred to a stainless steel hoop that resembles a springform pan. The words *Parmigiano-Reggiano,* formed by small holes in the hoop's side, are stenciled into the cheese as the curds are pressed, or molded.

Once firm, the cheeses are immersed in salt brine for 3 weeks, then transferred to drying shelves (or set outside in the sun). Finally, they are aged in temperature- and humidity-controlled rooms for two years.

Continued

Cheeses in the Parmesan family can vary in flavor, size, shape, region, method of production, and in the type of milk used. Grana Padano, which resembles Parmigiano-Reggiano in looks and flavor, is made in several Italian regions. Unlike Reggiano, Grana is made year-round, from partly skimmed milk; its curds are pressed into 52- to 88-pound wheels that are aged for one to two years before shipment. Grana Padano can be identified by the name stamped in the rind. Its production standards also are regulated by a consortium.

Domestic Parmesan cheeses are made primarily in Wisconsin and Michigan. Although they are cured for at least 14 months, they generally lack the mellow nuttiness of the imported varieties.

BUYING AND STORING

Since Parmesan is an aged cheese, it is a misnomer to call it "fresh." "Freshly cut" is a better way to describe Parmesan at its peak.

Some stores break down a wheel of cheese and wrap chunks in plastic. Since a small degree of flavor will be lost if the cheese is kept refrigerated over a long period of time, try to avoid purchasing prewrapped chunks or those that appear to have a white surface. It is best to have it cut to order from a large wheel rather than to depend on the vagaries of commercial storage.

At home, a good way to store Parmigiano-Reggiano is to put it in a single sheet of plastic wrap and place it in a plastic bag (I prefer zipper-lock bags) lined with a paper towel to trap excess moisture.

GRATING

With its snowy texture, hand-grated Parmesan melts quickly over hot foods. When hand-grated cheese is suggested in recipes, ingredients will specify a particular amount of "grated Parmesan cheese," rather than calling for Parmesan by weight.

When speed is of the essence, when a large quantity of grated cheese is required, or when cheese will be cooked or melted over direct heat or in the oven, it is practical, and certainly quicker, to grate it in the food processor. Processor-grated cheese can be substituted for hand-grated Parmesan. Before processing the cheese, bring it to room temperature, then chip off 1-inch cubes with the point of a sharp knife. Leftover rinds that are not plastic-coated can be kept in a bag and used in Milanese Minestrone (page 156).

CHICKEN STOCK

This recipe yields a substantial quantity of salt-free stock that can be used for soups, risottos, and sauces. It can be frozen in airtight plastic containers for up to three months, or refrigerated as long as 1 week, provided it is boiled every forty-eight hours to prevent souring. Should you wish to make a lightly salted stock, add ½ teaspoon salt to the recipe in step 2.

Over the years it has become my habit to throw vegetables for stock into the food processor and pulse them to a coarse texture so they will quickly give up their flavors. However, all of the vegetable preparation may be coarsely chopped by hand. *Makes about 4 quarts*

PREPARATION: 20 MINUTES
COOKING: 7 TO 8 HOURS

5 pounds chicken backs, necks, wings, and
*   carcasses, or a 5- to 7-pound stewing hen,*
*   cut up, fat removed*
2 medium onions, peeled, halved
Leaves from 2 medium leeks
2 carrots, peeled
6 medium celery ribs, with leaves
2 unpeeled crushed garlic cloves
1 cup parsley with stems
1 teaspoon dried thyme leaves
1 bay leaf, crushed

1. Put chicken in an 8-quart or larger stockpot. Add 6 quarts of cold water, or enough water to cover ingredients by 1 to 2 inches. Cover and heat to simmering. Uncover and remove fat and foam on the surface. Cover and slowly simmer 3 hours, skimming as necessary.

2. Prepare and add the vegetables to the stockpot as follows: coarsely chop the onion with the leek greens. Chop the carrots and celery. Add remaining ingredients to stockpot. Cover and simmer 4 hours longer.

3. Uncover and cool to room temperature. Remove vegetables with slotted spoon. Set a large strainer over a bowl. Press the vegetables to extract all possible liquid, then discard them.

4. Use a slotted spoon to transfer the chicken to the strainer. Pick over the chicken; discard skin and bones (meat can be reserved for soup, salad, or other uses). Strain liquid into storage containers, leaving 2 inches at the tops. Stock is ready to use, refrigerate, or freeze.

SHRIMP AND CURRY RISOTTO

The strong flavor of curry powder (page 147) works beautifully with shrimp and rice in this delicious and very different *Risotto Admirali*. As in so many Italian recipes that contain fish or shellfish, no cheese is added—it would work against the curry and overpower the shrimp.

If you plan to cook this risotto in the microwave, you will need to poach the shrimp in the hot stock just until they curl; remove and set them aside, then proceed with the microwave method, and stir the cooked shrimp into the finished risotto as the recipe directs.

FLEXIBLE MENU SUGGESTIONS

This is wonderful as a preface to Yogurt and Spice-Marinated Leg of Lamb (page 252) or Sage-Rubbed Veal Chops (page 242).

Or, get underway with Spinach Salad with Caviar and Chives (page 60), then follow with the risotto and Prosciutto Bread (page 354). Finish with Milanese Fruit Tart or Almond Soufflé Tart (page 408 or 414). *Makes 6 to 8 servings*

PREPARATION: 40 MINUTES
COOKING: 23 MINUTES

6 to 7 cups fish or Chicken Stock (page 165)
1 pound medium shrimp in shells, peeled, deveined (shells reserved), and halved lengthwise
14 tablespoons softened unsalted butter
2 medium garlic cloves, peeled
2 medium onions, peeled
1 pound Italian short-grain rice
½ cup dry white wine
1 to 1½ tablespoons curry powder
¼ teaspoon turmeric
Salt and ground black pepper

1. Combine stock and shrimp shells in a large saucepan. Cover and simmer for 20 minutes. Strain, pressing shells to extract all liquid. Discard shells, return stock to pan, cover, and keep the stock hot (can cool, refrigerate stock 24 hours, then heat to simmering and keep covered).

2. Cut 8 tablespoons (1 stick) butter into small dice. Mince the garlic and finely chop the onions. Put the vegetables and the remaining 6 tablespoons of butter in a 4- to 6-quart soup kettle. Cook over medium heat until onions begin to color slightly, about 8 minutes.

3. Add rice and stir to coat it with butter, about 2 minutes. Add wine and simmer until it evaporates. Stir in curry, turmeric, and ½ teaspoon salt.

4. Stir ½ cup of the hot stock into the rice and set a timer for 18 minutes. Simmer slowly, stirring until stock is absorbed and mixture thickens slightly.

5. Continue stirring, adding up to 5 cups stock in ½-cup batches, and keeping mixture at a steady simmer over the 18 minutes. Mixture will become creamy as the stock is absorbed by the rice.

6. After 18 minutes, taste the rice. If rice is just done, stir in the shrimp. If rice is still firm, continue adding stock in ¼-cup batches, stirring over low heat until rice is just tender, about 2 to 3 minutes; then add the shrimp.

7. Over very low heat, vigorously beat in the softened butter. If rice becomes too thick, stir in ¼ cup stock (it is normal to have 1 cup stock left over). Taste and adjust seasoning with salt (if needed) and pepper. Serve immediately.

TOP-GRADE GRAINS

For many years, Arborio rice, packed in small canvas sacks, was virtually synonymous with risotto. In fact it is the best known of the *superfino,* or top-grade varieties of Italian rice, and is not a brand name.

The quality of short-grain rice is determined by its size—the bigger the better. Rice is graded according to kernel size and length, based on standards established in 1931. Many risotto connoisseurs consider the rice known as Carnaroli to be equal, if not superior, to Arborio. The Roma variety is also good for risotto, although its grains can be slightly smaller than other varieties. Rice of lesser grades—*fino, semifino,* and *commune*—are normally used for soups.

Italian rice is carried in specialty stores and supermarkets. Whether packaged in bags or boxes, the only precaution is to check the label to be sure it is not precooked.

THE VENETIAN METHOD

There are a number of ways to cook risotto, but most Italian food authorities agree that basting the stubby kernels of rice with precisely enough hot broth to coax each grain to the point of tenderness—before beating in softened butter and a considerable quantity of grated Parmesan cheese—produces the best result.

This technique, which I call the Venetian method, requires more or less continuous stirring for approximately 23 minutes. Since the individual grains are permitted to swell and soften evenly during cooking, exuding their starch and absorbing stock, the rice is just tender and still firm—but not chalky—in the center when it is fully cooked.

Cooking risotto perfectly is simply a question of pacing. Stock is added evenly during the first 18 minutes while the mixture cooks at a slow, steady simmer. As stock is absorbed, the rice takes on a homogeneous texture. The moment it starts to thicken and lose its creaminess, more stock must be added so the rice does not become dry.

During a stay in Tuscany I had an opportunity to cook with chef Julie Lumia, who created Orso restaurants in New York, Toronto, London, and Los Angeles, and who learned to make risotto while working in the kitchen of a prominent Venetian restaurant. Her risotto, flavored by fresh *porcini* mushrooms and zucchini, still ranks as one of the most perfect and delicious I have ever tasted. The secret of the much-prized creamy texture was that once the rice was cooked, she vigorously beat a staggering quantity of butter and grated Parmesan cheese into the risotto with a wooden spoon, and adjusted the texture of the mixture with small quantities of hot stock. Working it in this manner, she explained, gave the rice its silky finish and exquisite taste.

I subsequently spent an hour in the kitchen of Bellini by Cipriani restaurant in New York (a branch of the renowned Harry's Bar in Venice), watching the chefs repeatedly prepare risotto in exactly the same manner. The sizable quantities of butter and cheese can be reduced to suit individual tastes and diets; however, expect the texture and flavor of the risotto to vary accordingly.

ADDITIONAL TIPS

Recipes that call for substantial quantities of grated Parmesan cheese must be made with salt-free stock to ensure that the risotto will not be oversalted. While homemade stock is ideal, salt-free canned chicken broths are available in health-food stores and supermarkets. Health Valley and Pritikin are good brands. Small quantities of leftover stock can be frozen.

To avoid oversalting, add butter and cheese to the rice mixture, then taste before adding salt. Generally, the cheese is sufficient to bring risotto to its peak of flavor.

If you must use salted, canned chicken broth, reduce the quantity of stock specified in the recipe by half and substitute water for the remainder.

To partially prepare risotto in advance: Follow the recipe for 12 minutes to cook the rice by two-thirds. Spread the hot rice onto a foil-lined baking sheet, cover it loosely with a sheet of plastic wrap, and set it aside until shortly before serving. To reheat the rice and continue cooking, add a batch of stock, slowly reheat the mixture, and taste the rice to gauge its doneness. Continue adding stock as the recipe directs, but taste the rice frequently, and take care not to overcook it.

THE 20-MINUTE MICROWAVE RISOTTO METHOD

Cooking Italian short-grain rice for risotto takes barely 20 minutes in a 700-watt microwave oven using the method that follows. (Appproximate times for lower-wattage ovens appear in parentheses.) As much as 1 pound of rice (six to eight risotto servings) can be cooked in a single batch with minimal stirring.

The key to this technique is microwaving the rice in three stages, as outlined in the basic instructions below. Although more than the usual amount of stock is added to the rice at one time, the fact that heat does not emanate from a single source promotes slow, even absorption of the cooking liquid. During the last few minutes of standing time, the rice continues to absorb stock, and beating in butter and cheese brings it to a creamy consistency in record time.

You will need to adapt these basic methods to each of the recipes in this chapter. When specific adjustments are required, notes appear with the recipes.

This method yields very good results, and since it is nearly effortless, I recommend it particularly when risotto will be served as an accompaniment. If risotto will be served as an appetizer or as a main course, some cooks may wish to cook it on top of the stove to ensure full depth of flavor.

METHOD FOR ½ POUND OF RICE

Cook the onion as the recipe directs, and transfer the warm onion to a 3-quart microwavable casserole. Stir in 5 tablespoons of butter and the rice; microwave on high power for 1 (2) minute. Stir in the wine and 2½ cups of the hot stock; microwave for 6 (7) minutes on high power. At this point, heat and stir in risotto flavorings as directed in the recipes. Microwave 3 (4) minutes longer on high power. Remove the casserole from oven and let it stand, covered, for 2 minutes. Then beat in the remaining butter, cheese, and seasonings. Adjust the risotto texture as each recipe directs.

METHOD FOR 1 POUND OF RICE

Cook the onion as the recipe directs, and transfer the warm onion to a 3-quart microwavable casserole. Stir in 6 tablespoons of butter and the rice; microwave on high power for 3 (4) minutes. Stir in the wine and 3 cups of the hot stock; microwave for 8 (9) minutes on high power. At this point, heat and stir in risotto flavorings as directed in the recipes. Add 1½ cups of hot stock and microwave 3 (5) minutes longer on high power. Remove the casserole from oven and let it stand, covered, for 3 to 4 minutes. Then beat in the remaining butter, cheese, and seasonings. Adjust the risotto texture as each recipe directs.

SAFFRON RISOTTO

Risotto alla Milanese is a historic "double" that can be served as a first course on its own, or as part of a main course such as osso buco, the famous braised veal shanks, or Milanese Beef Stew (page 185), also known as carbonata.

According to the late food historian Waverly Root, saffron was introduced to Italy after King Charles V of Spain made his son, Philip, duke of Milan in 1535. These crimson threads of the saffron crocus, harvested by hand in Spain and elsewhere in the Mediterranean, are scarce and costly. During mid-October, when the crocuses produce their vibrant purple blossoms, each flower must be stripped of its three stamens (pollen-bearing filaments) manually on the day the flowers are gathered. Then the stamens are dried by roasting. According to Spanish government reports, five pounds of crocus flowers produce five ounces of raw saffron, which weighs a mere one ounce when dried.

FLEXIBLE MENU SUGGESTIONS

A first course of Saffron Risotto can precede One-Side Grilled Fish (page 216) with Tomato Butter (page 220), Sage-Rubbed Veal Chops (page 242), Capretto with Lemon and Rosemary (page 246), Scampi alla Busara (page 272), Veal Scallops Giardino (page 284), or Cognac-Marinated Beef Fillet (page 298).

Serve it as a main-course accompaniment to Milanese Beef Stew (page 185), One-Side Grilled Fish (page 216) with Fresh Herb Butter (page 219), Veal Scallops Giardino (page 284), Veal Scallops with Black Olive Gremolada (page 286), Roasted Duck with Apples and Campari (page 289), Garlic-Roasted Leg of Lamb (page 295), or any of the dishes listed above, provided the rich, buttery rice is compatible with the appetizer and dessert. *Makes 4 to 6 servings*

PREPARATION: 15 MINUTES
COOKING: 30 MINUTES

½ pound unsalted butter
6 to 7 cups unsalted Chicken Stock (page 165)
¼ pound Parmesan cheese, rind removed, cubed
1 medium onion, peeled, cubed
1 pound short-grain Italian rice
⅛ teaspoon powdered saffron
½ cup dry white wine
Salt and ground black pepper

1. Cut 8 tablespoons (1 stick) butter into small dice and set it aside at room temperature. Heat the stock to simmering in a saucepan; cover and keep hot.

2. Fit a dry food processor with the metal blade. Process the Parmesan cheese until powdery; set aside. Chop the onion. Put the remaining butter into a 4- to 6-quart soup kettle, and heat until melted. Add the onion and stir over medium heat until softened, about 5 minutes.

3. Add rice and stir to coat with butter, about 2 minutes. Add the saffron; stir well. Add wine and slowly simmer until it evaporates.

4. Stir ½ cup hot stock into the rice mixture and set a timer for 18 minutes. Simmer slowly, stirring until stock is absorbed and mixture thickens slightly.

5. Continue stirring, adding up to 5 cups of stock in ½-cup batches, keeping mixture at a steady simmer over the 18 minutes. Mixture will become creamy as the stock is absorbed by the rice.

6. After 18 minutes, taste the rice. If still firm, continue adding stock in ¼-cup batches, stirring over low heat until rice is just tender—about 2 to 3 minutes longer.

7. Over very low heat, vigorously beat in the softened butter and grated cheese. If rice becomes too thick, stir in ¼ cup stock (it is normal to have 1 cup stock left over). Mixture will be creamy and porridgelike. Taste and adjust seasoning with salt (if needed) and pepper. Serve immediately.

A CONSUMING DILEMMA

Strictly speaking, risotto should be served in warm bowls and eaten with a soup spoon, but I believe it is correct to eat it either with a spoon or a fork. In fact, I prefer to use a fork because I find that a spoon, in contact with just-cooked rice, often can become too hot to use comfortably.

Always serve risotto immediately, because the mixture thickens woefully as it stands. The easiest and most informal method is to wrap the pot in a clean, attractive towel to cover up drips and bring it right to table, which also eliminates the need to add individual garnishes.

If you prefer to serve risotto from the kitchen, be sure the bowls are warm and that everyone is seated. If you are alone in the kitchen, keep the garnish simple—an herb sprig often will do. A well-organized host or hostess can serve risotto two portions at a time, then dash back to the kitchen for two more, and still get six or eight plates on the table within 3 minutes.

If you know there will be a delay getting dishes to table, plan to beat in the butter and cheese about 2 minutes before the rice is perfectly tender to give yourself some leeway—risotto will retain heat and continue to cook as it stands.

RISOTTO PRIMAVERA

Primavera—spring vegetable—risotto has a fifty-year-old pedigree at Harry's Bar in Venice. This recipe, from Bellini by Cipriani restaurant, the American branch of Harry's, includes nine vegetables and herbs, plus a *goccia,* or dash, of tomato sauce to tint the rice slightly and balance the richness of the cheese. Note that the tomato sauce must be prepared separately, unless you have some leftover sauce on hand in the refrigerator or freezer.

Despite the abundance of vegetables, this risotto has a more neutral flavor than many others, and the preparation is time-consuming. The critical ingredient here is cheese: only Parmigiano-Reggiano can do justice to the delicacy of the vegetables.

While this risotto sports a colorful assortment, many different vegetables may be substituted. Increase the amount of zucchini in substitution for the artichoke hearts; shiitake or portobello mushrooms can replace cultivated mushrooms; julienned snow peas can stand in for asparagus tips, and fresh, snipped chives can replace the parsley.

FLEXIBLE MENU SUGGESTIONS

A classic appetizer, this risotto can be served before One-Side Grilled Fish (page 216) with Orso Butter (page 221) and Garlic-Rubbed Chicken (page 278).

Alternately, make this the centerpiece of an easy menu that I suggested for one of my *New York* magazine entertaining articles: Begin with an appetizer of smoked or cured salmon, or cured Italian meats (prosciutto, dried beef, or country salami) and Rosemary Breadsticks (page 343), Tomato Flatbread with Two Herbs (page 346), or Black Olive Bread (page 356). Following the risotto, serve Espresso-Brownie Chunk Ice Cream (page 397) with Instant Hot Fudge Sauce (page 401) for dessert. *Makes 6 to 8 servings*

PREPARATION: 35 MINUTES
COOKING: 30 MINUTES

¼ cup My Favorite Tomato Sauce (page 126)
    or other tomato sauce
2 small onions, peeled
1 medium zucchini
1 medium yellow bell pepper
1 medium red bell pepper
½ pound unsalted butter
1 cup asparagus tips, sliced ¼-inch thick
½ cup finely diced mushroom caps
½ cup thinly sliced, cooked artichoke hearts
¼ pound Parmesan cheese, cubed
¼ cup firmly packed parsley leaves
7 to 8 cups unsalted Chicken Stock (page 165)

1 pound short-grain Italian rice
½ cup dry white wine
Salt
¼ cup julienned fresh basil leaves

1. Make or defrost the tomato sauce; set aside.

2. Chop one of the onions. Cut the zucchini and the bell peppers into ⅛-inch dice. Put the onion into a 4- to 6-quart soup kettle. Add 4 tablespoons butter and cook over low heat until softened, about 3 minutes. Stir in the bell peppers and asparagus and cook for

3 minutes. Then add the mushrooms, artichokes, and zucchini. Cook over low heat until the vegetables are softened slightly, but still colorful, about 5 minutes longer. Set vegetables aside (can cool, wrap airtight, and refrigerate overnight.)

3. If refrigerated, heat the vegetable mixture and keep it warm. Fit a dry food processor with the metal blade and process Parmesan cheese until powdery; set aside. Mince the parsley and set it aside. Chop the remaining onion.

4. Cut 8 tablespoons (1 stick) butter into small dice and set it aside at room temperature. Heat the stock to simmering in a saucepan; cover and keep hot.

5. Heat the remaining 4 tablespoons butter in the soup kettle. Add the onion and cook over low heat until softened, about 3 minutes. Add rice and stir over medium heat, about 2 minutes. Add wine and simmer, stirring until it evaporates.

6. Stir 1½ tablespoons of the tomato sauce and 1 cup hot stock into the rice mixture and set a timer for 18 minutes. Simmer rice slowly, stirring constantly, until stock is absorbed. Then continue stirring, adding up to 5 more cups stock in ½-cup batches over the 18 minutes. Mixture will become creamy as stock is absorbed by the rice.

7. After 18 minutes, stir the cooked vegetable mixture into the rice. Taste, and if rice is still very firm, continue adding stock in ¼-cup batches, stirring over low heat just until rice is tender, about 2 to 3 minutes longer. Over very low heat, vigorously beat in softened butter, parsley, Parmesan cheese, and remaining tomato sauce.

8. If rice becomes too thick, adjust consistency by stirring in ¼ cup stock (it is normal to have 1 cup stock left over). Mixture will be porridgelike. Taste and adjust seasoning with salt, if necessary. Stir in basil. Serve immediately.

RISOTTO SPINACCIOLA

Spinacciola is a combination of the Italian word for spinach, *spinaci* (spin-ah-chee), and Gorgonzola, Italy's principal blue cheese. This flavoring hails from Milan, where Gorgonzola often is added to risotto.

Mild Gorgonzola, or a high-fat cow's-milk blue cheese such as Saga Blue, Danablu, or Bavarian Blue, is required to give the rice a fabulous, mild blue-cheese flavor. It is important to distinguish between the sweet, spreadably creamy cow's-milk blues and the sharper, crumbly French and American blue cheeses, which also are very salty. Crumbly blue cheese should *not* be used in this recipe.

Depending on the strength of the cheese you select, there can be a wide variation in the amount that must be stirred into the recipe. For best results, purchase 10 ounces of a creamy blue cheese. Begin by adding 4 ounces, then stir in the remainder in 2-ounce batches, adding the cheese to taste.

FLEXIBLE MENU SUGGESTIONS

Risotto is always perfect as a first course and this one is particularly good before Sage-Rubbed Veal Chops (page 242), or even the lemony Garlic-Roasted Leg of Lamb (page 295).

As a light main course, this might particularly appeal to vegetarians. Begin with a simple salad of sliced tomatoes topped with fresh herbs and My Favorite Vinaigrette (page 72). Or, for nonvegetarians, thinly sliced prosciutto and melon is another good opener. Follow with Apple Crisp (page 424) or Almond and Lemon-Stuffed Pears (page 431). *Makes 4 to 6 servings*

PREPARATION: 15 MINUTES
COOKING: 35 MINUTES

*3 cups firmly packed stemmed spinach leaves
    (or a 10-ounce package thawed and well-
    drained frozen spinach)*
2 medium garlic cloves, peeled
1 medium onion, peeled
¼ pound unsalted butter
*3 to 4 cups unsalted Chicken Stock (page
    165)*
*4 to 10 ounces Saga blue or Gorgonzola
    Dolce (page 30) or other creamy cow's-
    milk blue cheese*
½ pound Italian short-grain rice
½ cup dry white wine
Salt and ground black pepper

1. Plunge fresh spinach leaves into 2 quarts boiling water. When water boils again, drain, cool, and twist the spinach in a cloth towel to remove all excess moisture (or drain, then twist defrosted spinach in towel); set aside.

2. Mince the garlic and finely chop the onion. Put them in a medium skillet with 3 tablespoons of the butter. Stir over low heat until vegetables soften, about 5 minutes. Chop the spinach finely, and transfer it to the skillet. Toss the spinach mixture over medium heat until excess liquid evaporates, about 3 minutes; set aside.

3. Heat stock to simmering in a saucepan; cover and keep it hot on the stove. Remove rind and cut cheese into ¼-inch dice; set aside at room temperature.

4. Melt remaining butter in a 4- to 6-quart soup kettle. Add the rice and stir to coat it with butter, about 2 minutes. Add wine and simmer until it evaporates. Stir ⅓ cup hot stock into the rice and set a timer for 18 minutes. Slowly simmer the rice, stirring until stock is absorbed and the mixture thickens slightly.

5. Continue stirring, adding up to 2 cups stock in ⅓-cup batches and keeping mixture at a slow, steady simmer over the 18 minutes. Mixture will become creamy as stock is absorbed by rice.

6. After 18 minutes, stir in the spinach mixture. Taste the rice, and if it is still firm, continue adding stock in ¼-cup batches, stirring over low heat until rice is just tender, about 2 minutes longer.

7. Over very low heat, vigorously beat in 4 ounces of the diced blue cheese; continue adding cheese until rice is strongly flavored. If rice becomes too thick, stir in ¼ cup stock (it is normal to have ½ cup or more stock left over). Taste and adjust seasoning with salt (if needed) and pepper. Serve immediately.

COUNTRY-STYLE RISOTTO

Porcini mushrooms add depth of flavor to any dish of rice, and here they are also combined with a simple mixture of vegetables and cooked sausage in the type of rustic risotto you might expect to find at a small trattoria or in a private Italian home.

Consider this recipe as open to interpretation—it can be a delicious way to use up leftover sausage, meat, or boneless poultry. While the porcini and their liquid are vital, you could substitute diced red bell peppers and zucchini for the carrots and peas, or tailor the vegetables to your menu with equanimity. If you prefer to discard, rather than use, the sausage drippings, a substitution is given in step 5.

Microwave note: undercook the sausage slightly in step 3, so that it does not become rubbery during the last minutes of microwaving.

FLEXIBLE MENU SUGGESTIONS

Sausage makes this a hearty first course that can be followed by Sage-Rubbed Veal Chops (page 242), Scampi alla Busara (page 272), or Garlic-Rubbed Chicken (page 278).

For a menu featuring the risotto as a main course, begin with Mozzarella, Tomato, and Olive Salad (page 62) or Lettuce, Radicchio, and Fennel Salad (page 70). Follow with fresh fruit and Gianduia Lace Cookies (page 386), Mixed Nut Sablés (page 442), or Chocolate-Walnut Linzer Torte (page 376). *Makes 8 to 10 servings*

PREPARATION: 30 MINUTES
COOKING: 25 MINUTES

1 ounce imported dried porcini mushrooms
6 ounces softened unsalted butter
1 pound mild Italian sausage
3 medium garlic cloves, peeled
2 medium onions, peeled
3 medium carrots, peeled
¼ pound Parmesan cheese, rind removed, cubed
6 cups unsalted Chicken Stock (page 165)
1 pound Italian short-grain rice
½ cup dry white wine
1 cup fresh cooked (or frozen, thawed, rinsed) peas
Salt and ground black pepper

1. Put mushrooms in a small saucepan with 1 cup of water. Cover and heat to boiling. Remove pan from heat and set it aside, covered, for 20 minutes. Swish mushrooms in the liquid to remove any sand that clings. Strain mushroom liquid through a paper-towel-lined sieve or through a coffee filter. Add enough water to make 1 cup and set the liquid aside. Coarsely chop and reserve the mushrooms.

2. Melt 3 tablespoons butter in a 4- to 6-quart soup kettle or Dutch oven. Add the sausage and brown it over low heat, turning it as necessary. Add ½ cup hot water and simmer the sausage, turning it once, until the liquid evaporates. Remove and cool the sausage; reserve the pan drippings.

3. Mince the garlic and chop the onion. Cut the carrots into ⅛-inch dice (or coarsely chop them), then add the vegetables and the chopped mushrooms to the kettle with 5 tablespoons of butter. Put a sheet of aluminum foil on top of the vegetables so that it directly touches their surface. Cook mixture over low heat until softened, about 15 minutes. Set the vegetable mixture aside. (Can prepare and refrigerate the sausage, vegetable mixture, and mushroom liquid overnight.)

4. In a food processor fitted with the metal blade, process the Parmesan until powdery; set aside. Cut the sausage into ¼-inch-thick rounds; set aside. Combine mushroom liquid with the stock in a saucepan and heat to simmering. Cover and keep the stock hot.

5. Cut remaining butter into small dice and set aside at room temperature. Heat the sausage drippings (or 3 tablespoons of the diced butter) in the soup kettle. Add the rice and stir over low heat until coated, about 2 minutes. Add wine and simmer until it evaporates.

6. Stir ½ cup of the hot stock into the rice and set a timer for 18 minutes. Simmer slowly, stirring rice until stock is absorbed and mixture thickens slightly.

7. Continue stirring, adding up to 5 cups stock in ½-cup batches and keeping the rice at a steady simmer over the 18 minutes. Mixture will become creamy as stock is absorbed by rice.

8. After 18 minutes, stir in the vegetables, sausage, and peas. Taste, and if the rice is still firm, continue adding stock in ¼-cup batches, simmering until rice is just tender, about 2 to 3 minutes longer.

9. Over very low heat, vigorously beat in the softened butter and grated cheese. If rice becomes too thick, stir in ¼ cup stock (it is normal to have 1 cup stock left over). Mixture will be creamy and porridgelike. Taste and adjust seasoning with salt (if needed) and pepper. Serve immediately.

PART THREE

The
MAIN COURSE

ONE-ACT PLAYS:
STEWS, BAKED ENTREES, AND
SUBSTANTIAL SALADS

FIRE AND SPICE—PART ONE:
GRILLING FISH AND SHELLFISH

FIRE AND SPICE—PART TWO:
BARBECUING POULTRY AND MEAT

CLASSICAL INSPIRATIONS:
FISH, SHELLFISH, POULTRY, AND MEAT

ONE-ACT PLAYS: STEWS, BAKED ENTREES, AND SUBSTANTIAL SALADS

*"A good play is a play which when acted upon the boards
makes an audience interested and pleased."*

MAURICE BARING

The spirit of abundance dwells in the savory contents of stockpots or casseroles that simmer peacefully on the stove or in the oven, filling the house with a fragrance that anticipates a good meal.

In this fast-paced world where time is of the essence, and the kitchen is often more of a stopover than a destination or a refuge, dinner parties based on one great dish—be it a stew or boiled dinner, a spicy baked main course, or a substantial salad—can be high-powered culinary one-act plays. Their focus creates an informality and approachability that immediately puts guests at ease.

Among the most successful evenings I can recall were my annual New Year's Sausage and Sauerkraut (page 186) dinners that played to an open house. The main course, assembled in a large copper pot, was kept warm on the cooktop in the center of my kitchen, with salad, good crusty bread, and a generous supply of wine available nearby. My friends were on their own to plumb the depths of the casserole at a leisurely pace, then settle in the various nooks and crannies of my Victorian parlor to eat and chat. As the evening progressed, I watched them freely return to the kitchen for second helpings—everyone felt very much at home.

Even when you are seated at table, serving a meal family-style—without the formal prelude of an appetizer—is an opportunity for everyone (including the cook) to relax. Since most of these self-contained main courses are prepared in advance, the strain of last-minute cooking is reduced, and accompaniments such as homemade breads or rolls (if you have time to make them) are never lost in the shuffle.

Foods that are suited to this type of presentation must be substantial enough to carry a meal, which is why I have included what I call "new-style" stews and ragouts, lively entrées baked in a single dish (which once would have been derisively relegated to the casserole category), and salads based on starch or meat.

THE NEW STEWS

What's old is what's new again in stews. While those included in this chapter are firmly rooted in various culinary traditions, their common denominator is direct, exciting taste—and correspondingly fewer enrichments—that gives them a contemporary turn. Flour is rarely used to thicken sauces, nor is there any dependence on cream. Stock, beer, wine, or vegetables, plus natural cooking juices, are the backbones of flavor.

Whereas old-fashioned stews offer a jumble of ingredients with no dominant element, these new-style stews place the emphasis on a single, hearty component such as beef, sausages, or a certain group of vegetables. In the case of Bollito Misto (page 188), which is a boiled dinner, the principal element is a medley of meats and poultry. The result of this reliance on primary ingredients is that these new stews have lost their sloppiness. In addition to more highly defined tastes, they offer greater opportunity for attractive presentations, free of most backward-looking pairings with pilaf or noodles. In short: they stand on their own.

BAKED ENTREES

At first, I referred to these quintessential one-dish meals as *casseroles*. Then I began to think about why that word made me so uncomfortable. Perhaps it is the fact that I grew up in the backlash of the macaroni-and-cheese, and tuna-noodle aesthetic.

The term *baked entrée* conveys the respect that this trio of ethnic "casseroles" commands. Each of these is an adventure in spice as well as a small taste of another culture that may interest cooks who relish the opportunity to experiment with a new type of fresh chile, mix up a batch of special curry powder, or learn the nuances of handling tortillas. With only one exception, these are easy dishes to assemble and bake well in advance of the time they are served.

Salads based on pasta or meat are particularly successful warm-weather fare, eminently suitable for casual dinners or early weekend suppers.

With the emphasis on eating light, we have become a salad-obsessed nation, and, thanks to the boom in supermarket salad bars and gourmet take-out stores, we are accustomed to having a wide choice of combinations.

A majority of the Italians I know consider pasta salad to be an abomination, and others might say that its time has come—and gone. I do not agree. A good pasta salad (that contains no cream or mayonnaise), with properly cooked noodles, interesting ingredients, and excellent seasoning, is a new "basic," and so I have included more than one here.

To complete the menu, follow any of these main courses with dessert. Fresh fruit or fruit salad is always great, particularly after spicy foods. However, a more elaborate dessert will never upstage the main course. Think of it as a surprise ending that can help to turn a terrific one-act play into a smash hit.

MILANESE BEEF STEW

———————

SAUSAGES AND SAUERKRAUT

———————

BOLLITO MISTO

———————

GREEN SAUCE

———————

HORSERADISH SAUCE

———————

ARIZONA CHICKEN WITH CORN RAGOUT

———————

Ancho Chile Powder

———————

CHILAQUILES

———————

The Immortal Herb

———————

CHICKEN ENCHILADAS VERDES

———————

The ABCs of Chiles

———————

Go for the Burn—Handling Peppers

———————

BAKED CURRIED BEEF

———————

BANANA RELISH

———————

SLIVERED CUCUMBERS

———————

TOMATO-ONION SALAD

———————

HOT CURRY POWDER

———————

FETTUCCINE WITH CHICKEN, ARTICHOKES, AND DILL

———————

PENNE WITH BROCCOLI AND SCALLOPS

———————

CHINESE CHICKEN SALAD

———————

An Oriental Pantry

———————

PORK AND VEGETABLE SALAD ORIENTALE

———————

SIMON'S HOISIN SAUCE

———————

MARINATED PORK TENDERLOIN

———————

MILANESE BEEF STEW

I first encountered this *carbonata di bue* while on a travel-story assignment in Milan. The recipe comes from the Alfredo Gran San Bernardo restaurant, and this mahogany-colored ragout is one of the few dishes accompanied by Saffron Risotto (page 170).

FLEXIBLE MENU SUGGESTIONS

Together with risotto, this is a bracing, filling, cold-weather main course that goes well with Snow Peas and Bell Pepper Ribbons (page 310) and Parmesan and Black Pepper Bread (page 348), Rosemary Breadsticks (page 346), or Tomato Flatbread with Two Herbs (page 346). Add Almond and Lemon-Stuffed Pears (page 431), Milanese Fruit Tart (page 408), or Lemon Tirami Su (page 429) for a grand finale. *Makes 6 servings*

PREPARATION: 30 MINUTES
COOKING: 2¼ HOURS

1 pound (or 28-ounce can) peeled, seeded Italian plum tomatoes, and their juice (strained and reserved)
1¾ pounds onions, peeled, halved
4 tablespoons butter
4 tablespoons olive oil
About ½ cup flour
2½ pounds boneless beef (chuck, neck, or shin) cut in 1½-inch cubes, patted dry
1 can (12 ounces) beer
Salt and ground black pepper
4 tablespoons minced parsley

1. Coarsely chop the tomatoes; set aside. Thinly slice the onions.

2. Heat half the butter and half the oil in a large (12-inch) ovenproof skillet. Add the onions and cook over medium heat until their liquid evaporates. Reduce heat, stirring until onions are golden and completely softened; set them aside. Wipe the skillet dry.

3. Sift flour over the meat, turning to coat the pieces lightly. Heat remaining butter and oil in the skillet and cook the meat on medium-high heat in batches (pieces should not touch), turning until deeply browned on all sides; set meat aside separately. Bottom of the skillet should become very dark.

4. Pour off any fat remaining in the hot skillet and immediately add the beer. Use a wooden spatula to scrape the bottom of the skillet until all particles adhering to the bottom are loosened. Simmer the beer over medium heat until it reduces by one-third.

5. Adjust oven rack to lowest position. Heat oven to 375 degrees. Return the onions to the skillet. Add the beef, tomatoes, and just enough reserved tomato juice to cover the beef. Cover with two overlapping sheets of aluminum foil, and press foil down to touch top of meat. Bake 1 hour 40 minutes to 2 hours, or until meat is very tender when pierced with a knife. Taste and adjust seasoning, adding ¼ teaspoon salt and ⅛ teaspoon pepper. (Can cool, cover, and refrigerate stew for 48 hours.)

6. If refrigerated, skim off all visible fat from the surface of the stew before reheating it. Adjust the seasoning, garnish with parsley, and serve immediately.

SAUSAGES AND SAUERKRAUT

For many years, this version of *Choucroute Garnie*—a stew of sauerkraut, smoked pork, bacon, and assorted sausages—has been the main-course focus of my New Year's dinner. *Choucroute* is among the best-known dishes of French Alsace, which shares a border and a culinary heritage with Germany. Ingredients such as homemade sauerkraut, smoked pork loin (called *Kassler rippchen*), and the various sausages called for in this recipe are often easiest to find at German or Eastern European butchers or delicatessens.

Choucroute requires little effort to prepare and reheats well; the recipe also doubles or triples effortlessly. It can be arrayed on a platter, on individual plates, or simply left in its pot, from which guests may enjoy serving themselves.

FLEXIBLE MENU SUGGESTIONS

It can be difficult to find a first course that will stand up to *choucroute,* and I generally do not serve one. However, Saga and Watercress Tart (page 106) is a good candidate should the need arise.

To complete a one-dish meal, add a mixed green salad with Hazelnut Vinaigrette (page 77), and Sunflower Rye (page 358) or French Dinner Rolls (page 360).

An elegant fruit dessert such as Classic Fruit Tart (page 416) or Lemon Tart Brulée (page 406) dresses up the menu. Or, Lemon-Praline Soufflé Glacé (page 433) can be made well in advance and kept frozen until serving time. *Makes 8 to 10 servings*

PREPARATION: 45 MINUTES
COOKING: 2 HOURS

½ pound slab bacon, rind removed and cubed, or sliced bacon, cut in 1-inch lengths
1 medium onion, peeled
1 carrot, peeled
1 tart green apple, peeled and cored
3 pounds German-style sauerkraut
1½ pounds smoked pork loin (Kassler rippchen), well trimmed
2 imported bay leaves
10 juniper berries
2 cups Riesling wine or Champagne
3 cups beef or Chicken Stock (page 165)
4 pounds assorted fresh and smoked German-style sausages, including weisswurst, bratwurst, and bauernwurst, or Hungarian kielbasa

Salt and ground black pepper
8 small red potatoes, peeled
2 tablespoons butter
2 tablespoons minced parsley

1. Bring 6 cups water to boil in a medium saucepan. Add the bacon. Boil slab bacon for 10 minutes (or sliced bacon 5 minutes); drain and rinse. Pat bacon dry in paper toweling; set aside.

2. Coarsely chop bacon, onion, carrot, and apple. Put bacon in a large ovenproof casserole or soup kettle and cook over medium heat for 2 minutes, then add chopped vegetables and apple. Cook over medium heat until the fat is rendered and vegetables soften, about 10 minutes longer.

3. Rinse, drain, and squeeze the sauerkraut dry; repeat.

4. Adjust oven rack to lowest position. Heat oven to 325 degrees. Add sauerkraut and pork loin to the casserole. Stir in the bay leaves, juniper berries, wine, and 2 cups stock. Cover and bake for 1 hour.

5. Pierce fresh sausages with a pin, but leave them whole. Cut smoked sausages into chunks. Move sauerkraut aside, add sausages to kettle, and arrange sauerkraut to cover the sausage completely. Add remaining broth and cover with aluminum foil directly touching the top of the sauerkraut; then cover with the casserole lid. Bake 45 minutes, or until fresh sausage juices run clear. Taste and adjust seasoning with salt and pepper, if necessary. (Can cool, cover, and refrigerate 24 hours.)

6. Shortly before serving, steam or boil potatoes until tender when pierced with a knife, about 30 to 35 minutes, depending on size. In a large skillet over low heat, toss steamed potatoes with butter and parsley.

7. To serve, reheat the sauerkraut and sausages, if necessary. Pile sauerkraut in center of a large serving platter, or put a generous portion on heated dinner plates. Slice and arrange the pork loin to the side of the sauerkraut. Put the potatoes around, and the sausages on top. (Or arrange sliced pork, potatoes, and sausage in the casserole over sauerkraut.) Serve immediately.

BOLLITO MISTO

Literally translated, Bollito Misto means "mixed boiled." However, words do little to convey the elegant beauty of this ensemble of cooked meat, poultry, and vegetables, served with green sauce and horseradish cream, and delicately moistened with hot, fragrant broth.

Every second Thursday, New York's Le Cirque restaurant serves an elaborate Bollito Misto composed of nine different meats and eight vegetables. It is accompanied by a cream-based *sauce suprême,* half of it colored by pureed spinach and herbs, the remainder fortified with horseradish. Le Cirque owner Sirio Maccioni and chef Daniel Boulud generously gave me access to their kitchen, and to their Bollito recipe. That recipe first appeared in a *New York* magazine issue on entertaining—this is an adaptation.

Bollito hails from northern Italy and is a cousin to the French *pot au feu.* Regional variations abound, and the ingredients and sauces for any single recipe vary accordingly. One requirement is a relatively large stockpot and a considerable measure of patience. The meats and poultry must simmer in broth to the point of melting tenderness. Once cooked, the meats are removed from the bone and neatly sliced; chickens are cut into serving segments. The carrots and zucchini may be boiled in the broth, but since the potatoes and cabbage must be cooked separately, it is easier to steam all the vegetables. The sauces are very simple to make. Leftover broth should be saved for soup, while leftover pieces of meat or poultry can be added to a soup, or turned into a salad.

Because of the time involved in its preparation (meats can be cooked a day in advance), and by its nature, Bollito Misto is destined to be the main course for an important dinner party. Rest assured that it is a showstopper.

Some notes on serving logistics: once you make Bollito, you will find it far less daunting than it first appears. With proper planning, even a cook working alone in the kitchen should be able to plate and serve this to guests as it appears in the photograph on the cover of this book. However, it is also easy to arrange the hot meats and vegetables on platters which can be passed at table, or set on a warming tray for guests to help themselves.

FLEXIBLE MENU SUGGESTIONS

Accompany Bollito with Rosemary Breadsticks (page 343), Parmesan and Black Pepper Bread (page 348), or French Dinner Rolls (page 360). Follow with a green salad with My Favorite Vinaigrette (page 72), and assorted Italian cheeses and the remaining bread. Perfect dessert choices include Milanese Fruit Tart (pictured on the back cover, recipe page 408), Lemon Tirami Su (page 429), or Rustic Apple Tart (page 410). *Makes 8 servings*

PREPARATION: 2 HOURS
COOKING: 3 TO 3½ HOURS

BROTH

2 carrots, peeled and halved
1 celery rib, halved
2 medium onions, peeled and quartered
1 head garlic, halved crosswise
1 leek, trimmed, split lengthwise, and rinsed
6 black peppercorns, cracked
Bouquet Garni of 3 thyme sprigs (1 teaspoon dried), ¼ cup packed parsley stems, and 1 bay leaf

MEAT

2 veal shanks (2 to 2½ pounds each), knuckles removed
3 pounds beef short ribs, well trimmed
2 whole frying chickens, cleaned
Green Sauce (page 191)
Horseradish Sauce (page 191)
1 pound French-style garlic sausage (available at specialty food stores), or cooked, warmed Homemade Garlic Sausage with Pistachios (page 92)

VEGETABLES

4 medium potatoes, peeled and halved
1 small green cabbage, cored and halved
4 large carrots, peeled, trimmed, cut crosswise in thirds
4 medium zucchini, trimmed and halved crosswise

1. One day in advance, begin the bollito by putting all the broth ingredients in a 12-quart stockpot with 6 quarts water. Cover and simmer the mixture for 30 minutes.

2. Tie veal shanks to keep the meat securely on the bones, leaving long strings attached so shanks can be retrieved from stockpot. Immerse shanks in the hot liquid. Tie beef ribs in bundles of two or three and attach long strings. Add to stockpot; cover and simmer for 1½ hours, skimming as necessary to remove foam that rises to the top of the liquid.

3. Test the short ribs and veal shanks for doneness (a knife inserted into thickest parts of meat should meet no resistance). It may be necessary to cover and simmer the short ribs for 30 minutes longer; the veal shanks may require 30 to 45 minutes of additional cooking to become tender. When ribs and shanks are done, carefully remove them (using the string to lift them carefully from the hot broth), transfer them to a bowl, and cover loosely with plastic wrap so the surfaces of the meats do not become dry.

4. Uncover and cool the broth in the stockpot, then refrigerate. Wrap cooled meats tightly in plastic and refrigerate. (Can refrigerate meat and broth overnight.)

5. With a spoon dipped in hot water, remove the layer of fat that solidifies on the surface of the broth, and bring the meats to room temperature.

6. Return the stockpot and broth to the stove and reheat to simmering. Truss the chickens and tie them with long strings for easy retrieval. Immerse chickens in the broth. Cover and simmer for 45 minutes, until just cooked; remove and cover loosely with plastic wrap. Strain the broth and skim off excess fat; set aside.

7. Make Green Sauce and Horseradish Sauce.

8. In a large saucepan, simmer the garlic sausage in 2 quarts water until thoroughly hot; remove and cover with plastic wrap. Discard cooking liquid. Do not simmer homemade garlic sausage in liquid; reheat by wrapping it in aluminum foil and baking at 325 degrees until hot.

9. Prepare Bollito for serving by trimming excess fat from the meats and removing the bones. Slice veal and beef ⅛-inch thick and arrange overlapping slices on a heatproof platter or a foil-lined jellyroll pan (if bollito will be plated). Separate chicken legs and thighs; arrange on platter. Cut each half of the chicken breasts off the bones in one piece, slice crosswise; arrange on platter (reserve the chicken backs and wings for another use). Slice and arrange the sausage on the platter. Ladle 1 to 2 cups hot broth over sliced meats, cover tightly with plastic wrap, and set aside at room temperature until serving time. Keep 3 additional cups of hot broth; reserve the remainder for other uses. (Leftover broth can be frozen.)

10. Up to 1 hour before serving, remove plastic wrap from the platter and cover it tightly with aluminum foil. Heat oven to 250 degrees. Put the platter into the oven for about 30 minutes, until meats and bouillon are hot, then turn oven down to 225 degrees and keep meat warm, if necessary.

11. To cook the vegetables, arrange potatoes and cabbage in a vegetable steamer; cover and steam 15 minutes. Add carrots and zucchini to the steamer; cover and steam 10 to 12 minutes longer, or until vegetables are tender. Cut the cabbage into eight wedges. Cut each carrot and zucchini segment in half lengthwise. Add vegetables to the meat platter or make a second platter of vegetables; moisten vegetables with ½ to 1 cup of hot broth. (Can cover vegetables with foil and keep warm in the oven for about 15 to 20 minutes.)

12. Serve the meat and vegetables on platters, or arrange ingredients on plates, accompanied by Green Sauce, Horseradish Sauce, and 2 cups of the hot broth.

GREEN SAUCE

Makes ½ cup

PREPARATION: 15 MINUTES

1 medium shallot, peeled
3 anchovy fillets, rinsed, patted dry
2 tablespoons drained, rinsed capers
1 cup loosely packed Italian parsley leaves
½ cup Herbed Oil (page 73) or mild extra-
*   virgin olive oil*
1 teaspoon grated lemon zest
Salt and ground black pepper

1. Mince the shallot and anchovies in a food processor fitted with the metal blade. Add the capers and parsley; process until mixture is finely chopped.

2. With the processor on, drizzle in the oil. Stir in the lemon zest, ¼ teaspoon salt, and pepper to taste. Serve sauce at room temperature. (Can transfer to an airtight storage container, cover, and refrigerate for 3 days; stir well before using.)

HORSERADISH SAUCE

Makes 1 cup

PREPARATION: 10 MINUTES

1 jar (4 ounces) savory grated horseradish
½ teaspoon finely grated lemon zest
Salt
1 cup chilled whipping cream

1. Drain horseradish in a fine strainer, then squeeze in your hands to remove excess moisture. Measure 1 tablespoon horseradish into a food processor fitted with the metal blade.

2. Add lemon zest, ⅛ teaspoon salt, and half the cream. Process for 30 seconds, then add the remaining cream in a thin stream. Process until cream whips to firm peaks. Taste and adjust seasoning. Cover and refrigerate sauce until serving time (up to 6 hours). Serve chilled.

ARIZONA CHICKEN WITH CORN RAGOUT

If you adore the flavor of hot chiles, as I do, this is one of the most wonderful dishes imaginable. Boned, frenched chicken breasts (with two-thirds of the wing removed and only the segment nearest the breast left attached) are rubbed with a fiery puree of chipotle chiles (canned, smoked jalapeños) and dipped in spiced cornmeal before browning and baking. The chicken is served atop a robust stew of corn and peppers.

You will need to make a trip to a store that carries Mexican products, since the recipe requires several different types of fresh, dried, and canned chiles, including the dried, leathery brown anchos that must be ground to a powder for the chicken coating. Fresh green Anaheim and poblano chiles (which range from mild to medium hot) will add their complex flavors to the ragout, but green bell peppers can be substituted, if necessary.

Like the Bollito Misto, this can be plated, or the chicken can be piled on a platter, and the ragout set aside in a bowl or soup tureen so that guests can help themselves. I prefer to see it plated since the colors are lively and especially appetizing. A dark dinner plate (particularly a black plate) will set this off to perfection.

The recipe from which this is adapted appeared in one of my *New York* magazine entertaining articles, and it was originally created by New York chef Brendan Walsh.

FLEXIBLE MENU SUGGESTIONS

Accompaniments can include American in Paris Biscuits (page 366), Ham and Jalapeño Cornbread (page 367), or Cheddar-Cumin Rolls (page 362). Chocolate desserts such as Chocolate Roulade (page 392), or Espresso-Brownie Chunk Ice Cream (page 397) with (or without) Bittersweet Chocolate Sauce (page 400) provide the best sweet counterpoint to the main course spicing, but any of the casual chocolate desserts can be substituted.

Don't overlook the possibility of serving these spicy chicken breasts without the ragout as a main course, accompanied by Corn and Jalapeño Pancakes (page 308), Black Beans (page 328), and a diced tomato-and-avocado salad lightly tossed with a few tablespoons of Chive Vinaigrette (page 61). Chocolate desserts are equally appropriate for this menu.
Makes 6 servings

PREPARATION: 30 MINUTES
COOKING: 40 MINUTES

CHICKEN AND COATING

¾ cup yellow cornmeal
*1 tablespoon finely ground ancho chiles (see
    page 194), or plain chili powder*
1 tablespoon ground cumin
¾ teaspoon cayenne pepper
Salt and ground black pepper
*1 can (4 ounces) chipotle chiles in adobo
    sauce*
*6 boned chicken breasts with skin on and
    wings frenched*

CORN RAGOUT

9 medium garlic cloves, peeled
1 large tomato, peeled and seeded
*2 green Anaheim chiles, halved, seeded, and
    cored (or 1 medium green bell pepper,
    halved, seeded, and cored)*
*1 poblano pepper, halved, seeded, and cored
    (or 1 medium green bell pepper, halved,
    seeded, and cored)*
*1 medium red bell pepper, halved, seeded, and
    cored*
½ pound chilled unsalted butter
*Raw kernels from 2 corn ears (or 2 cups
    thawed frozen corn kernels)*
6 tablespoons mild olive oil
1½ tablespoons arrowroot
2½ cups Chicken Stock (page 165)
*12 mustard greens (or spinach) leaves,
    shredded*
2 tablespoons lime juice
12 basil leaves

1. For the coating, thoroughly mix corn-meal, chili powder, cumin, cayenne pepper, 1 teaspoon salt, and 1¼ teaspoons black pepper; set the coating mixture aside.

2. Insert the metal blade in a dry food processor. Puree the entire can of chipotles with their seeds and sauce; carefully transfer puree to a small jar. Rinse chicken breasts, pat them dry, and check to be sure all small pieces of bone are removed. Brush the chipotle puree over the chicken on all sides, taking care not to let it touch your hands.

3. Using tongs, carefully press both sides of chicken breasts into the cornmeal mixture to coat them evenly on both sides. Put chicken breasts skin-side up on a wax-paper-lined baking sheet. (Can cover loosely and refrigerate chicken for several hours.) Cover and refrigerate remaining chipotle puree for another use.

4. Mince the garlic and transfer it to a 4-quart soup kettle. Coarsely chop tomato; set aside. Slice the Anaheim, poblano, and red bell pepper halves into thin strips; set the peppers aside.

5. Add 4 tablespoons butter to the kettle and cook garlic over medium heat until fragrant, about 1 minute. Add julienned peppers and toss over medium heat about 2 minutes. Add corn kernels and toss over medium heat 1 minute. (Can remove kettle from heat, cool, cover, and set aside at room temperature for 6 hours.)

6. In a 12-inch skillet, heat 3 tablespoons olive oil and 3 tablespoons butter until bubbling. Cook three chicken breasts, skin-side down, over medium-high heat, until coating is browned and crisp, about 5 minutes. Turn and cook 5 minutes longer. Transfer chicken, skin-side up, to an unlined baking sheet. Repeat to brown all the chicken, adding butter and oil to the skillet as necessary. (Can cook chicken simultaneously in two skillets. Chicken can be set aside uncovered up to 4 hours without refrigeration.)

7. Adjust oven rack to middle position. Heat oven to 500 degrees. Finish chicken by baking until topping is crisp and juices run clear when thickest part of breast is pierced, about 8 to 10 minutes.

8. Cut remaining 6 tablespoons butter into small cubes. While chicken cooks, return kettle with vegetables to medium heat. Dissolve arrowroot in chicken stock and add to kettle. Heat to boiling, then stir until mixture thickens slightly to make a light sauce.

9. Immediately stir in cubed butter, mustard greens (or spinach leaves), lime juice, tomato, and basil leaves. Heat to simmering and adjust seasoning as necessary. Ladle ⅔ to ¾ cup of the ragout onto warm dinner plates, and top each portion with a chicken breast placed in the center. Or, transfer chicken to a serving platter and ragout to a bowl or soup tureen. Serve immediately.

ANCHO CHILE POWDER

Ground ancho chiles can be an ingredient in chili powder, but pure ancho chili powder may be difficult to find. You can make your own at home according to the following method. If you like the deep, rich, and slightly acrid taste of ancho chiles, add this to your favorite chili powder.

FLEXIBLE MENU SUGGESTIONS
This ingredient appears in recipes for Arizona Chicken with Corn Ragout (page 192). It also can be mixed with prepared chili powder and used in Chilaquiles (page 195), Jalapeño Mayonnaise (page 271), and Two-Cheese Quesadillas (page 448), for the Chili-Rubbed Chicken (page 283), or over thinly sliced jicama in a menu based on Cognac-Marinated Beef Fillet (page 298). *Makes about ¼ cup*

PREPARATION: 15 MINUTES
COOKING: 10 MINUTES

6 ancho chiles

1. Put the chiles in a large skillet and place it over low heat. When chiles are warm and pliable, turn them continually until they have softened; remove from heat.

2. With scissors, cut off the stems, split the chiles lengthwise, and remove the seeds. Tear or cut the chiles into ½-inch pieces.

3. Process chile pieces in a food processor fitted with the metal blade until powdery (this may take 3 minutes). Or, grind chile pieces to a powder in a mortar, or in the small jar of a blender. Strain to separate larger pieces from powder; discard large pieces. Transfer powder to an airtight jar, cover, and store in a cool, dark place.

CHILAQUILES

Chilaquiles are best known as a dish of leftover fried tortillas, chili sauce, and melted cheese that usually accompanies eggs for breakfast, or refried beans for lunch. In this version, I have worked the tortillas into a zesty, earthy casserole—think of it as a Mexican lasagna—made with pork sausage. Should sausage not be to your taste, cooked shredded chicken or cooked ground beef may be substituted.

Corn tortillas are usually sealed by frying, but I eliminate that step, which adds unnecessary calories. Because corn tortillas become fragile in contact with moisture, this must be baked within 30 minutes of its assembly. It can be set aside after baking and reheated as the recipe directs.

FLEXIBLE MENU SUGGESTIONS

Chilaquiles are filling and rich. For contrast to the sour-cream garnish, they can be spiced up with Mixed Chile Salsa (page 258), or a small amount of potent Poblano Cream (page 225) can replace the sour cream. Add a green salad with Sherry-Walnut Vinaigrette (page 78) to the menu, and offer fresh fruit and Mixed Nut Sablés (page 442) or Coconut-Lime Tuiles (page 440), Espresso-Brownie Chunk Ice Cream (page 397) or Banana Ice Cream (page 438) for dessert. *Makes 6 to 8 servings*

PREPARATION: 45 MINUTES
BAKING: 25 TO 30 MINUTES

3 cups Salsa Mexicana (page 196)
1 pound preservative-free bulk breakfast
*   sausage*
½ pound Monterey Jack cheese, chilled
½ pound corn tortillas (6-inch diameter)
½ cup sour cream, or Poblano Cream (page
*   225)*
¼ cup loosely packed cilantro leaves

1. Prepare the Salsa and set aside.

2. Put the sausage in a skillet and cook over low heat until the meat turns pale and is thoroughly cooked. Transfer sausage to a strainer and drain it thoroughly to remove all fat. Chop the sausage finely in a food processor fitted with the metal blade. Stir the chopped sausage into the prepared Salsa.

3. Shred the cheese and set aside.

4. Put two tortillas into the bottom of an 11 × 7 × 2-inch baking dish. Spread ¾ cup Salsa and ½ cup loosely packed cheese over the tortillas. Top with two more tortillas and continue layering, finishing with cheese.

5. Adjust oven rack to lowest position. Heat oven to 350 degrees. Bake 25 to 30 minutes. Let stand 15 minutes. (Can set aside at room temperature up to 6 hours. Reheat by baking uncovered at 300 degrees until knife inserted into center is withdrawn hot.) Cut in squares. Garnish each serving with a spoonful of sour cream and cilantro leaves.

SALSA MEXICANA

⋙⋙⋙⋙⋙

Pale yellowish green chiles called "banana peppers" or "Hungarian wax peppers" are used in this sauce. Banana peppers are generally the milder of the two; the heat of this salsa can be adjusted by using the hot or mild variety. This salsa was created by Brenda Newman. *Makes about 3 cups*

PREPARATION: 25 MINUTES
COOKING: 30 MINUTES

2 medium garlic cloves, peeled
1 large banana pepper or Hungarian wax pepper, roasted, peeled, seeded
2 small onions, peeled
2 tablespoons olive oil
1 can Italian plum tomatoes (28 ounces), drained
1⅔ cups Chicken Stock (page 165) or beef stock
2 tablespoons chili powder
1 teaspoon dried oregano
½ teaspoon ground cumin
Salt and ground black pepper
¼ teaspoon cayenne pepper

1. Mince the garlic, and finely chop the banana pepper and onions. Heat the oil in a deep, nonreactive 10-inch skillet. Add the vegetables and cook over low heat until onions soften, about 5 minutes.

2. Puree the tomatoes. Strain the puree into the skillet; discard the seeds. Add stock, chili powder, oregano, cumin, ⅛ teaspoon salt, ¼ teaspoon pepper, and cayenne pepper. Simmer until slightly thickened, stirring occasionally, about 30 minutes. Puree the salsa in 2-cup batches until smooth. Cool to room temperature. (Can cover and refrigerate 4 days.) Salsa is ready to use.

THE IMMORTAL HERB

The first time I saw a bunch of cilantro in a cooking class, I mistook it for pale flat-leaf parsley and was all set to chop and add it to a recipe before someone stopped me. However, just one taste of these tangy, lime-green deckle-edged leaves clearly will set this herb apart from its much milder relative.

Cilantro is fresh coriander, the leaves of a hardy, annual plant (*Coriandrum sativum*) that is a member of the parsley family. To add to the confusion, this herb also is called Chinese or Mexican parsley.

Cilantro is the Spanish term for coriander, and I use it to avoid any possible confusion between coriander leaves and coriander seed (which actually is a berry). This herb is commonly used in Near Eastern, Middle Eastern, North African, Indian, and Asian cuisines, as well as in Mexican and Latin American dishes.

Cilantro has a distinguished origin: according to one source, records show it was placed in Egyptian tombs just after the time of Moses. It is mentioned in the Bible, and is believed to be the bitter herb eaten at the Jewish Passover seder. The ancient Chinese held that immortality could be achieved by eating coriander berries during a spiritual trance.

Many people cannot bear the flavor of fresh cilantro. I happen to adore this pungent, acidic, almost metallic-tasting herb, which is available with increasing frequency in supermarket produce sections.

Cilantro leaves may be stored successfully for a day or two in a plastic bag lined with a paper towel. If stems and roots are still attached to the leaves, a bunch of cilantro also does well in a jar of water, covered tightly with a plastic bag, in the refrigerator.

Flat-leaf parsley is not an adequate substitute for cilantro in recipes, although it would be acceptable for garnishes.

CHICKEN ENCHILADAS VERDES

My friend Elaine Gonzalez, a talented cook and chocolatier who lives in Chicago, makes an outstanding green chicken enchilada casserole which I am happy to include here. Tangy and filling, these enchiladas are sauced with a mixture of green poblanos, fresh tomatillos, and cilantro, and are very easy to make.

Tomatillos are pale-green tomato look-alikes with a cape of tan, papery skin. They are often mistakenly referred to as green tomatoes, but they actually are members of the species *physalis*—their relative is the Cape gooseberry. These and other fresh ingredients are available at Latin or Asian markets, and many supermarkets. As poblano peppers vary in piquancy, the heat of the sauce will depend on the chiles (see page 198).

For the filling, you will need one pound of boneless, cooked chicken. You can use a roasted or poached whole fryer (which provides white and dark meat), or boneless chicken breasts which can be tightly sealed in a large aluminum foil pouch, placed on a baking sheet, and baked in the oven at 450 degrees for 12 minutes.

Tortillas can be fried several hours in advance, drained on paper towels, and set aside until you are ready to assemble the enchiladas. Like the Chilaquiles (page 195), bake this within 30 minutes of its assembly to preserve the enchiladas' texture. Unfortunately, this dish suffers from advance preparation—plan to serve it the moment you remove it from the oven.

Elaine provides an interesting note about corn tortillas, which have two distinct sides. One is relatively smooth, and the other, rougher side is known as the *raspa*, or beard. When enchiladas are properly rolled, the rough side of the tortilla faces in.

FLEXIBLE MENU SUGGESTIONS

Either Yellow Rice (page 327) or Black Beans (page 328) are a good accompaniment for the enchiladas. Ham and Jalapeño Cornbread (page 367) or Cheddar-Cumin Rolls (page 362) also could be added to the menu. Follow dessert suggestions for Chilaquiles (page 195).
Makes 6 to 8 servings

PREPARATION: 1¼ HOURS
BAKING: 18 TO 20 MINUTES

1 pound fresh poblano peppers (4 medium)
1 pound skinned, boneless cooked chicken,
   room temperature or warm
½ cup lightly packed cilantro leaves
Salt
1½ pounds fresh tomatillos, husks removed
   and rinsed, or drained, rinsed, canned
   tomatillos

2 cups Chicken Stock (page 165)
1½ cups vegetable oil
12 corn tortillas (6-inch diameter)
2 ounces Chihuahua or Munster cheese,
   chilled
1 medium tomato, peeled and seeded
About ½ cup sour cream

Continued

1. Char, peel, and seed the poblanos as described on page 200; set the poblanos aside.

2. Shred the chicken by pulling it apart with your fingers or by processing it with the medium (4-mm) food-processor slicing disk. There should be 3 to 4 cups; set aside.

3. To make the green salsa, mince the cilantro in a dry food processor fitted with the metal blade. Add the roasted poblanos and ¼ teaspoon salt, and process until minced. Add the tomatillos and process until the mixture is pureed, slowly adding 1 cup of stock. Process until smooth.

4. Transfer the salsa to a nonreactive skillet large enough to hold a flat tortilla. Add 2 tablespoons oil and ¾ cup stock. Simmer until sauce thickens slightly, about 15 minutes. Adjust seasoning, adding ¼ teaspoon salt, or more as needed. Set the sauce aside in the skillet. (Can cover and refrigerate the sauce in a bowl for 48 hours.)

5. Heat the remaining oil in a large, heavy skillet to 325 degrees. Layer paper towels on a baking sheet with additional toweling nearby. To seal each tortilla, slip it into the hot oil for 15 to 20 seconds, turning it once. With tongs, transfer tortillas to paper towels; blot to remove excess oil. Repeat to seal all tortillas by frying.

6. Adjust oven rack to middle position. Heat oven to 350 degrees. To assemble the casserole, work on tortillas one at a time as follows: warm the sauce and dip a sealed tortilla into the sauce, coating each side. Rest the tortilla in a 15 × 10 × 3-inch baking dish (use glass, porcelain, enamel, or earthenware, as sauce is acidic). Put generous ¼ cup chicken on each tortilla, roll it up, and put it seam-side down in the dish, starting at one end. Place rolled tortillas snugly, side by side in the dish and work on top of the rolled tortillas as the dish fills up so that sauce is not lost.

7. Shred the cheese. Stir the remaining broth into the remaining sauce, and heat it to simmering—sauce will thicken slightly. Adjust the seasoning, and spoon all remaining sauce over enchiladas. Sprinkle with cheese, and cover the dish with aluminum foil. Bake until the tip of a sharp knife inserted into the enchiladas is withdrawn hot, about 18 to 20 minutes.

8. Coarsely chop the tomato. Serve the enchiladas by spooning them out of the dish. Garnish each portion with a generous spoonful of sour cream and some chopped tomato.

THE ABCs OF CHILES

Fresh chiles have broken the barriers of geography, becoming familiar throughout the country. Prized for the diversity of their flavors, they are sold in Asian, Latin, and Indian food markets and, increasingly, in supermarkets.

I have a passion for chiles that dates back to my earliest years when my father would take us on culinary excursions to Olvera Street, then the heart of the Mexican district in downtown Los Angeles. There we would eat *pollitos,* barbecued chickens slathered with spicy, fresh chile salsa and rolled in tortillas. Because Cal-Mex cuisine is one of my comfort foods, I like to use chiles liberally in recipes, but remembering their differences and similarities (not to mention mastering the intricacies of their names!) can be daunting.

The best source for detailed information about chiles is *Peppers, The Domesticated Capsicums,* by Jean Andrews (University of Texas Press, 1984), which I have consulted for technical information. More important than mastering the botanical complexities, however, is understanding what each type of pepper contributes to the flavor of a recipe.

The burning or stinging sensation in hot peppers comes from a phenolic compound, known as capsaicin, produced in the core and ribs. The amount of capsaicin in each pepper is controlled by a dominant gene—therefore heat varies not only among the different types of hot peppers, but from fruit to fruit as well. Other factors, such as climate and maturity, also influence hotness.

Jalapeños are the best-known and most widely available hot green chile. Named for the city of Jalapa, in Mexico, these are small (1 to 3 inches long) and dark green (or red when ripe) with a characteristic rounded or bullet-shaped tip. Their flavor is distinct and easy to identify, whether they are fresh or pickled; think of them as having a very pronounced, musty, and stinging green-pepper taste.

Smoked, dried jalapeños are called *chipotles.* Most commonly these are found canned in *adobo,* a brick-red sauce. Chipotles are searingly hot and must be carefully handled.

The slim, green *serrano* has a wicked sting; use it when maximum heat is required. In addition to its bite, the serrano has a slightly more herbal taste than other hot green peppers. It is relatively easy to identify by the smooth skin, medium-green color, small size (about 1½ inches), and narrow pointed tip.

Fresh red *cayenne* chiles are named after a river in French Guyana, where they are thought to have originated. These are incendiary, and their heat predominates, leaving only a marginal red-pepper taste. Thinner than a pinky finger, they usually measure about 4 inches (although they can be much longer). They tend to have gnarled bodies with pointed, curved tips. (The spice known as *cayenne pepper* is made from dried and ground hot red chiles, which may not necessarily be of the cayenne variety.)

Green or red *Anaheim* chiles also are called New Mexico No. 9, *chile verde* (when green), or *chile colorado* (when red). Shaped like skinny cucumbers with pointed tips, they measure 4 to 6 inches. Anaheims range from mild to hot and are the peppers you see dried and strung on wreaths, called *ristras,* at fall chile festivals. They are also ground for paprika and chili powder. When used fresh, they are often stuffed.

Fresh *poblano* chiles have a fabulous flavor that is deeper, richer, and less acidic than that of green bell peppers; and their piquancy varies from mild to very hot. The body of the pepper is an elongated heart shape, leathery and gnarled, ranging from 3 to 5 inches long. When green, their color is very dark; poblanos turn red when ripe.

Dried *poblanos,* called *Ancho* chiles, are reddish-brown to mahogany, flat, and leathery. They should be pliable (rather than brittle) at the time of purchase. Their pungent, slightly bitter flavor is wonderful and distinctive, even in a prepared chili powder or cooked salsa. See page 194 for information on grinding them into a chili powder.

GO FOR THE BURN—HANDLING PEPPERS

Fresh chiles and other peppers frequently need to be peeled, seeded, and deveined before cooking. Charring—either on top of a stove burner or under the broiler—is a good method for removing their skins.

Leave chiles or peppers in contact with a flame only until skins blacken, turning them constantly so that they do not overcook. Transfer the charred fruit to a plastic bag, twist it closed, and let them stand for 5 to 10 minutes. Remove blackened skins with the back of a small knife. Steam building up inside the peppers often extracts juice, which may be saved for use in recipes as peppers are split open and seeds removed. If necessary, rinse peppers or chiles under cold running water to remove any bits of skin that remain.

Whether hot chiles are peeled or unpeeled, removing the stem, seeds, and ribs is a process that can be painful for those with sensitive skin. I am less sensitive to hot peppers than many people, but occasionally I must reach for rubber gloves (the thin surgical, or hair-coloring, type are best) to protect my hands. Remember not to touch sensitive facial areas while working with chiles, especially your lips, eyes, and nose.

Store fresh chiles and bell peppers in plastic bags lined with paper towels to absorb moisture that may cause mildew. Peeled, seeded, small chiles may be preserved in alcohol (such as vodka). Larger peppers and chiles may be preserved in oil (a recipe appears on page 339).

Everyone facing an upcoming dinner party looks for a dish that is easy to make, a little bit different, relatively inexpensive, and delicious. If you also happen to like foods that have sweet, savory, and spicy elements, you will surely appreciate this curry-laced, South African *bobotie,* which is served hot, with several cold condiments to complete the meal.

The recipe comes from my friend Lindy Grobler, who made this for countless dinner parties while she lived in the United States. Like many dishes from southern Africa, India, and Malaysia, this one is spice-based. Lindy always used a special hot curry powder that packs more of a punch than store-bought blends—the little recipe appears below.

FLEXIBLE MENU SUGGESTIONS

This casserole doubles and triples well, and it freezes beautifully. It is made even more interesting by the variety of accompaniments—basically curry garnishes—that are served alongside. Accompaniments include Yellow Rice (page 327), the fruit and vegetable relishes that follow, mango chutney (or the chutneys on pages 337 and 338), and desiccated (dried, unsweetened) coconut, which is available at Indian food stores.

Good choices for dessert include Chocolate Truffle Cake (page 382), Milanese Fruit Tart (page 408), or Lemon-Praline Soufflé Glacé (page 433). *Makes 6 servings*

PREPARATION OF CASSEROLE: 30 MINUTES
PREPARATION OF RELISHES: 45 MINUTES
COOKING: 40 TO 50 MINUTES

½ cup firmly packed golden (sultana) raisins
Boiling water
1 piece (1-inch cube) fresh ginger, peeled
2 medium onions (½ pound), peeled
2 tablespoons vegetable or corn oil
2 pounds ground beef (preferably chuck)
2½ tablespoons hot or mild curry powder, or
   more to taste (page 203)
1 cup mango chutney, or Mixed Plum
   Chutney (page 338)
½ cup slivered almonds
2 tablespoons cider vinegar, or more to taste
2 teaspoons turmeric
Salt and ground white pepper
3 tablespoons sugar
5 eggs
4 bay leaves
1¼ cups half-and-half

1. Put raisins in a small, heatproof bowl and cover with boiling water; set aside. Mince the ginger, and coarsely chop the onions. Put the oil in a large skillet. Add the ginger and onions and stir over low heat until onions soften, about 8 minutes.

2. Add the beef to the skillet and stir it over medium heat until it turns pinkish-brown and separates into ground consistency, about 6 to 8 minutes. Sprinkle 2½ tablespoons curry powder over the meat; cool.

3. Coarsely chop the large pieces of chutney, and stir it, along with the almonds, vinegar, turmeric, 1 teaspoon salt, ½ to ¾ teaspoon white pepper, and sugar, into the beef mixture. Taste and adjust the seasoning, increasing the curry, vinegar, salt, and pep-

Continued

per to taste. (Can cool completely, cover, and refrigerate mixture 2 days.)

4. Adjust oven rack to middle position. Heat oven to 350 degrees. Beat 1 egg and mix it thoroughly into the beef. Transfer the mixture to a deep 2- to 2½-quart casserole or baking dish. Insert bay leaves upright and halfway into meat mixture.

5. Mix 4 eggs with the half-and-half until blended. Pour over the beef. Bake 40 to 50 minutes, or until meat is hot in center and custard is set and lightly glazed. Remove bay leaves before serving. Pass garnishes separately. (Can keep casserole warm in 200-degree oven for 30 to 45 minutes.)

BANANA RELISH

Makes 3 cups

PREPARATION: 10 MINUTES

1 thin (quarter-size) slice fresh ginger, peeled
1 can (14 ounces) sweetened condensed milk
1 cup sour cream
⅛ teaspoon ground pepper
⅛ teaspoon ground nutmeg
¼ cup fresh lemon juice
About ¼ to ⅓ cup milk, or more as needed
4 large bananas

1. Mince the ginger and put it in a mixing bowl. Stir in condensed milk, sour cream, pepper, nutmeg, lemon juice, and ¼ cup milk. If very thick, thin to saucelike consistency with additional milk. Refrigerate until serving time.

2. At serving time, peel the bananas and slice them thinly. Gently mix the slices into the cream. Serve immediately.

SLIVERED CUCUMBERS

Makes 1½ cups

PREPARATION: 10 MINUTES

1 pound cucumbers, peeled, seeded, quartered

Cut the cucumbers into 1½-inch by ⅛-inch julienne strips. Cover and refrigerate until serving time, up to 4 hours.

TOMATO-ONION SALAD

Makes 2 cups

PREPARATION: 15 MINUTES

1 small red onion, peeled
2 tablespoons cider vinegar
2 teaspoons sugar
2 pounds ripe tomatoes, peeled, seeded, and
  drained

1. Coarsely chop the onion and transfer it to a medium bowl. Stir in vinegar and sugar.

2. Cut tomatoes into ⅛-inch dice, drain them well, and stir them into the onion mixture. Adjust the seasoning with vinegar or sugar, if necessary. Refrigerate until serving time. (Can refrigerate up to 4 hours.)

HOT CURRY POWDER

Makes ¼ cup

PREPARATION: 5 MINUTES

¼ cup prepared, salt-free curry powder
½ teaspoon chili powder
¾ to 1 teaspoon cayenne pepper
¼ teaspoon ground coriander

Mix spices and store in an airtight jar.

FETTUCCINE WITH CHICKEN, ARTICHOKES, AND DILL

Finding just the right balance of ingredients for a chicken and pasta salad is always a challenge: either the pasta seems bland, or the chicken is trumped by other components. Several years ago, a friend who owned a restaurant asked me to develop a grilled chicken salad. This was the result, and it became a popular summer main course.

In the restaurant, the chicken breasts were grilled (they also can be barbecued or sautéed) in the morning and set aside. At home, this could be done the night of a barbecue for a salad to be served the next day. Pasta can be cooked, well drained, tossed with oil (so it doesn't become gummy), then covered very loosely and set aside to cool until serving time.

To prevent the salad from becoming bland and dry (pasta absorbs seasonings), mix the components together just before serving and carefully double-check the seasoning.

FLEXIBLE MENU SUGGESTIONS

Since the dressing does not contain egg yolk and the salad is not especially rich, it can be followed by a luxurious dessert—try Gianduia Cheesecake (page 384), Dome Cake (page 388), Chocolate-Walnut Linzer Torte (page 376), or Double Chocolate Ice Cream (page 399) with Instant Hot Fudge or Caramel Sauce (pages 401 and 444). *Makes 4 servings*

PREPARATION: 25 MINUTES
MARINATION: 2 HOURS
COOKING: 20 MINUTES

DRESSING

¼ cup packed dill leaves
1 medium garlic clove, peeled
¼ cup lemon juice
⅔ cup mild olive or vegetable oil
Salt and ground black pepper

SALAD INGREDIENTS

1 can (14 ounces) artichoke hearts, drained, rinsed, quartered
1 medium avocado, peeled, pitted, rinsed, cut in ¾-inch dice
1 to 2 tablespoons vegetable oil
2 whole chicken breasts (2 pounds) with skin on, boned, split

½ pound dry pasta (fettuccine or penne), cooked and cooled
½ pint cherry tomatoes, rinsed and halved
1 can (5 ounces) black pitted olives, drained and halved

1. For the dressing, mince the dill in a food processor fitted with the metal blade. Add the garlic and lemon juice and process, adding the oil in a thin stream. Season with ¼ teaspoon salt and ⅛ teaspoon pepper.

2. Pour the dressing into a large mixing bowl. Add the artichokes and avocado cubes. Cover and refrigerate for 2 hours to marinate.

3. Rub chicken breasts with half the oil and grill or broil over moderate heat until juices run pale pink. (Or, sauté with 2 tablespoons vegetable oil, turning once, until juices run clear.) Set the chicken aside at room temperature. When cool, slice crosswise into ¼-inch-wide strips, leaving skin intact for color.

4. About 1 hour before serving time, bring the artichoke mixture to room temperature. At serving time, toss the artichoke mixture with the cooked pasta. Gently mix in the chicken strips, tomatoes, and olives, taking care not to smash the avocado. Adjust seasoning with salt and pepper. Serve immediately at room temperature.

PENNE WITH BROCCOLI AND SCALLOPS

Scallops, broccoli, red pepper, and olives are felicitous and surprisingly delicate partners in a salad made with tubular penne, ziti, or corkscrew-shaped fusilli. A small amount of the scallop steaming liquid replaces acid in the dressing, and minced lemon zest adds zip.

Whole Oil-Marinated Olives (page 63) can be substituted for the sliced olives, and Red (or yellow) Peppers Preserved in Oil (page 339) can replace the roasted red bell pepper.

FLEXIBLE MENU SUGGESTIONS

Loaves of Prosciutto Bread (page 354) or Tomato Flatbread with Two Herbs (page 346) complement the salad. Milanese Fruit Tart (page 408), Classic Fruit Tart (page 416), Mixed Berry Cobbler (page 420), or fresh fruit with Chocolate Madeleines or Mixed Nut Sablés (pages 394 and 442) round out the menu. *Makes 4 servings*

PREPARATION: 35 MINUTES
COOKING: 30 MINUTES

1 pound broccoli, stems peeled, rinsed
1 pound bay scallops, rinsed
1 medium red bell pepper
¾ pound dry penne, fusilli, or ziti
3 tablespoons mild olive oil

DRESSING

1 medium lemon
3 medium garlic cloves, peeled
Salt and ground black pepper
1 tablespoon Dijon mustard
1 cup mild olive oil
3 tablespoons minced parsley
1 cup loosely packed black pitted olives or
   Oil-Marinated Olives (page 63)

1. Fit large saucepan with steamer basket, add the broccoli, cover, and steam until tender, 8 to 10 minutes; set aside. Steam scallops until opaque, about 3 to 4 minutes. Remove scallops and reserve 4½ tablespoons steaming liquid.

2. Char, peel, and seed the bell pepper as described on page 339. Set the pepper aside.

3. Heat 4 quarts water to boiling. Add pasta and boil until nearly tender. Drain, then return pasta to the pot with the oil. Toss over very low heat until oil is absorbed, then transfer it to a bowl and set it aside to cool, tossing it occasionally.

4. For the dressing, grate the lemon zest into a food processor. Turn the machine on, and drop in the garlic. Add ¾ teaspoon salt, several grinds of pepper, the mustard, and scallop steaming liquid. Process, adding oil. Pulse in the parsley, and set the dressing aside.

5. Separate the broccoli florets from the stems; add florets to the pasta. Thinly slice and add the stems. Cut large olives crosswise into rounds (leave small olives whole); add olives to the pasta mixture. Slice the pepper into julienne strips and add it to the pasta.

6. Add scallops and dressing to the pasta. Gently toss, then adjust seasoning to taste. Serve within 2 hours, adjusting seasoning again, if necessary.

CHINESE CHICKEN SALAD

Thin rice stick noodles expand like popcorn in contact with hot vegetable oil, making a crunchy background for this fairly formal, colorful salad, which looks stunning on black dinner plates. I always think of serving this for a special lunch, but it also makes a fine late spring or summer dinner entrée that goes particularly well with beer.

This recipe is adapted from a salad created by my friend and Chinese cooking instructor, chef Simon Teng. I passed it along to my sister, Bette Publicker, who is the corporate chef for a major film studio. She has served the salad countless times, and her modifications are included here. A description of the Oriental products used in the recipe appears on page 208; many of these items are also available in supermarkets.

FLEXIBLE MENU SUGGESTIONS

Follow the salad with something rich yet not overpowering, such as Orange Crème Brulée (page 426), Mixed Berry Cobbler (page 420), or Banana Ice Cream with Caramel Sauce (pages 438 and 444). *Makes 6 servings*

PREPARATION: 30 MINUTES
MARINATION: 2 HOURS
COOKING: 25 MINUTES

4 cups vegetable oil
½ package rice stick noodles, broken in 2-inch lengths

CHICKEN AND MARINADE

2 tablespoons dark soy sauce
1 tablespoon sesame oil
2 whole chicken breasts (2 pounds), boned, skinned, split
2 tablespoons vegetable oil

DRESSING

½ medium garlic clove, peeled
1 small piece ginger (½-inch cube), peeled
1 tablespoon sugar
1½ tablespoons dry mustard
1 tablespoon peanut butter or sesame paste
1 tablespoon sesame oil
Salt and ground white pepper
1½ tablespoons rice or cider vinegar
2 tablespoons all-purpose soy sauce
½ cup Chicken Stock (page 165)
½ cup vegetable oil

GARNISHES

½ pound (½ medium head) iceberg lettuce
½ bunch medium scallions, rinsed, patted dry
Handful cilantro leaves
½ red bell pepper, seeded, thinly julienned
1½ teaspoons toasted sesame seeds

1. Heat 4 cups oil in wok or deep skillet to 375 degrees. Add one-third of the dry rice

Continued

stick noodles and cook 30 seconds; turn and cook just until noodles are opaque and expanded. Transfer noodles to paper towels with a slotted spoon, and repeat to cook all the noodles. (Can cook 48 hours ahead and store in an airtight tin. Oil can be strained and reused.)

2. For the marinade, mix dark soy sauce and sesame oil in a nonreactive dish, add chicken breasts, and turn until coated. Cover and refrigerate, turning once or twice, for 2 hours (can cover and refrigerate overnight).

3. Pat chicken breasts dry with paper towels. Heat remaining 2 tablespoons oil in a large skillet. Sauté chicken breasts until lightly colored, about 2 minutes on each side. Cover skillet tightly with a lid or aluminum foil. Set aside off heat until lukewarm, about 30 minutes. Uncover and reserve pan juices for dressing (or discard). Cool, wrap, and refrigerate chicken until chilled. (Can refrigerate 24 hours.)

4. For the dressing, insert the metal blade in a dry food processor. Mince the garlic and ginger. Add sugar, mustard, peanut butter, sesame oil, ¼ teaspoon salt, ¼ teaspoon pepper, vinegar, and soy sauce. Add ½ cup combined chicken cooking liquid and stock (or use ½ cup stock). Then process, adding the oil in a thin stream; set dressing aside. (Can cover and refrigerate 24 hours.)

5. To assemble the salads, shred 3½ cups of lettuce, and slice the scallions into rings. Cut chicken crosswise into ⅛-inch julienne strips. Divide noodles evenly over six dinner plates. Divide shredded lettuce over each portion of noodles, top each portion with chicken pieces, scallion rings, cilantro leaves, bell pepper strips, and ¼ teaspoon sesame seeds. Spoon 2 to 3 tablespoons dressing over each salad. Serve immediately.

AN ORIENTAL PANTRY

Many Chinese ingredients need no introduction to those cooks who can easily discern the differences in soy sauce, find their way through the vast maze of bean pastes, or identify unfamiliar (and sometimes weird-looking) vegetables.

For most people, the number of products available is disconcertingly vast, and translations on labels are not always clear. The following ingredients are those most regularly used in recipes, and having them on hand will provide you with a good, basic larder.

If stored in airtight containers, many sauces and dry ingredients will last for several months or longer; having them on hand eliminates a trip to the Oriental market. Many products are now also available in supermarkets, but if you get stuck, a Chinese restaurant often will sell you ingredients.

SOY SAUCE
Soy sauce is derived from fermented soy beans, and each type or brand of sauce will vary in pungency, saltiness, and viscosity. The particular type of soy sauce used can drastically affect the flavor of a dish.

All-purpose soy sauce: Japanese-style soy sauce (such as the Wisconsin-made Kikkoman) is suitable for most uses because its saltiness, sweetness, and consistency are moderate.

Dark soy sauce: Also known as thick or black soy, this sauce is intensely flavored. Partially derived from molasses, it is relatively viscous, making it good for marinades and sauces.

NOTE: Don't confuse "lite" soy sauce (which is reduced in sodium) with what Chinese call "light" soy sauce, which is used for dipping. Reduced-sodium soy sauce can be substituted for all-purpose soy, but the seasoning balance may be altered.

OILS AND PASTES

Sesame oil: A fragrant nut-brown oil made from toasted sesame seeds. Either Japanese or Chinese brands are good.

Hot sesame oil: Fiery amber-colored sesame oil flavored with hot red peppers. (To make at home, add dried red chiles to gently heated sesame oil; let stand overnight.)

Hot red chili oil: Oil flavored with Szechwan peppercorns, hot red chilies, sesame oil, and sometimes aniseed. (To make at home, combine 50 percent vegetable oil and 50 percent sesame oil, and heat with dried red chiles and roasted Szechwan peppercorns. Let stand 1 hour to 2 days).

Chili paste with garlic: Made from mashed red chiles and garlic, this paste often contains salt and vinegar. Use carefully as a seasoning, adjusting salt to taste.

Hoisin sauce: A brownish-red (canned) bean paste and the primary ingredient in Simon's Hoisin Sauce (page 211). Keeps indefinitely when refrigerated.

Sesame paste: A paste made from toasted sesame seeds. (Substitute creamy peanut butter.)

WINE AND VINEGAR

Shaohsing wine: Whiskey-colored Chinese rice wine from Shaohsing, near Shanghai, is a staple Chinese cooking ingredient. I use a brand made in Taiwan (simply called Shaohsing) which has a bright red label. Substitute dry sherry or Japanese sake.

Chinese red vinegar: Fermented (malted) rice, vinegar, and water give this its characteristic reddish color and pungent taste. I use Koon Chun brand. While there is no actual substitute, the closest Western ingredient would be sherry wine vinegar.

Rice vinegar: A sweet, pale vinegar (can use Chinese or Japanese brands).

SPICES AND DRIED INGREDIENTS

Szechwan peppercorns: These brick-red pepper berries, the size of buckshot, split open as they dry and are filled with small weedlike stems or radicles (remove stems before using). When roasted in a dry skillet, the peppercorns emit a pungent aroma, and their flavor becomes fiery. A good brand is Kung Wo Ho (but note that these are labeled "dried red pepper").

Rice stick noodles: Brittle, opaque white "mi fen" noodles are the size of angel hair pasta, and are sold in bricklike bunches. Inedible in their packaged state, they must be fried in oil, which causes them to puff to crisp white strands that can be used in salads (see Chinese Chicken Salad, page 207), or softened in hot water and stir-fried (see Curried Rice Stick, page 326).

PORK AND VEGETABLE SALAD ORIENTALE

Robust and colorful, this assemblage of meat and vegetables, tossed with an Oriental-inspired dressing, can be conveniently prepared and left at room temperature for 2 hours before serving. It is an ideal salad for a lazy Sunday dinner, and it can be beautifully presented in a large bowl or on a platter that is passed at table.

FLEXIBLE MENU SUGGESTIONS

Add a bowl of tiny, cold boiled new potatoes as an accompaniment to the salad. For dessert, choose between slices of Peach Turnover (page 418) topped with vanilla ice cream, Apple Crisp (page 424) with whipped cream, or Crème Brulée (page 426). Or, dessert can be pared down to fresh berries and Quick Custard Sauce (page 443). *Makes 4 servings*

PREPARATION: 20 MINUTES
COOKING: 8 MINUTES

Marinated Pork Tenderloin (page 211),
  cooked and chilled

SESAME DRESSING

2 tablespoons lemon juice
2 tablespoons sesame oil
3 tablespoons reserved pork marinade or soy
  sauce
2 teaspoons sesame seeds
1 tablespoon Simon's Hoisin Sauce (page 211)
1 teaspoon hot red pepper oil
1 teaspoon sugar
½ teaspoon powdered ginger
½ teaspoon dry sherry or Chinese Shaohsing
  wine
⅔ cup mild olive oil or vegetable oil

VEGETABLES

¾ pound broccoli, stems peeled
¼ pound snow-pea pods, tips and strings
  removed
1 medium cucumber (about ½ pound), peeled,
  halved lengthwise, and seeded
1 medium yellow crookneck squash, halved
  lengthwise

1 medium red bell pepper, halved, cored, and
  seeded
3 medium scallions, roots removed
2 medium celery stalks, pared

1. Prepare and refrigerate the Marinated Pork Tenderloin.

2. For the sesame dressing, put all ingredients except oil into a food processor fitted with the metal blade. Process, adding oil in a thin stream. (Can cover and refrigerate overnight.)

3. For the vegetables, separate broccoli florets from the stems, and cut the stems diagonally into ⅛-inch-thick slices. Put sliced stems and florets in a vegetable steamer basket (page 317). Steam for 3 minutes, add the pea pods, and steam 3 to 4 minutes longer. Remove and immediately plunge vegetables in cold water, then transfer to a cloth towel to drain.

4. Thinly slice the cucumber and squash into half-round pieces. Cut the red pepper into thin julienne strips, and slice the scallions into rings. Cut the celery into 2-inch-long segments, then cut it into long, thin julienne strips. Transfer all the vegetables to a large salad or pasta bowl. (Can cover and refrigerate up to 6 hours.)

5. Shortly before serving, slice the pork ⅛-inch thick and add it to the salad. Toss well with salad dressing and let the mixture stand for 30 minutes (but no longer than 3 hours) before serving. Adjust the seasoning and serve immediately.

SIMON'S HOISIN SAUCE

xxxxxxxxxx

Each Chinese chef creates his own Hoisin sauce by adding ingredients to a jarred or canned commercial paste, which tends to be bitter and very thick. When Hoisin sauce is specified in recipes, use the sauce mixture below. *Makes 1¼ cups*

PREPARATION: 10 MINUTES

1 cup prepared Hoisin sauce
1½ tablespoons sugar
2 tablespoons Shaohsing wine or pale dry sherry
2 tablespoons sesame oil
1½ teaspoons rice vinegar

Put all ingredients in a food processor fitted with the metal blade, and process until smooth. Transfer the sauce to a plastic or glass storage container and refrigerate. (If tightly covered, sauce keeps indefinitely in the refrigerator.)

MARINATED PORK TENDERLOIN

xxxxxxxxxx

Marinate the pork three days ahead, and roast it a day in advance for easy preparation. Substitute a well-trimmed piece of boneless pork loin if the tenderloin (fillet) is not available. *Makes about 1 pound*

PREPARATION: 15 MINUTES
MARINATION: 4 TO 24 HOURS
COOKING: ABOUT 25 MINUTES

1 slice fresh ginger (¼ inch thick), peeled
2 medium garlic cloves, peeled
¼ cup Chinese Shaohsing wine or dry sherry
¼ cup dark soy sauce
2 teaspoons sugar
1 pound pork tenderloin, excess fat removed, well trimmed

1. Mince the ginger and garlic and transfer to a glass (or other nonreactive) loaf pan. Add wine, soy sauce, and sugar and stir until mixed.

2. Put the pork tenderloin in the pan and turn to coat it thoroughly with the marinade. Cover and refrigerate 4 hours (or overnight), turning pork several times in the marinade.

3. Adjust oven rack to middle position. Heat oven to 450 degrees. Reserve 3 tablespoons pork marinade for the salad. Remove the pork from the marinade and pat it dry. Transfer it to a small pan and roast, turning it several times, until an instant-read thermometer registers 145 degrees, usually 20 to 25 minutes. Cool to room temperature. Wrap and refrigerate until thoroughly chilled before slicing (as long as 2 days).

FIRE AND SPICE—PART ONE: GRILLING FISH AND SHELLFISH

ndoor grilling at home is an idea whose time has come. Taking a cue from European kitchens, where fish and meat have been cooked over natural wood fires for centuries, California and Southwest chefs were the first to initiate this move toward simple cooking and easy but flavorful sauces. Smart home cooks are following their lead.

While the notion is not new on this side of the Atlantic, it received a boost during the rise in popularity of grill restaurants, a trend that began as a reaction to the excesses of *nouvelle cuisine*. However, chefs and restaurateurs in many parts of the country—notably Jovan Trboyevic, in Chicago—served grilled fish for nearly a decade before it became fashionable.

Although there was a built-in electric grill in my mother's kitchen during the mid-1970s, my family used it primarily to cook steaks and hamburgers. I actually learned to grill fish in the course of writing an article about Trboyevic's Le Perroquet restaurant, where I spent a week in the kitchen. There, for the first time, I saw a portable, cast-iron French grill (about the size of a pancake griddle), which the chef used over two burners on top of the range. I also encountered the excellent one-side fish-grilling technique on which much of this chapter is based.

That method calls for marking the fish, then transferring it to a baking sheet, grilled-side up. When cool, the fish is refrigerated until shortly before serving time, and finished quickly in the oven.

My purchase of a cast-iron grill, similar to the one I saw in the restaurant, put me into the business of conveniently grilling fish several hours in advance, eliminating the smokiness that results from placing it over an open fire at the last minute, as well as the perils of overcooking the delicate flesh.

Whether you purchase a grill like mine (which is no more difficult to clean than a frying pan, and can be tucked away like a cookie sheet) or opt for installing a built-in unit, an indoor grill should be standard equipment at home.

To me, the very spirit and spice of life seems implicit in the sizzle of foods cooked in this manner, and today, grilled fish and seafood (as well as poultry, meats, and vegetables) are dinner party basics. Whenever possible, I prefer to grill (rather than to sauté) in order to impart a distinct flavor with a minimum of cooking fat. Best of all, composing beautiful plates around fresh grilled fish is a snap.

The dramatic effect of a fillet of salmon, handsomely crosshatched and moistened by a thin glaze of Roasted Garlic and Saffron Butter, belies the ease of its preparation. If saffron seems a bit too exotic, you can serve classic Fresh Herb Butter instead.

A succulent wedge of swordfish, perfumed by a smoky veil of shallot-infused oil, is irresistible in an avocado- and tomato-studded sauce, while a garnish of peppery, green-chile cream adds spice.

And while a tender medley of grilled shellfish with Bouillabaisse Sauce may require slightly more attention to detail than other recipes included here, it is a stellar main course that will pamper guests with a touch of luxury and make them feel particularly welcome at your table.

ONE-SIDE GRILLED FISH

Marketing and Mongering

Points of Perfection

FRESH HERB BUTTER

TOMATO BUTTER

ORSO BUTTER

ROASTED GARLIC AND SAFFRON BUTTER

Compounding Flavor

_____

AVOCADO VINAIGRETTE

_____

POBLANO CREAM

_____

CITRUS SALSA

_____

WINTER PESTO

_____

BOUILLABAISSE SAUCE

_____

A Saucy Legend in Its Own Time

_____

GRILLED CEVICHE

_____

SHRIMP AND SCALLOPS WITH CHILE-PEANUT SAUCE

_____

ONE-SIDE GRILLED FISH

Fish is among the top-selling main courses in restaurants, yet many people do not think of grilling it at home. Here is a master recipe for grill-marking fish fillets or skewered shellfish, then finishing them in the oven. This two-step cooking process gives you the attractive grilled look and taste without the smokiness of last-minute cooking.

Among the best fish for grilling are salmon, swordfish, tuna, tilefish, mahimahi, mako shark, bluefish, bass (particularly striped bass), grouper, and red snapper. Boneless sole and flounder fillets are too delicate to grill.

I recommend using skinned, boned fish fillets. However, red snapper or rockfish, mackerel, and striped bass fillets—which have lovely skins—can be grilled skin-side down, and then served with the grilled skin side up.

Fillets vary in thickness from side to side, even after pounding. To ensure even cooking, it is necessary to rotate fish 90 degrees during grilling, which also produces attractive cross-hatch markings on one side.

Within 2 to 3 minutes on a hot grill, most well-oiled fish will be clearly marked and sufficiently charred to release easily with the aid of a metal spatula (excess moisture can cause it to stick). Keep in mind that grills have hot spots (stovetop grills are hottest directly above the heat source), so foods may cook more quickly on some parts of the grill than on others.

FLEXIBLE MENU SUGGESTIONS

Recipes for nine simple sauces that can be served with grilled fish and seafood follow. Since the varying combinations of fish and sauce affect the choice of appetizers and desserts, menu suggestions are included with sauces. *Makes 6 to 8 servings*

PREPARATION: 5 MINUTES
MARINATION: 1 TO 12 HOURS
COOKING: 8 TO 12 MINUTES (DEPENDING ON THICKNESS)

2 to 2½ pounds boned fish fillets (skinned if desired)
Salt and ground black pepper
2 medium shallots, peeled and quartered (optional)
½ cup olive oil or Herbed Oil (page 73)

1. Rinse and pat fish fillets dry with paper toweling and put them skin-side down on a work surface. Check for bones by running your finger down the center line of each fillet, toward the widest end. With a tweezer or small pliers, extract any bones, pulling with the grain. (If fish tears, you are pulling against the grain. Turn fillet around and work from the opposite direction.)

2. Cut fillets crosswise into 6- to 8-ounce portions (each about 4 to 5 inches long). If pieces are uneven in thickness, pound them lightly with the flat side of a cleaver—this is optional.

3. Transfer fish to a glass (or other nonreactive) baking dish and sprinkle lightly with

salt and pepper. Mix shallots with oil, pour over fish, and turn to coat pieces completely with oil. Cover tightly with plastic wrap and refrigerate 1 hour, turning pieces several times. (Can refrigerate overnight.)

4. To cook, preheat a ridged, cast-iron stove-top grill, indoor grill, or broiler. (If cast-iron grill is used, it must be sizzling hot—drops of water sprinkled on it must evaporate immediately.) With pastry brush, coat grill irons with a small amount of oil from the fish marinade.

5. Remove fish from marinade and blot off excess oil with paper toweling. Put fillets on the grill, skin-side up (or skin-side down if desired). Grill until fillets are clearly marked and release easily, about 2 minutes. Rotate each fillet 90 degrees (to make a crosshatch) and grill 2 minutes longer (it is not necessary to rotate fish under broiler).

6. Transfer fillets, marked-sides up, to a buttered or oiled jelly-roll pan. (Can cool, cover, and refrigerate up to 6 hours.)

7. Heat oven to 425 degrees. Bake fillets (without turning) until the tip of a small knife inserted into the thickest part of the fillets is withdrawn hot, or to an internal temperature of 125 degrees, about 10 minutes.

8. Use a pancake turner to transfer hot fillets quickly from baking sheet to warm dinner plates. Add the appropriate sauce. Serve immediately.

MARKETING AND MONGERING

"Fresh" has come to be a relative term where fish is concerned. In a market it can mean anything from truly fresh to recently defrosted. What I mean by fresh is minimal time out of water and off the bone.

Whenever possible, buy at a fish market. Look for shiny, firm, whole fish with clear, smooth eyes, and ask to have it cleaned and filleted while you wait. Count on purchasing ½ pound of fish per person.

When I buy fillets or steaks, I look for bright, shiny pieces that have no dark bruises or bloody areas (a sign that the fish was injured at some stage, which can affect its flavor). Look for a smooth surface and tight grain, since a spongy texture or flesh that is separating usually indicates that the fish has been frozen and defrosted. Fresh fish never has a "fishy" odor, and it should be displayed or stored on crushed ice.

Some fish experts believe that rinsing fillets and shellfish prior to cooking removes water-soluble proteins from the surface and destroys flavor. However, I rinse fish and shellfish in cold tap water to remove any stray scales, small bones, or debris that may cling to its surface. I then pat it dry, cut it into portions, and coat it with oil as the recipe directs.

Rinsing is not a necessary step and comes down to what chef Eberhard Müller, of Le Bernardin restaurant in New York, calls "a question of trust" between you and the fish market. If you are sure your market handles fish impeccably, it is not necessary to rinse it. Chef Müller also points out that cooking fish at a surface temperature of 180 degrees (the approximate temperature of poaching liquid) or more, effectively destroys any bacteria on the surface.

POINTS OF PERFECTION

Fish fillets or steaks will grill most evenly when they are 1 to 1¼ inches thick (very thin pieces tend to curl on the grill). Fillets of uneven thickness can be pounded lightly with the flat side of a cleaver.

Swordfish and tuna, which are usually precut into large boneless steaks, should be skinned. If desired, each steak can be portioned into triangles according to the grain of the fish; if steaks exceed 1½ inches in thickness, it may be wise to split them horizontally into two portions of equal thickness.

If fish must be stored in the refrigerator unmarinated, it should be iced as follows: put ice cubes or crushed ice on a jelly-roll pan, and cover the ice with plastic wrap. Put unwrapped fish or shellfish (such as shrimp or scallops) on the plastic. Cover loosely with plastic and refrigerate no longer than overnight.

Shellfish such as shrimp or scallops should be handled like fish fillets and marinated in oil prior to grilling. If shrimp and scallops are small, skewer them to facilitate their removal from the grill or baking sheet. Large shrimp (whether in or out of shells) and giant sea scallops can be grilled individually or skewered.

COOKING CONTROL

There are numerous methods for calculating cooking time and determining when fish is done. The Canadian Cooking Theory, which estimates cooking time at 10 minutes per inch of thickness, will cook fish to medium-well or well done, which for me is overcooked.

For many years—in situations that range from department-store cooking demonstrations to formal dinner parties—I have used two methods for judging doneness, which I define as fish that is moist, juicy, and just cooked through.

The simplest method is to insert the tip of a thin metal paring knife into the thickest part of the fish for about 5 seconds. When the knife tip feels hot to the touch (your lower lip will be more sensitive than your finger), fish is sufficiently cooked.

The most reliable method is to use an instant-read thermometer (or meat/yeast thermometer), which is inserted into the thickest part of the fish. When the dial registers 125 degrees, the fish is just cooked. Serve it as soon as possible.

BROILING AS AN ALTERNATIVE TO GRILLING
Fish may be broiled on a very hot, lightly oiled, preheated broiler tray about 2 inches from the heat source.

FRESH HERB BUTTER

The flavor of garden-fresh minced herbs transfers effortlessly to hot, grilled fish or shellfish with this butter as a vehicle. It can be be made with a single herb, or elaborated with a classical *fines herbes* mixture of chervil, chives, tarragon, and parsley. Plan to mince the herbs just before making the butter to capture their essences fully.

FLEXIBLE MENU SUGGESTIONS

While this butter is lovely as a sauce for fish or chicken, it also can be softened and used as all-purpose herb butter for steamed vegetables, pasta, or for Snow Pea and Bell Pepper Ribbons (page 310), in place of plain butter.

For a hearty menu that begins with Wild Rice Soup (page 50) or Pasta with Milanese Meat Sauce (page 130), serve slices of the butter over grilled salmon or shrimp. Add steamed spinach tossed in Herbed Oil (page 73) in a menu with the soup, or a sautéed julienne of red, yellow, and green bell peppers following the pasta. Fresh tropical fruits with Coconut-Lime Tuiles (page 440), Lemon Tirami Su (page 429), or Pomegranate Granita (page 439) are good desserts for either menu.

During the summer, a meal for herb lovers could begin with Mozzarella, Tomato, and Olive Salad (page 62), grilled swordfish, salmon, or shrimp with the rosemary-butter variation, and Yellow Rice (page 327). For dessert, consider Peach Turnover with Quick Custard Sauce (pages 418 and 443) or à la mode.

A spring or fall dinner could begin with the cold Three-Vegetable Terrine and Coral Sauce (pages 83 and 85). Grill bass, grouper, swordfish, or tilefish fillets, top them with this butter, and serve Saffron Risotto or Yellow Rice (pages 170 and 327) and French Dinner Rolls (page 360) with the main course. Finish with Almond and Lemon-Stuffed Pears (page 431).

Makes 8 to 10 servings

PREPARATION: 10 MINUTES

1 medium shallot, peeled
¼ cup minced fresh herbs (tarragon, basil, chervil, chives, dill, or cilantro leaves), or 2 tablespoons minced rosemary leaves
1 teaspoon lemon juice
Several dashes hot red pepper sauce (optional)
¼ pound unsalted butter, softened
Salt and ground white pepper

1. Mince the shallot. Insert the metal blade in a dry food processor. Add shallot and remaining ingredients, including ¼ teaspoon salt and ¼ teaspoon pepper. Process until herbs are thoroughly mixed with butter.

2. Spoon butter onto a 12-inch-long sheet of plastic wrap. Roll into a 1-inch-diameter log shape, about 8 inches long. Use immediately or refrigerate up to 3 days. (Can double-wrap in aluminum foil and freeze up to 3 months.)

TOMATO BUTTER

A small amount of tomato paste punches up the flavor of this butter, and also gives grilled grouper, bass, halibut, or scrod a rosy luster. This butter is a convenient way to use leftover tomato paste (see My Favorite Tomato Sauce, page 126).

FLEXIBLE MENU SUGGESTIONS

Several different menus can be constructed around any white-fleshed fish and this butter. One, with an Italian flavor, begins with Saffron Risotto (page 170) and features steamed asparagus and Prosciutto Bread (page 354) as accompaniments to the fish, and Apple Crisp (page 424) for dessert.

Mushroom Pizzas on Prosciutto Crust (page 114) could be quartered as a light appetizer of a menu for four. Half the suggested quantity of grilled fish (so it will serve four), topped with slices of this butter, can be served with steamed new potatoes and broccoli or sugar snap peas. End with Crème Brulée or Chocolate Roulade (page 426 or 392).

For a no-nonsense spring dinner, start with Milanese Asparagus Soup (page 162). Serve Yellow Rice (page 327) and a julienne of mixed bell peppers with the fish. Consider Lemon Tirami Su (page 429) or Almond Soufflé Tart (page 414) for dessert.

Following Onion and Chèvre Tart (page 104) or Four-Vegetable Tart (page 100), serve grilled bass or grouper with the butter. Add steamed broccoli or spinach, or Snow Pea and Bell Pepper Ribbons (page 310) following the cheese tart, and Yellow Rice and Rosemary Breadsticks (pages 327 and 343) after the vegetable tart. Complete the menu with Pink Grapefruit Sorbet or Pomegranate Granita (pages 435 and 439), plus Gianduia Lace Cookies or Mixed Nut Sablés (pages 386 or 442). *Makes 8 to 10 servings*

PREPARATION: 10 MINUTES

1 medium shallot, peeled
1½ tablespoons tomato paste
1 teaspoon lemon juice
Several dashes hot red pepper sauce
(optional)
¼ pound unsalted butter, softened
Salt and ground white pepper

1. Mince the shallot and put it in a food processor fitted with the metal blade. Add remaining ingredients, including ¼ teaspoon salt and ¼ teaspoon pepper. Process until thoroughly mixed.

2. Spoon butter onto a 12-inch-long sheet of plastic wrap. Roll into a 1-inch-diameter log shape, about 8 inches long. Use immediately or refrigerate up to 3 days. (Can double-wrap in aluminum foil and freeze up to 3 months.)

ORSO BUTTER

I first tasted this butter, made with small Niçoise olives, at Orso restaurant in Toronto. Because the olives are cured in salt brine, the butter requires no other seasoning. It is marvelous over grilled swordfish, striped bass, or red snapper. Don't overlook the possibility of swirling it into baked or mashed potatoes.

FLEXIBLE MENU SUGGESTIONS

For a rustic menu, start with slim wedges of Sausage and Artichoke Pizzas (page 108), Pasta with Milanese Meat Sauce (page 130), Scallion and Goat-Cheese Agnolotti (page 142), or Risotto Primavera (page 172). Since the appetizers provide both vegetables and starch, a mixed green salad with Lemon-Basil Vinaigrette (page 74) can be served "family style" on the same plate with the fish. Baked Stuffed Apples (page 425) are a homey dessert.

An equally good menu could begin with Pasta with Broccoli Raab (page 134) as a first course. The fish and butter, together with steamed carrots and Tomato Flatbread with Two Herbs (page 346) complete the main course. Almond and Lemon-Stuffed Pears (page 431) are a refreshing finale in the Italian spirit.

With Milanese Asparagus Soup (page 162) as an appetizer, serve the fish, steamed potatoes, and sautéed strips of red and yellow bell peppers. Add Tomato Flatbread with Two Herbs (page 346) if you like. Then, either Lemon Tart Brulée (page 406) or Pomegranate Granita (page 439) adds a pleasantly acerbic finish. *Makes 6 to 8 servings*

PREPARATION: 10 MINUTES

*¼ cup drained Niçoise olives, or Oil-
    Marinated Olives (page 63)*
6 tablespoons unsalted butter, softened

1. Pat olives dry and remove pits by cutting away flesh with a small sharp knife; discard pits. Puree olive flesh with butter in a food processor fitted with the metal blade, until mixture makes a thick paste.

2. Spoon butter onto a 10-inch-long sheet of plastic wrap. Roll into a 1-inch-diameter log shape. Use immediately or wrap in plastic and refrigerate up to 3 days. (Can double-wrap in aluminum foil and freeze up to 3 months.)

ROASTED GARLIC AND SAFFRON BUTTER

Roasting tempers the flavor of garlic and gives it a wonderful richness that sets off the astringency of the saffron, adding a complexity of flavor to this butter.

Toasting the delicate saffron threads briefly helps to break the filaments into tiny pieces that garnish and flavor fish at the same time. If you wish to substitute powdered saffron, add a scant ⅛ teaspoon to the butter, then adjust the flavor to taste.

FLEXIBLE MENU SUGGESTIONS

Like Orso Butter, this is very well suited to Italian-style menus. During the summer, I like to serve Mozzarella, Tomato, and Olive Salad (page 62) as an appetizer, then follow with this butter over grilled swordfish, chicken breasts, or veal chops. Accompany the fish with thinly sliced, grilled zucchini (use grilling method in Mediterranean Sauce, page 150) that has been sprinkled with fresh basil or oregano. End with Mixed Berry Cobbler (page 420) or Black Plum Sorbet and Chocolate Madeleines (pages 437 and 394).

For an all-fish menu, present Pasta with Tomato-Seafood Sauce (page 124) as an appetizer. Swordfish, mako shark, striped bass, or red snapper are good choices for the butter, and Snow Peas and Bell Pepper Ribbons (page 310) is a fine accompaniment. Serve Classic Fruit Tart (page 416) or Almond Soufflé Tart (page 414) for dessert.

Pasta with Milanese Meat Sauce (page 130) is a classical first course for a casual meal that continues with swordfish topped with the butter, and accompanied by fresh broccoli. Complete the menu with Milanese Fruit Tart (page 408) or Almond and Lemon-Stuffed Pears (page 431).

If serving fish to guests seems the least bit daring, plan the main course around a lively menu that begins with Milanese Asparagus Soup (page 162). Accompany the fish (striped bass) with Stuffed Tomatoes (page 312) and herbed basmati rice made like Yellow Rice (page 327) without turmeric. You may wish to add Black Olive Bread (page 356), and end with Lemon Tart Brulée (page 406). *Makes 8 to 10 servings*

PREPARATION: 15 MINUTES
COOKING: 25 MINUTES

10 small garlic cloves, unpeeled
¼ teaspoon saffron threads
¼ pound unsalted butter, softened
1 teaspoon lemon juice
Salt
Hot red pepper sauce (optional)

1. Adjust oven rack to middle position and heat oven to 350 degrees. Put garlic in a small dish and bake until softened, about 25 minutes. Set garlic aside until warm.

2. Put the saffron in a small skillet or metal pie plate and heat until threads are crisp enough to break with your fingers, about 2 minutes; set aside. Peel the garlic and put cloves in a food processor fitted with the metal blade; puree. Add the saffron and re-

maining ingredients, including ¼ teaspoon salt. Process until smooth and thoroughly mixed.

3. Spoon butter onto a 12-inch-long sheet of plastic wrap. Roll into a 1-inch-diameter log shape, about 8 inches long. Use immediately, or wrap in plastic and refrigerate up to 3 days. (Can double-wrap in aluminum foil and freeze up to 3 months.)

COMPOUNDING FLAVOR

I love to thumb through the pages of my copy of *The Cookery Repertory (Le Repertoire de la Cuisine)*. It makes me giggle to read the introduction, which notes that "every day some well-intentioned chef or cook will either give a new name to a dish which is already known to everyone as something else or he will introduce under a well-known name a preparation different from that which the name normally implies. These are bad practices which . . . will debase the culinary art beyond redemption."

Here I am discussing compound butters, but the closest recipes I can find bear scant resemblance to the butters that follow in this chapter. Fortunately, home cooks need not concern themselves with culinary debasement. Whipping up a compound butter is virtually guaranteed to enhance the flavor of many foods.

These butters are simple but sophisticated minimal sauces composed of chopped or pureed herbs, vegetables, or seasonings mixed with softened butter. Just 1 tablespoon (only 100 calories) will coat a piece of hot, grilled fish with a velvety blanket of flavor as it melts.

Swirl the butters into soups, stews, or risottos, toss them with steamed vegetables, add them to mashed or baked potatoes, or use them as emergency sauces for pasta.

AVOCADO VINAIGRETTE

Although this is called a vinaigrette it contains no vinegar, and is actually closer in spirit to a Latin salsa or chopped salad than to a sauce. There is a delicate balance between the richness of avocado, black olives, and olive oil, offset by the acidity of lemon juice and tomato. The entire ensemble receives a last-minute boost of flavor when it is warmed slightly from the heat of the grilled fish or seafood. A small amount of spicy Poblano Cream, sprinkled randomly over each portion, is an attractive and powerful garnish.

FLEXIBLE MENU SUGGESTIONS

For a menu that combines tropical and sunshine flavors, serve Papaya-Melon Soup (page 41) for an appetizer. Continue with the sauce served over grilled tuna, swordfish, shrimp, or sea scallops. With the diversity of vegetables in the sauce, additional accompaniments seem unnecessary. Yellow Rice (page 327) is the best choice if you insist on a starch. Add breadsticks made with oregano, rather than rosemary (page 343), and wind up with Almond Soufflé Tart (page 414) or Espresso-Brownie Chunk Ice Cream (page 397). *Makes 1½ cups*

PREPARATION: 15 MINUTES

Poblano Cream (page 225)
1 medium garlic clove, peeled
1 teaspoon Dijon mustard
½ teaspoon dry mustard
Salt and ground black pepper
2½ tablespoons lemon juice
¾ cup olive oil or Herbed Oil (page 73)
½ medium avocado, peeled
1 medium tomato, peeled, seeded
2 tablespoons pitted black olives, or Oil-
  Marinated Olives (page 63), cut into
  ⅛-inch dice

1. Make the Poblano Cream.

2. Mince the garlic and put it in a mixing bowl. Whisk in the mustards, ¼ teaspoon salt, ⅛ teaspoon pepper, lemon juice, and the olive oil. Cover and set aside (up to 4 hours).

3. At serving time, cut avocado and tomato into ¼-inch dice; add to bowl and stir in the diced olives. Adjust the seasoning. Heat the Poblano Cream. Spoon 3 to 4 tablespoons of the sauce over each piece of fish, then drizzle the entire mixture with 1 to 2 teaspoons of Poblano Cream. Serve immediately.

FAVORING CURRY

As the first course of a dinner for guests who love curry, these narrow, fragrant noodles are mounded into individual hillocks, and graced with a cascade of tiny bay scallops and nuggets of freshly diced tomato. The deceptively simple sauce also contains snippets of serrano chiles and cilantro—for color and snap. The sculptural arrangement of the pasta is a dramatic flourish that helps to underscore this artful blending of seafood and spice.

The recipe and menus for Curry Noodles with Scallops and Cilantro appear on page 146.

RUSTIC PIZZA

Turn on the oven, break out the beer, and set the table in the kitchen. Crisp, crusty, individual pizzas are the perfect focus of a casual meal. Whether you pick one topping, or make an assortment and share the bounty, the sight of these homey "pies" emerging bronzed and blistered from the oven is a mouth-watering signal that dinner is served.

Recipes and menus for Smoked-Salmon Pizza (bottom, right), Prosciutto and Leek Pizza on Oregano Crust (center, left), Mushroom Pizza on Prosciutto Crust (top), and Sausage and Artichoke Pizza (center, right) appear on pages 110, 112, 114, and 108.

THE FLEXIBLE MENU

COLD CATCH

It is, quite simply, a dream entrée for a steamy midsummer night: chilled seafood, refreshing vegetable-rice salad, and crackling rolls, sparked by glasses of bubbling rosé wine. Linger at the table to pursue every morsel of these lobsters simmered in chicken stock (for maximum flavor), and dip right into twin coral-colored sauces—one spiked with Armagnac; the other spiced with fresh chiles—nestled side by side in the shells.

Recipes and menus for Cold Chicken-Poached Lobster, Zucchini Rice Salad, Jalapeño Mayonnaise, Coral Sauce, and French Dinner Rolls appear on pages 270, 331, 271, 85, and 360.

ALL THAT GLITTERS

On some special occasions, nothing short of formality will do. That's the time to go for the glamor of chargers under the china, show off the silver, and set out champagne flutes. A great match for all the finery is this roasted duck, sauced with Campari (Italian orange bitters), garnished with sautéed apples, and accompanied by asparagus custards and an earthy potato gratin—a dazzling main course that is bound to make the meal a 24-carat success.

Recipes and menus for Roasted Duck with Apples and Campari, Two-Potato Gratin, and Asparagus Timbales appear on pages 289, 319, and 313.

THE FLEXIBLE MENU

CHOCOLATE SUITE

When a passion for dessert demands a creation that unites the best qualities of pastry and candy, this unique tart composed of chocolate, nuts, caramel, and cream may be the ultimate confection of its kind. Poised on an ethereal cocoa triangle, the tart needs no further embellishment. And for those who find that too much of a good thing is never enough, there are chocolate-hazelnut cookies and more *après* dessert.

Recipes and menus for The Barry Tart, Gianduia Lace Cookies, and Coconut-Lime Tuiles appear on pages 380, 386, and 440.

POBLANO CREAM

I think of this as a potent liquid spice, to be sprinkled in a thin web over food it will enhance. Use this cream cautiously—2 teaspoons will adequately season a 6- to 8-ounce portion of fish or poultry, even if the peppers are tame. However, there is virtually no way to predict whether poblanos (see page 198) will be mild or fiery until you taste the sauce. The recipe doubles easily, but if the peppers seem to sting as you are coring and seeding them (see page 200), use no more than three for a double recipe.

FLEXIBLE MENU SUGGESTIONS

This sauce accompanies the Avocado Vinaigrette (page 224). It can be a garnish for Chilaquiles (page 195), or a condiment for sliced Chili and Garlic-Rubbed Flank Steak (page 245).
Makes ¼ cup

PREPARATION: 8 MINUTES
COOKING: 15 MINUTES

2 medium poblano peppers, cored, seeded
½ cup whipping cream
Salt

1. Chop the poblanos finely and transfer them to a small saucepan. Add cream and simmer until mixture reduces to ⅓ cup, about 10 minutes.

2. Strain firmly to extract all possible liquid from the peppers; discard the solids. Adjust the seasoning of the cream with salt to taste. Sauce is ready to use warm or at room temperature. (Can cover and refrigerate 2 days.)

CITRUS SALSA

Like the Mixed Chile Salsa (page 258), this sauce has a wonderfully refreshing taste as well as terrific color when served over grilled foods. Since it contains absolutely no fat, it is the perfect counterpoint to oily, dark-fleshed grilled fish such as tuna, bluefish, or mackerel; the salsa also is superb with salmon and is delicious over grilled chicken breasts and pork tenderloins.

This recipe comes from Betsy Schultz, an outstanding cook and a native Texan, who has a way with citrus and spice. After cutting up the citrus segments, she advises, you should have about 1⅓ cups of diced orange sections, a scant ½ cup of lime sections, and 1 cup of grapefruit sections. Add enough fruit juice to moisten, but not drown, the ingredients.

FLEXIBLE MENU SUGGESTIONS

A very casual dinner can be planned around a main course of grilled fish (add swordfish, prawns, and sea scallops to the list above) and salsa. Finding a first course can be troublesome, unless you reach into the accompaniment section, garnish Corn and Jalapeño Pancakes (page 308) with sour cream, cooked crumbled chorizo sausage, and snipped chives, and serve them for a first course as you would blini, three or four per person. Otherwise, guacamole would be a good appetizer. Accompany the main course with Black Beans (page 328) and warm corn tortillas. For dessert, present Almond Soufflé Tart with Caramel Sauce (pages 414 and 444), or opt for Double Chocolate Ice Cream (page 399) and Chocolate Madeleines (page 394). *Makes about 2 cups*

PREPARATION: 30 MINUTES

2 medium navel oranges
2 small limes
1 medium pink grapefruit
2 medium radishes, trimmed
1 celery stalk, pared
1 small onion, peeled
1 to 2 serrano chiles, stemmed and seeded
2 tablespoons minced cilantro leaves
1½ teaspoons sugar
Salt

1. Peel oranges, limes, and grapefruit, completely removing the pith and membrane from the flesh. Working over a mixing bowl to catch the juices, use a paring knife to remove the sections from each side of the interior membrane. Cut the orange, grapefruit, and lime sections crosswise into ¼-inch pieces; add the sections to the bowl. Hold the membranes over the bowl and squeeze them to remove as much juice as possible.

2. Cut the radishes, celery, and onion into ⅛-inch dice and add them to the bowl. Mince and add the serrano. Stir in the cilantro, sugar, and a scant ⅛ teaspoon salt. Adjust seasoning with additional sugar as necessary. Salsa should be tart but not sour. (Can cover and refrigerate for 2 hours before serving.)

3. At serving time, bring salsa to room temperature, stir it well, and spoon ¼ cup over each portion. Serve immediately.

WINTER PESTO

Green sauces appear in numerous versions throughout the Mediterranean as accompaniments to meats, fish, vegetables, and pasta. Pesto, which originated in Italy's Liguria region, is the best known of these *salse verde,* and although this mixture does not contain basil or cheese, I call it Winter Pesto to distinguish it from other similar sauces (see page 191) that do not contain garlic.

This sauce gives grilled swordfish, tilefish, salmon, or bass (in addition to chicken or veal) a wonderful garlic-and-herb accent, but unlike pesto made with basil, it will not discolor. A heaping tablespoon (or slightly more, if you prefer) is attractive when placed in a neat mound on one side of each portion of fish.

FLEXIBLE MENU SUGGESTIONS

For a simple menu for four, start with pasta and My Favorite Tomato Sauce or Tomato-Seafood Sauce (pages 126 and 124). Serve sautéed yellow squash and Black Olive Bread (page 356) with the fish and pesto. Then end with Orange Crème Brulée (page 426), or fresh fruit and Quick Custard Sauce (page 443).

A summer menu could include cold Tomato Soup with Garlic and Basil (page 44) and cold poached salmon with the pesto, accompanied by Zucchini Rice Salad (page 331), plus Mixed Berry Cobbler (page 420) for dessert.

Another alternative is to begin with cold Three-Vegetable Terrine and Coral Sauce (pages 83 and 85). Follow with grilled bass, grouper, swordfish, or tilefish and the pesto, accompanied by Saffron Risotto or Yellow Rice (pages 170 and 327) and French Dinner Rolls (page 360). End with Pomegranate Granita (page 439).

This pesto also can be used as a dressing for potato salad, or served with Mesquite-Grilled Cornish Hens (page 240). *Makes 4 to 6 servings*

PREPARATION: 5 MINUTES

1 medium garlic clove, peeled
½ cup pine nuts
½ cup curly parsley leaves
½ cup Italian parsley leaves
½ to ¾ cup mild extra-virgin olive oil
Salt and coarsely ground black peppper

1. Insert the metal blade in a dry food processor container. Mince the garlic, then add the pine nuts and parsley; process until mixture makes a rough puree.

2. With motor on, drizzle ½ cup olive oil into machine to make a thick paste. Add ¼ teaspoon salt and 1½ teaspoons pepper. Taste and adjust the seasoning. Use the pesto immediately, or transfer it to an airtight storage container, top with remaining ¼ cup olive oil, and refrigerate until 2 hours before serving. (Can refrigerate up to 1 week.) Stir well, adjust seasoning, and serve at room temperature.

Adapted from a recipe of New York chef Gino Piserchio.

BOUILLABAISSE SAUCE

Gleaming black mussels are a gorgeous garnish for this robust butter sauce of garlic, saffron, tomato, and herbs that is reminiscent of the broth that accompanies bouillabaisse, the French fish stew. The sauce is designed to cover the entire surface of a warm dinner plate—about ¼ cup per portion is required. Grilled fish is then positioned in the center of the plate, over the sauce. Three to four mussels are placed around the fish, and the final sprinkling of parsley can go over the mussels and sauce (but not over the fish).

The base of this sauce is a *beurre blanc.* I have always found it convenient to make this in the food processor, which is unconventional. When this recipe ran in a *Cook's* magazine entertaining article, the test kitchen did a comparison of stove-top and processor methods. The testers found "no difference in taste, texture, or stability" between the two methods, and concluded that "the food processor method has the advantage of being fast, foolproof, and requiring less attention than the standard technique."

FLEXIBLE MENU SUGGESTIONS

This sauce is a natural for almost any type of grilled white-fleshed fish, or for shellfish.

Lead off a menu with Spinach Salad with Caviar and Chives (page 60). As the fish and sauce occupy most of the plate, little room is left for anything else—at most a few tiny steamed potatoes. The best accompaniment is crusty French Dinner Rolls (page 360) or French bread that can be used to soak up the sauce. Offset the richness of the sauce with a sorbet (pages 435 to 437) and Mixed Nut Sablés (page 442) for dessert.

The meal featured in *Cook's* included Scallion and Black Pepper Lasagne with Black Olive Pesto (page 144). The fish and sauce were accompanied by Rosemary Breadsticks (page 343), and followed by a mesclun salad (see page 71) with Chive Vinaigrette (page 61). Lemon Tart Brulée (page 406) made a fabulous dessert. *Makes 6 servings (1¾ cups)*

PREPARATION: 30 MINUTES
COOKING: 20 MINUTES

1 pound fresh mussels, rinsed and scrubbed
2 cups dry white wine (preferably chardonnay)
4 medium garlic cloves, unpeeled
2 shallots, peeled
⅛ teaspoon powdered saffron
⅛ teaspoon each: dried basil, dried marjoram, dried savory, dried thyme, dried sage leaves (½ teaspoon in all when mixed)
2 medium tomatoes, peeled and seeded

1½ cups hot melted unsalted butter (160 to 180 degrees)
Salt and ground black pepper
Hot red pepper sauce
3 tablespoons minced parsley

1. Remove the filaments from the sides of mussels. Put the mussels, ½ cup cold water, and ½ cup white wine in a 6-quart soup kettle. Cover and heat to boiling, then boil until mussels open, about 3 to 5 minutes; do

not overcook. Transfer mussels to a bowl with slotted spoon. (Can refrigerate overnight.)

2. Use a fine sieve lined with a coffee filter to strain mussel liquid into a medium, non-reactive saucepan. Stir in the remaining wine. Peel, crush, and add three of the garlic cloves. Slice the shallots and add to the pan, along with the saffron and the herbs; then simmer until mixture reduces to ½ to ⅔ cup. (Can cover and refrigerate reduction overnight.)

3. Coarsely chop 1 tomato. Cut the remaining tomato into ⅛-inch dice and set it aside for garnish. Peel and cut the remaining garlic clove in half.

4. Strain the sauce reduction into a saucepan or microwavable measuring cup, pressing firmly to extract all possible liquid (discard solids). Reheat the reduction to boiling (on the stove or in the microwave) and transfer it to a food processor fitted with the metal blade. Add the chopped tomato and remaining garlic clove and process until pureed. Then process, pouring the hot melted butter slowly into the reduction. Add salt, pepper, and hot red pepper sauce to taste.

5. Return sauce to a large saucepan and add the diced tomato and mussels in their shells. (Can cover with plastic and set aside at room temperature no more than 4 hours; do not refrigerate.) Stir over low heat until mussels are just hot to touch. Do not allow sauce to simmer. Adjust seasoning. Serve immediately, and garnish the sauce with the hot mussels and parsley.

In his book *The Food of France,* the late food writer Waverly Root devotes nine pages to bouillabaisse and relates the legend that this chowder "was invented by Venus to put her husband Vulcan to sleep when she had a rendezvous with Mars."

In addition to discussing lobster and mussels, two disputed ingredients, Root mentions the various Mediterranean fish used in the stew. "I know their names in French, I know what they look like, I know what they taste like—but have they any names in English?"

One of the most reliable and accurate sources of information about fish is the *Multilingual Dictionary of Fish and Fish Products,* compiled by the Organization for Economic Cooperation and Development (O.E.C.D.). The dictionary, which identifies species according to scientific names and in fifteen different languages, should be available at bookstores that specialize in culinary matters.

A SAUCY LEGEND IN ITS OWN TIME

Butter sauce based on a white-wine reduction is generally known as *beurre blanc.* Its origin is French regional cookery, rather than the classical kitchen, although this sauce has now become a restaurant standard.

Many legends exist about its origin. One holds that *beurre blanc* was created by accident around 1900, when a cook's helper in the employ of a certain Marquis de Goulaine forgot to add egg yolks to a Sauce Béarnaise —plausible enough.

White-wine butters are traditionally associated with the preparation of pike and shad, but they have become a base for a family of improvisational sauces with infinite variations based on vegetable and fruit purees, vinegars, herbs, spices, or even soy sauce.

Strictly speaking, there is no one correct recipe or method. As chef Roger Vergé points out in his book *Ma Cuisine du Soleil,* this sauce is "one of the great subjects of controversy and discussion. . . . One hundred recipes exist, all leading to the same result."

Still, the sauce is usually made in two basic steps. First, white wine is simmered (usually with shallots) until it reduces, generally by three-quarters or more; this is called the *reduction.* Then butter is whisked into the reduction—quickly or slowly. One technique calls for adding butter all at once and heating the sauce to boiling. Each method produces a slight variation in consistency, but the rule of thumb is that the faster the butter is added, the thinner the sauce will be.

This type of sauce is considered to be difficult or tricky because the emulsion, or blend of liquids, is chemically linked. Heat and physical agitation (such as whisking or processing) are essential to emulsify or hold the sauce together. If the sauce is overheated, the emulsion breaks down, causing it to separate.

Processing (or blending) can replace conventional on-the-stove whisking. The key is to be sure that hot melted butter is added slowly to the hot wine mixture. Melted butter approaches 160 to 170 degrees when the milk solids begin to foam and rise to the surface.

GRILLED CEVICHE

Fresh fish and shellfish, marinated in an acidic liquid such as citrus juice, is the major component of ceviche, the Latin American seafood cocktail. I like to pluck the fish chunks from their fruity bath and grill them on skewers, where they remain juicy and partially infused with citrus flavor. The marinade can be used as a sauce or discarded.

FLEXIBLE MENU SUGGESTIONS

The delicate flavor of the grilled fish demands a first course that will not be overpowering. Papaya-Melon Soup (page 41) is the best bet. Accompany the fish skewers with Curry Noodles (page 148), Corn and Jalapeño Pancakes (page 308), or Black Beans (page 328). Then either Mixed Berry Cobbler (page 420) or Banana Ice Cream with Caramel Sauce (pages 438 and 444) is a good ending. *Makes 4 servings*

PREPARATION: 30 MINUTES
MARINATION: 8 TO 24 HOURS
COOKING: 10 TO 12 MINUTES

MARINADE

¼ cup lightly packed cilantro leaves
½ medium onion, peeled
1 medium tomato, seeded
⅓ cup lime juice
⅓ cup orange juice
Salt
⅛ teaspoon sugar
Hot red pepper sauce
5½ tablespoons mild olive oil

BROCHETTES

1 pound boneless fish steaks (tuna, swordfish, halibut, or striped bass), cut 1-inch thick
¾ pound sea scallops (of even size), rinsed, patted dry
¾ pound medium shrimp, shelled, deveined, patted dry

1. For the marinade, coarsely chop the cilantro, onion, and tomato and transfer them to a shallow glass (or other nonreactive) dish at least 9 inches long. Stir in lime and orange juices, ¼ teaspoon salt, sugar, hot pepper sauce, and 3 tablespoons olive oil; set aside.

2. Cut the fish into cubes the size of the scallops for uniform cooking (remove and discard any fish bones).

3. Soak ten 9-inch-long bamboo skewers in hot water for 20 minutes. Leaving ½ inch at each end, thread fish pieces on the skewers as follows: scallop, shrimp (through the back to curl on skewer), fish; repeat. Add the skewers to the marinade, and turn to coat fish on all sides. Cover and refrigerate for 8 hours, turning skewers several times. (Can refrigerate overnight.)

4. Heat a grill or a broiler pan (placed 2 inches below a heat source). Brush the grill or pan with 2 teaspoons oil. Remove skewers from the dish, reserve the marinade, and pat the fish dry. Brush skewers with remaining oil. Grill or broil brochettes, 3 to 5 minutes per side (depending on size), turning once. Serve immediately on skewers with about 1 tablespoon marinade spooned alongside each portion.

SHRIMP AND SCALLOPS WITH CHILE-PEANUT SAUCE

Like a Thai or Indonesian saté, these skewers of seafood, marinated with serrano chiles, are drizzled lightly with a hot and spicy peanut sauce. While this combination may seem unusual, spice-lovers will find it to be surprisingly good.

The heat of the sauce will vary according to the piquancy of the serrano pepper, while the texture can range from creamy to pasty, depending upon the consistency of the peanut butter. I prefer a sauce that is thick, but pourable—a thin webbing of sauce should garnish the brochettes. It may be necessary to thin the sauce slightly with chicken stock.

FLEXIBLE MENU SUGGESTIONS

The brochettes lend themselves to a spicy summer menu beginning with Curried Vichyssoise (page 48). Add steamed snow peas and follow with Mixed Berry Cobbler (page 420) or Lemon Tart Brulée (page 406).

Alternately, start the menu with green salad dressed with Chive Vinaigrette (page 61), then pair brochettes with the vegetable-studded Curried Rice Stick (page 326) or plain Curry Noodles (dough recipe on page 148). Pink Grapefruit Sorbet and Coconut-Lime Tuiles (pages 435 and 440), Peach Turnover, (page 418), or Lemon Tirami Su (page 429) offer a range of choices for dessert. *Makes 4 servings*

PREPARATION: 10 MINUTES
MARINATION: 2 TO 24 HOURS
COOKING: 4 TO 6 MINUTES

BROCHETTES AND MARINADE

¾ pound medium sea scallops (of even size),
  rinsed and patted dry
¾ pound medium shrimp (with tails left on),
  shelled and deveined
Juice of 1 medium lime
1 serrano chile, stemmed, seeded, minced (or
  ½ small jalapeño)
¼ cup mild olive oil

PEANUT SAUCE

1 medium garlic clove, peeled
½ cup natural peanut butter
½ to ¾ cup Chicken Stock (page 165)
1½ teaspoons sesame oil
1½ teaspoons rice vinegar
1½ teaspoons all-purpose soy sauce
1 teaspoon hot red chili oil
1 teaspoon red-wine vinegar
¼ teaspoon cayenne pepper
Salt
¼ cup parsley leaves

1. For the brochettes and marinade, soak eight 9-inch bamboo skewers in warm water for 20 minutes. Alternate scallops and shrimp on skewers. Put lime juice, serrano, and olive oil in a glass baking dish; stir well.

Put skewers in the dish and turn to coat with marinade; cover and refrigerate. (Can refrigerate 2 hours or overnight.)

2. For the sauce, insert the metal blade in a dry food processor. Mince the garlic and add the peanut butter to the machine. Heat chicken stock to boiling and add ½ cup to the processor with the motor on. Pulse in remaining sauce ingredients, adding salt to taste (about ⅜ teaspoon if peanut butter is unsalted). Thin sauce to creamy consistency by adding chicken stock as necessary; refrigerate until cooking time. (Can cover and refrigerate overnight.)

3. Bring sauce to room temperature. Mince the parsley. Heat a grill or broiler. Grill or broil brochettes 3 to 5 minutes (depending on size), turning once. Transfer brochettes to warm dinner plates. Drizzle sauce lightly over brochettes and garnish with parsley.

A SPECIAL NOTE ABOUT INDOOR GRILLS

In order to build a wood or charcoal fire in an indoor grill, the base of the grill must be specially constructed, and an adequate ventilation system (comparable to those in restaurants) may be required. The flue or chimney must be professionally cleaned periodically to prevent the build-up of flammable lacquer. Never use wood or charcoal indoors unless you are absolutely sure your grill meets these specifications.

FIRE AND SPICE—PART TWO: BARBECUING POULTRY AND MEAT

An open fire—sputtering, hissing, and sending smoke aloft—performs magical acts of transformation as ordinary foods emerge bronzed and fragrant from its searing heat. What boiled, fried, or stewed meat can compare with the lightly charred surface of a sparerib, the crispness of tangy barbecued chicken skin, or the chewy crust of a sirloin steak? Certainly no one could forget the childish thrill of tending a marshmallow over white-hot coals until the outside blackens and the center becomes warm and gooey.

Cooking science tells us that intense heat applied to the exterior of a piece of meat actually makes it taste better by virtue of certain chemical browning reactions. This helps to explain why a charcoal-grilled steak seems superior to one that is broiled, and why barbecued lamb is so superb.

I can vividly recall, from my childhood, the air of excitement and anticipation that accompanied the prospect of meals cooked outdoors. When I was four or five, my father built a large barbecue in our backyard. Following weeks of construction—when the bricks, concrete, and a pile of sand were transformed into a stately edifice with metal doors, a grate, and a chimney—Sunday dinner became something of an event, for he was an intrepid griller.

My conviction that a natural wood fire makes a difference in the flavor of barbecued food is something I always took for granted. The notion dates back to my father's practice of using wood as fuel, something he no doubt picked up from the Mexican restaurants my family frequented during the fifties in Los Angeles.

Years later, when I taught an annual summer barbecue class, my technique of burning oak logs, floor boards, and kindling in the bellies of the three Weber kettles (which were used to cook everything from pizzas to half a baby lamb) always seemed to astonish my students.

If you have never cooked over a natural wood fire, I urge you to try. If you are reluctant, plan to begin by embellishing charcoal with aromatic wood chunks or chips. I believe that smoke from wood such as oak, mesquite, hickory, or even a few of the sweeter fruit woods improves the taste of recipes included in this chapter, as well as many other grilled foods.

To enhance the effect of the grill even further and play off the smoky taste of wood or charcoal, I like to season poultry and meats with marinades or oil-based rubs. Several are pungent and a few are downright spicy.

A terrific marinade for veal chops can be as simple as garlic oil steeped with shredded sage leaves, or as elaborate as the soy sauce-and-port wine mixture that first bathes a hickory-grilled pork loin and then is simmered to create a spirited, mahogany-colored sauce.

One of my easiest recipes calls for giving chicken pieces an overnight soak in an Oriental-style mixture chock-full of scallions and cilantro. The result is a kind of updated "teriyaki" with a particularly herbaceous kick.

Leg of lamb is a dinner party basic and the red meat of choice these days. Pick any of the lamb recipes as a point of departure for an interesting but approachable menu. Invoke the aura of Provence by rubbing lamb with minced garlic, anchovies, and herbs. Or, tenderize the meat in a melange of yogurt, ginger, cumin, cardamom, and turmeric for Indian-inspired food without the fuss. Barbecue a whole butterflied leg of lamb, or cut it into nuggets to create exotic curry-drenched kabobs skewered with green peppers and plump apricot halves.

Each recipe here offers a special taste adventure plus an opportunity to welcome guests with rustic, relaxed meals infused with the romance of fire and spice.

SOY-MARINATED CHICKEN

Fueling the Fire

MESQUITE-GRILLED CORNISH HENS

SAGE-RUBBED VEAL CHOPS

Grilling with Aromatic Woods

CHILI AND GARLIC-RUBBED FLANK STEAK

CAPRETTO WITH LEMON AND ROSEMARY

LEG OF LAMB WITH NICOISE SEASONING

The Joys of Boneless Lamb

LEG OF LAMB WITH MALAY SEASONING

LEG OF LAMB WITH ORIENTAL SEASONING

YOGURT AND SPICE-MARINATED LEG OF LAMB

SKEWERED LAMB WITH CURRY AND FRUIT

JALAPENO AND JACK CHEESE SAUSAGES

MIXED CHILE SALSA

HICKORY-GRILLED BABY BACK RIBS

BARBECUE SAUCE

SOY-MARINATED CHICKEN

Staples from the Chinese pantry—vinegar, soy sauce, and sesame oil—plus garlic, ginger, and scallions comprise a pungent marinade for easy barbecued chicken. Despite the predominance of soy sauce, the chicken fits into a variety of menus in which Eastern and Western dishes can be mixed. Consult page 208 for information on ingredients in the marinade.

FLEXIBLE MENU SUGGESTIONS

For an informal menu, begin with quickly made Cream of Watercress Soup (page 43). With the chicken, serve Sweet Potato Flans (page 324), Shoestring Vegetables with Whole-Grain Mustard (page 335), Curry Noodles, or Curried Rice Stick (pages 148 and 326). For a cool finish, add Banana Ice Cream (page 438).

Curry Noodles with Scallops and Cilantro (page 148) is a first course that sets up a more formal menu. Then steamed asparagus, plus a julienne of Red Peppers Preserved in Oil (page 339) or Snow Peas and Bell Pepper Ribbons (page 310) can accompany the chicken. End with a substantial dessert such as Chocolate-Walnut Linzer Torte (page 376) or Peach Turnover (page 418).

Spicy Homestyle Beef Soup (page 160) is a bracing Oriental-style first course. Continue the theme by serving rice and Thai-Taste Coleslaw (page 336) with the main course, then serve Black Plum Sorbet or Pink Grapefruit Sorbet (page 437 or 435) with fresh fruit and Mixed Nut Sablés (page 442) for dessert. *Makes 6 to 8 servings*

PREPARATION: 20 MINUTES
MARINATION: 24 HOURS
COOKING: 25 TO 35 MINUTES

3 medium garlic cloves, peeled
1 chunk (1½ inches) fresh ginger, peeled
¼ cup packed stemmed cilantro (or parsley) leaves
4 medium scallions, roots removed
¾ cup all-purpose soy sauce
¼ cup Chicken Stock (page 165)
½ cup sugar
¼ cup vegetable oil
2 tablespoons dark soy sauce
2 tablespoons Chinese red vinegar, sherry vinegar, or red-wine vinegar

3 tablespoons sesame oil
½ cup dry sherry or Shaohsing wine
Ground white pepper
4 pounds chicken legs and thighs (or 2 small frying chickens, cut into serving pieces)

1. Mince the garlic, ginger, and cilantro, and coarsely chop the scallions. Transfer ingredients to a large nonreactive roasting pan or to a plastic container.

2. Stir in the soy sauce, chicken stock, sugar, vegetable oil, dark soy, vinegar, sesame oil, sherry or wine, and ¼ teaspoon pepper. Add the chicken pieces and turn to coat them in the marinade. Cover and refrigerate the chicken, turning once, overnight, or up to 24 hours.

3. At cooking time, remove the chicken from its marinade; pat the pieces dry. Put chicken on a hot grill, cover, and cook (basting occasionally with marinade) until juices run clear when thickest part of thighs are pierced with a fork, usually 20 to 25 minutes depending on heat of fire. (Or, adjust broiler rack to 3 inches below heat source. Broil, turning once, and test as described above after 20 minutes.) Serve immediately.

FUELING THE FIRE

Creating a natural wood fire in a barbecue is no more difficult than using charcoal. During the renovation of my house in Chicago, a surplus of unvarnished oak floor boards became my regular barbecue fuel. Later, I was astounded to learn that oak floor boards are used at a Parisian restaurant celebrated for its grilled and roasted food. Today, many restaurants that feature food cooked in wood-burning ovens regularly use oak.

If you can secure them, small oak logs or boards make the best fires and give food a fabulous flavor. Alternately, oak chunks (available in many hardware stores), in combination with charcoal, will greatly improve flavor on the grill.

To start a fire, tightly crumple whole sheets of newspaper and pack them into a snug layer on the bottom grill shelf, until the layer begins to buckle and the shelf is full. Top off the pile with twigs (and charcoal if you are using it). Pack the twigs and charcoal tightly, since it will shift slightly, creating air drafts, as the paper burns away. Put logs or wood close together over the twigs and charcoal.

Wood fires burn hotter and faster than charcoal fires. Light the paper and step back. Initially, flames will be much higher than is normal for charcoal.

While I prefer natural wood barbecues, charcoal is the most popular fuel, whether it is used alone or in combination with wood logs, chunks, chips, vines, or herbs. However, I believe it is best to avoid briquettes that contain harmful chemical binders. Those bound with food-grade corn or wheat starch are better—look for labeling that indicates this type of "natural" binder.

I also start charcoal with crumpled newspapers and dry twigs, or with an electric starter. I believe that chemical charcoal-lighting fluid is a health hazard. I never use it, nor do I recommend using it to light a barbecue.

Prescribing the ideal size and duration of a barbecue fire is difficult, since these will vary with fuel, weather, and type of grill, as well as the amount of food being cooked. However, dry wood and small logs or chunks can stoke a fire as the initial mass burns down.

Once the fire starts, watch it carefully until the wood or coals begins to burn. A hot fire gives off a red glow and low flames. A medium fire has a red glow and no flame, and the coals or wood will be covered with white ash.

The heat of the fire can be adjusted conveniently in a Weber grill or other kettle-type barbecues by adjusting the vents in the cover and in the bottom of the drum.

A covered barbecue can be improvised by enclosing food in a tent of heavy-duty aluminum foil, or covering it with a disposable aluminum-foil turkey-roasting pan. Be sure the foil is vented so the fire does not go out, and feel your way on cooking times, which may vary from the times indicated in recipes.

If you are improvising a covered barbecue and also want to use damp wood chips on the fire, add the chips slowly and be sure there is a smoke build-up before covering the food.

MESQUITE-GRILLED CORNISH HENS

The full-blown taste of mesquite can be transferred to poultry (or meats) by barbecuing on a covered grill and stoking the coals of a red-hot fire with damp mesquite wood chips—these hens emerge deeply bronzed from the billows of fragrant wood smoke.

The hens can be grilled over other fuels, or in a conventional oven, and brushing them with Herbed Oil (page 73) will help to enrich the oven-roasted flavor. Splitting the hens down the back and opening them flat prevents them from rolling on the grill and makes them easy to handle and serve. Since this method also permits heat to penetrate evenly from both sides, the legs seem to cook faster, and the breast meat remains juicy.

FLEXIBLE MENU SUGGESTIONS

Either Beet-Salad Mimosa (page 59) or cold Three-Vegetable Terrine with Coral Sauce (pages 83 and 85) will give a polished start to a barbecue meal (about half the terrine will be left over). Since each of the hens takes up most of a dinner plate, accompaniments can be minimal. After the salad, corn on the cob would be appropriate, and Cheddar-Cumin Rolls (page 362) also could be served. Following the terrine, pair the hens with French Potato Salad (page 332); Winter Pesto (page 227) could be added as a sauce. Choose between Mixed Berry Cobbler (page 420), Peach Turnover (page 418), or Espresso-Brownie Chunk Ice Cream (page 397) for dessert.

Avocado, Grapefruit, and Seafood Salad (page 58) or Papaya-Melon Soup (page 41) are two first courses for informal menus. The soup yields four servings (to serve eight, double the soup and add two hens). Following a fruit-based first course, the hens are good with spicy Corn and Jalapeño Pancakes (page 308) or Black Beans (page 328), and American in Paris Biscuits (page 366). Ultra-Fudge Brownies (page 395) served with fresh raspberries are one good dessert possibility; others include Double Chocolate Ice Cream with Instant Hot Fudge Sauce (pages 399 and 401) or Chocolate-Walnut Linzer Torte (page 376).

A highly styled menu could begin with Mixed Lettuces with Shrimp and Ginger-Lime Vinaigrette (page 68), followed by the hens, served with Yellow Rice (page 327). Crème Brulée (page 426) provides a luscious ending.

Another approach is to omit a first course and offer Two-Cheese Quesadillas (page 448). Then put a substantial salad such as Potato Salad Puttanesca (page 334), Quinoa Tabbouleh (page 330), or Rosemary-Roasted Potato Salad (page 333) with the hens, and complete the menu with any dessert suggested for the menus above. *Makes 6 servings*

PREPARATION: 20 MINUTES
COOKING: 40 TO 60 MINUTES

6 rock Cornish hens (about 1 pound each),
  cleaned
2 tablespoons olive oil, or Herbed Oil
  (page 73)
Salt and ground black pepper

1. Soak 3 cups mesquite chips in water as package directs; drain well and set aside until cooking time.

2. To remove backbones from hens, put them breast-side down with legs pointing toward you. With poultry shears or a cleaver, cut through tail and split hens down the backs, then cut away center backbones (set bones aside for use in stock or discard).

3. Rinse, drain, and pat hens dry. Put hens, skin-side up, on work surface; flatten by pressing on breastbones with your palm. Rub the hens with olive oil and sprinkle all over with salt and pepper. Refrigerate until cooking time.

4. When grill fire is hot, add the drained mesquite chips. Put the hens flat on the grill. Cover and grill 25 minutes. Then check for doneness every 5 minutes until juices run clear when the thickest part of the thigh is pierced with a metal skewer, about 10 to 15 minutes longer. (Alternately, put hens flat on two jelly-roll pans. Preheat oven to 425 degrees. Roast 20 minutes, reduce heat to 375 degrees, then start testing for doneness after another 30 minutes as described above.) Serve immediately.

SAGE-RUBBED VEAL CHOPS

Grapevine shards, added to the barbecue, will round out the flavor of these very simple chops. Other pungent herbs, such as summer or winter savory, or rosemary, can be substituted for sage and will not cook away in contact with the intense heat of the grill.

The veal chops—veritable menu workhorses—are compatible with nearly all the Italian-inspired foods (see below). This recipe is similarly adaptable. To vary the number of servings, simply adjust the number of chops you purchase.

FLEXIBLE MENU SUGGESTIONS

Either of the mozzarella salads (pages 62 and 66) or Spinach Salad with Caviar and Chives (page 60) is a good opener. Follow with the veal and Bistro Potatoes (page 322) or Scallion and Black Pepper noodles (page 140). For dessert, try Gianduia Cheesecake (page 384), Dome Cake (page 388), or Double Chocolate Ice Cream (page 399).

A heftier menu would start with Milanese Asparagus Soup (page 162). Serve Tomato Pasta (page 128), Stuffed Tomatoes (page 312), or Italian Baked Vegetables (page 306) with the veal, and any dessert suggested above.

After Onion and Chèvre Tart (page 104), pare side dishes down to something as simple as steamed spinach or carrots tossed with Balsamic Butter (page 311), and bake Prosciutto Bread (page 354) or Tomato Flatbread with Two Herbs (page 346). Finish with Almond and Lemon-Stuffed Pears (page 431) or Apple Crisp (page 424).

The following pastas (pages 124 to 145) make hearty first courses: Pasta with Tomato-Seafood Sauce, Pasta with Four Cheeses, Pasta with Broccoli Raab, Spinach and Herb Pasta with Goat-Cheese Sauce, Scallion and Goat-Cheese Agnolotti, or Scallion and Black Pepper Lasagne with Black Olive Pesto. If the pasta includes tomato sauce, accompany the veal with a steamed green or yellow vegetable, and follow with Milanese Fruit Tart or Lemon Tirami Su (pages 408 and 429). For the pastas with creamy sauces, or very little or no tomato, serve Stuffed Tomatoes (page 312) with the veal, then follow with the tart (above) or Almond and Lemon-Stuffed Pears (page 431).

Since Lemon-Garlic Capellini with Mediterranean Sauce (page 150), which makes six appetizer servings, is a hot-cold dish, plan to serve hot broccoli tossed with Balsamic Butter (page 311) with the veal. Then add Espresso-Brownie Chunk Ice Cream (page 397), fruit and Gianduia Lace Cookies (page 386), or Chocolate-Walnut Linzer Torte (page 376).

Risotto (pages 166 to 177) as an appetizer eliminates the need for starch with the main course, but take care not to repeat vegetables. Following Saffron Risotto or Shrimp and Curry Risotto, consider steamed spinach, pea pods, green beans, broccoli, or Snow Pea and Bell Pepper Ribbons (page 310) with the chops. Substitute carrots after Risotto Spinacciola, or Stuffed Tomatoes (page 312) after Country-Style Risotto. Milanese Fruit Tart (which has minimal custard, page 408), the pears (above), or Pomegranate Granita (page 439) adds a light ending.

The affinity between prosciutto and veal makes wedges of Mushroom Pizzas with Prosciutto Crust (page 114) a natural first course. Serve the veal with steamed broccoli, spinach, carrots, or pea pods. For dessert, add Chocolate Truffle Cake, Gianduia Cheesecake, or Chocolate Roulade (pages 382, 384, and 392)—you may find that the first two courses are surprisingly light. *Makes 6 servings*

PREPARATION: 15 MINUTES
COOKING: 10 MINUTES

¾ *cup mild olive oil or Herbed Oil (page 73)*
⅓ *cup thinly julienned fresh sage leaves*
   (loosely packed)
4 *medium garlic cloves, peeled*
6 *veal rib chops, each cut 1-inch thick, well*
   trimmed
Salt and ground black pepper

1. In a shallow, nonreactive baking dish, stir together the oil and sage. Mince and stir in the garlic. Trim veal chops carefully (excess fat causes flare-ups on grill or broiler, which can cause chops to burn). Add veal chops and turn to coat them evenly with the marinade. Set dish aside, covered, at room temperature up to 4 hours. (Can refrigerate in marinade 2 days.)

2. Prepare fire in the grill, or heat the broiler. For the grill, soak grapevine or wood chips in cold water to cover, 15 to 30 minutes; drain. When fire is ready, scatter chips or vines on top.

3. Remove chops, reserving marinade. Pat chops dry with paper towels to remove excess oil and sprinkle them lightly with salt and pepper. Grill (or broil) 4 to 5 minutes per side, or until juices run pink, for medium-rare. Brush lightly with reserved oil from the marinade before serving.

GRILLING WITH AROMATIC WOODS

Of all the natural fuels, *mesquite,* with its rich, pungent smoke, imparts the most distinctive taste to food. A hardwood tree indigenous to the arid American Southwest and Mexico, mesquite can be found in logs, chunks, chips, and charcoal.

Most commercially packaged mesquite is sold as heat-dried chunks or chips. When dry, chunks and chips burn quickly on a hot fire, adding a light mesquite flavor to food. If chunks or chips are soaked in water and drained before burning, they emit a fragrant, dense smoke that permeates food with the maximum flavor of this wood. I am an enthusiastic fan of mesquite barbecue, particularly for cooking shellfish, pork, veal, lamb, baby goat, or beef.

Hickory, in the form of chunks or chips, gives food a familiar sweet taste often associated with Southern barbecue. Like mesquite, hickory chips and chunks can be added wet or dry to a hot fire. I prefer to restrict the use of hickory chips to pork, since I find it overpowers poultry and is slightly too assertive for beef.

Fruitwood chips, such as *apple* or *elder,* tend to make foods very sweet, which makes them best for chicken and pork.

Dried grapevine cuttings (often called *grapesmoke* or *sarments de la vigne*) have long been used—particularly where grapes are grown—to impart a delicate fruity flavor to foods. Dried vine cuttings are far less assertive than wood chunks or chips. When used dry, they provide an initial boost of heat, followed by light smoke, and I recommend trying them for veal, lamb, poultry, fish, and vegetables.

Dried mixed herbs (page 105), dried citrus rinds, and fruitwood scraps also can be added to the barbecue to obtain a range of sweet, subtle tastes.

TIPS ON CHIPS

Be certain woods used on the barbecue are unvarnished, and that they have not been sprayed with chemicals.

For maximum flavor, soak wood chips as the package directs, then drain them for half an hour. Add damp chips carefully to avoid extinguishing a fire. You have added a sufficient quantity when a good veil of smoke rises.

Be sure to stand downwind after adding wood chips to a fire. Otherwise, your clothing can take on the same odors as the food!

Chips, chunks, and logs are available in hardware stores, supermarkets, and specialty food stores, as well as from wood dealers. In addition, here are some special sources.

Mesquite chips are available from Lazzari Fuel Co., Box 34051, San Francisco, CA 94134, 415-467-2970.

Kitchen Bazaar, 4401 Connecticut Ave., N.W., Washington, DC 20008, 202-244-1550, carries mesquite and hickory chips and chunks.

Weber-Stephens, makers of covered grills, distributes 7½-pound bags of mesquite, natural oak, and hickory chunks to stores that carry their grills and accessories.

CHILI AND GARLIC-RUBBED FLANK STEAK

Adding soaked, drained, mesquite chips to the grill gives the steak an assertive, smoky flavor that is underscored by the Tex-Mex-inspired seasoning rub; use dry chips for a less pronounced mesquite taste. Or, grill the steak over a plain wood or charcoal fire—it cooks quickly, slices into lovely strips, and is great stuffed into warm flour or corn tortillas.

FLEXIBLE MENU SUGGESTIONS

For a three-course menu, start with Avocado, Grapefruit, and Seafood Salad (page 58), then serve Mixed Chile Salsa (page 258), Yellow Rice (page 327), and Black Beans (page 328) with the steak. Or, replace rice and beans with Corn and Jalapeño Pancakes (page 308) and French Potato Salad (page 332). Espresso-Brownie Chunk Ice Cream (page 397) will stylishly offset the heat and spice.

This steak also can be the focus of a taco dinner by changing accompaniments. Start with guacamole and corn chips; then, in addition to warm flour or corn tortillas, present the steak with salsa (above) or Poblano Cream (page 225), sliced tomatoes, and shredded lettuce.

If you prefer grilled sandwiches to tacos, make Cheddar-Cumin Rolls (page 362). Pass wedges of Two-Cheese Quesadillas (page 448) while the steak cooks, then give it a sprinkling of fresh lime juice as it comes off the grill. Spread the rolls with hot or flavored mustard. Double Chocolate Ice Cream (page 399) with Instant Hot Fudge Sauce (page 401), the espresso ice cream (above), Ultra-Fudge Brownies (page 395), or Gianduia Cheesecake (page 384) are dessert options for a taco or sandwich menu. *Makes 4 to 6 servings*

PREPARATION: 20 MINUTES
MARINATION: 4 TO 24 HOURS
COOKING: 15 MINUTES

1 flank steak (about 2½ pounds), trimmed
2 medium garlic cloves, peeled
2 tablespoons olive oil
1 tablespoon mild chili powder
½ teaspoon ground cumin
Salt

1. With a sharp knife, score steak lightly at 1-inch intervals. Mince the garlic and mix with the oil, chili powder, and cumin in a flat nonreactive dish large enough to hold the steak. Rub the mixture all over the steak; sprinkle with salt. (Cover and refrigerate 4 to 24 hours.)

2. Heat a grill (or broiler). Soak, drain, and add mesquite chips to the grill when the coals are white-hot (or use chips dry). Grill (or broil) steak 5 to 7 minutes per side for medium-rare. Slice thinly across the grain. Serve immediately.

CAPRETTO WITH LEMON AND ROSEMARY

Don't be put off by the idea of cooking baby goat (*capretto* in Italian). Its flavor is similar to (and often mistaken for) lamb, and it is just as easy to prepare. This recipe comes from Nicola Civetta, of Primavera Restaurant in New York, where baby goat is a specialty of the house. In fact, it is such a popular main course, this recipe was featured in one of my entertaining articles for *New York* magazine.

The goats weigh 12 to 14 pounds and can be purchased at specialty meat markets or ethnic markets in Greek, Latin, or Italian neighborhoods. Ask the butcher to saw the meat into 3-inch pieces and remove (and keep) the head. Goat has an aroma that is slightly stronger than lamb when raw, but it disappears with marination.

Apart from the loin chops, there are just scraps of meat on many of the bones. Since a considerable amount of trimming is required, you will need the full 10 pounds of meat called for in the recipe.

FLEXIBLE MENU SUGGESTIONS

Capretto can be substituted in any of the menus for Sage-Rubbed Veal Chops (page 242).

For a fall meal that begins with Wild Mushroom Soup (page 49), serve colorful Italian Baked Vegetables (page 306) with the capretto. Prosciutto Bread (page 354) is a splendid addition to the menu, and Almond and Lemon-Stuffed Pears (page 431) are a light dessert to offset the creamy soup. If the bread is omitted from the menu, consider making Rustic Apple Tart (page 410) for dessert.

For a more formal meal, start with Three-Vegetable Terrine (page 83) served hot, with Tomato-Basil Sauce (you will need a double recipe, page 267). Since the appetizer has a rich sauce as well as abundant vegetables, add roasted potatoes to the main course, then offer a mixed green salad tossed with My Favorite Vinaigrette (page 72). For a more abbreviated menu, serve Polenta Diamonds (page 450) in place of the appetizer, and Potato Salad Puttanesca (page 334) with the goat. End either menu with Dome Cake (page 388) or Milanese Fruit Tart (page 408).

Although there will be several portions left over, Two Soups in One Bowl (page 52) makes a stunning first course. Stuffed Tomatoes (page 312), Bistro Potatoes (make a double recipe, page 322), and Black Olive Bread (page 356) will be good with the main course. For dessert, the options include Classic or Milanese Fruit Tart (pages 416 and 408), Lemon Tart Brulée (page 406), Chocolate Macadamia Torte (page 374), or The Barry Tart (page 380).

For a pasta or risotto first course, choose between Pasta with Tomato-Seafood Sauce (page 124), Scallion and Black Pepper Lasagne with Black Olive Pesto (page 144), or Saffron Risotto (page 170). Serve the goat with Snow Pea and Bell Pepper Ribbons (page 310) or steamed spinach. To the dessert list of fruit tarts, pears, or the Dome Cake included in other menus (above), add Lemon Tirami Su (page 429). *Makes 6 to 8 servings*

PREPARATION: 20 MINUTES
MARINATION: 2 TO 24 HOURS
COOKING: 15 TO 20 MINUTES

3 medium garlic cloves, peeled
3 fresh rosemary sprigs (about 2½ inches
long), plus additional rosemary sprigs
Salt and ground black pepper
Juice of 2 medium lemons
½ cup dry white wine
½ cup mild pure olive oil
10 pounds baby goat with bones, cut in 3-inch
chunks

1. Mince the garlic. Strip rosemary leaves off the branches and chop the rosemary finely. Mix the garlic, rosemary, ¼ teaspoon salt, ¼ teaspoon pepper, lemon juice, wine, and olive oil in a nonreactive baking dish that will hold the meat in a single layer (or divide ingredients and use two dishes).

2. Trim goat pieces to remove the tough skinlike fell and excess fat. Put the goat in the marinade, and turn to coat all the pieces. Let stand 2 to 3 hours. (Can cover and refrigerate overnight.)

3. Heat the barbecue (or heat a grill or broiler on highest setting). Barbecue (or broil) meat in batches, turning as necessary, until it is tender and medium rare, about 10 to 15 minutes. Transfer meat to a roasting pan, and keep it warm (uncovered) in a 250-degree oven until all the meat is cooked. Serve immediately, garnished with whole rosemary sprigs.

"There's rosemary,
that's for remembrance...
and there is pansies,
that's for thoughts."

—SHAKESPEARE

LEG OF LAMB WITH NICOISE SEASONING

In the south of France, the trio of garlic, anchovies, and herbs is often used in conjunction with lamb. This paste gives the meat a natural affinity for other foods with Provençal seasonings, yet it does not restrict menus from crossing the border into Italy.

FLEXIBLE MENU SUGGESTIONS

Cold Salt-Cod Terrine with Tomato, Garlic, and Black Olive Sauce (pages 88 and 89) highlights the Provençal spirit of the lamb. Add a double recipe of Bistro Potatoes (page 322) and a green vegetable to the main course, and end with Lemon-Praline Soufflé Glacé (page 433).

Onion and Chèvre Tart (page 104) is another logical first-course choice. Accompany the lamb with Stuffed Tomatoes (page 312) and *haricots verts,* then serve Almond and Lemon-Stuffed Pears (page 431) for dessert.

A fairly formal menu (which can stretch to ten servings if the lamb leg is large) begins with hot Three-Vegetable Terrine (page 83) and Tomato-Basil Sauce (page 267). Serve Two-Potato Gratin (page 319) and a julienne of red and yellow peppers with the main course; add French Dinner Rolls (page 360) if time permits. Almond and Lemon-Stuffed Pears (page 431) will cut the richness of the terrine and potatoes (you would need a double recipe), whereas Chocolate Macadamia Torte (page 374) would add opulence (and easily serve ten).

Colorful Four-Vegetable Tart (page 100) makes vegetables and potatoes or rice redundant with the main course. In this case, turn to the exotic Mixed Grains (page 325) as a match for the lamb. Lemon-Praline Soufflé Glacé (page 433) or Lemon Tirami Su (page 429) adds a finishing flourish without competing with the delicate pastry in the first course.

Mozzarella salad, hot or cold (pages 66 or 62), is a good beginning for a warm-weather menu. Follow with French Potato Salad (page 332) or Rosemary-Roasted Potato Salad (page 333), whether the lamb is served hot or at room temperature. Add Mixed Berry Cobbler (page 420) or fresh berries for dessert.

A dinner late in the spring is right in season with Milanese Asparagus Soup (page 162). Add Bistro Potatoes (page 322) and steamed carrots tossed in Balsamic Butter (page 311) to the main course. Lemon Tart Brulée (page 406) balances the menu beautifully.

Pasta with Tomato-Seafood Sauce (page 124), Scallion and Goat-Cheese Agnolotti (page 142), Scallion and Black Pepper Lasagne (page 144), Pasta with Broccoli Raab (page 134), or Lemon-Garlic Capellini with Mediterranean Sauce (page 150) are filling first courses in the Italian spirit. After the Broccoli Raab or the Mediterranean Sauce, add a tossed green salad with My Favorite Vinaigrette or Lemon-Basil Vinaigrette (pages 72 and 74) family-style to the plate with the sliced lamb. Zucchini or eggplant can be sliced lengthwise, brushed with Herbed Oil (page 73), and grilled lightly to accompany the lamb after the pasta with tomato sauces. Follow with Espresso-Brownie Chunk Ice Cream (page 397), Double Chocolate Ice Cream and Bittersweet Chocolate Sauce (pages 399 and 400), or if the pasta is not too rich, with Lemon Tirami Su (page 429). *Makes paste for 1 leg of lamb (6 to 8 pounds)*

2 medium garlic cloves, peeled
¼ cup firmly packed parsley leaves
5 medium anchovies, rinsed, patted dry
½ teaspoon dried mixed herbs: marjoram or
    savory, oregano, and rosemary in equal
    amounts (or 2 teaspoons minced mixed
    fresh herbs)
Salt and ground black pepper
⅓ cup olive oil or Herbed Oil (page 73)

1. Mince garlic, parsley, and anchovies by adding them to a food processor fitted with the metal blade, with the motor on.

2. Add the herbs, ¼ teaspoon salt (depending on the saltiness of the anchovies), and ⅛ teaspoon pepper. Process, slowly adding oil to the mixture in the machine. Paste is ready to use (see page 249).

THE JOYS OF BONELESS LAMB

Boned, butterflied leg of lamb, rubbed with pungent seasonings and barbecued to medium rare, is a joy to cook and savor and is as easy to slice as a steak.

Any one of three seasoning pastes (pages 248 to 251) is sufficient to cover a 6- to 8-pound lamb leg with a thin blanket of flavor. After refrigerating the seasoned meat overnight (it should be placed in a nonreactive—glass, enamel, or porcelain —dish), bring it to room temperature at least 2 hours before cooking.

Skewers may be inserted horizontally into various sections of the leg to keep the lamb perfectly flat and prevent thin areas of the meat from curling on the barbecue. Use metal skewers, or long, wooden skewers that have been soaked for 30 minutes in warm water.

On a hot barbecue (or in a broiler about 3 inches from the heat source), it will take approximately 20 to 25 minutes for the thickest section of a boned, butterflied leg of lamb to cook. Check the temperature after 20 minutes, and every 5 minutes thereafter. Removing lamb at 125 degrees will ensure that it arrives rare at table; remove it at 130 degrees for medium-rare.

As the meat will continue to cook, and the temperature will rise slightly after removing it from the barbecue, you can let the lamb stand (loosely covered with foil) for 5 to 8 minutes before slicing.

In order to capture the lovely natural juices and spoon them over the meat, be sure to slice the lamb on a carving board with a well, on a warm platter, or on a foil-lined cutting board.

The best carving utensil is a long, sharp, flexible knife. To make the widest possible slices, hold the knife at a slight diagonal to the meat while slicing, and be sure to slice across the grain. Barbecued lamb may be served hot or cold.

LEG OF LAMB WITH MALAY SEASONING

The notion of using seasoning pastes on meat began with this recipe, which my friend, Lindy Grobler, and I concocted one icy winter weekend when we were determined to barbecue a butterflied leg of lamb. We whirled a small quantity of ingredients we had on hand—garlic, spices, and oil—together in the food processor and rubbed them on the meat. The spicing was sensational, and the crust that formed on the surface of the cooked meat helped to keep it especially succulent.

FLEXIBLE MENU SUGGESTIONS

Strong Malay-style spicing dictates soothing or refreshing first courses and desserts to balance menus. Sweet Potato and Apple Bisque (page 45), Avocado, Grapefruit, and Seafood Salad (page 58), or Mixed Lettuces with Shrimp and Ginger-Lime Vinaigrette (page 68) are good first-course choices.

After the soup, Stuffed Tomatoes (page 312) and a steamed green vegetable can accompany the lamb. Following either salad, consider Two-Potato Gratin (page 319) and Asparagus Timbales or Potato Croquettes (page 313 or 320), and steamed carrots or yellow squash. Mixed Plum Chutney (page 338) makes a lovely garnish. Adding Cheddar-Cumin Rolls (page 362) will reinforce the spicing in the lamb.

For dessert select the Almond Soufflé Tart (page 414), Classic Fruit Tart (page 416), or if one of the salads is served first, the big Rustic Apple Tart (page 410). *Makes paste for 1 leg of lamb (6 to 8 pounds)*

PREPARATION: 5 MINUTES

2 medium garlic cloves, peeled
1½ tablespoons ground cumin
1 tablespoon medium chili powder
1 tablespoon medium or hot curry powder
  (page 147)
Salt
⅓ cup olive oil or Herbed Oil (page 73)

Mince garlic by dropping it into a food processor fitted with the metal blade, with the motor on. Add cumin, chili powder, curry powder, ¼ teaspoon salt, and 1 tablespoon oil. Process, pouring the remaining oil slowly into the machine. Paste is ready to rub over butterflied lamb (see page 249).

LEG OF LAMB WITH ORIENTAL SEASONING

Chinese oyster sauce and soy sauce are the dominant flavors in this paste. Because each is sufficiently salty, no additional salt is required. For information on Chinese ingredients, see page 208.

FLEXIBLE MENU SUGGESTIONS

Begin one East-West menu with Avocado, Grapefruit, and Seafood Salad (page 58), then pair the lamb with colorful hot Curried Rice Stick noodles (page 326). Orange Crème Brulée (page 426) or Banana Ice Cream (page 438) with Caramel Sauce (page 444) are compatible desserts.

Mixed Lettuces with Shrimp and Ginger-Lime Vinaigrette (page 68) is another good cross-cultural opener. Add Yellow Rice (page 327) and Snow Pea and Bell Pepper Ribbons (page 310) to the main course, then top off the meal with Lemon-Praline Soufflé Glacé (page 433).

For a one-dish barbecue menu, serve Thai-Taste Coleslaw (page 336) and corn on the cob with the lamb; add Mixed Berry Cobbler (page 420) for dessert. *Makes seasoning for 1 leg of lamb (6 to 8 pounds)*

PREPARATION: 5 MINUTES

1 quarter-size slice fresh ginger, peeled
2 medium garlic cloves, peeled
¼ teaspoon ground coriander seed
¼ teaspoon ground black pepper
2 teaspoons Dijon mustard
1 teaspoon dry sherry or Shaohsing wine
1 teaspoon sesame oil
1 teaspoon hot red pepper oil
2 tablespoons all-purpose soy sauce
1 tablespoon Chinese oyster sauce
¼ cup peanut or vegetable oil

Mince the ginger and the garlic in a food processor fitted with the metal blade by adding them to the machine with the motor on. Add the remaining ingredients and process until thoroughly mixed. Paste is ready to use (see page 249).

YOGURT AND SPICE-MARINATED LEG OF LAMB

A marinade of yogurt and spices often is used by Indian chefs for foods cooked in the tandoor, the Indian-style clay oven. The natural acidity in yogurt acts as a meat tenderizer and a flavor enhancer. Apply the mixture to a barbecued, butterflied leg of lamb, and the result is velvety lamb with a lovely, spicy crust, whether the meat is served hot or cold.

This recipe calls for some little-used spices which I always seem to have left over from other recipes—in fact, I designed the spice mixture specifically to deplete an overabundant and underutilized supply of ground coriander, cardamom, and cumin.

FLEXIBLE MENU SUGGESTIONS

A menu for six can begin with Fennel-Leek Soup (page 52). Along with the lamb, serve Yellow Rice (page 327), Apple-Pear Chutney (page 337), Tomato-Onion Salad (page 203), and Slivered Cucumbers (page 203). Finish the meal with Crème Brulée (page 426) or Banana Ice Cream (page 438).

Curried Vichyssoise (page 48) is a great cold appetizer that eliminates the need to serve rice or potatoes with the lamb. Instead, try Shoestring Vegetables with Whole-Grain Mustard (page 335) or Quinoa Tabbouleh (page 330), plus Almond Soufflé Tart (page 414).

Curry Noodles with Scallops and Cilantro (page 146) is a practical appetizer for four. For a menu serving six, either Shrimp and Curry Risotto (page 166), Wild and Brown Rice Soup (page 50), or Sweet Potato and Apple Bisque (page 45) is suggested. Present the lamb with one of the chutneys (page 337 or 338) and Snow Peas and Bell Pepper Ribbons (page 310); substitute Asparagus Timbales (page 313) after the noodles. End with Lemon Tart Brulée (page 406).

For a casual menu that begins with Avocado, Grapefruit, and Seafood Salad (page 58), serve cold, sliced lamb sandwiches on French Dinner Rolls (page 360) or Cheddar-Cumin Rolls (page 362). Follow with a dessert such as Lemon Tirami Su (page 429) or Banana Ice Cream (page 438).

A cold meal for eight could begin with a double recipe of Papaya-Melon Soup (page 41). Serve the lamb cold with Quinoa Tabbouleh (page 330) and Cheddar-Cumin Rolls (page 362). Then add fresh fruit with Quick Custard Sauce (page 443) and Coconut-Lime Tuiles (page 440). *Makes 6 to 8 servings*

PREPARATION: 20 MINUTES
MARINATION: 24 TO 48 HOURS
COOKING: 30 TO 35 MINUTES

2 medium garlic cloves, peeled
1-inch cube ginger (1/2 ounce), peeled
1 small onion, peeled
1 1/2 teaspoons dried oregano leaves
1 teaspoon ground cumin
1/2 teaspoon ground coriander
1/2 teaspoon chili powder
1/2 teaspoon turmeric
1/4 teaspoon ground cardamom
1 1/2 cups plain yogurt
3 tablespoons olive or vegetable oil
Salt and ground black pepper
1 leg of lamb (6 to 8 pounds), boned,
*   butterflied, trimmed*

1. Mince the garlic and ginger, chop the onion, and transfer the ingredients to a bowl. Stir remaining ingredients (except lamb) into the marinade, including 1 teaspoon salt and 1/4 teaspoon black pepper.

2. Open the leg of lamb flat and insert 4 metal skewers (or soak 9-inch bamboo skewers in cold water 30 minutes before insertion) horizontally into the meat to prevent it from curling during cooking. Pour half the marinade into a nonreactive baking dish. Add the lamb and the remaining marinade. Cover and refrigerate overnight. (Can refrigerate up to 48 hours.)

3. Heat the barbecue (or a broiler with the broiler tray in place for 10 minutes). Shake the excess marinade off the lamb and put it on the barbecue (or under the broiler). Cook until the internal temperature registers 125 degrees (for rare) or 130 degrees (for medium-rare) in the thickest section of the meat. Let the meat stand for about 5 minutes after removing from the barbecue (or broiler). Slice it thinly; serve immediately.

"Yogurt has always been a guardian of good health."

—YAMUNA DEVI

SKEWERED LAMB WITH CURRY AND FRUIT

Once again, curry takes center stage in a sweet, hot, and sour marinade that is cooked with chicken stock to become a palate-searing sauce for the brochettes. The vegetables grilled with nuggets of skewered lamb—red onions, green peppers, and dried apricot halves—make this a colorful centerpiece for an informal dinner.

FLEXIBLE MENU SUGGESTIONS

Because the skewers are served atop the spicy sauce, mixed green salad with Ginger-Lime Vinaigrette (page 69) is a good opener. Then serve brochettes with Yellow Rice (page 327) and curry condiments—Slivered Cucumbers (page 203), Banana Relish (page 202), and Mixed Plum Chutney (page 338)—for a play of color and flavor. Or, the skewers can be served with the rice and Black Beans (page 328), or simply with Quinoa Tabbouleh (page 330) and warm pita bread. Following the curry, opt for a soothing dessert. Crème Brulée (page 426) or the creamy Lemon-Praline Soufflé Glacé (page 433) are good choices. *Makes 4 to 6 servings*

PREPARATION: 50 MINUTES
MARINATION: 24 TO 48 HOURS
COOKING: 35 MINUTES

MARINADE

*1 serrano or jalapeño chile, stemmed, halved,
   seeded*
3 medium garlic cloves, peeled
2 medium onions, peeled
*1½ tablespoons hot or mild curry powder
   (page 147)*
½ teaspoon ground coriander
½ teaspoon turmeric
1 tablespoon brown sugar
2 bay leaves
⅓ cup lime juice
½ cup vegetable oil
Salt and ground black pepper

SKEWERS

*2 pounds boneless leg of lamb, trimmed and
   cut in 1¼-inch cubes*
*2 medium green peppers, cored and cut in
   1-inch squares*
2 medium red onions, cut in 1-inch squares
*½ pound dried apricots, plumped in cold
   water*

SAUCE

1¼ cups Chicken Stock (page 165)
2 tablespoons olive oil
*3 tablespoons minced cilantro or parsley
   leaves*

1. For the marinade, mince the serrano and garlic, and chop the onions. In a shallow nonreactive dish long enough to hold 9-inch-long skewers, mix the chopped vegetables with the remaining marinade ingredients, including ¼ teaspoon salt, ¼ teaspoon pepper, and ½ cup cold water.

2. For the skewers, soak ten 9-inch-long bamboo skewers in hot water for 30 minutes. Leaving ¼ inch at each end, thread lamb and vegetables closely together on skewers as follows: lamb, green pepper, onion, apricot, onion, lamb. Repeat. Turn skewers in the marinade until they are coated on all sides. Cover and refrigerate overnight (or as long as 48 hours), depending on spiciness desired.

3. Remove skewers from the marinade, pat them dry with paper toweling, and set aside until ready to grill.

4. For the sauce, combine marinade with Chicken Stock in a medium saucepan. Simmer until mixture reduces and thickens to a saucelike consistency, about 20 minutes. Adjust seasoning (sauce is extremely spicy). Set aside until serving time.

5. Heat a grill (or broiler). Brush brochettes lightly with oil. Grill (or broil) 6 to 8 minutes, turning once, for medium-rare. Reheat sauce, if necessary. To serve, spoon a thin strip of sauce on one side of dinner plates. Put skewers over sauce and sprinkle with cilantro. Serve immediately.

JALAPENO AND JACK CHEESE SAUSAGES

Pork, jalapeño peppers, and Monterey Jack cheese is a tasty, spicy combination that warrants the time it takes to make these sausages at home. Barbecuing with mesquite chips enriches their flavor. It will be necessary to obtain sausage (hog) casings from a supermarket or a butcher. A mail-order source for casings and other equipment is Richard Kutas, The Sausage Maker, 177 Military Road, Buffalo, NY 14207, 716-876-5521.

FLEXIBLE MENU SUGGESTIONS

Although the sausages are made of pork rather than beef, menus are quite similar to those for the flank steak. Avocado, Grapefruit, and Seafood Salad (page 58) solves the problem of what to serve first, and the Mixed Chile Salsa (page 258), Black Beans (page 328), and Yellow Rice or French Potato Salad (pages 327 and 332) are good accompaniments. American in Paris Biscuits (page 366) would add a down-home touch to the menu, or chile lovers might find that Ham and Jalapeño Cornbread (page 367) is not too much of a good thing. Espresso-Brownie Chunk Ice Cream (page 397) is a logical choice for dessert. *Makes 6 servings*

PREPARATION: 40 MINUTES
RIPENING: 6 TO 24 HOURS
COOKING: 15 MINUTES

3 medium jalapeño chiles (about 1½ inches long)
1¼ pounds boneless pork butt, trimmed, cubed, chilled
8 ounces fresh (unsalted) pork fatback, chilled, cut in ½-inch cubes
2 medium garlic cloves, peeled
1 medium onion, peeled
Salt and ground black pepper
¼ teaspoon mild chili powder
¼ teaspoon ground cumin
½ pound Monterey Jack cheese, chilled, cut in 1-inch cubes
3 strands natural hog casings
2 tablespoons olive oil

1. Roast, peel, and seed the jalapeños as described on page 200.

2. Combine pork cubes and fatback in a roasting pan; cover and refrigerate. Mince the garlic, and coarsely chop the onion. Scatter the garlic and onion evenly over the meat and fat cubes. Mix 1¼ teaspoons salt, ½ teaspoon pepper, chili powder, and cumin. Sprinkle spices over meat, cover, and refrigerate.

3. Working with rubber gloves, mince the jalapeños and sprinkle them evenly over the meat cubes. Meat is ready for grinding. (Can cover tightly with plastic wrap and refrigerate overnight.)

4. Sprinkle the cubes of cheese evenly over the meat mixture. Insert the metal blade in clean, dry food processor (or set up a sausage grinder). Working in 1½-cup batches, process meat mixture to coarse-sausage consistency with four to five 2-second pulses;

do not overprocess. Set ground mixture aside. Repeat as needed to grind all the meat and cheese. Fry 1 tablespoon ground sausage mixture until juices run clear (never taste uncooked pork). Adjust seasoning of remaining pork mixture to taste, cooking 1 tablespoon again if needed. (Or, continue steps 5 and 6, and grind and stuff all the sausage mixture into casings using the sausage attachment of a heavy-duty mixer, according to manufacturer's directions.)

5. Cover casings with cold water; soak 15 minutes. Drain, then fit one end of each casing over the nozzle of the kitchen sink faucet. Holding casing firmly, run a thin stream of cold water slowly through casing to rinse the interior, and untwist casing as necessary. If casing leaks, cut off the section with the hole. Return rinsed casing to a clean bowl and cover with cold water.

6. Run your fingers down the length of one casing to remove excess water inside. Gather the casing onto the nozzle of a sausage stuffer. Using your thumbs, press some sausage mixture through the nozzle to the end. Pull enough casing off the nozzle to knot the end. Then gather the knotted end back up and onto the nozzle until knot is placed at its mouth—the knot will be the end of the first stuffed sausage.

7. Fill stuffer completely with meat and use your thumbs or a small spoon to push the mixture into the casing. (Can use another stuffing method, if desired.) Casing will be eased off nozzle as it is filled. Be sure the ground-meat mixture is evenly packed into the casing, which should be uniformly thick.

8. Repeat to stuff all ground-meat mixture into casings. (If overpacked, casings can burst. If casing breaks, cut away, remove meat and stuff into another casing.) To form 3-inch sausages, pinch the casing gently at 3½-inch intervals until mixture moves aside to create a ¼-inch space (this also helps remove air pockets, which can cause spoilage). Twist casing several times between each sausage, then tie off sausages with butcher's string. Use a thin, sterilized needle to pierce the casing as needed to remove any large air pockets. Cover and refrigerate sausages (without cutting apart) for 6 hours (or overnight) to ripen.

9. To cook, heat 3 quarts of water to simmering. Add sausages (without cutting them apart); turn heat to low. Poach at a bare simmer for 3 minutes. Remove, drain, and rub the sausages with oil.

10. To grill the sausages, scatter 2 cups soaked, drained mesquite chips over a white-hot fire (if mesquite flavor is desired). Grill sausages without cutting them apart, turning until browned, about 10 minutes. (Sausages may also be pan-fried over low heat, adding ½ cup water after initial browning.) Cook, turning frequently, over low heat until juices run pale pink when pierced. Cut sausages apart and serve immediately.

MIXED CHILE SALSA

Fresh jalapeño, serrano, and güero chiles are finely diced to ensure a balance between hot and mild peppers in this lively salsa. Be sure to consult page 200 for information on handling the chiles.

FLEXIBLE MENU SUGGESTIONS

Salsa is a perfect match for Chilaquiles (page 195), Jalapeño and Jack Cheese Sausages (page 256), Chili and Garlic-Rubbed Flank Steak (page 245), Chili-Rubbed Chicken (page 278), Cognac-Marinated Beef Fillet (page 298), or grilled chicken, pork, shellfish, tuna, or bluefish.
Makes 3 cups

PREPARATION: 30 MINUTES
MARINATION: 30 MINUTES

2 jalapeño chiles, cored and seeded
2 serrano chiles, cored and seeded
1 banana pepper, cored and seeded
1 small bunch red radishes, rinsed and
*   trimmed*
1 small cucumber, peeled and seeded
5 medium tomatoes, cored
4 medium scallions, trimmed
¼ cup minced cilantro leaves
¼ cup mild olive or vegetable oil
2 tablespoons lime juice
Salt
Hot red pepper sauce (optional).

1. Using rubber gloves, cut the hot chiles into ⅛-inch dice (to make 3 tablespoons jalapeños and 1½ tablespoons serranos). Cut the banana pepper into ⅛-inch dice (¼ cup). Trim and cut the radishes into ¼-inch dice (about 1 cup). Cut cucumber into ¼-inch dice (1 cup) and repeat to dice the tomato (2 cups). Chop the scallions finely (½ cup).

2. Transfer all the vegetables to a bowl and stir in the cilantro, oil, lime juice, and ½ teaspoon salt. Cover and refrigerate the salsa for 30 minutes. At serving time taste, and adjust seasoning with hot pepper sauce if desired.

HICKORY-GRILLED BABY BACK RIBS

Even cooks who have their own time-tested barbecued ribs may want to try this recipe for meaty baby back pork loin ribs. The sauce imparts flavor and tang without burning on the barbecue. I like to add a strong hickory-smoked flavor by putting a layer of damp drained hickory chips over the hot barbecue fire. The ribs will also be good without hickory chips, but they should be cooked over moderate heat to prevent excessive charring.

FLEXIBLE MENU SUGGESTIONS

Barbecued rib dinners are generally a one-course affair. I like to include Corn and Jalapeño Pancakes (page 308), Rosemary-Roasted Potato Salad (page 333), or corn on the cob and sliced tomatoes. I also recommend Soft Rolls (page 364). Either Mixed Berry Cobbler (page 420) or Apple Crisp (page 424) is ideal for dessert. *Makes 4 to 6 servings*

PREPARATION: 15 MINUTES
MARINATION: 24 TO 36 HOURS
COOKING: 50 MINUTES

3 racks (5 pounds) baby back ribs
Barbecue Sauce (page 260)

1. Soak 2 to 3 cups hickory wood chips in water to cover for 30 minutes; drain and set aside.

2. Remove the membrane from the underside of each rack of ribs by catching it with the tip of a sharp knife and pulling or scraping it free. Score the backs of the ribs at 1-inch intervals, making a crisscross pattern. For easy handling, cut ribs into mini-slabs four to five ribs wide.

3. Generously brush ribs with 2½ cups Barbecue Sauce and transfer them to a large, nonreactive baking dish or plastic container. Cover and refrigerate ribs overnight (or up to 36 hours) to marinate. Separately refrigerate the remaining sauce.

4. Heat the barbecue. When fire is red-hot, add the damp hickory chips. Put the ribs on the barbecue, cover (or improvise a heavy-duty aluminum foil cover), and cook until tender, about 40 to 50 minutes, turning once and basting with additional sauce. Serve immediately with additional Barbecue Sauce.

BARBECUE SAUCE

This recipe comes from my friend Thayer Wine, whose housekeeper, Pearl Williams, made this sauce as long as anyone in Thayer's family can remember. The sauce has a low sugar content, which keeps the ribs from burning on the barbecue, and it has a mild enough taste to be served at room temperature on the table. It works equally well for 5 pounds of ribs or two cut-up frying chickens, doubles beautifully to yield 1½ quarts, and is great to have on hand in the refrigerator. *Makes 3 cups*

PREPARATION: 10 MINUTES

2 tablespoons dry mustard
1 cup cider vinegar
2⅓ cups tomato ketchup
¼ cup Worcestershire sauce
2 tablespoons sugar
1 tablespoon hot red pepper sauce
Salt and ground black pepper

Combine dry mustard and vinegar in a jar or bowl and stir until the mustard dissolves. Whisk in the remaining ingredients, including 1½ teaspoons salt and ½ teaspoon pepper. Store covered in refrigerator. (Can refrigerate 30 days.) Serve at room temperature to accompany barbecued foods.

CLASSICAL INSPIRATIONS: FISH, SHELLFISH, POULTRY, AND MEAT

I once saw a Roz Chast cartoon entitled "Young Professional Recipe Test." The first frame poses the question: "Does recipe contain at least four different kinds of flavored vinegars?"

The second: "Does it require one tremendously expensive ingredient that you will use once *and never again for as long as you live?*"

And the third: "Do you have to go out and buy a type of pan you've never even heard of?"

Even when a recipe calling for unique ingredients and specialized cookware is valid and interesting, Chast's parody seems all too accurate. However, most of us *do* want to serve something just a little different, individual, and exciting for a dinner party, which raises another question. How do you go about balancing creativity with the kind of common sense that always seems to put guests at ease?

In the course of writing a *Harper's Bazaar* article on entertaining trends, I interviewed several New York caterers. Not too long ago, one observed, extravagance was often confused with elegance. Many people believed that giving a successful dinner party meant impressing guests with meticulously arranged, lavish food landscapes, garnishing plates with every ingredient in the garden, or serving meals composed of dishes that were immediately recognizable as chic, or stylish restaurant or cookbook clones. As a result, rather than relaxing, guests were forced to work at dinner parties—identifying unknown ingredients, determining why a dish seemed so familiar, or spending an evening trying to cope with eating an "elaborate presentation."

Today, that attitude has changed. As we gain more knowledge about food, a new simplicity has moved to the forefront. Instead of wanting to impress and overwhelm guests, the idea is to purchase the best and freshest possible ingredients, and make people feel comfortable by serving food that is captivating and easy to appreciate.

So when it gets to the meat of the matter, I like to serve main courses that are classically inspired, but never totally predictable. Some of these dishes offer variations on major culinary themes: lobster poached in chicken stock for additional flavor, and served with a piquant Jalapeño Mayonnaise (pictured in the color section). Chicken, roasted in a veil of herbs or spices, takes on an extra helping of flavor. Sautéed veal scallops "sauced" with a flurry of colorful salad greens and dressing is a rustic presentation that adds welcome acidity and color to a dish that can be drab.

Everyone appreciates the fresh strong flavors of herbs and spices, which are used liberally here, often in place of sauces. But for those occasions when something with a rich sauce seems appropriate, recipes such as Scallop and Basil-Stuffed Sole with Tomato-Basil Sauce (page 265), or Roasted Duck with Apples and Campari (pictured on page 289) should help say to guests that you have gone out of your way to make a special and original dinner.

Whether you consider them to be simple or inspired, these are main courses that have withstood the test of time in my kitchen, in the dining room, and in the recollections of my guests.

SCALLOP AND BASIL-STUFFED SOLE

TOMATO-BASIL SAUCE

HALIBUT WITH WARM VINAIGRETTE

COLD CHICKEN-POACHED LOBSTER

JALAPENO MAYONNAISE

SCAMPI ALLA BUSARA

MUSHROOM AND PROSCIUTTO-STUFFED CHICKEN BREASTS

WHOLE-GRAIN MUSTARD-CHIVE BUTTER

HERB- OR SPICE-RUBBED CHICKEN

HERB RUB

GARLIC RUB

CURRY RUB

CHILI RUB

VEAL SCALLOPS GIARDINO

VEAL SCALLOPS WITH BLACK OLIVE GREMOLADA

SZECHWAN PEPPER RIBEYES

ROASTED DUCK WITH APPLES AND CAMPARI

BROWN VEAL STOCK

PORK WITH PORT WINE SAUCE

Aging Gracefully

GARLIC-ROASTED LEG OF LAMB

A French Cut

COGNAC-MARINATED BEEF FILLET

SCALLOP AND BASIL-STUFFED SOLE

Imagine lettuce-wrapped packages containing a "sandwich" of fresh sole filled with a thin layer of basil-flecked scallop mousseline, and tied with a ribbon of scallion. The hot bundles, afloat on a pool of rosy tomato butter sauce, are garnished with fresh basil shreds. Here is a fish main course that looks and tastes as good as it sounds. It is surprisingly easy to make, and it doubles effortlessly.

FLEXIBLE MENU SUGGESTIONS

Choosing a first course can be tricky because the fish and sauce are rich and the course contains tomato, lettuce, and herbs. Country Pork Terrine (page 90) is one good choice. Another strategy is to serve an all-fish dinner composed of a Smoked Fish Rillettes hors d'oeuvre (page 454), followed by an appetizer of Spinach Salad with Caviar and Chives (page 60). The sole occupies the entire plate, but tiny peeled, steamed new potatoes are a good garnish, and French Dinner Rolls (page 360) or Black Olive Bread (page 356) are other good additions to the menu. Classic Fruit Tart (page 416), Lemon Tart Brulée (page 406), or Lemon-Praline Soufflé Glacé (page 433) are fine dessert choices. *Makes 4 servings*

PREPARATION: 45 MINUTES
BAKING: 20 MINUTES

SCALLOP-BASIL MOUSSELINE

¼ *pound chilled bay scallops, rinsed, patted*
   dry
1 *egg white*
Salt and ground white pepper
Hot red pepper sauce
½ *cup chilled whipping cream*
1 *tablespoon chopped fresh basil leaves*

FISH FILLETS

4 *large sole fillets (10 ounces each), rinsed*
   and halved crosswise
Salt and ground black pepper
Green part of 4 large scallions
1 *large head Boston lettuce, cored*
3 *tablespoons softened butter*
Tomato-Basil Sauce (page 267)

1. For the scallop-basil mousseline, put scallops, egg white, ⅛ teaspoon salt, ⅛ teaspoon pepper, and several dashes of hot red pepper sauce in a food processor fitted with the metal blade. Process until pureed. With the motor on, add the cream to the pureed scallops in a thin stream, then thoroughly mix in the chopped basil.

2. Cover a baking sheet with plastic wrap. Pat the fish pieces dry and put them on the plastic wrap with skinned-sides down; season with salt and pepper. Spread the mousseline on four pieces (using all of it), and cover with four matching pieces to make neat sandwiches; refrigerate.

3. Heat 1 quart water to boiling in a large saucepan. Add scallion greens. When the water boils again, remove the scallions with a slotted spoon; drain. Remove the eight

Continued

largest leaves from the lettuce and push them down into the boiling water. When the water boils again, drain the leaves in a colander and gently rinse them with cold water.

4. Carefully unfurl each lettuce leaf on a separate sheet of wax paper. Four single leaves large enough to wrap fish pieces completely are needed; it may be necessary to combine two leaves with stem ends facing each other, slightly overlapping. Put a fish "sandwich" on each large leaf. Gently peel away wax paper, folding lettuce over to enclose fish completely and make a neat package.

5. Tie the scallion greens together to make strands long enough to encircle the lettuce packages. Wrap each package with a scallion, and make a knot to hold it in place. If necessary, trim ends of scallions to within 1 inch of knots.

6. Use 2 tablespoons butter to coat the bottom of a baking dish large enough to hold lettuce packages in a single layer. Transfer packages to the dish, cover them with aluminum foil coated with remaining butter, and refrigerate. (Can refrigerate 6 to 8 hours, but not overnight.)

7. Make the Tomato-Basil Sauce.

8. Heat the oven to 350 degrees. Bake the fish, covered with the foil, for 12 to 18 minutes, or until center of mousseline is just set and the tip of a knife inserted into the packages is withdrawn hot.

9. To serve, ladle ¼ cup of the hot sauce over the surface of four heated dinner plates. With a spatula, carefully transfer a fish package to the center of each plate, over the sauce. Serve immediately.

TOMATO-BASIL SAUCE

∼∼∼∼∼∼∼∼

Here is the delicious first cousin to Bouilla-baisse Sauce—a white-wine-and-tomato butter (see box, page 230) garnished with a sprightly fresh-basil julienne. Designed to coat the entire plate with flavor and color, this sauce provides a stunning backdrop for fish, shellfish, or chicken.

The recipe multiplies easily to make 2 cups (eight servings), or even 3 cups (twelve servings). For a double batch use only six shallots and reduce wine to ½ cup in step 1. For a triple batch increase to only eight shallots and reduce wine to ⅔ cup in step 1. In each instance, you will need to add vinegar to taste.

FLEXIBLE MENU SUGGESTIONS

The sauce is essential for Scallop and Basil-Stuffed Sole (page 265). In addition, it can be served with the hot Three-Vegetable Terrine (page 83) that is included in a menu based on Capretto with Lemon and Rosemary (page 246). *Makes about 1 cup*

PREPARATION: 15 MINUTES
COOKING: 20 MINUTES

½ medium garlic clove, peeled
4 medium shallots, peeled
1 cup dry white wine
1 tablespoon white-wine vinegar
Salt and ground white pepper
1 small ripe tomato, peeled, seeded, chopped
1 cup hot (170 degrees) melted unsalted butter
Hot red pepper sauce
4 to 6 fresh basil leaves

1. Mince the garlic and shallots and transfer them to a medium nonreactive saucepan. Add wine and slowly simmer until the mixture reduces to ¼ cup.

2. Stir in the vinegar, ¼ teaspoon salt, and a pinch of pepper. Strain, pressing the shallots to extract as much of the liquid as possible. Discard the solids. Return the reduction to the saucepan. (Or, can cool, cover, and refrigerate reduction overnight.)

3. Add the tomato to the reduction and heat the mixture to simmering. Immediately transfer the hot tomato mixture to a food processor fitted with the metal blade. With the motor on, add hot melted butter to the machine in a slow stream, and process until the tomato is completely pureed. Add ⅛ teaspoon pepper and hot red pepper sauce, adjusting seasoning to taste. (Can cover processor and hold sauce for 5 minutes.)

4. Return the sauce to the pan if necessary to keep it warm, but do not allow the sauce to simmer. (Can cover in saucepan with plastic touching top of sauce, cool to room temperature, and set aside for 4 hours. Do not refrigerate. Whisk while reheating slowly.)

5. At serving time, adjust seasoning to taste. Make a thin basil julienne by stacking the leaves and slicing them crosswise. Stir basil into the sauce. Serve immediately (do not reheat sauce after adding basil).

HALIBUT WITH WARM VINAIGRETTE

Halibut was hardly noticed in restaurants before this popular dish was introduced at New York's Le Bernardin, where these fish steaks, cooked just to the point of translucency and topped with a warm vinaigrette, occupy an entire dinner plate.

This recipe was included in one of my *New York* magazine entertaining articles as the centerpiece of an elegant all-fish dinner. It is particularly delicious because the warmth and acidity of the sauce lifts, and brilliantly highlights, the delicate flavor of the halibut. If you must find a substitute for halibut, use swordfish or tuna steaks; the warm vinaigrette also can be spooned over grilled fish.

FLEXIBLE MENU SUGGESTIONS

An all-fish menu can begin with Smoked Fish Rillettes or Wild Rice Blini with caviar (pages 454 and 456). Or, serve Wild and Brown Rice Soup (page 50). Follow with the halibut and steamed asparagus or snow peas served on the side. Pink Grapefruit Sorbet or Pomegranate Granita (pages 435 and 439) with Coconut-Lime Tuiles (page 440) are light, refreshing desserts, while Chocolate Macadamia Torte (page 374) would give the menu a sumptuous finish. *Makes 6 servings*

PREPARATION: 20 MINUTES
COOKING: 23 MINUTES

POACHING LIQUID

½ carrot, peeled
½ small onion, peeled
¼ celery stalk
½ tomato, peeled, seeded
1½ cups dry white wine
1 cup white-wine vinegar
⅛ teaspoon dried thyme leaves
Salt
½ bay leaf
12 black peppercorns

VINAIGRETTE

¼ cup sherry-wine vinegar
¼ cup red-wine vinegar
½ cup mild extra-virgin olive oil
½ cup vegetable oil
1 teaspoon Dijon mustard
Salt and ground black pepper
2 medium shallots, peeled

FISH AND GARNISH

6 halibut steaks (8 ounces each) with skin and
    bones
¼ cup minced fresh herbs (equal amounts of
    chives, tarragon, and chervil) or ¼ cup
    fresh minced chives

1. For the poaching liquid, thinly slice carrot, onion, and celery. Chop the tomato, and transfer the ingredients to a 4-quart nonreactive soup kettle. Add 2 quarts of cold water, the wine, vinegar, thyme, 2 teaspoons salt, bay leaf, and peppercorns. Cover and heat to boiling. Simmer 15 minutes, then strain the liquid into a nonreactive roasting pan large enough to hold the fish in one layer. Discard the vegetables. Cool the poaching liquid to room temperature. (Can cover and refrigerate overnight; bring liquid to room temperature before proceeding with recipe.)

2. For the vinaigrette, whisk the .vinegars, oils, and mustard with salt and pepper to taste in a medium nonreactive saucepan; set aside until serving time. Mince the shallot and set aside.

3. At serving time, rinse the halibut steaks and pat dry. Put the halibut into the poaching liquid. Heat until liquid begins to approach a simmer—the liquid will move rapidly and bubbles will begin to form. Turn off the heat and let the fish stand in the liquid until the flesh appears slightly translucent when the point of a small knife is inserted between center bone and flesh (about 125 degrees on an instant-read thermometer), 2 to 3 minutes, depending on thickness.

4. Heat the vinaigrette just until warm to the touch; stir in the shallots and herbs. Use a pancake turner to lift the halibut steaks carefully from the poaching liquid, letting each steak drain for a few seconds. Transfer halibut to warm dinner plates; carefully remove the skin. Pour ¼ cup warm vinaigrette over each portion of fish. Serve immediately.

COLD CHICKEN-POACHED LOBSTER

Simmering lobsters in chicken stock is similar to the Italian notion of cooking certain fish and shellfish in meat stock to enrich their subtle flavors. Even when served cold, the lobsters benefit from the taste of the cooking liquid. In turn, reuse the liquid as a stock for soups or sauces or in the following recipes: Scallop Bisque (page 40), Shrimp and Corn Chowder (page 46), My Favorite Tomato Sauce (page 126), or Shrimp and Curry Risotto (page 166).

FLEXIBLE MENU SUGGESTIONS

Cold lobsters are quintessential summer fare. They are pictured in the color section with Zucchini-Rice Salad (page 331), Jalapeño Mayonnaise (page 271), Coral Sauce (page 85), and French Dinner Rolls (page 360).

Several menus can be constructed around the lobsters, with variations in sauce and accompaniments to balance the first course. Following Beet-Salad Mimosa (page 59), serve Green Sauce (page 191) and French Potato Salad (page 332). After Curried Vichyssoise (page 48), try Jalapeño Mayonnaise (page 271) and Shoestring Vegetables with Whole-Grain Mustard (page 335). After Homemade Garlic Sausage with Pistachios (page 92), consider Green Sauce and Italian Baked Vegetables (page 306); switch to Coral Sauce and French Potato Salad if Spinach Salad with Caviar and Chives (page 60) is served first.

To complete the menus, serve the Classic Fruit Tart (page 416), which will nicely balance any menu except the one beginning with the soup. Other dessert possibilities include Peach Turnover (page 418) or Mixed Berry Cobbler (page 420). *Makes 8 servings*

PREPARATION: 25 MINUTES
COOKING: 40 MINUTES
CHILLING: 4 HOURS

2 medium onions, peeled
2 medium celery stalks
2½ quarts Chicken Stock (page 165)
8 sprigs parsley
10 white peppercorns
*2 to 3 branches fresh thyme (½ teaspoon
    dried thyme leaves)*
8 live lobsters (each 1 to 1¼ pounds)

1. Slice the onions and celery and put them in an 8- to 10-quart stockpot with the Chicken Stock, 1½ quarts of water, the parsley, peppercorns, and thyme. Cover and simmer rapidly for 20 minutes. Remove vegetables with slotted spoon and discard them.

2. Cover and heat the liquid to boiling. Add two lobsters, heads first. Cover and simmer for 7 minutes per pound, until lobsters are just cooked. Transfer lobsters to a foil-lined jelly-roll pan to drain. Repeat to cook remaining lobsters, returning the juices that drain from lobsters to the pot. (It may be necessary to add a small amount of water if the liquid in the pot reduces.)

3. When lobsters are cool, use a sharp knife to make a small slit in each of the heads. Hold each by the tail over a bowl (or over

the cooled pot of broth) until all the excess liquid drains from the body. (Reserve the broth for uses suggested above.) Wrap and refrigerate lobsters until chilled, 4 hours (or overnight).

4. When thoroughly chilled, put lobsters on a cutting board. Using a cleaver and beginning at the tail end, split each in half lengthwise. Remove and discard sacks from the heads. Use a knife tip to remove the dark veins from the tails. Clean body cavity of lobster with spoon (tomalley may be blended with softened butter and used to enrich soup, or discarded; coral may be finely chopped and used as a garnish for a sauce).

5. Cover and refrigerate lobsters until serving time. Serve one lobster per person, spooning sauce into space in body cavities, or passing it separately.

JALAPEÑO MAYONNAISE

The distinctive flavor of jalapeño chiles (see page 198) gives this mayonnaise a special complexity.

FLEXIBLE MENU SUGGESTIONS

A lively partner for Cold Chicken-Poached Lobster (page 270), this mayonnaise is also delicious on sandwiches or as a sauce for grilled fish, chicken, or pork, cold roasted meat or poultry, or vegetables such as tomatoes, avocados, and onions. *Makes 1½ cups*

PREPARATION: 6 MINUTES

1 large egg
1 large egg yolk
Salt
2 to 3 teaspoons red-wine vinegar
1 teaspoon chili powder
1 teaspoon ground cumin
1 medium jalapeño pepper, roasted, skinned, seeded, quartered
1¼ cups mild olive oil

1. Put the egg, egg yolk, ½ teaspoon salt, vinegar, chili powder, and cumin in the container of a food processor fitted with the metal blade. Add the jalapeño, and with the motor on, drizzle the oil very slowly into the machine until the mayonnaise "takes" and thickens slightly. Then pour in the remaining oil in a thin stream and process until mayonnaise is very thick.

2. Transfer the mayonnaise to a glass or plastic container. Cover and refrigerate until serving time. (Can refrigerate 36 hours, covered.) Adjust seasoning before serving.

SCAMPI ALLA BUSARA

I once wrote a short piece on Italian knitwear designers Tai and Rosita Missoni as part of a travel article on Milan, and visited their sprawling home and office complex just outside the city, in Sumirago. Tai loves to cook, and he took me straight to the kitchen to prepare this dish of scampi—crustaceans that resemble small, pale, skinny lobsters, cooked live and whole in their shells. The dish is named after his home town on the Dalmatian coast.

On this side of the Atlantic we occasionally find scampi. Spanish prawns and large shrimp are acceptable substitutes. Fresh shrimp, with heads and bodies intact, are occasionally seen in Chinese markets; these would be ideal because the character of the tomato-dominated sauce comes from the shellfish. Crayfish or lobster halves also are suitable.

The Missonis served the scampi Italian-style, with only a few tablespoons of the tomato mixture, and suggested that leftover sauce be saved and used the next day on pasta. The juice from canned tomatoes can be frozen for sauces or soup, or reduced for use as tomato paste.

FLEXIBLE MENU SUGGESTIONS

Three hearty preludes to scampi include Onion and Chèvre Tart (page 104), Pasta with Four Cheeses (page 132), and Saffron Risotto (page 170). All three eliminate the need to serve a starch with the main course, although you may wish to add a green vegetable tossed with Balsamic Butter (page 311), and Black Olive Bread (page 356), Rosemary Breadsticks (page 343), or Prosciutto Bread (page 354).

Since Pasta with Broccoli Raab (page 134) and Country-Style Risotto (page 176) mix vegetables and starch, they eliminate the need to serve either with the scampi, which then can be presented Italian-style, perhaps accompanied by one of the breads (above).

Sausage and Artichoke Pizzas (page 108) are another appetizer possibility that can be followed by scampi with boiled potatoes, and green beans tossed with a julienne of yellow bell pepper along the lines of the snow-pea recipe on page 310. Bread, however, would be redundant here.

Almond and Lemon-Stuffed Pears (page 431) are the best dessert for a menu that begins with the Chèvre Tart. To balance other appetizers, try Lemon Tirami Su (page 429), Dome Cake (page 388), or Milanese Fruit Tart (page 408), but two tarts—chèvre and fruit—are not a good idea in the same menu. *Makes 4 to 6 servings*

PREPARATION: 10 MINUTES
COOKING: 40 MINUTES

3 medium garlic cloves, peeled
1 large onion, peeled
1/4 cup Herbed Oil (page 73), or olive oil
2 cans (28 ounces each) Italian plum
    tomatoes, or 2 1/2 pounds ripe plum
    tomatoes
1/2 cup beef or fish stock, or 4 tablespoons
    meat glaze
2 pounds large shrimp with shells on, cleaned
    and deveined, or 2 1/2 pounds prawns,
    scampi, or crayfish with heads left on,
    rinsed, or 4 small lobsters, halved
1/2 cup dry white wine
Salt and ground black pepper

1. Mince the garlic and chop the onion finely. Transfer the mixture to a large nonreactive skillet, add the oil, and stir over medium heat until onion softens, about 5 minutes.

2. Drain, seed, and coarsely chop the tomatoes (peel and seed fresh tomatoes before chopping) and add them to the skillet. Stir in the stock, and cook over medium heat until mixture thickens to tomato-sauce consistency and excess liquid evaporates, about 30 minutes.

3. At serving time, add shrimp (or other shellfish) and wine to the skillet, and simmer until just cooked, about 5 minutes. Do not overcook. Stir in 1/2 teaspoon salt and 1/4 teaspoon pepper, or more as needed to taste. Serve shrimp lightly covered with sauce.

The menu term "shrimp scampi" is an oxymoron. Scampi is the Italian name for *Nephrops norvegicus*, also called "Norway lobsters," "Dublin bay prawns," or "langoustines." Although shrimp are often used as a substitute, these pale apricot-colored crustaceans belong to the same family as lobsters (*Nephropsidae*).

MUSHROOM AND PROSCIUTTO-STUFFED CHICKEN BREASTS

Paper-thin slices of prosciutto make a wonderfully flavorful lining for the interior of skinned, boned chicken breasts, baked in a big aluminum-foil pouch so they literally steam in their own juices. Adding mushrooms and bits of diced chicken to the stuffing ensures that the chicken breasts present well when they are sliced crosswise and fanned out slightly on the plate.

Creating a pocket in each half of a chicken breast is not difficult. The trick is to exert pressure with one hand while feeling your way with a boning knife, so that each piece of meat is evenly split but not cut apart. There is no need to sew or skewer the stuffed breasts before steaming, since the chicken clings to itself when raw, and seals up perfectly when cooked.

This recipe calls for carving and plating each hot chicken breast as soon as the pouch emerges from the oven, which can turn into a logistical problem. If you are working alone, the best way to serve quickly and get all the food to the table hot is to have the plates warmed and all the vegetable accompaniments ready (if possible) before baking the chicken.

The best strategy is to carve the breasts and return them to the warm pouch (keep it covered with towels) in a 200-degree oven. Then, working on two plates at a time, arrange the chicken and accompaniments, spread a dollop of the mustard butter over the chicken, and serve.

FLEXIBLE MENU SUGGESTIONS

Because first courses such as Spinach Salad with Caviar and Chives (page 60) or Four-Vegetable Tart (page 100) are vegetable-intensive, and the chicken has mushrooms in the filling, plan to serve the chicken with Yellow Rice (page 327) or thin tomato noodles (dough, page 128). Add color to the plates with a watercress garnish. Slices of toasted Black Pepper Brioche (page 352), or French Dinner Rolls (page 360), would round out the main course.

After wedges (plan on two per person) of Smoked-Salmon Pizzas (page 110), the chicken can be accompanied by Potato Croquettes (page 320) or thin spinach and fresh herb noodles (dough, page 139), and Stuffed Tomatoes (page 312); add the dinner rolls (above) if you like.

With a first course of Spinach Salad, serve Almond Soufflé Tart (page 414), the elegant Milanese Fruit Tart (page 408), or the super rich Barry Tart (page 380) for dessert. If the meal begins with the vegetable tart or pizza, then Almond and Lemon-Stuffed Pears, a sorbet, or the Pomegranate Granita (pages 431 and 432, 434 to 437, and 439) with Gianduia Lace Cookies (page 386) provide a light, refreshing finish; Orange Crème Brulée (page 426) is an alternative. *Makes 6 servings*

PREPARATION: 45 MINUTES
COOKING: 30 MINUTES

3 whole chicken breasts, skinned, boned, and
    split
3 tablespoons butter
4 small shallots, peeled
½ pound mushrooms, trimmed, wiped clean
Salt and ground black pepper
¼ cup fresh white bread crumbs
3 tablespoons minced parsley
4 to 5 ounces prosciutto, sliced paper thin
Whole-Grain Mustard-Chive Butter (page
    277)

1. Remove the small fillet from the under-side of each chicken breast lobe, and cut the fillets into ¼-inch dice. Heat 1 teaspoon butter in a medium skillet. Toss the diced chicken until the color turns and pieces are just cooked; transfer a heaping ½ cup cooked diced chicken to a large bowl (reserve remainder for another use).

2. Mince the shallots, and finely chop the mushrooms. Add the shallots to the skillet with 2 tablespoons of the butter and cook over low heat until softened, about 3 minutes. Add the mushrooms and toss over medium heat until liquid evaporates, then cook over low heat until mushrooms are dark and dry, about 15 to 20 minutes. Season mushrooms to taste with salt and pepper and add them to the bowl with the diced chicken. Stir in the bread crumbs and parsley. Cool, then refrigerate stuffing until thoroughly chilled. (Can cover and refrigerate overnight.)

3. To make a pocket in each chicken breast lobe, begin at the thickest side: press down firmly with one hand and use the tip of a sharp knife to split each chicken-breast lobe into a half-moon-shaped pocket that is attached by ¼ inch at the top and along the curved edge (down to the point). Put each piece of chicken on the work surface and open each pocket flat, cut-sides up.

4. Cover the entire inside surface of each chicken "pocket" with a single layer of prosciutto (one to two slices, depending on size). Put 2 tablespoons mushroom mixture in the center, and fold one side of the chicken over the filling, tucking in the edges of the prosciutto as necessary. Press to enclose the filling in each lobe of the now very plump chicken breasts.

5. Lightly butter a 30 × 12-inch sheet of aluminum foil and put the foil on a baking sheet. Put the chicken pieces (smooth sides up) on one half of the foil. Carefully fold the foil in half, over chicken, pressing gently to remove excess air. Double-fold all edges of the foil to enclose the chicken in a rectangular, airtight pouch. Be sure folds are sharp and foil has no small tears (or pouch will not puff). Refrigerate pouch on baking sheet until ready to cook (up to 6 hours).

6. Prepare Whole-Grain Mustard-Chive Butter and keep the butter soft at room temperature (do not let it melt).

7. At serving time, adjust oven rack to middle position, and heat oven to 450 degrees. Bake until pouch puffs, or no longer than 12 minutes. Remove pouch from oven and pierce the center to let steam escape. Open one edge and carefully drain off the liquid in the pouch (reserve it for use as chicken stock). Cover pouch with towels to keep chicken warm.

Continued

8. To serve chicken breasts, quickly transfer pieces one-by-one from the pouch to a cutting board. Slice chicken lobe crosswise and on a diagonal into four pieces to expose the filling. Using the knife or a spatula, carefully transfer sliced chicken to warm dinner plates, fanning out slices slightly in a crescent shape. Then spread a dollop of the mustard butter (about 1 to 1½ tablespoons) over each chicken breast. Garnish plates as desired and serve immediately.

WHOLE-GRAIN MUSTARD-CHIVE BUTTER

Mustard grains are the seeds of flowering plants cultivated throughout the world. They have a slightly crackly texture and have been used as a condiment since ancient times in Greece and China. In the New Testament (St. Matthew: 13, 31, and 32), mustard is mentioned as "the least of all seeds . . . ," but a tablespoon or two of this butter melting over steamed, grilled, or roasted chicken, grilled or broiled fish, veal chops, or steak adds a tremendous punch of flavor. It can work wonders on a baked potato, and on plain pasta or spaghetti.

Whole, or coarse-grain, old-fashioned mustards vary according to brand. They should have a mild flavor without being overly salty or vinegary. Taste the mustard before using it in the butter since its flavor is of paramount importance here. Notes on compound butters appear on page 223.

FLEXIBLE MENU SUGGESTIONS

In addition to the menus based on steamed chicken breasts, this butter is excellent for menus based on grilled fish.

Omit mustard from the garnishes for Country Pork Terrine (page 90) or Homemade Garlic Sausage with Pistachios (page 92), and serve the butter with grilled striped bass or swordfish (page 216), accompanied by Italian Baked Vegetables (page 306), Snow Peas and Bell Pepper Ribbons (page 310), or Stuffed Tomatoes (page 312). French Dinner Rolls (page 360) or toasted slices of Black Pepper Brioche (page 352) then can be served throughout the meal. Almond and Lemon-Stuffed Pears (page 431) or Apple Crisp (page 424) are good desserts to complete the menu.

After a bowl of robust Duck and Sausage Gumbo (page 158), top the grilled fish (page 216) suggested above with this butter, and put Corn and Jalapeño Pancakes (page 308) alongside. Complete the menu with Pomegranate Granita (page 439) or Banana Ice Cream with Caramel Sauce (pages 438 and 444).

Lemon-Garlic Capellini with Mediterranean Sauce (page 150) (a vegetable- and herb-intensive pasta underlined with garlic) would be delicious before grilled salmon (page 216) or grilled chicken breasts. Accompany the main course with fresh baby carrots and Tomato Flatbread with Two Herbs (page 346). Complete the meal with Almond and Lemon-Stuffed Pears (page 431), Chocolate-Walnut Linzer Torte (page 376), or fresh fruit and Gianduia Lace Cookies (page 386). *Makes ¼ pound*

PREPARATION: 10 MINUTES

¼ cup minced fresh chives
1½ tablespoons whole-grain mustard
⅛ teaspoon ground black pepper
1 teaspoon lemon juice
¼ pound softened unsalted butter
Salt

1. Put all the ingredients, including a pinch of salt, into a food processor fitted with the metal blade and process until thoroughly mixed.

2. Spoon butter onto a 12-inch-long sheet of plastic wrap. Roll into a 1-inch-diameter log shape, about 8 inches long. Use immediately or refrigerate up to 3 days. (Can double-wrap in aluminum foil and freeze up to 3 months.)

HERB- OR SPICE-RUBBED CHICKEN

Herb- or spice-rubbed chicken is a staple for informal dinners. The chickens (as well as the little rub recipes) can easily be doubled or tripled to feed eight to twelve, and can be oven-roasted or barbecued with equal ease.

Rubs, made from simple but powerful seasonings such as dried herbs, garlic, or mixed spices, are a particularly easy way to add flavor to chicken, whether they are put on the skin, or between the skin and the meat. Letting rubbed chicken stand for several hours or refrigerating it overnight helps to intensify the flavor.

Splitting baby chickens or Cornish hens down the back and flattening them is a technique that is found in French, Indian, and some Asian cuisines. The French refer to this shape as *à la crapaudine* (*crapaud* translates as "toad").

The advantages of preparing birds in this manner are that they have an attractive appearance, they cook evenly, and they do not need to be turned or basted. Nor do the chickens roll in the oven, on the grill, or on the plate. To carve them neatly into quarters, simply lift off each leg and second joint in one piece, then split the breast down the center.

Roasting on high heat helps render fat from beneath the surface of the skin (although it tends to create a slightly smoky kitchen). Steam forming under the skin puffs it slightly, which makes it very crisp—these chickens are at their peak the moment they emerge from the oven or grill.

FLEXIBLE MENU SUGGESTIONS

Numerous menus can be created for this chicken. Follow serving suggestions given for each rub (pages 278 to 283). *Makes 4 servings*

PREPARATION: 10 MINUTES
COOKING: 55 TO 60 MINUTES

2 frying chickens (2 to 2½ pounds each), or 4
 Cornish hens or baby chickens (poussins)
¼ cup Herbed Oil (page 73) or olive oil
Seasoning Rub

1. Working on one chicken at a time, place each one breast-side down on a work surface, with the legs facing you. To split the chicken down the back, use poultry shears or heavy scissors to cut down center of tail, then continue cutting through backbone and to one side of remaining neck bone. Flatten the chicken by grasping and pulling down the two cut sides.

2. Use a small, sharp knife to cut away the glands, veins, and fat from neck area. Remove the remaining part of the neck at its base if it protrudes. Remove any other visible fat or matter that clings to the bones.

3. Rinse, pat the chickens dry with paper towels, and return them to the work surface with the breast-sides up. Pat both sides of chickens dry with paper towels.

4. Firmly press the breastbone to flatten each chicken for roasting. With a small sharp knife, remove the small appendages from the wing tips.

5. Make the rub. Mix the oil with the rub and use half to coat the surface of each chicken completely. (If you wish to season the meat rather than the skin, begin at the neck end, work your fingers between the breast meat and skin, then continue working with your hands until the skin is separated from the breast and leg meat. Coat as much of the meat as possible with the rub, then oil the skin lightly.) Transfer the chickens to shallow metal roasting pans, skin side up; tuck wing tips under the neck skin. (If desired add neck and giblets; reserve liver for another use.) Cover and set aside 1 hour. (Can cover and refrigerate overnight.)

6. Adjust oven rack to lowest position. Heat oven to 435 degrees by setting oven dial between 425 and 450 degrees. Roast chickens 50 to 55 minutes, until leg joint moves freely and skin is golden, without basting or turning them. (Can cook 45 to 55 minutes in covered grill, depending on heat of fire.) Serve chickens immediately, or cool and serve at room temperature.

HERB RUB

Mixed herbs are hardly an uncommon way to season chicken or poultry, but their great flavors make this an enduring recipe that I have used for many years. If you like, the herbs can also be made into a paste with finely minced garlic.

FLEXIBLE MENU SUGGESTIONS

Choose Cream of Watercress or Tomato Soup with Garlic and Basil (pages 43 and 44) to begin a straightforward menu for four, and accompany chicken with Bistro Potatoes (page 322) and green beans or broccoli. Finish with Chocolate-Walnut Linzer Torte (page 376).

For a spring dinner for six, start with Mozzarella, Tomato, and Olive Salad or Beet-Salad Mimosa (pages 62 and 59). Add Mixed Grains (page 325) and steamed broccoli tossed with Balsamic Butter (page 311) to the main course; finish with the torte (above).

For menus beginning with appetizers that contain no tomatoes, start with Pasta with Four Cheeses (page 132), Sausage and Artichoke Pizzas, or Mushroom Pizzas on Prosciutto Crust (pages 108 and 114) to serve four; or Pasta with Broccoli Raab (page 134), Scallion and Black Pepper Lasagne with Black Olive Pesto (page 144), or Onion and Chèvre Tart (page 104) to serve six. Accompany the chicken with Stuffed Tomatoes (page 312) and Black Olive Bread (page 356). Wind up with Pomegranate Granita and Mixed Nut Sablés (pages 439 and 442).

For a winter menu that serves four, either Pasta with Tomato-Seafood Sauce (page 124) or Pasta with Milanese Meat Sauce (page 130) is a great beginning. Steamed carrots (page 316) and Prosciutto Bread (page 354) are good with the chicken; then follow with creamy Dome Cake or Chocolate Roulade (pages 388 and 392) for a rich finale (with leftovers).

A sophisticated late-summer dinner could include Lemon-Garlic Capellini (or spaghettini) with Mediterranean Sauce (page 150) followed by the chicken and grilled shiitake mushrooms. Add Black Plum Sorbet (page 437) with a mixed plum compote.

For a very summery menu, start with Mozzarella, Tomato, and Olive Salad (page 62), then present the chicken with a garnish of julienned red, yellow, and green peppers tossed with Balsamic Butter (page 311). Mixed Berry Cobbler (page 420) is an alternative to fresh fruit.

In addition to the chicken, a casual two-course meal for eight to ten could feature a vibrant array of salads including Potato Salad Puttanesca (page 334), Shoestring Vegetables with Whole-Grain Mustard (page 335), and Quinoa Tabbouleh (page 330), plus grilled chunks of Japanese eggplant, zucchini, and red or orange bell peppers with my Favorite Vinaigrette (page 72). Add Prosciutto Bread (page 354), and choose a big dessert such as Lemon Tirami Su (page 429) or the Rustic Apple Tart (page 410). *Makes rub for 2 chickens*

PREPARATION: 3 MINUTES

3 tablespoons Mixed Herbs (page 105)
Salt and ground black pepper

Crush the herbs in a small mortar or shallow bowl with ¼ teaspoon salt and ¼ teaspoon pepper, using a pestle or the back of a spoon.

GARLIC RUB

The idea for this rub comes from my paternal grandmother, Rose, with whom I lived for many years. She was no ordinary cookie-baking grandmother. Dinner was a chore Rose normally dispatched early in the morning, for she was always in a hurry to go off to her poker game. My grandmother, you see, was a professional gambler. Poker notwithstanding, Rose always cooked Thanksgiving dinner (her turkeys were outstanding), and she often made a roasted chicken coated with a garlic paste that was my inspiration here.

FLEXIBLE MENU SUGGESTIONS

For a simple Italian-style meal for six, start with Milanese Minestrone (page 156), and serve the chickens with Stuffed Tomatoes (page 312). Finish with Double Chocolate Ice Cream and Gianduia Lace Cookies (pages 399 and 386).

With rustic Risotto Primavera, Country-Style Risotto (pages 172 and 176), or Pasta with Milanese Meat Sauce (page 130) as a prelude to a menu for six, serve chicken with a green salad tossed with Lemon-Basil Vinaigrette (page 74). For dessert try Almond and Lemon-Stuffed Pears (page 431).

An interesting East-West menu for four can begin with half the recipe for Mixed Lettuces with Shrimp and Ginger-Lime Vinaigrette (page 68) as an appetizer. Accompany the chicken with Curried Rice Stick noodles (page 326), Curry noodles (dough, page 148) or Tomato noodles (dough, page 128) tossed with Fresh Herb Butter (page 219). Baked Stuffed Apples (page 425) or Banana Ice Cream (page 438) and Caramel Sauce (page 444) are easy, compatible desserts.

As the first course of a substantial menu for four, try Pasta with Tomato-Seafood Sauce or Milanese Meat Sauce (pages 124 and 130), or the Agnolotti (page 142). Add Snow Peas and Bell Pepper Ribbons (page 310) and Umbrian Cheese Bread (page 350) to the main course; then you may wish to follow with green salad tossed with My Favorite Vinaigrette (page 72). Choose Crème Brulée or Dome Cake (pages 426 and 388) for dessert.

Creamy Pasta with Four Cheeses (page 132) is another luscious first course for four, and Italian Baked Vegetables (page 306) are a good partner for the chicken, even though the dish contains potatoes. Apple Crisp (page 424) or Almond and Lemon-Stuffed Pears (page 431) offer a sweet, but relatively light, ending to this meal. *Makes rub for 2 chickens*

PREPARATION: 5 MINUTES

2 medium garlic cloves, peeled
1 teaspoon paprika
¼ teaspoon dried thyme
⅛ teaspoon cayenne pepper
Salt and ground black pepper

Mince the garlic together with the remaining ingredients, including ¼ teaspoon salt and ¼ teaspoon pepper, until it is extremely fine. Transfer the mixture to a small bowl.

CURRY RUB

Like the chili rub, this paste never fails to improve the taste of chicken. You can crank up the heat of the curry as you like—please be sure to read the notes on curry powder (page 147). Leftover chicken makes a wonderful salad.

FLEXIBLE MENU SUGGESTIONS

Cold Papaya-Melon Soup (page 41) is a good beginning for a summer meal for four. Along with the chicken, serve Shoestring Vegetables with Whole-Grain Mustard or Thai-Taste Cole-slaw (pages 335 or 336), and Soft Rolls (page 364). End with Chocolate Roulade (page 392) or Ultra-Fudge Brownies (page 395) and fresh cherries or strawberries.

For a menu for six that features an hors d'oeuvre and a main course, but no appetizer, start with Chutney Toasts (page 449). To the chicken course add Yellow Rice (page 327), Tomato-Onion Salad, Slivered Cucumbers, and Mixed Plum Chutney (pages 203 and 338). Dessert can be as buttery as Peach Turnover (page 418) or as rich as Lemon Tirami Su (page 429).

For a two-course menu for six to eight, serve room-temperature chicken with Quinoa Tabbouleh (page 330) or Zucchini Rice Salad (page 331). End with Strawberry Bread (page 422) à la mode. *Makes rub for 2 chickens*

PREPARATION: 5 MINUTES

2 tablespoons mild or hot curry powder
    (page 147)
1½ teaspoons paprika
Salt and ground black pepper

Mix the spices with ¼ teaspoon salt and ¼ teaspoon pepper in a small dish.

CHILI RUB

If you like the pungent taste of ancho chiles (see page 198), which are an ingredient in many chili powder blends, substitute Ancho Chile Powder (page 194) in the recipe below.

FLEXIBLE MENU SUGGESTIONS

Avocado, Grapefruit, and Seafood Salad (page 58) is an interesting start for an informal menu for six. Serve Corn and Jalapeño Pancakes (page 308) and Soft Rolls (page 364), or Sweet Potato Flans (page 324) and a plain variation of Ham and Jalapeño Cornbread (page 367) with the chicken. End with Espresso-Brownie Chunk Ice Cream (page 397).

Fruit can provide a good counterpoint to the spicing of chili in a menu for six. Begin with Sweet Potato and Apple Bisque (page 45). Accompany the chicken with a steamed green vegetable or salad tossed with Hazelnut Vinaigrette (page 77) and Cheddar-Cumin Rolls (page 362). Conclude with Almond Soufflé Tart (page 414).

A two-course cold menu for six to eight can include the chicken served at room temperature with French Potato Salad (page 332) or Rosemary-Roasted Potato Salad (page 333), plus diced tomatoes and avocado tossed lightly in Lemon-Basil Vinaigrette (page 74) or Shoestring Vegetables with Whole-Grain Mustard (page 335). End with Espresso-Brownie Chunk Ice Cream (page 397), or fresh berries with Quick Custard Sauce (page 443), and Mixed Nut Sablés (page 442).

A casual dinner for four could begin with Two-Cheese Quesadillas (page 448), and continue with the chicken served with Black Beans (page 328), Yellow Rice (page 327), and Mixed Chile Salsa (page 258). In warmer weather, substitute Zucchini Rice Salad (page 331) for both the rice and salsa, and serve slices of Peach Turnover (page 418) topped with peach ice cream for dessert. Alternately, Chocolate-Walnut Linzer Torte (page 376), Gianduia Cheesecake (page 384), or Double Chocolate Ice Cream (page 399) are suitable for this menu.
Makes rub for 2 chickens

PREPARATION: 3 MINUTES

1 tablespoon chili powder
2 teaspoons ground cumin
2 teaspoons ground coriander
Salt and ground black pepper

Mix the spices with ¼ teaspoon salt and ¼ teaspoon pepper in a small dish.

VEAL SCALLOPS GIARDINO

When is a salad served as a sauce? That may sound like an odd question, but main courses of sautéed or grilled meat, poultry, or seafood are frequently being served with vegetables, greens, salsas, or dressings on top.

The mixture of greens and vegetables adds wonderful color to the plate, and acid (such as vinegar or lemon juice) in the dressing points up the flavor of the meat—particularly this breaded, sautéed veal.

Giardino means "garden" in Italian and these veal scallops, topped with peppery watercress (or arugula), crunchy leaves of endive, and a tomato dressing made with balsamic vinegar, have a sensationally fresh taste.

New York restaurants such as Il Mulino in Greenwich Village regularly serve a similar dish —made with huge pounded veal chops that cover the entire surface of a dinner plate. I included the Il Mulino recipe in one of my *New York* magazine entertaining articles—this is a simplified adaptation.

To ease last-minute preparation, the cheese coating in step 3 can be prepared and refrigerated for as long as two days in advance.

FLEXIBLE MENU SUGGESTIONS

Either Butternut Squash Soup (page 52) or Wild Mushroom Soup (page 49) are good appetizers for a fall dinner. Accompany the veal (which will occupy at least half the surface of a dinner plate) with Saffron Risotto (page 170) and Rosemary Breadsticks (page 343), or Parmesan and Black Pepper Bread (page 348). Choose between Chocolate Truffle Cake (page 382) or Chocolate Macadamia Torte (page 374), two large cakes that are so good, guests may ask for seconds.

Wedges of Prosciutto and Leek Pizzas on Oregano Crust (page 112) would make a rustic first course. Follow with the veal and Lemon-Garlic capellini (dough, page 149) tossed in Herbed Oil (page 73). Complete the menu with Almond and Lemon-Stuffed Pears (page 431), or fresh fruit with Gianduia Lace Cookies (page 386). *Makes 4 servings*

PREPARATION: 30 MINUTES
COOKING: ABOUT 15 MINUTES

DRESSING

1 medium garlic clove, crushed
1 tablespoon balsamic vinegar
3 tablespoons olive oil
Salt and ground black pepper
¼ small red onion, peeled
2 medium tomatoes, rinsed

SALAD

1 cup packed, trimmed watercress or arugula
* leaves*
1 medium Belgian endive, rinsed

2 ounces Parmesan cheese (four 1-inch cubes)
1½ cups dried bread crumbs
Nutmeg
Ground white pepper
2 eggs
¼ cup vegetable oil
¼ cup olive oil
1 pound veal scallops (8 pieces), pounded
  paper thin

1. At least 30 minutes in advance, make the salad dressing in a medium bowl: mix garlic, vinegar, and oil with a pinch of salt and pepper. Slice the onion paper thin and add it to the bowl. Cut the tomatoes into ½-inch dice and add them to the bowl. Let the mixture stand at room temperature, stirring occasionally, until serving time—as long as 1 hour. Remove the garlic with a fork before serving.

2. In a large mixing bowl, toss watercress leaves (or arugula) with the endive; cover with damp towels and refrigerate (up to 2 hours).

3. Grate the Parmesan cheese in a food processor fitted with the metal blade by processing until the cheese is powdery. Add bread crumbs, ⅛ teaspoon nutmeg, and 1½ teaspoons pepper and process until mixed; transfer mixture to a flat dish and set it aside (can wrap and refrigerate).

4. At serving time, beat the eggs lightly in a small bowl; set aside. Mix and set the oils aside. Dip each veal scallop, one or two at a time, into the egg, then press each side into the bread-crumb mixture, turning the scallops over and over in the crumbs until they are coated and no spots of egg show through. Transfer scallops to a clean sheet of wax paper. With a veal pounder or the flat side of a cleaver, pound on one side, very gently, to press on the crumbs.

5. Heat 3 tablespoons of the mixed oils in a large skillet. Sauté the scallops until cooked on each side; transfer scallops to a paper-towel-lined baking sheet, gently blot them dry, and keep them warm in a 250-degree oven (do not cover). Repeat, adding oil as necessary, to sauté the remaining veal. (Discard any leftover bread crumbs or reserve for another use.)

6. Quickly toss the salad mixture thoroughly with the dressing. Transfer veal scallops to warm dinner plates and top each portion with a heaping cup of salad. Serve immediately.

VEAL SCALLOPS WITH BLACK OLIVE GREMOLADA

The late culinary historian Waverly Root noted in his 1971 treatise *The Food of Italy* that after checking seven different cookbooks he found seven different formulas for *gremolada*, a seasoning paste stirred into the sauce for osso buco. And, Root admitted, "If I consulted seven more . . . I would wind up with fourteen." He went on to note that lemon peel was the common denominator in the recipes, many of which also contained parsley, garlic, anchovies, and herbs.

This gremolada, made with orange rind, garlic, black olives, and chopped cilantro, is mixed into butter before being stirred into the pan drippings of the sautéed veal. It gives this sauce a terrific jolt of flavor, but care should be taken not to allow the mixture to boil, or the sauce can separate. (Leftover gremolada can be used as a quick sauce for pasta.)

FLEXIBLE MENU SUGGESTIONS

The natural affinity between asparagus and oranges makes Milanese Asparagus Soup (page 162) a superb first course. Round out the menu with Potato Croquettes (page 320) or Saffron Risotto (page 170), and consider Almond and Lemon-Stuffed Pears (page 431) for dessert.

Wild and Brown Rice Soup (page 50) is an appetizer that eliminates the need for starch with the veal, which then can be accompanied by Asparagus Timbales (page 313), or fresh steamed asparagus or pea pods, and Prosciutto Bread (page 354). End with the pears or Baked Stuffed Apples (page 425) for dessert. *Makes 4 servings*

PREPARATION: 25 MINUTES
COOKING: 20 MINUTES

GREMOLADA

Zest of 1 medium orange
Salt
2 to 3 medium garlic cloves, peeled
1 cup pitted black olives, well drained
6 tablespoons unsalted butter, softened
¼ cup minced cilantro leaves

VEAL

2 tablespoons butter
4 tablespoons mild olive oil
1 to 1¼ pounds veal scallops (8 to 10 pieces), pounded paper thin
Salt and ground black pepper
Flour
⅔ cup dry white wine
2 tablespoons minced cilantro leaves

1. For the gremolada, grate the orange zest and put it in a food processor fitted with the metal blade. Add ¼ teaspoon salt. With the motor on, drop the garlic into the machine and process until minced. Add olives and coarsely chop the mixture. Add the butter

and cilantro and process until mixture forms a paste. Measure and set aside ⅓ cup in refrigerator. (Wrap and refrigerate or freeze remainder.)

2. At serving time, heat butter and oil in a large skillet. Sprinkle each veal scallop with salt and pepper, and dust the scallops lightly with flour. Sauté the veal, turning once, just until scallops are done, about 2 minutes. Transfer veal scallops to a foil-lined dish and put the dish in a 225-degree oven.

3. Off heat, add wine to the skillet, scraping with a spoon or spatula to deglaze the pan. Adjust heat to medium, and simmer until wine reduces to ¼ cup. Add veal juices that accumulate on the foil to the skillet; heat mixture to simmering.

4. Over low heat, vigorously whisk ⅓ cup of the chilled gremolada into the skillet. Continue whisking for about 1 minute, just to cook the garlic slightly. Do not allow pan juices to boil. Transfer veal scallops to dinner plates. Adjust the seasoning, and spoon the sauce over the veal slices. Garnish with cilantro and serve immediately.

SZECHWAN PEPPER RIBEYES

A blend of three peppercorns—black, white, and the fiery, tiny rust-colored Szechwan peppercorns (see page 209)—are roasted, ground, and pressed onto each steak for a new twist on an old favorite. Sautéing (rather than grilling or broiling) the steaks helps to keep the pepper in place. Be sure steaks are very well trimmed to avoid an overabundance of fat in the skillet.

Ribeye steaks are a luxurious and juicy cut. I think of them as great fare for a casual but very sophisticated dinner for pepper-loving friends.

FLEXIBLE MENU SUGGESTIONS

Since the steaks cook quickly, they can be the basis of a relatively easy menu for four. Scallop Bisque (page 40) or Mozzarella, Tomato, and Olive Salad (page 62) require minimal preparation, and plain blanched spinach (to accompany the steaks) cooks in a trice. Bistro Potatoes (page 322) are a good addition here, as are French Dinner Rolls (page 360). Crème Brulée (page 426) gives the meal a silky finish.

With appetizers such as the Agnolotti, or Pasta with Tomato-Seafood Sauce (pages 142 and 124), the menu takes on a very different tone (there is no need for another starch after pasta, and the Agnolotti makes spinach redundant). Serve a simple sauté of assorted julienned bell peppers, or Snow Pea and Bell Pepper Ribbons (page 310) with the main course. Espresso-Brownie Chunk Ice Cream (page 397) or Lemon Tart Brulée (page 406) help balance flavors and textures. *Makes 4 servings*

PREPARATION: 20 MINUTES
REFRIGERATION: 4 TO 8 HOURS
COOKING: 10 TO 12 MINUTES

Fresh Herb Butter (page 219)
3 tablespoons whole black peppercorns
1 tablespoon whole white peppercorns
1 teaspoon Szechwan peppercorns
4 ribeye steaks (10 to 12 ounces each)
Salt
1 tablespoon olive oil

1. Prepare 4 tablespoons of the Herb Butter and bring to room temperature.

2. Mix the peppercorns in a small dry skillet. Shake the pan over medium-low heat until peppercorns are lightly roasted and fragrant, about 5 minutes. Cool.

3. Grind the roasted peppercorns into a small bowl or custard cup. Pat steaks dry on paper toweling. Sprinkle 1 teaspoon ground pepper and ⅛ teaspoon salt evenly over each side of the steaks; press to be sure pepper adheres to steaks.

4. At serving time, heat 1 tablespoon oil in a large, heavy-duty skillet, or divide the oil between two medium skillets. When oil is very hot, add the steaks and cook 3 to 4 minutes per side for medium-rare.

5. Transfer steaks to warm dinner plates. Top each with a tablespoon of Herb Butter and serve immediately.

ROASTED DUCK WITH APPLES AND CAMPARI

This recipe falls into the "labor of love" category, but it also could be seen as a cooking adventure. Brown Veal Stock is needed for the sauce, and the ducks must be dried for twenty-four hours in the refrigerator prior to cooking them and carving the legs and breasts for presentation (the duck is pictured in the color section).

Also, I should warn that the ducks must be basted with their hot rendered fat, a technique I have found best for thoroughly removing it from beneath the skin. In order to be basted successfully and brown properly, the skin must be dry; otherwise a great deal of splattering may occur. When basting the birds, your hands must be protected by potholders or oven mitts, and your arms covered by long sleeves.

These caveats aside, I prefer this duck dish over most others for, in addition to rosy breast meat, there is a sensational sauce tempered by Campari—the red Italian bitters spiced with herbs and orange zest—to offset the sweetness of the sautéed apples.

FLEXIBLE MENU SUGGESTIONS

A very elaborate dinner could begin with wedges of Smoked-Salmon Pizza (page 110) for hors d'oeuvres; Chutney Toasts (page 449) or Wild Rice Blini (page 456) are good alternatives. For an elegant first course, begin the meal with half a recipe of Wild Mushroom Soup (page 49) or Milanese Asparagus Soup (page 162). Accompany the duck, sauce, and apples with Two-Potato Gratin, Potato Croquettes (pages 319 and 320), Saffron Risotto (page 170), half a recipe of Sweet Potato Flans (page 324), or Mixed Grains (page 325). Add Asparagus Timbales (page 313) after Mushroom Soup, or opt for a steamed vegetable (such as pea pods) that does not repeat the first course. Following the asparagus soup, consider grilled (or sautéed), sliced shiitake mushrooms, or sautéed escarole or kale as vegetable accompaniments that are particularly compatible with potatoes or risotto.

Lemon-Praline Soufflé Glacé (page 433) or Lemon Tart Brulée (page 406) will end the meal on a festive note; either will provide sweet leftovers. *Makes 4 servings*

PREPARATION: 1½ HOURS
STANDING: 6 TO 24 HOURS
COOKING: 3 HOURS

2 fresh ducks (4 to 5 pounds each) at room temperature, wing tips removed and reserved with the necks and giblets
8 medium shallots (¼ pound), peeled
1 medium carrot, peeled
1 stalk celery

1 cup mushrooms (or stems)
3 green apples, peeled and cored
¼ cup minced parsley
½ teaspoon thyme leaves
3 cups Brown Veal Stock (page 291)
2 tablespoons sugar
¼ cup cider or honey vinegar
2 tablespoons butter
½ cup Campari
Salt and ground black pepper

Continued

1. One day in advance, remove excess fat from cavity of ducks. Trim the neck skins close to body and remove any fat that clings to the interiors. Rinse ducks, pat dry, and put them—unwrapped—directly on the refrigerator shelf rack (put a paper towel on the shelf below to catch any drippings). Or, put ducks 2 inches apart on a large cake rack set over a baking sheet and refrigerate them overnight (or up to 2 days) to allow the air to circulate around the ducks and slightly dry out the skins and interiors.

2. Mince the shallots, and chop the carrot, celery, mushrooms, and one of the apples. Transfer the chopped mixture and the parsley to a 4-quart saucepan. Add thyme, veal stock, and the reserved duck pieces (do not add livers). Cover and simmer for 45 minutes. Uncover and slowly simmer until liquid reduces to 1½ cups when strained, about 30 minutes longer. (Can cool, cover, and refrigerate this enriched, strained stock as long as 24 hours.)

3. Bring the stock to room temperature if refrigerated. Combine sugar and vinegar in a small nonreactive saucepan. Cover and simmer for 3 minutes. Uncover and simmer rapidly until the mixture is thick and syrupy. Stir the vinegar mixture into the reduced stock; set aside near the stove.

4. Cut each of the remaining apples into wedges. Heat butter in large skillet and toss apples over high heat until golden. Remove apples to aluminum foil with slotted spoon.

5. Add the vinegar-stock mixture to the skillet and heat to boiling, loosening cooked-on particles in the pan with a wooden spatula. Add the Campari and simmer until the sauce reduces to 1¼ cups. Adjust seasoning with salt and pepper. Cover with plastic wrap directly touching the top of the sauce and set it aside at room temperature until serving time. (Can cover cooled sauce, wrap the apples, and refrigerate both overnight.)

6. Adjust oven rack to lowest position. Heat oven to 450 degrees. Pierce the duck breasts and legs with the tip of skewer or with a trussing needle at ½-inch intervals to permit fat to escape. Put the ducks, breast-sides down, in the roasting pan. Roast 15 minutes. Carefully remove pan from oven and baste the ducks with the hot rendered fat. Turn the ducks breast-sides up. Roast 15 minutes longer, then baste, and transfer excess fat from the pan to a heatproof cup or bowl as necessary. Rotate the ducks breast-sides down, and roast 15 minutes longer, basting again with the fat. Remove ducks from the oven, and set them aside.

7. When ducks are cool enough to handle, remove each leg and thigh in one piece, by cutting in a wide arc at the base of the leg to expose the thigh joint nearest the body. Detach the thigh at the joint. Remove the second joint bones from the legs so that each piece can stand, cut-side down, on the plate.

8. Carefully cut down midline of the breasts and, working away from the breast bone in each direction, lift each lobe off the bone in one piece (leave skin attached to the breast meat). Set the legs and breasts aside. (Can wrap and set aside for 4 hours; reserve juices that accumulate in wrapping.) Use meat that is left on carcasses for salad or pizza.

9. At serving time, heat the oven to 450 degrees. Put duck legs in a baking dish, placing them upright as they will rest on plates. Bake for 7 minutes. Add breasts, skin-side down, to the dish. Roast 5 to 6 minutes longer or until juices run pink when legs are pierced with a skewer.

10. Meanwhile, reheat apples in the sauce, adding any roasting juices that have accumulated from carving the ducks. Season the sauce with salt and pepper. Put the duck legs on warm dinner plates. Blot skin sides of breasts with paper towels, then cut breasts into thin slices. Transfer the duck breasts to the plates, fanning them slightly. Spoon the apples and sauce around the duck. Serve immediately.

BROWN VEAL STOCK

I find it easier and faster to brown veal bones under the broiler, but they also can be roasted in a hot (425 degrees) oven—be sure to turn them frequently.

FLEXIBLE MENU SUGGESTIONS

This stock can be substituted for beef stock in Garlic-Roasted Leg of Lamb (page 295) and in the sauce for Cognac-Marinated Beef Fillet (page 298). *Makes 3½ to 4 quarts*

PREPARATION: 45 MINUTES
COOKING: 6 TO 7 HOURS

5 pounds veal bones (including a cracked knuckle bone)
1 pound beef shin bones with meat
2 medium onions (skins on), cubed
4 carrots, cubed
3 celery stalks, with leaves
2 cloves unpeeled crushed garlic
1 cup parsley with stems
1 bay leaf, crumbled
1 teaspoon dried thyme

1. Adjust oven rack to high position and heat the broiler. Put veal and beef bones in a shallow roasting pan. Broil, turning the bones frequently, until they are golden brown, taking care not to allow edges to burn.

2. Transfer the hot bones to an 8- to 10-quart stock pot. Cover with 6 quarts cold water, or enough to cover the bones by 2 inches. Heat to simmering, then skim off the foam that rises to the surface of the stock. Turn heat to low, set cover ajar, and simmer for 2 hours.

3. Coarsely chop the onions, carrots, and celery and add them to the pot with the remaining stock ingredients. Set the cover ajar and simmer the for 4 to 6 hours longer.

4. Uncover and cool the stock to room temperature. Lift out the large bones with a slotted spoon, draining them well, and discard them. Pour the stock through a double-mesh sieve or through a cheesecloth-lined strainer. Press vegetables firmly to extract all possible liquid.

5. Transfer the stock to 1-quart storage containers, leaving several inches at the tops. Refrigerate until completely chilled; cover. (Can refrigerate 2 days or freeze up to 6 months.)

PORK WITH PORT WINE SAUCE

Whether you serve it hot or cold, hickory-grilled on the barbecue or oven-roasted, don't overlook this pork loin. Both the meat and its rich sweet-savory sauce are so irresistible, even leftovers, such as a sandwich of thinly sliced pork on Umbrian Cheese Bread (page 350), with sauce, are fabulous.

Plan ahead, as the pork absolutely requires a forty-eight-hour soak in the wine-based marinade so its flavor can penetrate. Then the marinade is transformed into a marvelous mahogany-brown sauce while the pork cooks to a rosy, juicy (and very safe) 145 degrees. The meat can be served hot or cold.

FLEXIBLE MENU SUGGESTIONS

For a cold, high-summer menu, serve Curried Vichyssoise (page 48) as the first course. Shoestring Vegetables with Whole-Grain Mustard (page 335) were created as a special partner for the pork, and while it might seem odd, Umbrian Cheese Bread is a spectacular addition. Chocolate-Walnut Linzer Torte (page 376), filled with peach jam, makes a delicious dessert.

When the pork is served hot, try Milanese Asparagus Soup (page 162) as a starter. Potato Croquettes (page 320) help to soak up the Port Wine Sauce, while steamed carrots add color. Almond Soufflé Tart (page 414) or the Linzer Torte (above) gives the menu a terrific finish.

Either Sweet Potato and Apple Bisque (page 45) or Fennel-Leek Soup (page 52) is good for a classic menu. Accompany the pork with Mixed Grains (page 325); add watercress for garnish, and end with Classic Fruit Tart (page 416) or Lemon Tart Brulée (page 406).

Mixed Lettuces with Shrimp and Ginger-Lime Vinaigrette (page 68) sets off a meal with an exotic note. Add Sweet Potato Flans (page 324) and steamed broccoli to the main course, then close with the Lemon Tart (above) or Crème Brulée (page 426). *Makes 6 to 8 servings*

PREPARATION: 20 MINUTES
MARINATION: 48 HOURS
COOKING: 40 TO 50 MINUTES

1 boneless, center-cut pork loin (3 to 3½ pounds), tied

MARINADE

6 medium garlic cloves
2 cups tawny port wine
½ cup dark brown sugar
¼ cup all-purpose soy sauce
2 tablespoons dry mustard
1 teaspoon hot chili oil or pinch cayenne pepper

1. Pierce pork loin with a sharp skewer all over at 2-inch intervals. Put the pork into a glass loaf pan. Crush the garlic cloves and mix them with the remaining ingredients. Pour the marinade over the pork, cover, and refrigerate for 2 days.

2. To oven-roast the pork, heat oven to 425 degrees. Transfer marinade (including garlic) to a small saucepan and simmer until the mixture reduces to ⅔ cup, about 20 minutes. (Can cool, cover, and refrigerate the sauce overnight.)

3. Pat the pork dry and put it in a small metal roasting pan. Roast for 20 minutes, turning it several times, until evenly brown. Lower oven to 375 degrees. Roast until an instant-read thermometer registers 145 degrees in the thickest section of the roast, about 20 to 30 minutes longer. Transfer pork to a platter or dish and cover it loosely with aluminum foil. Let it sit up to 10 minutes before carving, or set it aside, uncovered, to cool to room temperature. (If you wish to barbecue pork, make a fire, as discussed on page 239. When coals are red-hot, put 3 cups soaked, drained hickory chips on the fire. Add the meat, cover, and grill until thickest part registers 145 degrees, usually 40 to 50 minutes. Remove meat from grill.)

4. Immediately pour off excess fat from the roasting pan (or barbecue drip pan—do not worry if drippings are unusable, do not deglaze pan or add them to sauce). Add ⅓ cup cold water to the roasting pan and stir over low heat with wooden spoon to deglaze. Add this to the prepared sauce and simmer until the mixture reduces once again to ⅔ cup.

5. Strain and keep the sauce warm; discard the garlic. Slice the pork thinly, spoon sauce onto warm plates and arrange slices over the sauce. (Or pork and sauce can be served at room temperature.)

AGING GRACEFULLY

For a number of years I lived in Chicago and taught cooking classes at home. Early one Thursday morning in the dead of winter I awoke to a blizzard and, with nearly three feet of snow outside the door, I was forced to cancel my morning lesson.

The class was to have been focused on a boned saddle of lamb, and the ingredients already had been purchased, making the refrigerator a muddle. A week later I was shocked to discover that the very expensive lamb saddle had been totally forgotten on the bottom refrigerator shelf. I cooked the meat that very night and found it—quite remarkably—to be among the most delicious lamb roasts I had ever tasted.

I have always left large cuts of meat unwrapped in the refrigerator for a day or so, a practice I learned from Richard Olney, with whom I studied. I knew that circulation of air around unwrapped ducks, for example, helped to dry out the skin, which let them brown better in the oven. But I never actually considered aging meat at home.

My cooking students often did express shock at finding meat unwrapped on my refrigerator shelf. But aging large cuts of meat —including legs and saddles of lamb, veal roasts or saddles, beef roasts, and ducks—in the refrigerator for three to five days generally improves their flavor and texture, tenderizes the meat, and makes it easier to carve. One exception is beef fillet, which benefits from no more than one to two days of aging.

Whenever I purchase a large roast, I unwrap it completely and put it directly on the refrigerator shelf rack (with paper towels on the shelf below to catch drips) for at least three days (and preferably five days) before trimming, seasoning, or marinating the meat. An alternate method, for refrigerators with glass shelves, is to elevate the meat on a large cake rack set over a jelly-roll pan.

This method simulates butcher-shop aging, during which enzymes in the muscles of meat are thought to be responsible for the beneficial changes in flavor and tenderness.

After aging a leg of lamb, remove the outer membrane (or fell) by catching it and pulling it off (use a small, sharp knife to remove stubborn parts). Removing the fell will eliminate the strong, or gamey, taste and permit you to trim off all but the thinnest layer of fat. Then the lamb can be marinated, rubbed, or treated as the recipe suggests.

Trim off all dry or dark sections from other home-aged meats and roasts before marinating or proceeding with recipes.

GARLIC-ROASTED LEG OF LAMB

Years ago, no one liked lamb very much, and the late James Beard was fond of saying it was "the most hated meat in America." That is no longer true. Lamb has become the red meat of choice for dinner parties.

A marinade of garlic, mustard, and lemon zest is used both as a rub for this leg of lamb, and as the principal flavoring for a simple sauce made from the pan juices. The beauty of the mixture is that it provides the full-blown taste of garlic without the troublesome process of inserting garlic slivers into the meat.

Frenching the lamb shank bone (see page 297) makes it particularly easy to turn and hold the leg steady for slicing. You will need to purchase a leg of lamb that has the shank bone intact, and not cracked. Plan to age the lamb for at least two days (see page 294) before removing the fell as indicated in step 1 of the recipe.

FLEXIBLE MENU SUGGESTIONS

The dominance of garlic in the recipe dictates a soothing balance of complementary appetizers and desserts.

Since Spinach Salad with Caviar and Chives (page 60) is a vegetable-intensive first course for six, serve colorful Saffron Risotto (page 170), or a double recipe of Bistro Potatoes (page 322) with the lamb, and Classic Fruit Tart (page 416) for dessert.

Be sure all eight guests are garlic lovers before offering Cold Salt-Cod Terrine (page 88) with its robust Tomato, Garlic, and Black Olive Sauce (page 89) as a first course. Add French Dinner Rolls (page 360) or Black Olive Bread (page 356). Then accompany lamb with roasted potatoes and a "bouquet" of steamed yellow squash, carrots, and pea pods or asparagus tips, or Snow Pea and Bell Pepper Ribbons (page 310). End with Almond Soufflé Tart (page 414).

Risotto Spinacciola (page 174) or Saga and Watercress Tart (page 106) are sensationally rich appetizers based on blue cheese. Follow with the lamb and baby carrots and baby beets (or cubed larger beets). Since the menu is so substantial, end with fresh fruit and Gianduia Lace Cookies (page 386), Pomegranate Granita (page 439) with Coconut-Lime Tuiles (page 440), or splurge and offer Chocolate Macadamia Torte (page 374) for dessert.

Scallion and Goat-Cheese Agnolotti (page 142) or Scallion and Black Pepper Lasagne with Black Olive Pesto (page 144) are excellent preludes to the lamb, although the Agnolotti makes only four portions. Pasta with Broccoli Raab (page 134) is an unusual appetizer but it, too, is garlic-intensive. The small amount of scallion in two of the pastas does not rule out small steamed leeks and grilled (or broiled) eggplant or zucchini slices as accompaniments; Stuffed Tomatoes (page 312) are best following the broccoli raab. Then, Dome Cake (page 388), Crème Brulée (page 426), or Chocolate Truffle Cake (page 382) are smooth endings to a flavor-packed menu.

Continued

If you prefer to begin with Two Soups in One Bowl (page 52), consider the offbeat Mixed Grains (page 325) paired with Snow Peas and Bell Pepper Ribbons (page 310), or Italian Baked Vegetables (page 306), which need no further accompaniment, as partners for the lamb. Add Chocolate Roulade (page 392), Milanese Fruit Tart (page 408), or Classic Fruit Tart (page 416) for dessert. *Makes 6 to 8 servings*

PREPARATION: 20 MINUTES
STANDING: 2 TO 48 HOURS
COOKING: 60 TO 70 MINUTES

LAMB AND MARINADE

1 aged leg of lamb (5 to 7 pounds)
1 medium lemon
Ground black pepper
⅛ teaspoon cayenne pepper
3 medium garlic cloves, peeled
3 tablespoons Dijon mustard
Salt
2 teaspoons fresh minced rosemary or thyme
  (or 1 teaspoon dried)
⅓ cup Herbed Oil (page 73), or olive oil

SAUCE

2 medium shallots, peeled
1 cup beef or veal stock
1½ teaspoons Dijon mustard
1 tablespoon Cognac

1. With a small sharp knife, carefully remove the tough outer membrane or fell that covers the lamb leg. Trim off all but a ¹⁄₁₆-inch layer of the visible fat. French the shank bone (see page 297), and put the leg in a large dish.

2. Strip off 3 long strips of lemon zest with a vegetable peeler, wrap them in plastic, and refrigerate. Grate the remaining lemon zest and put it in a food processor fitted with the metal blade. Add ⅛ teaspoon black pepper and cayenne pepper. With the motor on, add the garlic, the mustard, ⅛ teaspoon salt, and the rosemary. Process, adding the oil

until the mixture has the consistency of a light mayonnaise.

3. Brush the garlic marinade evenly over the lamb. Cover and refrigerate overnight. (Can leave in a cool place as long as 4 hours.)

4. If refrigerated, bring the lamb to room temperature. Adjust the oven rack to the lowest position. Heat oven to 425 degrees. Transfer lamb to a metal pan and roast for 15 minutes. Turn heat to 375 degrees and roast until an instant-read thermometer inserted into the thickest part of leg registers 125 degrees (for rare) or 130 degrees (for medium-rare), about 45 to 55 minutes longer. (Check temperature at 5-minute intervals after a total of 1 hour of roasting.) Remove the lamb from the oven and let it stand loosely covered with aluminum foil for 10 to 12 minutes while preparing the sauce.

5. For the sauce, pour off fat from the roasting pan. Mince the shallots. Put the pan on the stove over medium heat. Add shallots to pan drippings and stir with a wooden spoon or spatula until lightly colored. Add stock and the reserved strips of lemon zest. Stir in the mustard and Cognac and simmer rapidly, using spoon to loosen the cooked-on drippings, until the mixture reduces to ⅔ cup.

6. Strain the sauce, and press the solids well to extract all the liquid possible. Discard solids in the strainer. Adjust sauce seasoning with salt and pepper. Slice the lamb thinly, stirring any juices that accumulate into the sauce. Spoon sauce over each serving.

A FRENCH CUT

Browsing through the meat case in a supermarket, I often see legs of lamb packed in cellophane with the shank bones sawed through and bent backwards so they will not pierce the wrapper. I find this to be a particularly annoying practice since, in effect, it mutilates an otherwise lovely roast.

Whenever possible, ask the butcher in the supermarket meat department (or butcher shop) to set aside a leg of lamb with the shank bone intact but with the tendon (called the *gambrel cord*) at the base of the leg removed, and the shank bone trimmed one inch above the break joint.

With the shank bone cut in this manner, "frenching" the leg—freeing the tendons of the bulbous shank meat by scraping them free of the bone with the tip of a sharp knife—is a simple task. Thus loosened, the meat and tendons retract during roasting, conveniently leaving an inch or two of bone to serve as a handle for carving. The bone can be grasped with a small napkin, a towel, or with a *manche à gigot*.

Gigot is French for "leg of lamb," and *manche* translates as "sleeve"; the *manche à gigot* is nothing more than an old-fashioned carving handle that slips over the narrow shank bone. A pointed screw anchors the *manche* and permits the lamb leg to be turned and sliced easily.

COGNAC-MARINATED BEEF FILLET

From time to time, I like to serve beef fillet at dinner parties because it is a conservative main course, "tried and true." My choice is to serve the beef plain, without sauce, but a very simple sauce, similar to the one for Garlic-Roasted Leg of Lamb (page 295), can be created from pan juices. Directions are given below. Beef fillet should be well trimmed and nearly fat-free before cooking, making it as lean as possible.

Aging the meat for a day (see page 294), then marinating it before cooking helps to improve its flavor. This marinade includes Cognac or brandy, and it is important to use a top-quality brand; otherwise the meat can have a sweet taste. Be sure to pat the fillet dry with paper towels before rubbing it with oil so that it sears and browns (rather than steams) during cooking. Directions are given here for oven-roasting, but the fillet can be barbecued over oak (page 239) to the same internal temperature.

To make a simple sauce from the pan juices, follow the guidelines in the lamb recipe, but add two minced shallots and a chopped tomato to the roasting pan; then add 1¼ cups beef stock or Brown Veal Stock (page 291), and reduce the liquid to about ¾ cup. The better the stock, the better the sauce. Add a tablespoon of Cognac, then simmer the sauce with some arrowroot dissolved in a tablespoon or two of cold water to give it a lovely sheen and good, light body.

FLEXIBLE MENU SUGGESTIONS

A majority of the following menus serve six. However, desserts that yield more than the number of menu servings allow for second helpings or leftovers.

For an entertaining menu in *Cook's* magazine, Two Soups in One Bowl (page 52) made a colorful first course. The beef was served with Snow Peas and Bell Pepper Ribbons (page 310), Mixed Grains (page 325), and Parmesan and Black Pepper Bread (page 348), and the menu ended with Chocolate Macadamia Torte (page 374).

Wild Mushroom Soup (page 49) is another good soup choice. Add Spinach and Fresh Herb noodles (dough, page 139) and Stuffed Tomatoes (page 312) to the main course, then wrap up the meal with the stunning Lemon-Praline Soufflé Glacé (page 433) or tangy Lemon Tart Brulée (page 406).

Wild and Brown Rice Soup (page 50) is another option. Pair the beef with Stuffed Tomatoes (page 312) and steamed asparagus tips or spinach tossed in Balsamic Butter (page 311), braised fennel, or sautéed zucchini. A green salad with Sherry-Walnut Vinaigrette (page 78) can be served before the dessert. Round out the menu with Rustic Apple Tart (page 410) or the rich Lemon Tirami Su (page 429).

For a lighter touch, start with the delicate Avocado, Grapefruit, and Seafood Salad (page 58). Accompany the beef with Saffron Risotto (page 170) and Snow Peas and Bell Pepper Ribbons (page 310), or broccoli with Balsamic Butter (page 311), then wind up the menu with The Barry Tart or Chocolate Truffle Cake (pages 380 and 382).

With a preface of Spinach Salad with Caviar and Chives (page 60), serve Two-Potato Gratin (page 319) with the main course. Then follow with the Chocolate Roulade (page 392), Chocolate Macadamia Torte (page 374), or Rustic Apple Tart (page 410) for dessert.

For an Italian-style menu for four, begin with Scallion and Goat-Cheese Agnolotti (page 142), then serve the beef with grilled Japanese eggplants (page 316) and steamed baby carrots. Consider a variety of desserts: Dome Cake (page 388) for richness, Pomegranate Granita (page 439) for a light ending, or Almond Soufflé Tart (page 414) for elegance.

For a casual menu based on cold, sliced beef, begin with Beet-Salad Mimosa (page 59). Serve French Potato Salad (page 332) and sliced tomatoes with the main course. End with Gianduia Cheesecake (page 384), Espresso-Brownie Chunk Ice Cream (page 397), or Strawberry Bread à la mode (page 422).

For a two-course menu with Tex-Mex flair, serve Two-Cheese Quesadillas (page 448) as an hors d'oeuvre, then accompany cold, sliced beef with Mixed Chile Salsa (page 258), Corn and Jalapeño Pancakes (page 308), or French Potato Salad (page 332). Add julienned jicama sprinkled with lime juice and Ancho Chile Powder (page 194), and Cheddar-Cumin Rolls (page 362). End with Double Chocolate Ice Cream or Espresso-Brownie Chunk Ice Cream (pages 399 and 397). *Makes 6 servings*

PREPARATION: 10 MINUTES
MARINATION: 24 HOURS
COOKING: 30 TO 35 MINUTES

1 medium garlic clove, peeled
2 medium shallots, peeled
½ teaspoon dried thyme leaves
½ teaspoon summer savory
Salt and ground black pepper
3 tablespoons Cognac or brandy
⅓ cup Herbed Oil (page 73) or olive oil
3 pounds aged center-cut beef fillet, trimmed and tied

1. Mince the garlic and shallots and transfer them to a nonreactive baking dish large enough to hold meat. Add the thyme, savory, ¼ teaspoon salt, ⅛ teaspoon pepper, Cognac, and ¼ cup oil. Turn the meat in the marinade, cover, and refrigerate overnight.

2. Adjust oven rack to the lowest position. Heat oven to 425 degrees. Remove meat from the marinade, pat it dry with paper towels, and rub it with the remaining olive oil. Transfer meat to a roasting pan.

3. Roast for 15 minutes, turning to sear meat on all sides. Continue roasting until an instant-read thermometer registers 120 degrees (for rare) when inserted into thickest area, about 15 to 20 minutes longer. Remove meat from the oven and cover it loosely with aluminum foil for about 5 minutes. Remove the strings, cut the beef into ¼-inch-thick slices, and serve immediately.

PART FOUR

ACCOMPANIMENTS

CAMEO CROP:
VEGETABLES, RICE, GRAINS, AND RELISHES

ON THE RISE:
BREADS AND ROLLS

CAMEO CROP:
VEGETABLES, RICE, GRAINS, AND RELISHES

There is something quite noble about tending a vegetable garden, filling the earth with tiny seeds and watching them sprout and grow into lovely plants that bear delicious fruits for the table. If I had a little plot of land, instead of a concrete balcony cantilevered from the twentieth floor of a high-rise, I might even brave the travails of mosquito and other bug bites and try my hand at growing things.

My history with herbs has been pretty good, perhaps because I was lucky enough to keep sage, rosemary, and chives, which are quite happily fed by my neglect. But if I only had a little plot of land I know that I would risk sunburn to gather a bunch of hyssop flowers, harvest more than thirty leaves of basil at one time, or watch a purple eggplant grow so that I would know *for sure* that it once really was green.

Of course, I could try tomatoes in pots, and herbs in olive-oil cans on the balcony, and I probably could even grow arugula out there if I tried. But all of us cannot be tillers of the soil and, quite frankly, I find that a trip to my local greengrocer (where one afternoon I was astonished to find a box of fresh tree ears—the black fungus you find in Chinese mu shu pork—plopped down casually next to the hot chiles) or to a supermarket with a large, well-stocked, and adventurous produce section is consolation enough for me.

Long ago I determined that if by some chance I was permitted to eat only one type of food, I would probably choose tomatoes—even over ice cream. Asparagus runs a close second, and mushrooms are next, although fresh porcini mushroom caps—which I ate at lunch and dinner for seven days during a trip to Italy—give tomatoes a definite run for their money.

My preference for the clear, sharp flavors of plainly cooked vegetables is stated in numerous menus. I was fascinated to see banana buds in a produce market in Berkeley, and actually encounter someone who knew how to fix them. Tasting a dessert sauce made from prickly-pear puree was delightful and I certainly would try it—sometime. The world of tropical fruits and vegetables is indeed vast and interesting.

However, when I am planning a special dinner, I try to rely on vegetables that are compatible, rather than competitive, with the major focus of the main course, and I think of them, as well as rice, grains, and relishes, as actors that have cameo roles on each plate.

Whether they are spooned from a dish, stuffed, molded and baked, served hot as a side dish, or cold as a salad, matching vegetables with fish, meat, or poultry can be critical to the success or failure of the ensemble.

For every guest who adores a special creamy potato gratin, ethereal asparagus flans, or spirited Corn and Jalapeño Pancakes (page 308), there is someone else who is grateful to be served a slice or two of grilled eggplant sprinkled with fresh herbs, or a few chubby, perfectly cooked asparagus spears glazed with a whisper of flavored butter or a drizzle of herb-infused olive oil—delicate sauces that enhance plain vegetables to just the right degree. Both the plain and the fancy appear here.

This section also seems a natural place to begin to explore the rapidly expanding world of grains and legumes, as well as their exciting tastes and textures. Fragrant basmati rice from India (both white and brown) is a joy to cook and eat. Quinoa, a protein-rich South American grain, will excite and satisfy anyone who is counting calories, and the combination of lentils, barley, bulgur, and wild rice that I call Mixed Grains (page 325) seems fresh and new, although two of these ingredients have been eaten since biblical times.

In addition, there are preparations with distinct personalities to explore: curry-laced Singapore noodles, coleslaw inspired by a Thai pickle, and potato salad adapted from one of Italy's most famous dishes of spaghetti—the lusty puttanesca, or harlot's-style pasta. While they may play a cameo role in a menu, their harmonious array of color and artful arrangement on each plate are what make vegetables and grains important in every dinner scene.

ITALIAN BAKED VEGETABLES

CORN AND JALAPENO PANCAKES

SNOW PEAS AND BELL PEPPER RIBBONS

BALSAMIC BUTTER

STUFFED TOMATOES

ASPARAGUS TIMBALES

Nuggets and Kernels

The Favored Fourteen

Steam Heat

TWO-POTATO GRATIN

POTATO CROQUETTES

BISTRO POTATOES

SWEET POTATO FLANS

MIXED GRAINS

CURRIED RICE STICK

—————

YELLOW RICE

—————

BLACK BEANS

—————

QUINOA TABBOULEH

—————

ZUCCHINI RICE SALAD

—————

FRENCH POTATO SALAD

—————

ROSEMARY-ROASTED POTATO SALAD

—————

POTATO SALAD PUTTANESCA

—————

SHOESTRING VEGETABLES WITH WHOLE-GRAIN MUSTARD

—————

THAI-TASTE COLESLAW

—————

APPLE-PEAR CHUTNEY

—————

MIXED PLUM CHUTNEY

—————

RED OR YELLOW PEPPERS PRESERVED IN OIL

—————

ITALIAN BAKED VEGETABLES

A colorful mixture of layered vegetables, baked in a casserole with olive oil, is both attractive and delicious. The variety included in the recipe eliminates the need to serve two different vegetables, or a vegetable and a starch, with many main courses.

This recipe comes from Italian knitwear designer Tai Missoni, and in the Italian tradition, the vegetables are baked with a considerable quantity of olive oil until they are soft enough to be spooned from the dish. Fresh chopped herbs (summer savory or oregano) can be added to each layer, and any oil left over after cooking can be strained and used for salad dressing. A mild, relatively unassertive olive oil is a good choice here.

The food processor will speed up the slicing chores dramatically—you will need the thin (2-mm), medium (4-mm), and thick slicing disks. Vegetables can be cut in half if needed to make them fit into the machine. However, the tomatoes should be sliced by hand.

FLEXIBLE MENU SUGGESTIONS

The vegetables can be served warm or at room temperature, and are included in menus based on Homemade Garlic Sausage with Pistachios (page 92), One-Side Grilled Fish (page 216) with Whole-Grain Mustard-Chive Butter (page 277), Sage-Rubbed Veal Chops (page 242), Capretto with Lemon and Rosemary (page 246), Cold Chicken-Poached Lobster (page 270), or Garlic-Rubbed Chicken (page 278). *Makes 6 to 8 servings*

PREPARATION: 30 MINUTES
BAKING: 70 MINUTES

1¼ pounds small eggplants
Salt
½ cup mild olive oil
1 pound Idaho russet potatoes, peeled
Ground black pepper
1 pound onions, peeled
2 medium green bell peppers, cored and
*   seeded*
1 pound ripe tomatoes, cored
1 can (5 ounces) black pitted olives, drained
*   and rinsed*

1. With a vegetable peeler, make ½-inch-wide stripes down the sides of the eggplants. Cut them crosswise into ¼-inch-thick slices. Spread the slices on a large platter and sprinkle them with ½ teaspoon salt; set aside 15 minutes, then rinse and pat slices dry on paper toweling.

2. Coat the bottom of a 15 × 10-inch baking dish with 2 tablespoons of oil; set aside. Adjust oven rack to lowest position. Heat oven to 450 degrees.

3. Thinly slice the potatoes and spread in an even layer in the bottom of the baking dish. Sprinkle with salt and pepper. Slice the onions and spread them over the potatoes in an even layer; add salt and pepper. Cut the bell peppers into ⅜-inch rings and arrange them over the onions, then put eggplant in an even layer over the peppers and sprinkle with salt and pepper.

4. Cut the tomatoes into ⅛-inch-thick slices and put them over the eggplant. Cut the olives in half, pat them dry, and put them over the tomatoes. Sprinkle salt and pepper lightly over the vegetables, then drizzle the remaining olive oil over the top.

5. Cover the dish loosely with aluminum foil. Bake 25 minutes. Lower oven heat to 325 degrees and bake 45 minutes longer, or until a knife inserted into vegetables meets no resistance.

6. Uncover and cool. (Can prepare, cool, and set aside loosely covered up to 6 hours.) Serve warm or at room temperature.

"We all know that vegetables are good for us. It does not mean that we all love vegetables, any more than the average school boy loves soap because it is good for him."

—ANDRE SIMON

CORN AND JALAPEÑO PANCAKES

One summer, I shared a beach house with several friends who are food professionals, and each weekend one of us was responsible for cooking dinner. No matter who cooked, two people usually went shopping. Because it often was the same two, the menu invariably included corn on the cob and fresh jalapeño peppers.

Often, there were half a dozen or more ears of corn left over from dinner, as well as numerous chiles. Since Sunday brunch was the last meal of the weekend, we always tried to make do. One morning, I made these pancakes, which everyone asked for every weekend thereafter.

It never is easy to predict how hot chiles (see page 198) will be. You can use only one or two, if you like, or make the pancakes milder by substituting half of a small green bell pepper for all the jalapeños. The sour-cream garnish, which will ease the burn of the chiles, can be included or omitted as appropriate for the dish or the menu.

FLEXIBLE MENU SUGGESTIONS

These pancakes are delicious for a brunch with bacon or sausage, or as blinilike appetizers (topped with sour cream, cooked and crumbled chorizo sausage, and snipped chives) in the menu based on One-Side Grilled Fish (page 216) with Citrus Salsa (page 226) or Whole-Grain Mustard-Chive Butter (page 277). They make a terrific vegetable accompaniment for menus based on Grilled Ceviche (page 231), Arizona Chicken with Corn Ragout (page 192), Mesquite-Grilled Cornish Hens (page 240), Chili-Rubbed Chicken (page 278), the Chili and Garlic-Rubbed Flank Steak (page 245), and Hickory-Grilled Baby Back Ribs (page 259).
Makes about 2 dozen

PREPARATION: 20 MINUTES
COOKING: 15 MINUTES

2 ears fresh corn, husked
4 medium jalapeño peppers, cored, halved,
   seeded
½ red bell pepper, cored, seeded
3 medium scallions, trimmed
1 egg
½ cup all-purpose flour
¼ cup yellow cornmeal
½ teaspoon baking powder
Salt
1 tablespoon white or white-wine vinegar

¾ cup milk
Vegetable oil
Sour cream (optional)

1. Heat 4 quarts water to boiling in a large soup kettle. Add the corn and boil until tender, about 2 or 3 minutes; cool. Trim the kernels off the cobs and discard the cobs. There should be 1 cup of kernels.

2. Mince the jalapeños, cut the bell pepper into ⅛-inch dice, and slice the scallion bottoms into thin rings; wrap and refrigerate the tops.

3. In a large mixing bowl (or in the container of a food processor fitted with the metal blade), whisk together (or process) the egg, flour, cornmeal, baking powder, ½ teaspoon salt, and vinegar until mixed. Whisk in the milk (or process) until the batter is smooth. Stir in the minced vegetables and corn kernels.

4. Heat 2 tablespoons oil in a large skillet or griddle. Stir the batter well, then ladle it (about 2 tablespoonfuls at a time) onto the hot skillet or griddle, and spread it to form 2-inch pancakes, with corn and vegetables distributed evenly over the surface. Cook until the bottoms of the pancakes are set, about 2 minutes, then turn and cook until done; transfer to paper towels. Repeat to cook all the pancakes. Serve immediately, garnished with a dollop of sour cream and scallion tops (optional). (Can wrap in aluminum foil and keep pancakes warm in a 225-degree oven for 15 minutes. Or, cool and serve at room temperature, or transfer to aluminum foil, cool, and refrigerate overnight. Reheat refrigerated foil-wrapped pancakes in a 325-degree oven.)

SNOW PEAS AND BELL PEPPER RIBBONS

The delicate flavor of the pea pods and bell peppers is retained by cooking them separately. Tossing them at the last minute with a small amount of softened butter gives the vegetables a buttery gloss. If you wish to use Fresh Herb Butter or Balsamic Butter instead of plain butter in step 4, omit the seasoning in step 3, then adjust seasoning to taste after adding the flavored butter.

FLEXIBLE MENU SUGGESTIONS

Among the most delicious and serviceable of all vegetable accompaniments, this recipe can be included in menus based on One-Side Grilled Fish (page 216) with Tomato Butter (page 220), Roasted Garlic and Saffron Butter (page 222), or Whole-Grain Mustard-Chive Butter (page 277). It also goes well with Milanese Beef Stew (page 185), Soy-Marinated Chicken (page 238), Sage-Rubbed Veal Chops (page 242), Capretto with Lemon and Rosemary (page 246), Leg of Lamb with Oriental Seasoning (page 251), Yogurt and Spice-Marinated Leg of Lamb (page 252), Chili-Rubbed Chicken (page 278), Szechwan Pepper Ribeyes (page 288), Garlic-Roasted Leg of Lamb (page 295), and Cognac-Marinated Beef Fillet (page 298).
Makes 8 servings

PREPARATION: 20 MINUTES
COOKING: 8 MINUTES

½ pound snow peas
Salt
Ice water
2 medium red bell peppers (¾ pound)
2 medium yellow bell peppers (¾ pound)
2 tablespoons olive oil
1 tablespoon softened unsalted butter, Fresh Herb Butter (page 219), or Balsamic Butter (page 311)
Ground black pepper

1. Remove the stem ends and strings from the snow peas. Bring 2 quarts of water to a boil in a large saucepan with ½ teaspoon salt. Add the peas and cook just until the water returns to a boil. Drain and immediately immerse the pea pods in ice water. Drain and pat dry with paper toweling. (Can cover and refrigerate overnight.)

2. Core and slice the bell peppers lengthwise into ⅛-inch julienne strips; set aside.

3. Heat the oil in a large skillet with ⅛ teaspoon salt and ⅛ teaspoon pepper. Sauté the julienned peppers over high heat, stirring constantly, until they soften slightly, about 1 minute.

4. Add the snow peas in two batches, stirring constantly until vegetables are heated through, about 1 minute longer. Remove skillet from heat and stir in the butter. Serve immediately.

BALSAMIC BUTTER

Think of this butter as vegetable polish: one tablespoon softened and tossed with steamed vegetables at the last moment—off heat—gives them a lovely finish. Take care, however, that vegetables such as green beans do not become discolored in contact with acid in the butter.

In addition, this can be swirled into pan juices to make a very simple sauce for sautéed veal, chicken breasts, or fish fillets. The small quantity of vinegar also helps to perk up the flavor of potatoes or rice.

FLEXIBLE MENU SUGGESTIONS

Depending upon menu specifics, this butter can be used interchangeably with Fresh Herb Butter (page 219), and it is called for in recipes based on Sage-Rubbed Veal Chops (page 242), Leg of Lamb with Niçoise Seasoning (page 248), Herb-Rubbed Chicken (page 278), and Cognac-Marinated Beef Fillet (page 298). *Makes 8 to 10 servings*

PREPARATION: 10 MINUTES

1 medium shallot, peeled
2½ teaspoons balsamic vinegar
Salt and ground white pepper
Several dashes hot red pepper sauce
   (optional)
¼ pound softened unsalted butter

1. Mince the shallot in a food processor fitted with the metal blade. Add the remaining ingredients and process until thoroughly mixed.

2. Spoon the butter onto a 12-inch-long sheet of plastic wrap. Roll into a 1-inch-diameter log shape, about 8 inches long. Use immediately or refrigerate up to 3 days. (Can double-wrap in aluminum foil and freeze up to 3 months.)

STUFFED TOMATOES

Stuffing tomatoes is hardly a new idea, yet it is surprising how often you can serve these, which are simply tufted with anchovy, capers, and Parmesan cheese. This is a traditional recipe that has been served for years at Bagutta restaurant in Milan.

Most delicious when made from home-grown, vine-ripened tomatoes and served warm, rather than hot, the baked tomatoes also could be garnished with small dabs of Black Olive Pesto (page 145).

FLEXIBLE MENU SUGGESTIONS

Unless there is tomato elsewhere in a menu, plan to include these in grill menus based on One-Side Grilled Fish (page 216) with Whole-Grain Mustard-Chive Butter (page 277), Sage-Rubbed Veal Chops (page 242), Capretto with Lemon and Rosemary (page 246), or Leg of Lamb with Niçoise Seasoning (page 248). They are equally good in menus with the classical Mushroom and Prosciutto-Stuffed Chicken Breasts (page 274), Garlic- or Herb-Rubbed Chicken (pages 281 and 278), Cognac-Marinated Beef Fillet (page 298), or Garlic-Roasted Leg of Lamb (page 295). *Makes 6 servings*

PREPARATION: 20 MINUTES
BAKING: 12 MINUTES

3 medium tomatoes, rinsed
1 small onion, peeled
3 tablespoons olive oil
¼ cup dry bread crumbs
2 anchovy fillets, rinsed, patted dry, minced
2 tablespoons minced parsley
1 tablespoon capers, drained, minced
⅛ teaspoon dried basil leaves
Worcestershire sauce
Salt and ground black pepper
¼ cup grated Parmesan cheese

1. Cut tomatoes in half, remove the seeds and put them, cut-sides down, on paper toweling; drain 30 minutes.

2. Chop the onion and put in a medium skillet with 1 tablespoon oil. Stir over medium heat until onion softens, about 4 minutes. Cool. Stir in the bread crumbs, anchovies, parsley, capers, basil, Worcestershire sauce, ⅛ teaspoon salt, ⅛ teaspoon pepper, and 1 tablespoon cheese.

3. Adjust oven rack to lowest position. Heat oven to 450 degrees. Lightly oil an ovenproof baking dish; set aside.

4. Divide the stuffing among tomato halves, packing it lightly. Sprinkle remaining cheese over tops of tomato halves, put them in the dish, then drizzle them with the remaining 2 tablespoons of the oil. Bake until soft, about 10 to 12 minutes. Serve hot, warm, or at room temperature. (Can bake, cover loosely with aluminum foil, and leave at room temperature 4 hours.)

ASPARAGUS TIMBALES

Toward the end of asparagus season, when the emerald spears are just past their prime, asparagus timbales add pale green notes of jewel-like glamor to dinner plates (the recipe is pictured in the color section).

The baked timbales are very delicate, since the cooked, pureed asparagus is sieved to remove fibrous matter (be sure to press the fiber in the strainer until it becomes dry and matted). Small metal dariole molds are either thimble shaped (hence the French *timbale*), or oval. The asparagus mixture will fill six ½-cup or nine ⅓-cup darioles. Round porcelain ramekins or Pyrex custard cups can be substituted for metal molds, but the wide, flat shape tends to give the timbales a clunky look. To avoid problems unmolding the timbales, butter all the molds with a very heavy hand.

FLEXIBLE MENU SUGGESTIONS

Serve these in menus based on Leg of Lamb with Malay Seasoning (page 250) and Yogurt and Spice-Marinated Lamb (page 252), Veal Scallops with Black Olive Gremolada (page 286) and Roasted Duck with Apples and Campari (page 289). *Makes 6 to 8 servings*

PREPARATION: 25 MINUTES
BAKING: 25 MINUTES

1 pound fresh thin asparagus, trimmed
1½ cups whipping cream
3 eggs
2 egg yolks
Salt and ground white pepper
Nutmeg
2 to 3 tablespoons softened butter

1. Cut the asparagus into 1-inch lengths and put them in a vegetable steamer basket (page 317). Steam until soft, about 8 to 10 minutes; drain.

2. Put the cooked asparagus in a food processor fitted with the metal blade, and process until pureed. With the motor on, slowly pour the cream into the machine. Pass contents through a fine sieve, pressing firmly to extract all the asparagus possible, then discard the fiber left in the sieve.

3. Lightly beat the eggs, egg yolks, ¾ teaspoon salt, ¼ teaspoon pepper, and several dashes of grated nutmeg, then stir the egg mixture into the asparagus cream.

4. Adjust oven rack to lowest position. Heat oven to 400 degrees. Generously coat six ½-cup (or nine ⅓-cup) dariole molds with butter. Stir the asparagus custard well, and pour it into the molds (there may be enough to fill an extra mold).

5. Put the molds close together in a baking dish lined with a thin tea towel to prevent sliding. Add enough hot tap water to reach halfway up the sides of the molds. Bake 20 to 25 minutes. (Can cover and keep warm in water bath for 30 minutes.)

6. To serve, carefully invert the molds on warm plates. Serve immediately.

NUGGETS AND KERNELS

In many restaurants, vegetables are prepared in advance and reheated by a sauté in clarified butter—a method to which I have a particular aversion as it always makes vegetables look and taste greasy. I prefer to steam vegetables and give them the simplest possible finish with a small amount of olive oil, Herbed Oil (page 73), or a tablespoon of softened butter or flavorful compound butter, or serve them plain.

I am also particularly fond of saucing vegetables with room-temperature vinaigrette or salsa, provided the vegetables will not discolor in contact with acids such as vinegar or lemon juice. Hot asparagus with Sherry-Walnut Vinaigrette (page 78) is delicious, and those same verdant spears are equally wonderful with a garnish of Citrus Salsa (page 226), particularly alongside barbecued chicken or pork.

Substituting plain vegetables in menus that call for specific recipes often saves preparation time. Since many of these vegetable recipes are rich, this is an area of the menu where you can crank down the calorie load by simplification.

The sheer number of vegetables and critical judgments about which go well with certain foods, plus the numerous ways that vegetables can be cut, shaped, combined, arranged, and sauced, expand the spectrum of choices.

At the risk of producing shrieks of protest from gardeners, an argument could be made that air shipment has made strict seasonal consideration of vegetables more or less irrelevant. Tomatoes, bell peppers, eggplants, and *haricots verts* shipped in from Israel, Holland, Mexico, and Chile are physically available in January. However, it is helpful and important, I believe, to think about the season a menu suggests and to select vegetables accordingly. The best choices are invariably the freshest vegetables one can obtain in season, and often they hail from a home garden.

Vegetables should be compatible with fish, poultry, or meat from the standpoint of flavor and color. When I serve Szechwan Pepper Ribeyes (page 288)—large steaks that will occupy nearly half the surface of a dinner plate—I have learned to balance the steak with a colorful vegetable such as steamed spinach, and I chose the diced Bistro Potatoes (page 322) sautéed with mushroom shreds because they offer a different shape, texture, color, and size on the plate.

When uniformly cut and arranged symmetrically on a plate, vegetables seem to be more formally presented than those that are placed asymmetrically. As a corollary, large vegetable pieces (such as whole asparagus), mounds (such as spinach, kale, or chard), and chunky or irregular segments (of carrot, celery, or zucchini) seem less formal than neatly trimmed asparagus spears, diced vegetables, or elegant juliennes—even when they are positioned in the same way.

I particularly recall a swordfish entrée that consisted of a wedge of grilled fish surrounded by a ring of thinly cut carrots—formal food from a formal restaurant room. As I began to eat, I noticed that some of the carrots were cut into rounds, some into flat strips, and others into long julienne. Clearly, this was intended as an artful vegetable mélange, but it did not work. The shapes seemed odd and randomly mixed, leaving me with the impression that someone in the kitchen was either playing games or that a mistake had been made.

THE FAVORED FOURTEEN

In addition to the specific vegetable recipes included in this chapter and in menus throughout the book, it can be helpful to have guidelines for presenting and saucing what I call "plain" vegetables—those with minimal embellishments that often can be workhorse accompaniments.

Many suggestions are included in the menus, but here are some general ideas for preparing more than a dozen vegetables that can be matched with sauces, oils, and compound butters, or served plain.

Count on about 1 to 1½ pounds to make four servings of vegetables that do not yield a great deal of waste when trimmed, or 2 to 2½ pounds of vegetables (such as broccoli or asparagus) that do require considerable paring. Cooking times are approximate, and will vary with quantity and vegetable size.

Using the food processor and the microwave oven are added bonuses that I highly recommend. Due to the variety of microwave cooking methods for vegetables, however, space does not permit their inclusion here.

Asparagus: Allow 5 to 6 stalks per serving (depending on size). Remove the woody ends from large stalks, and use a sharp knife or vegetable peeler to pare off the fibrous surface of the lower two-thirds of each stalk. Pencil asparagus can be served whole, without peeling. Asparagus can be left whole, cut short (about 4 inches including the tip), or halved lengthwise. Serve them loose, or arranged in bundles, with points facing in the same direction, and "tied" with blanched leek or scallion greens prior to steaming. Steam until crisp-tender, about 4 to 8 minutes depending on thickness.

Hot asparagus can be garnished with any of the vinaigrettes, Anchovy-Lemon Oil, Tomato, Garlic, and Black Olive Sauce, Gremolada Oil, Goat-Cheese Sauce, Mediterranean Sauce and shaved Parmesan cheese, any of the compound butters, or Citrus Salsa. Cold asparagus can be garnished with the oil-based sauces or the salsa.

Beets: Trim and steam beets until tender (see page 317), or rinse and wrap whole beets in aluminum foil and bake them in a 350-degree oven until tender, about 35 minutes to 1 hour depending on size. Beets can be sliced, diced, shredded, or cut into julienne strips. Hot beets are especially good when tossed with Fresh Herb Butter, Balsamic Butter, or Whole-Grain Mustard-Chive Butter. When cold, consider Chive Vinaigrette, Dill Dressing, or Hazelnut Vinaigrette.

Bell Peppers: Cut off each end of raw (unpeeled) peppers, then gently run a knife around the interior to remove the core and seeds. Cut peppers into rounds, long or short julienne strips, squares, or triangles. Peppers can be sautéed in olive oil or Herbed Oil. Halves can be rubbed with oil and grilled. Cooked peppers (warm or room temperature) can be drizzled with Gremolada Oil, Anchovy-Lemon Oil, My Favorite Vinaigrette, or Chive Vinaigrette. After a quick sauté, they can be tossed with softened Fresh Herb Butter, Orso Butter, or Balsamic Butter.

Roasted, peeled bell peppers can be handled and sauced in the same way as raw peppers although care must be taken not to overcook when heating them.

Broccoli: Trim off the tough base of broccoli stems. Stalks can be left whole, or sliced lengthwise through the florets into long, graceful pieces. Or, remove florets from raw broccoli and peel the stems by catching the tough fiber with the tip of a sharp knife and pulling it off. Prior to cooking, slice stems diagonally, or into

Continued

rounds. Steam until crisp-tender, about 4 to 8 minutes.

Serve broccoli hot with Fresh Herb Butter, Roasted Garlic and Saffron Butter, or Whole-Grain Mustard-Chive Butter;; or cold with Gremolada Oil, Anchovy-Lemon Oil, Chive Vinaigrette, Ginger-Lime Vinaigrette, My Favorite Vinaigrette, or Tomato, Garlic, and Black Olive Sauce.

Carrots: Remove tops and peel large raw carrots. Cut them into diagonal or round slices, thin julienne, coarse dice, roll-cut, or segments. Baby or finger carrots should be scrubbed with a teflon pad to remove skin. About ½ inch of the greens can be left attached (these can be eaten with the fingers, using the greens as a convenient "handle"). Steam just until tender, 4 to 14 minutes depending on size. Toss hot carrots with Fresh Herb Butter or Balsamic Butter. Carrots served at room temperature are good with Chive Vinaigrette, Dill Dressing, Ginger-Lime Vinaigrette, or Hazelnut Vinaigrette.

Eggplant: Whenever possible, select small eggplants (about 4 per pound) or purchase long, narrow Japanese eggplants. Rinse eggplants and remove stem ends. Eggplants can be completely peeled or skin can be striped with a vegetable peeler. Cut eggplants into round or long slices for sautéeing, grilling, or baking. Salt slices lightly and let stand 30 minutes, then rinse well and press dry with paper towels.

Sauté eggplant in olive oil or Herbed Oil. Before grilling or broiling eggplant, brush it with olive oil or Herbed Oil. Grill or broil eggplant until marked or lightly browned, and completely soft. Serve hot or at room temperature, topped with Anchovy-Lemon Oil, Gremolada Oil, Tomato, Garlic, and Black Olive Sauce, or a spoonful of Mediterranean Sauce.

Fennel: Trim off stalks and fronds from the fennel bulb. Halve bulb, and remove the tough core at the base. Slice fennel crosswise into strips for sautéing, or cut bulbs lengthwise into quarters or sixths and steam just until tender, about 8 to 12 minutes, depending on size.

Sauté fennel in Herbed Oil or olive oil until tender, and serve with minced fennel fronds; or toss with Fresh Herb Butter, Tomato Butter, Orso Butter, or Balsamic Butter. Hot steamed fennel hearts can be drizzled with Anchovy-Lemon Oil, or with Tomato, Garlic, and Black Olive Sauce or My Favorite Tomato Sauce.

Haricots Verts and Green Beans: Rinse and cut off the tips, leaving ends cut blunt. Steam until crisp-tender, about 4 to 6 minutes, then toss with Herbed Oil, Anchovy-Lemon Oil, Fresh Herb Butter, or Roasted Garlic and Saffron Butter, or drizzle with Poblano Cream.

Mushrooms: Wipe with a damp cloth; do not rinse. Trim off stem ends of cultivated mushrooms; completely remove shiitake stems; remove woody sections of portobello stems. Mushroom caps can be sliced thinly or thickly, cut into wedges, or diced. Sauté in Herbed Oil, then lightly drizzle with Anchovy-Lemon Oil or Gremolada Oil. Or, sauté in olive oil, then toss with a compound butter at the last moment. Fresh Herb Butter, Roasted Garlic and Saffron Butter, and Balsamic Butter all go well with mushrooms.

Potatoes: Scrub small new potatoes, and steam in their jackets until tender (can peel if desired). Larger potatoes can be peeled and steamed whole, or halved, quartered, or diced before cooking to reduce steaming time. Steam until completely tender (time will vary with size of potatoes). Season cooked potatoes lightly with salt and pepper, then drizzle with Gremolada Oil or Poblano Cream, or toss with Fresh Herb Butter, Tomato Butter, Orso Butter, Roasted Garlic and Saffron Butter, Black Olive Pesto, or Winter Pesto. Use Herbed Oil or compound butters in baked potatoes.

Snow Peas: Steam pea pods 3 to 4 minutes, then toss with Herbed Oil, Fresh Herb Butter, or Balsamic Butter. Peas will discolor in contact with the acids in vinaigrette.

Spinach: Steam until wilted, or blanch in 4 quarts of boiling water just until water returns to the boil; drain well and press to squeeze dry. Sauté in Herbed Oil, then drizzle with Gremolada Oil. Or, sauté in oil or sweet butter and stir in Fresh Herb Butter, Whole-Grain Mustard-Chive Butter, or Balsamic Butter.

Turnips: Peel and steam turnips as you would potatoes, then toss with Fresh Herb Butter, Tomato Butter, Balsamic Butter, Whole-Grain Mustard-Chive Butter, or a dab of Winter Pesto.

Zucchini (also Yellow Squash): Slice in rounds, lengthwise, cut into ¼-inch dice, or julienne. Sauté with Herbed Oil, then drizzle very lightly with Gremolada Oil, dress with Tomato, Garlic, and Black Olive Sauce, or toss with Orso Butter, Tomato Butter, Roasted Garlic and Saffron Butter, or Balsamic Butter. Can slice lengthwise and grill (page 151).

STEAM HEAT

Even before I set foot in a Chinese kitchen, where steaming is a primary cooking method, testing vegetable recipes proved to me that the standard French technique of blanching—or boiling—generally produces vegetables that lack an edge of flavor and color. I find that steaming vegetables gives the best results.

PREPARING VEGETABLES

Rinse, pare, or trim vegetables as necessary. Depending on their shape, vegetables can be cut in myriad ways: wedges, quarters, diagonal or straight slices, a thin or matchstick julienne, or a fat julienne (about ¼ inch × 2 inches). They can be diced, roll-cut in the Chinese manner, or turned by the classical French technique of paring them into graceful, bowed hexagonal cylinders with blunt ends. Always try to keep the pieces uniform in size so they will cook evenly. The food processor can give a lightning assist to standard vegetable preparation such as slicing, julienne, and rough dicing.

CHOOSING A STEAMER

For a majority of steaming chores, I use an inexpensive stainless steel vegetable steamer basket placed in a 2- to 3-quart saucepan with a tight-fitting lid. Since stainless steel is nonreactive, the basket will not discolor vegetables, and its flexible outer rim contracts or expands to fit into the pan. The short, straight legs of the steamer help to elevate it above the water (about 2 to 2½ cups) in the bottom of the saucepan.

For large quantities of vegetables, or for some Chinese recipes, I use a three-tier Oriental bamboo steamer that fits over my wok. The baskets can be lined with cheesecloth or cabbage leaves to allow steam to penetrate the layers, but prevent foods from falling through the wide mesh. Firm vegetables (such as carrots or turnips) can be arranged in the bottom tier for maximum steam, while

Continued

softer foods (e.g., cauliflower or pea pods) receive gentler gusts in the center, or on top of the stack. The only drawback to using a wok is that you must check frequently to be sure it contains a sufficient quantity of water at all times; it often must be refilled with boiling water.

Friends in Paris recently presented me with a glorious, tin-lined, two-tier copper steamer. The bottom is equivalent to a 6-quart stockpot, and the top level has a perforated bottom and a tight-fitting lid. While this definitely falls into the luxury category, similar steamers made of aluminum—with earlike handles—are sold in Chinese equipment stores. These offer the same large surface area and they are relatively inexpensive. The perforated bottom of a large aluminum steamer can be easily lined with cheesecloth, a Handiwipe, or even cabbage leaves, to prevent aluminum oxide from discoloring vegetables.

The microwave may be the most convenient way to steam vegetables. Tender pea pods, green beans, or asparagus can be placed in a microwavable plastic bag with as little as 1 tablespoon of water (or in a microwavable dish covered with plastic wrap) and cooked on high power for 3 to 6 minutes (in a 700-watt oven). Prior to opening the bag or uncovering the dish, pierce the plastic carefully with a sharp knife to permit steam to escape. Several microwave cookbooks contain useful charts that give basic cooking information for an extensive number of vegetables.

Alternately, there are steamers with basket inserts, as well as tiered electric steamers made of heatproof plastic. A surprisingly wide choice of equipment is available in supermarkets, cookware stores, and even hardware stores.

TESTING FOR DONENESS

In recipes, steaming time is calculated from the moment the pot goes on the stove. To check for doneness, probe with the tip of a small, sharp paring knife. Vegetables are crisp-tender when the knife tip meets slight resistance (as opposed to well-done, when the knife tip meets no resistance) and colors remain bright. When in doubt, remove a piece of vegetable from the steamer, run it under cold water for 30 seconds, then taste it.

Be particularly careful when opening the steamer lid or piercing the microwave plastic wrap. Hot vapor buildup in the pan or cooking utensil can cause burns. Be sure that your hands are protected and your face is kept well away from the lid.

If you plan to reheat steamed vegetables, remove them from the steamer when they are three-quarters cooked. Immediately plunge them into a shallow dish or sink filled with ice water. Let stand just until cool to the touch, then transfer to dry cloth towels to drain. Always wrap cooked vegetables in plastic before refrigerating to prevent dehydration.

TWO-POTATO GRATIN

One of my hobbies is reading about fashion, and it always amuses me to see thinner-than-a-julienne French society matrons referred to as the *gratin*—French slang for the upper crust. Technically, the term refers to the brown crust that forms on top of food that is baked with cream to the point of melting tenderness.

Here, fresh sweet potato and Idaho potato slices are interlaced with lovely results (the recipe is pictured in the color section); turnips could be substituted for the sweet potatoes, if desired. Since this gratin is as rich as French society, there are bound to be leftovers, which can make a wonderful, if offbeat, addition to breakfast.

FLEXIBLE MENU SUGGESTIONS

These potatoes are a fine accompaniment to Leg of Lamb with Niçoise or Malay Seasoning (pages 248 and 250), Roasted Duck with Apples and Campari (page 289), and Cognac-Marinated Beef Fillet (page 298). *Makes 6 servings*

PREPARATION: 45 MINUTES
BAKING: 1 HOUR 30 MINUTES

1 pound russet potatoes, peeled and soaked in
    cold water
1 pound sweet potatoes, peeled and soaked in
    cold water
1 small garlic clove, peeleld
2 tablespoons softened unsalted butter
Salt and ground black pepper
Nutmeg
3 eggs, lightly beaten
3 cups half-and-half
½ cup whipping cream

1. Insert thin (2-mm) slicing disc in food processor container, and slice the russet potatoes. Transfer potato slices to cloth towel and pat dry. Slice the sweet potatoes and pat dry separately in a towel. (Or, cut the potatoes by hand into ⅛-inch-thick slices.)

2. Mince the garlic and mix into the butter. Use the butter to coat a 9 × 7 × 2½-inch baking dish; set the dish aside.

3. Adjust oven rack to lowest position. Heat oven to 450 degrees. To assemble the gratin, make a layer of russet potatoes on bottom of baking dish; sprinkle lightly with salt and pepper. Top with a layer of sweet potatotes; sprinkle lightly with salt and pepper. Continue layering until all the potatoes are used.

4. In a mixing bowl, whisk eggs with half-and-half, cream, ⅛ teaspoon salt, ⅛ teaspoon pepper, and several dashes of grated nutmeg. Taste and adjust seasoning, then pour the mixture through a strainer and over potatoes in the dish.

5. Bake 30 minutes. Lower oven heat to 350 degrees and bake 1 hour longer, or until top is lightly browned. Cool 10 minutes before serving.

POTATO CROQUETTES

There is something quite irresistible about the crisp brown exterior and soft, mashed center of old-fashioned potato croquettes. Perhaps it is the contrast in textures, or the way they tend to complement natural juices and sauces on the plate.

The best mashed potatoes are made from cooked russets, which are slightly mealy because their cells tend to separate easily during cooking. This type of potato can be mashed for croquettes by ricing, or as a shortcut, acceptably shredded in the food processor without becoming gluey.

Instead of a traditional heavy flour and egg *panade* to hold the croquettes together, the light binder, described on page 86, is used to give these potatoes a slightly fluffy texture and fresh flavor.

FLEXIBLE MENU SUGGESTIONS

These potatoes are included in menus based on Leg of Lamb with Malay Seasoning (page 250), Mushroom and Prosciutto-Stuffed Chicken Breasts (page 274), Veal Scallops with Black Olive Gremolada (page 286), Pork with Port Wine Sauce (page 292), and Roasted Duck with Apples and Campari (page 289). *Makes 6 to 8 servings*

PREPARATION: 30 MINUTES
COOKING: ABOUT 35 MINUTES

2 pounds russet potatoes, rinsed
2 egg yolks
Salt and ground black pepper
Nutmeg
2 tablespoons milk
6 tablespoons hot melted unsalted butter
2 quarts vegetable oil
2 eggs
1½ cups plain bread crumbs

1. Put potatoes in a 6-quart soup kettle with water to cover. Cover and boil until soft, about 30 to 40 minutes. Drain, peel, and return peeled potatoes to the pot. Toss over medium heat about 2 minutes to dry the potatoes thoroughly.

2. To make the binder, insert the metal blade in a food processor. Add egg yolks, ½ teaspoon salt, ¼ teaspoon pepper, two dashes of nutmeg, and 1 tablespoon milk. Process, adding the hot melted butter to the machine in a thin stream; transfer the mixture to a mixing bowl.

3. Mash the potatoes with a ricer, or very gently shred them in the food processor, using the medium shredding disk. Thoroughly stir the mashed potatoes into the egg-yolk mixture in the bowl, and adjust the seasoning to taste.

4. Coat a sheet of wax paper with ½ teaspoon oil and put paper on a baking sheet, oiled-side up. With wet hands, shape potatoes into fifteen to eighteen ovals, each 2 × 1 inches. Put the ovals on the wax paper and freeze for 30 minutes.

5. Heat remaining vegetable oil in a dry soup kettle or deep skillet to 350 degrees on a deep-fry thermometer. Lightly beat the eggs with the remaining tablespoon of milk. Put the bread crumbs on a sheet of wax paper.

6. To finish the croquettes, roll each potato oval in the beaten egg mixture, then roll it in bread crumbs. Deep-fry croquettes in small batches until puffy and brown, about 3 minutes. Transfer to paper towels with slotted spoon; gently blot croquettes dry. Serve immediately. (Can keep croquettes warm on paper towels in 250-degree oven up to 1 hour.)

BISTRO POTATOES

Duxelles is a classical French preparation that calls for mincing and squeezing mushrooms to remove juices, then slowly cooking them with shallots and butter until the mixture is dry and the flavor is concentrated. The food processor offers a shortcut: when shredded rather than minced, mushrooms have a surface area large enough to permit moisture to evaporate easily during cooking, eliminating the need for squeezing.

I always think of these diced, sautéed potatoes, tossed with *duxelles,* as something one would find in French bistros. Indeed, they are wonderful with roasted poultry, meats, or game, but there are two slightly tedious aspects to the recipe.

The potatoes must be cut into ¼-inch dice. This can be done by hand or, more quickly, in a food processor, using the French-fry disk. To process by machine, make vertical, lengthwise slits ¼ inch apart in the potatoes, but do not cut the potatoes apart. Leave them attached at the top. Insert the potato in the processor feed tube with the cut sides facing forward, and process. As the raised teeth of the French-fry disk move sideways through the potatoes, small, irregularly "diced" pieces are formed.

Once diced, the potatoes must be patted dry and carefully sautéed—the pieces should not be crowded, otherwise they will not brown nicely. I recommend initially sautéeing them in two 10-inch skillets, or in two batches.

FLEXIBLE MENU SUGGESTIONS

Although it may be necessary to double this recipe, these potatoes are included in menus based on Sage-Rubbed Veal Chops (page 242), Capretto with Lemon and Rosemary (page 246), Leg of Lamb with Niçoise Seasoning (page 248), Herb-Rubbed Chicken (page 278), Szechwan Pepper Ribeyes (page 288), and Garlic-Roasted Leg of Lamb (page 295).
Makes 4 servings

PREPARATION: 40 MINUTES
COOKING: 1 HOUR

2 medium garlic cloves, peeled
1 medium shallot, peeled
5 tablespoons butter
¾ pound mushrooms, wiped clean
2 pounds russet potatoes, peeled
Salt and ground black pepper
¼ cup minced parsley

1. Mince the garlic and shallot and put them in a 10-inch skillet with 2 tablespoons butter. Insert the medium shredding disk in the food processor, and shred the mushrooms.

2. Heat the butter and cook the garlic mixture until fragrant, about 2 minutes. Add the mushrooms and cook over medium heat until they are dark, dry, and give up all their liquid, about 40 minutes. (Can cover and refrigerate up to 1 week, or freeze.)

3. Cut the potatoes into ¼-inch dice and soak them in cold water for 10 minutes. Drain them in a colander, then spread them on cloth towel; pat very dry.

4. Heat 1½ tablespoons butter in a large skillet (or use the remaining 1½ tablespoons butter in a second skillet). Sauté half the diced potatoes in the skillet (or cook them simultaneously in the two skillets) on medium heat, for 5 minutes, turning frequently. Cover, increase the heat slightly, and cook 5 minutes longer, tossing frequently. Decrease heat slightly and cook until potatoes are browned and soft when pierced with a sharp knife, 5 to 8 minutes longer; set aside. Repeat if necessary to cook all the potatoes.

5. Reheat all the potatoes in a large skillet. Stir in *duxelles* and add salt and pepper to taste. Toss over medium heat until hot, thoroughly mixed, and any liquid remaining in the *duxelles* has evaporated. Stir in the parsley and serve immediately.

"At a dinner party one should eat wisely but not too well, and talk well but not too wisely."

—W. SOMERSET MAUGHAM

SWEET POTATO FLANS

Cooked sweet potatoes, pureed with a special binder (see page 86), bake into lovely little "flans" that are marvelous as a holiday alternative to sweet potato casserole, and are terrific accompaniments for chicken, turkey, ham, or pork.

Because I originally created these to accompany a Thansgiving dinner, they make a large number of servings. For some menus, you may wish to halve the recipe. Unmolded leftover flans can be successfully reheated in a microwave oven on medium power.

FLEXIBLE MENU SUGGESTIONS

The flans make a special contribution to menus based on Soy-Marinated Chicken (page 238), Pork with Port Wine Sauce (page 292), Chili-Rubbed Chicken (page 278), and Roasted Duck with Apples and Campari (page 289). *Makes 10 servings*

PREPARATION: 20 TO 25 MINUTES
COOKING: ABOUT 1 HOUR

1¾ pounds sweet potatoes
3 eggs
3 egg yolks
1 to 2 tablespoons lemon juice
½ cup hot (170 degrees) melted unsalted
*   butter*
Salt and ground white pepper
Nutmeg
Hot red pepper sauce
3 tablespoons softened unsalted butter

1. Put potatoes in 4-quart soup kettle; cover with cold water. Cover and boil until potatoes are soft, about 35 to 40 minutes. Drain, cool, peel, and cut potatoes into 1½-inch chunks; set aside.

2. Put eggs, egg yolks, and 1 tablespoon lemon juice in a food processor fitted with the metal blade. Process, adding hot melted butter. Pulse in ¼ teaspoon salt, ⅛ teaspoon pepper, a pinch of nutmeg, and several dashes hot pepper sauce. Adjust seasoning to taste.

3. Add half the potatoes and process until minced. Add remaining potatoes and process to a fine, silky puree. Adjust seasoning, adding lemon juice, salt, pepper, nutmeg, and hot red pepper sauce to taste.

4. Adjust oven rack to lowest position. Heat oven to 350 degrees. Use softened butter to generously coat ten ½-cup porcelain ramekins or heatproof custard cups. Spoon puree into the molds. Cover each mold with a buttered wax-paper square, buttered side down.

5. Put filled molds in a baking dish lined with a thin tea towel. Add enough hot tap water to reach halfway up the sides of the molds (do not allow dishes to float). Bake 30 to 35 minutes. (Can turn off oven, leave door ajar, cover with foil, and keep warm for 30 minutes.)

6. To serve, remove wax paper, and loosen each flan from its mold by carefully passing a thin knife around the inside edge. Carefully invert the molds on warm plates. Serve immediately.

MIXED GRAINS

Grains and legumes such as barley, wild rice, lentils, and cracked wheat (bulgur) can be mixed and cooked in the manner of rice and served in the same way. This mélange is wonderfully tasty, and several of the grains also are very high in fiber.

FLEXIBLE MENU SUGGESTIONS

Minced ham or bacon adds zing to the grain mixture but can occasionally conflict with main-course meats (you can omit the ham but the grains will be slightly lacking in flavor). This recipe is a particularly good match for Leg of Lamb with Niçoise Seasoning (page 248), Herb-Rubbed Chicken (page 278), Roasted Duck with Apples and Campari (page 289), Pork with Port Wine Sauce (page 292), Garlic-Roasted Leg of Lamb (page 295), or Cognac-Marinated Beef Fillet (page 298). *Makes 6 to 8 servings*

SOAKING: OVERNIGHT
PREPARATION: 20 MINUTES
COOKING: 90 MINUTES

½ cup barley
3 medium garlic cloves, peeled
1 large red onion, peeled
5 medium scallions, trimmed
½ cup (2 ounces) ham
4 tablespoons olive oil
1 quart Chicken Broth (page 165)
½ teaspoon dried oregano
½ cup lentils, rinsed
¼ cup wild rice
¼ cup medium bulgur
Salt and ground black pepper
¼ cup minced parsley

1. Put the barley in a bowl and cover with 2½ cups cold water; set aside overnight.

2. Mince the garlic, chop the onion, and slice the scallions into thin rings. Cut the ham into ¼-inch dice.

3. Heat the oil in a 4-quart saucepan. Add the ham and cook until fat is rendered. Add the garlic, onions, and scallions and cook until the vegetables soften, about 6 to 8 minutes.

4. Drain and add the barley to the pan with 2 cups broth, 1 cup water, and oregano. Cover and simmer 30 minutes, stirring occasionally. Stir in lentils, wild rice, the remaining broth, and 1 cup water. Cover and simmer 20 minutes.

5. Stir in the bulgur. Cover and simmer until all the grains are tender, about 25 minutes. Uncover and simmer 5 to 7 minutes longer, or until most of the liquid has been absorbed and mixture is hot. Taste; adjust seasoning with salt and pepper. Garnish with parsley and serve immediately.

CURRIED RICE STICK

Stir-fried rice stick noodles—common to several Asian cuisines including Thai, Japanese, Vietnamese, Filipino, Indonesian, and Malaysian—are also served in many Cantonese restaurants. When spiced with curry powder they often are called Singapore-style noodles, since that nation's Nonya cooking blends Chinese ingredients and Malay spices.

A limitless number of variations for this dish exist—Chinese versions often include pork, shrimp, or hot chiles. This is a colorful, but rather tame, vegetarian version that can be spiced with a minced green chile. Additional information about the noodles appears on page 209.

FLEXIBLE MENU SUGGESTIONS

These noodles add spice to menus based on Shrimp and Scallops with Chile-Peanut Sauce (page 232), Soy-Marinated Chicken (page 238), Leg of Lamb with Oriental Seasoning (page 251), or Garlic-Rubbed Chicken (page 278). *Makes 4 servings*

PREPARATION: 20 MINUTES
COOKING: 6 MINUTES

¼ pound rice stick noodles
14 small water chestnuts (2 ounces), drained
2 medium red bell peppers, julienned
1 pound small zucchini, quartered lengthwise
6 medium scallions, roots removed
1 chunk fresh ginger (2 × 1 inch), peeled
1 large garlic clove, peeled, crushed
½ cup Chicken Stock (page 165)
3 tablespoons all-purpose soy sauce
2 tablespoons Shaohsing wine or dry sherry
Salt
¼ teaspoon sugar
5 tablespoons vegetable oil
1 tablespoon curry powder
1 tablespoon sesame oil

1. Put noodles in a large bowl, cover with 1 quart of warm water, and let them soak for 10 minutes; drain and set aside.

2. Thinly slice the water chestnuts and transfer them to a bowl. Add the bell-pepper julienne. Cut the zucchini crosswise to make ¼-inch-thick triangles; add to the bowl. Cut the scallion bottoms into thin rings and set aside; then make 2 tablespoons of thin green scallion rings for garnish; reserve the remaining tops for another use. Slice the ginger diagonally into ⅛-inch-thick pieces.

3. Mix stock, soy sauce, Shaohsing wine, ¼ teaspoon salt, and sugar in a cup; set aside. Put remaining ingredients nearby.

4. Heat 2 tablespoons of oil in a wok. Add ginger and garlic; stir-fry until fragrant, then remove and discard. Add the mixed vegetables to the wok and stir-fry until crisp-tender, about 2 minutes; return to the bowl.

5. Put 3 tablespoons oil into the hot wok. Add the noodles and sprinkle them with curry powder; toss to coat with oil. Add the sauce mixture, and toss until liquid is absorbed but noodles are not dry. Add the vegetables, white scallion rings, and sesame oil. Stir-fry until hot and thoroughly mixed, about 1 minute. Garnish with scallion greens and serve immediately.

YELLOW RICE

Vibrant and colorful, the yellow hue of this pilaf comes from turmeric, a tropical plant that is a relative of ginger. The turmeric rhizome (or rootlike stem) is dried and ground to produce the spice, which has a slightly acrid flavor and is a prominent ingredient in curry powder. Turmeric has long been used in India for medicinal purposes, as a dye and a cosmetic. No doubt the spice found its way to Africa via Indian settlers there; this recipe was adapted from one my friend Lindy Grobler regularly served with her Baked Curried Beef.

Basmati, a narrow, long-grain rice from northern India and Pakistan, has an unmistakably nutty taste and distinct fragrance. This is the aromatic rice you find in many Indian, Pakistani, and Afghan restaurants, and when cooked, these grains nearly double in length. According to Indian food expert Julie Sahni, the word *basmati* means "queen of fragrance."

Texmati, a crossbreed of Texas long-grain with basmati strains, came on the U.S. market in 1985. It is similar in flavor and aroma to basmati and also will give this pilaf an extra dimension of flavor. However, any type of long-grain rice can be used in this recipe.

Despite the exotic ingredients, pilaf is a simple preparation that calls for coating grains of rice in butter, then cooking it slowly with onion and liquid in a covered pot. When cooked in this manner, the rice remains relatively firm, dry, and separate.

FLEXIBLE MENU SUGGESTIONS

This recipe is suitable for numerous main courses including Baked Curried Beef (page 201), Chicken Enchiladas Verdes (page 197), One-Side Grilled Fish (page 216) with Tomato Butter (page 220), Fresh Herb Butter (page 219), or Winter Pesto (page 227), Mesquite-Grilled Cornish Hens (page 240), Leg of Lamb with Oriental Seasoning (page 251), Yogurt and Spice-Marinated Leg of Lamb (page 252), Skewered Lamb with Curry and Fruit (page 254), Jalapeño and Jack Cheese Sausages (page 256), Chili and Garlic-Rubbed Flank Steak (page 245), Mushroom and Prosciutto-Stuffed Chicken Breasts (page 274), or Chili- or Curry-Rubbed Chicken (pages 283 and 278). *Makes 6 to 8 servings*

PREPARATION: 10 MINUTES
COOKING: 30 TO 35 MINUTES

2 tablespoons butter
2 cups basmati, Texmati, or other long-grain
   rice
2 teaspoons turmeric
Salt
5 cups Chicken Stock (page 165)

1. Melt the butter in a 4-quart saucepan with a tight-fitting lid. Add rice and turmeric. Stir over low heat until the rice becomes shiny. Stir in ½ teaspoon salt (increase the salt to 2 teaspoons if unsalted broth is used).

2. Add the stock and heat to simmering. Stir the rice very well to prevent grains from sticking. Cover and cook over low heat until liquid is absorbed and rice is fluffy, usually 30 to 35 minutes. (Can set aside, covered, 20 minutes.) Serve immediately.

BLACK BEANS

For me, black beans are inextricably linked to a memorable Cuban meal eaten in a San Juan restaurant during a visit to Puerto Rico. Although I was raised on refried pinto beans, each rich bite of *frijoles negros,* with their hint of mushroom flavor, was so sensational I was hooked immediately.

Once a relatively obscure Latin American and Caribbean cooking ingredient, today turtle beans (*phaseolus vulgaris*) are widely available in supermarkets and health-food stores. Their popularity is no doubt due to their heartiness as well as their inky color, which adds drama and visual contrast to many different food combinations.

Due to their low moisture content, dried beans require an overnight soak in cold water, or parboiling. They will produce less foam if one tablespoon of fat per cup of beans is added to the cooking liquid. While this recipe calls for salt pork—a traditional Latin ingredient that gives these beans enormous flavor—Herbed Oil (page 73) or olive oil may be substituted (however, this change will require additional seasoning so the beans are not bland). Once cooked, an extra-creamy texture can be achieved by pureeing several cups of the beans and stirring the puree back into the pot, but this is not an essential step.

While their flavors are not equivalent, small red or pink beans can be substituted for black beans in this recipe.

FLEXIBLE MENU SUGGESTIONS

The beans are wonderful with Arizona Chicken with Corn Ragout (page 192) or Chicken Enchiladas Verdes (page 197). In addition, they are excellent for grills and barbecued foods, including One-Side Grilled Fish (page 216) with Citrus Salsa (page 226), Grilled Ceviche (page 231), Mesquite-Grilled Cornish Hens (page 240), Skewered Lamb with Curry and Fruit (page 254), Chili and Garlic-Rubbed Flank Steak (page 245), Jalapeño and Jack Cheese Sausages (page 256), and Chili-Rubbed Chicken (page 278). *Makes 6 to 8 servings*

SOAKING: 1 HOUR OR OVERNIGHT
PREPARATION: 30 MINUTES
COOKING: ABOUT 1½ HOURS

1 pound black (turtle) beans, picked over to
*   remove broken pieces or stones*
¼ pound salt pork, rind removed
5 medium garlic cloves, peeled
2 medium onions, peeled
1 large celery stalk
½ teaspoon vinegar
Salt and ground black pepper

1. Put beans in a 4-quart soup kettle. Cover with cold water and heat to boiling. Boil 2 minutes, then set beans aside for 1 hour. Drain, reserving 1 quart of the parboiling liquid. (Or, can cover beans with cold water and soak at room temperature overnight.)

2. Cut the salt pork into ¼-inch dice and put it in the soup kettle. Toss over medium heat until browned, about 10 to 15 minutes. Remove pork with a slotted spoon, leaving the drippings in the kettle.

3. Mince the garlic, and chop the onions and celery. Heat the pork drippings (or 3 tablespoons oil), add the vegetables, and cook over medium heat until they soften, about 10 minutes.

4. Stir in the beans, diced salt pork, and 1 quart of the parboiling liquid or cold water. Heat the liquid to boiling, cover, and simmer for 45 minutes. Uncover and simmer 45 minutes to 1 hour longer, or until most of the liquid has evaporated and the beans are very tender when mashed with a spoon. (It is best not to disturb the beans by stirring while they cook since this can cause breakage, which may cause them to stick to the bottom of the pan and burn.)

5. Remove 3 cups of the cooked bean mixture from the kettle and puree it in a food processor fitted with the metal blade. Return the pureed beans to the kettle, and stir in vinegar. Taste and adjust seasoning with salt (if needed) and pepper. Beans are ready to serve. (Can cool to lukewarm and refrigerate uncovered 48 hours. Reheat slowly, stirring to prevent burning; beans will thicken slightly.)

QUINOA TABBOULEH

Sometime during 1985, a mysterious and little-known grain from the highlands of Bolivia and Peru appeared in health-food stores. This was quinoa (pronounced keen-wah), touted as a super grain with a high protein content and relatively low calorie count (about 130 calories in a 1½-ounce serving), and said to have been the 7,000-year-old staple of the ancient Inca diet.

Quinoa resembles sesame seeds, although it swells nearly to the size of barley when soaked or cooked. It has a delicious, nutty flavor and is an excellent substitute for rice, couscous, or bulgur (cracked wheat) in many salads. When used instead of bulgur for this new-wave *tabbouleh,* the added plus is reducing the quantity of olive oil (100 calories per tablespoon—no cholesterol) in the salad.

This grain can be cooked on top of the stove, or in the microwave (initial microwave cooking times are given for 700-watt ovens; secondary times are a guideline for ovens with lower wattage). Quinoa is now available in many supermarkets.

FLEXIBLE MENU SUGGESTIONS

This salad is suggested in menus based on Mesquite-Grilled Cornish Hens (page 240), Yogurt and Spice-Marinated Leg of Lamb (page 252), Skewered Lamb with Curry and Fruit (page 254), and Herb- or Curry-Rubbed Chicken (pages 278 and 282). *Makes 6 to 8 servings*

PREPARATION: 25 MINUTES
STANDING: ABOUT 1 HOUR

1½ cups quinoa
Salt
½ pound cucumber, peeled and seeded
½ pound firm ripe tomatoes, cored
½ small red onion, peeled
¼ cup lemon juice
¼ cup olive oil
Ground black pepper
Hot red pepper sauce
½ cup minced parsley

1. Put the quinoa in a fine strainer, rinse with cold water, and drain. Transfer it to a 2-quart saucepan. Add 2 cups water and ¼ teaspoon salt. Cover and heat to boiling. Reduce heat and simmer until water is absorbed and quinoa is tender, about 20 minutes; cool. (Or, put quinoa, 2 cups water, and the salt in a 2-quart microwavable casserole. Cover and microwave on high power for 5 to 7 minutes, then on medium power for 5 to 7 minutes longer. Let stand, covered, for 5 minutes. Uncover and cool.)

2. Cut the cucumber and tomatoes into ¼-inch dice; transfer the vegetables to a large mixing bowl.

3. Slice the onion into ½-inch-long julienne strips and add it to the bowl with the lemon juice, olive oil, ½ teaspoon pepper, and a dash of hot red pepper sauce. Stir in the quinoa and parsley and adjust seasoning to taste. (Can set salad aside up to 4 hours.) Serve at room temperature.

ZUCCHINI RICE SALAD

Colorful and refreshingly simple, zucchini rice salad is a lighthearted partner for numerous cold foods (the recipe is pictured in the color section). If you have a food processor French-fry disk on hand, the zucchini is easy to roughly dice in the machine (see step 4).

FLEXIBLE MENU SUGGESTIONS

This recipe is included in menus based on One-Side Grilled Fish (page 216) with Winter Pesto (page 227), Cold Chicken-Poached Lobster (page 270), and Curry- or Chili-Rubbed Chicken (pages 278, 282, and 283). *Makes 6 to 8 servings*

PREPARATION: 30 MINUTES
COOKING: 25 MINUTES

1 medium ear fresh corn, halved
½ cup mild olive oil
2 cups basmati or long-grain rice
Salt
1 small red onion, peeled
¼ cup white-wine vinegar
1 medium red bell pepper, cored and seeded
½ pound medium zucchini, rinsed
2 tablespoons fresh minced oregano
*   (1½ teaspoons dried)*

1. Put the corn into a large saucepan fitted with a vegetable steamer (page 317). Cover and steam until corn is just cooked, about 5 minutes; set aside to cool. Strain the steaming liquid and add enough water to measure 1 quart; set aside.

2. Heat 1 tablespoon oil in the same saucepan. Add the rice and stir over low heat about 2 minutes. Stir in 1 teaspoon salt and the corn liquid. Cover and heat to boiling. Stir well to prevent rice from sticking, then cover and simmer until liquid is absorbed, about 18 to 20 minutes. Spread the hot, cooked rice on a foil-lined baking sheet; set aside to cool.

3. Cut the onion into thin, ½-inch-long julienne strips, transfer it to a large bowl, and stir in the vinegar; set aside. Cut the bell pepper into ½-inch-long julienne strips and add it to the bowl. (Or, cut the onion into eighths and cut the bell peppers lengthwise into ½-inch-wide strips. Use the processor medium slicing disk to slice the onion and peppers across the grain.)

4. Cut the zucchini into ¼-inch dice. (Or, insert the French-fry disk in a food processor. Slit each zucchini lengthwise into three "fingers" leaving all pieces attached at the stem ends. Stand zucchini upright in the food chute with cut side facing front. Process with a firm push to processor-dice.)

5. Remove corn kernels from the cob. Discard the cob and add the kernels to the bowl with zucchini and the remaining oil. Stir in the cool rice and oregano. (Can cover and set aside up to 6 hours.) Adjust seasoning to taste; serve at room temperature.

FRENCH POTATO SALAD

French cooks often season potato salad with shallots and white wine in addition to vinegar and mustard, giving it a distinctive flavor. Take care to adjust seasoning immediately prior to serving so salad will not be bland.

FLEXIBLE MENU SUGGESTIONS

Think of this as a basic potato salad that can replace most others in a menu. The recipe doubles easily, and is suitable for menus based on Country Pork Terrine or Homemade Garlic Sausage with Pistachios (pages 90 and 92); barbecued Leg of Lamb with Niçoise Seasoning (page 248), Chili and Garlic-Rubbed Flank Steak (page 245), Jalapeño and Jack Cheese Sausages (page 256), Cold Chicken-Poached Lobster (page 270), Chili-Rubbed Chicken (page 278), or Cognac-Marinated Beef Fillet (page 298). *Makes 4 to 6 servings*

PREPARATION: 30 MINUTES
COOKING: 30 MINUTES
CHILLING: 3 TO 4 HOURS

2 pounds waxy white potatoes, rinsed
1 medium shallot, peeled
¼ cup white-wine vinegar
2 tablespoons dry white wine
2 teaspoons Dijon mustard
Salt and ground black pepper
½ cup mild olive oil
¼ cup minced parsley
2 teaspoons fresh minced chives

1. Put potatoes in a 6-quart soup kettle with water to cover. Cover and boil until tender when pierced with a knife, about 30 minutes. Drain and let them stand, uncovered, until cool. Refrigerate until chilled. (Can refrigerate overnight.)

2. Mince the shallot and transfer it to a large mixing bowl. Whisk in the vinegar, wine, mustard, ¼ teaspoon salt, ¼ teaspoon pepper, and the oil (or mix together in a food processor fitted with the metal blade); set aside.

3. Peel the chilled potatoes and cut them with a wet knife into ⅛-inch-thick slices (can use thick processor slicing disk).

4. Add the parsley to the dressing. Carefully toss potatoes with the dressing in the bowl. Adjust seasoning to taste. Garnish with chives and serve immediately. (Can refrigerate the salad up to 6 hours. If refrigerated, bring salad to room temperature and adjust seasoning before serving as potatoes absorb flavor.)

ROSEMARY-ROASTED POTATO SALAD

Few salads are simpler than this one made from very small, new potatoes that have been roasted with oil and herbs, and dressed with fresh lemon juice and parsley. The salad is most delicious at the point when the potatoes have just cooled to room temperature and some of the edges are still oven-crisp.

FLEXIBLE MENU SUGGESTIONS

This recipe is included in menus based on Country Pork Terrine (page 90), Mesquite-Grilled Cornish Hens (page 240), Leg of Lamb with Niçoise Seasoning (page 248), Hickory-Grilled Baby Back Ribs (page 259), Chili-Rubbed Chicken (page 278), and Cognac-Marinated Beef Fillet (page 298). *Makes 6 servings*

PREPARATION: 25 MINUTES
COOKING: 35 TO 40 MINUTES

3 medium shallots, peeled
1½ teaspoons fresh minced rosemary leaves
1 teaspoon fresh minced thyme leaves
Salt and ground black pepper
Cayenne pepper
⅓ cup olive or vegetable oil
3 pounds small new potatoes, rinsed and well-scrubbed
Juice of ½ medium lemon
¼ cup minced parsley

1. Adjust oven rack to lowest position. Heat oven to 425 degrees.

2. Mince the shallots and put them in a small bowl with the rosemary, thyme, ¾ teaspoon salt, ¼ teaspoon black pepper, ⅛ teaspoon cayenne pepper, and the olive oil; stir well.

3. Quarter the potatoes and pat dry, and put them on a 13 × 10-inch jelly-roll pan. Pour the oil mixture over the potatoes and turn to coat potatoes completely. Roast the potatoes until they are browned and soft when pierced with a knife, turning them several times with a pancake spatula, about 35 to 40 minutes.

4. Cool potatoes to room temperature. Adjust seasoning to taste with salt and pepper. Squeeze lemon juice over potatoes, sprinkle with parsley, and toss to mix thoroughly. Serve at room temperature.

POTATO SALAD PUTTANESCA

One of my newest potato salads is based on a robust pasta: the famous puttanesca, or "harlot's-style" spaghetti, that is said to be a specialty of Ischia, an island off the coast of Naples. There are, of course, many versions of puttanesca sauce, but garlic, tomatoes, capers, and the black olives of nearby Gaeta are some of the standard ingredients. Anchovies are often added, although tuna is sometimes substituted.

Here the sauce is made with Niçoise olives (preferably the Oil-Marinated Olives, page 63), and tossed with tiny new-potato quarters. Directions for cooking potatoes in the microwave are included because I find this method particularly useful on hot days. (Initial microwave cooking times are given for 700-watt ovens; secondary times are a guideline for ovens with lower wattage).

FLEXIBLE MENU SUGGESTIONS

Include this salad in menus based on Mesquite-Grilled Cornish Hens (page 240), Capretto with Lemon and Rosemary (page 246), and Herb-Rubbed Chicken (page 278).
Makes 6 servings

PREPARATION: 45 MINUTES
COOKING: 35 MINUTES

2½ pounds very small new potatoes
3 medium garlic cloves, peeled
1½ teaspoons dried oregano
½ cup olive oil
1 pound (8 medium) Italian plum tomatoes,
* peeled*
1 small green pepper, cored
5 anchovies, rinsed and patted dry
3 tablespoons drained capers
¼ cup minced parsley
Salt and ground black pepper
¼ cup (about 25) Oil-Marinated Olives (page
* 63), or Niçoise olives, drained*

1. Put the potatoes in a 6-quart soup kettle, add 3 quarts water, and boil until tender, about 20 minutes. Cool, peel, quarter, and set potatoes aside. (Or, put potatoes in a microwavable 3-quart casserole with ⅓ cup water. Cover and microwave on high power for 12 to 15 minutes, stirring once. Let stand, covered, for 5 minutes. Cool, peel, quarter, and set the potatoes aside.)

2. Mince the garlic and transfer it to a medium skillet. Add the oregano and 3 tablespoons oil and cook over low heat until fragrant, about 2 minutes. Coarsely chop the tomatoes and add them to the skillet. Simmer until most of the liquid evaporates, about 20 minutes; set the tomato sauce aside in a large mixing bowl.

3. Cut the green pepper into thin, ½-inch-long julienne pieces and add them to the tomato sauce. Mash and stir in the anchovies and the remaining oil. Add potatoes, capers, and parsley. Mix the salad thoroughly and adjust seasoning to taste with about ¾ teaspoon salt and ¼ teaspoon pepper. Let salad stand for 30 minutes (or up to 6 hours). Stir in the olives and adjust the seasoning again. Serve at room temperature.

SHOESTRING VEGETABLES WITH WHOLE-GRAIN MUSTARD

White or yellow mustard seeds (*brassica hirta*) resemble tiny pale beads. They are coarsely ground or crushed, then mixed with water, wine or vinegar, and salt to make whole- or coarse-grained (also called old-fashioned or farmhouse) mustard. This type of mustard is older than the smooth version, which was invented during the early eighteenth century.

A coarse mustard adds acidity and tang to this dressing, in addition to a slightly grainy texture that is eminently compatible with the shoestring vegetables. Always taste the mustard before using it in the recipe to be sure you like its flavor. Depending on the brand, it can vary from mild to relatively pungent.

FLEXIBLE MENU SUGGESTIONS

The salad was created to offset the sweetness of Pork with Port Wine Sauce (page 292), but the mustard dressing makes it equally good with Country Pork Terrine (page 90), Homemade Garlic Sausage with Pistachios (page 92), Soy-Marinated Chicken (page 238), Yogurt and Spice-Marinated Leg of Lamb (page 252), Cold Chicken-Poached Lobster (page 270), or Curry-, Chili-, or Herb-Rubbed Chicken (pages 282, 283, and 278). *Makes 8 servings*

PREPARATION: 25 MINUTES

SALAD

2 small yellow squash, rinsed
2 small zucchini, rinsed
1 bunch (½ pound) radishes, rinsed, stemmed
8 medium scallions, roots removed

DRESSING

1½ to 2 tablespoons lemon juice
1 egg white
Salt and ground black pepper
2 tablespoons whole-grain mustard
½ cup mild olive oil

GARNISH

8 large Bibb lettuce leaves

1. To prepare the salad ingredients, cut the yellow squash and zucchini into thin shoe-string strips (3 inches by ⅛ inch) and transfer the julienne to a large bowl. Slice the radishes thinly and cut the scallions into thin rings; add each to the bowl. Toss to mix the vegetables.

2. To make the dressing, fit a food processor with the metal blade. Process the lemon juice with the egg white and a pinch of salt until foamy. Add ⅛ teaspoon pepper and the mustard. Process, quickly pouring oil into the machine. Adjust seasoning to taste. (Can cover and refrigerate vegetables and dressing separately for 6 hours.)

3. At serving time, toss vegetables with dressing. Spoon the salad onto lettuce-leaf "cups," and serve immediately.

THAI-TASTE COLESLAW

Peanuts, hot green chiles, and a curry-spiked dressing transform shreds of green cabbage, curly Savoy cabbage, or crunchy Napa (celery) cabbage into an exotic sweet and spicy salad inspired by the pickled vegetable garnishes served in Thai restaurants. This is very quickly prepared if you use the medium or fine slicing disk of a food processor to cut the cabbage across the grain into shreds, and slice the cucumbers and scallions.

FLEXIBLE MENU SUGGESTIONS

This coleslaw is included in menus based on Soy-Marinated Chicken (page 238), Leg of Lamb with Oriental Seasoning (page 251), and Curry-Rubbed Chicken (page 278).
Makes 6 to 8 servings

PREPARATION TIME: 20 MINUTES

2 medium garlic cloves, peeled
2 medium serrano chiles, cored, seeded
1 pound Savoy or green cabbage, cored, cut in
   wedges
½ pound cucumber, peeled, seeded, quartered
   lengthwise
4 medium scallions, roots removed
¼ cup rice vinegar
2 tablespoons sugar
½ teaspoon curry powder
½ cup vegetable oil
½ cup dry-roasted peanuts
2 tablespoons minced cilantro leaves
Salt and ground pepper

1. Mince the garlic and chiles and put them in a large mixing bowl.

2. Shred the cabbage across the grain in a food processor or with a chef's knife or cleaver; add it to the bowl. Cut the cucumbers into thin triangular slices and the scallions into thin rings (cucumbers and scallions also can be sliced together by processing vertically); add them to the bowl.

3. In a measuring cup, mix the vinegar, sugar, curry, and oil. Pour the dressing over the cabbage. Coarsely chop and add the peanuts and the cilantro; then toss to mix thoroughly. Adjust seasoning with salt and pepper. (Can cover and refrigerate 6 hours before serving.) Serve at room temperature.

APPLE-PEAR CHUTNEY

Green apples and firm pears make a delightful fall or winter chutney that is an excellent condiment for veal, chicken, pork, or duck.

FLEXIBLE MENU SUGGESTIONS

Serve this in place of Mixed Plum Chutney (page 338) if desired. It is included in menus based on Baked Curried Beef (page 201) and Yogurt and Spice-Marinated Leg of Lamb (page 252), and it can help dress up Pork with Port Wine Sauce (page 292) leftovers. *Makes 3½ cups*

PREPARATION: 30 MINUTES
MARINATION: 48 HOURS
COOKING: 1½ TO 2 HOURS

1 chunk (1 ounce or a 1½ by 1-inch piece) ginger, peeled
1 medium onion, peeled
1½ pounds Granny Smith apples, peeled and cored
1 pound Bosc or Bartlett pears, peeled and cored
1 cup sugar
½ cup white (sultana) raisins
¾ cup cider vinegar
½ teaspoon cinnamon
½ teaspoon powdered mustard
¼ teaspoon cayenne pepper
1 cup (4 ounces) blanched slivered almonds

1. Mince the ginger, coarsely chop the onion, and transfer the vegetables to a large, nonreactive bowl.

2. Cut the apples into ¼-inch slices (apples can be sliced in the food processor with the thick slicing disk). Cut the pears into ¼-inch dice. Combine all ingredients except the almonds in the bowl, cover it tightly with plastic wrap, and set it aside in a cool place for 48 hours.

3. Transfer the contents of the bowl to a large (at least 10 inches), deep, nonreactive skillet. Simmer over low heat, stirring frequently, until the mixture thickens to the consistency of a chunky jam, about 1½ to 2 hours. (Can transfer chutney to sterilized jars, cool, tightly cover, and refrigerate up to 1 month, or can the mixture as described below.)

4. Transfer the hot chutney to hot, wet sterilized canning jars. Cover with hot, wet sterilized lids. Adjust caps according to manufacturer's directions. Process in a boiling water bath, with water covering jars by 2 inches, for 10 minutes. Cool and check the seals according to manufacturer's instructions. (Can store jars in a cool dry place up to 1 year.)

MIXED PLUM CHUTNEY

Let me quote Indian cooking expert Julie Sahni on the subject of chutney "or *chatni* as it is pronounced in India, . . . a Sanskrit word meaning 'for licking'." The difference between a chutney and a pickle, she explains, "is the texture. Chutney . . . can be in the form of a sauce, dip, thick pulpy spread, or finely minced preserve, while a pickle contains clearly distinguishable pieces of vegetable or fruit."

This recipe satisfies both definitions: it is cooked to a sweet-sour jamlike consistency, yet it still retains chunks of fruit. The best time to make this chutney is late August or September, when the markets are filled with an assortment of plums. Use it as a condiment to accompany the recipes below, as a glaze for roasted baby chickens or Cornish hens, or in salads. It is lovely to put by for holiday gifts.

FLEXIBLE MENU SUGGESTIONS

This chutney is delicious to use for Chutney Toasts (page 449), with Baked Curried Beef (page 201), Leg of Lamb with Malay Seasoning (page 250), Yogurt and Spice-Marinated Lamb (page 252), Skewered Lamb with Curry and Fruit (page 254), or Curry-Rubbed Chicken (page 278). *Makes about 1 quart*

PREPARATION: 30 MINUTES
MARINATION: 48 HOURS
COOKING: 1½ TO 2 HOURS

1 chunk (½ ounce or 1-inch cube) ginger, peeled
1 medium onion, peeled
2½ pounds mixed dark plums, including Santa Rosa, Granada, Friar, Zonas, or other red plums, halved, pitted
1 cup sugar
½ cup firmly packed white (sultana) raisins
¾ cup cider vinegar
½ teaspoon cinnamon
½ teaspoon Hot Curry Powder (page 203), or mild curry powder
¼ teaspoon cayenne pepper
½ teaspoon powdered mustard

1. Mince the ginger, coarsely chop the onion, and transfer the vegetables to a large, nonreactive bowl.

2. Cut the plums into ⅛- to ¼-inch slices and add them to the bowl (plums can be processed using the medium slicing disk). Stir all the remaining ingredients into the bowl, cover it tightly with plastic, and set it aside in a cool place for 48 hours.

3. Transfer the contents of the bowl to a large, deep, nonreactive skillet. Simmer over low heat, stirring frequently, until the mixture thickens to the consistency of a chunky jam, about 1½ to 2 hours.

4. Transfer the hot chutney to hot, wet sterilized canning jars. Cover with hot, wet sterilized lids. Adjust caps according to manufacturer's directions. Process in a boiling water bath, with water covering jars by 2 inches, for 10 minutes. Cool and check the seals according to manufacturer's instructions. (Can store jars in a cool dry place up to 1 year.)

RED OR YELLOW PEPPERS PRESERVED IN OIL

Preserved red or yellow (or even orange) peppers are wonderful to have on hand in the refrigerator because they can be substituted for roasted bell peppers in any number of recipes, and they eliminate last-minute preparation.

Salting them lightly to draw out excess water and packing them in olive oil (mild pure olive oil or mild extra-virgin oil) preserves their fresh flavor. After the peppers are used, recycle the oil in salad dressings, soups, and pasta sauces.

FLEXIBLE MENU SUGGESTIONS

These peppers are marvelous to wrap around tiny tender balls of fresh mozzarella (*ciliegine*) for a quick hors d'oeuvre. Present them on Bibb lettuce leaves, toasted, garlic-rubbed French or Italian toast, or around slices of soft cheese. A mound of julienned yellow peppers also looks great on small radicchio leaves.

Use them in Penne with Broccoli and Scallops (page 206) or for Mushroom Pizzas on Prosciutto Crust (page 114). They also can be julienned and put on the plate as a bright accompaniment to Soy-Marinated Chicken (page 238) or Herb-Rubbed Chicken (page 278). *Makes 1½ pints*

PREPARATION: 45 MINUTES
CONSERVATION: 2 MONTHS IN REFRIGERATOR

8 medium red or yellow bell peppers
Salt
1 to 1¼ cups mild pure or extra-virgin olive
  oil

1. Turn gas jets on the stove to high (or heat the broiler).

2. Arrange peppers on stove burners (or broiler pan). Turn them frequently on top of the stove (or broil 4 inches from heat source, turning frequently) until skins are charred and blistered on all sides, about 8 minutes. Transfer the blackened peppers to a heavy-duty plastic bag, and twist it closed. Set the bag aside until skins loosen and peppers are cool to touch, about 15 minutes.

3. Slit each pepper down one side, and open it flat, with the skin-side up. Scrape away the charred skin and remove and discard the seeds, veins, and stems. Sprinkle the peppers very lightly with ¼ teaspoon salt, and let them stand for 20 minutes.

4. Pour ⅛ inch olive oil into two 1-pint plastic or glass storage containers. Blot the peppers with paper towels, and pack them in the containers, adding oil to cover each layer. Cover the peppers completely with oil, seal, and refrigerate the containers. (Peppers can be stored up to 2 months.) Oil will congeal during refrigeration but liquefy again at room temperature. Bring the containers to room temperature before using peppers. If necessary, blot them with paper towels to remove excess oil.

ON THE RISE:
BREADS AND ROLLS

When Billy Joel wrote the song about the "uptown girl . . . living in a white-bread world," he aptly described my exposure to bread before I started baking. Although my family was always interested in food, pursuits such as bread baking were not particularly emphasized or understood.

My very first glimpse of raw bread dough was in the kitchen of the late James Beard, from whom I took cooking lessons for many years. At the time, Jim was testing recipes for *Beard on Bread,* and I shall never forget the sight of him kneading dough in one of his great hands, or the aromas of his yeasty loaves rising and browning in the ovens.

Naturally, I was one of the first to sign up for a bread-baking class—those sights and smells immediately inspired me to try *my* hand at the alchemy of yeast and flour. As I tend to be impatient in the kitchen, I was delighted to discover that the food processor—which had just arrived in America—quickly dispatched what I considered to be the boring part of making bread: kneading the dough. Once I devised a way to knead Jim's Cuban Bread in less than a minute, I became hooked on bread baking.

Happily, cuisinary consciousness-raising has spawned a wonderful new generation of bread bakers, and the demand for loaves of quality with real flavor and texture has fostered a rebirth of artisanal bakeries. Great American and European breads, including French baguettes, *pain au levain, focaccia,* Tuscan whole-wheat loaves, croissants, and brioche (to name only a few) have become nearly as familiar in this country as pizza. With good bread available, and cooking time at a premium, one might argue that baking bread for a special dinner seems like a waste of time.

However, I do think bread baking is here to stay, and for good reason. While I often will purchase rolls that are similar to my French Dinner Rolls, it is rare to find the equivalent of my special, flavored breads that can make such a distinctive contribution to meals. One of my most discriminating guests, a man who prides himself on eating exclusively and often in the finest restaurants (and believe me, he is a finicky eater), polished off two loaves of Parmesan and Black Pepper Bread all by himself, and never fails to mention it when the subject of bread arises.

Breads flavored with cheese, spices, and herbs are sensational accompaniments to many menus. Even when a dinner party gets pared down to a single course of soup, pasta, or risotto, adding a generous slice of homemade Prosciutto Bread, or squares of Tomato Flatbread with Two Herbs can make it memorable.

Bread baking becomes a less time-consuming prospect when you realize that ingredients such as dry active yeast and bread flour are widely available in supermarkets, and that the mechanics of kneading dough are no trouble at all. In my kitchen, the plastic zipper-lock bag and the handy refrigerated rise have eliminated messy clean-up chores and permitted me to bake when I (and not the dough) am ready.

Would I bake bread if I had to knead it by hand? Probably not as often. Unlike many cooks, I do not find bread baking to be either therapeutic or relaxing. For me, the thrill lies in seeing how the dough is transformed in the oven, when it is on the rise. Then, while it cools I can dash out to the market, and when I return with my bundles I am greeted by the most tantalizing smells. Each time, I can hardly wait for guests to arrive and share in tasting the results.

ROSEMARY BREADSTICKS

Rising Signs

TOMATO FLATBREAD WITH TWO HERBS

It's in the Bag

PARMESAN AND BLACK PEPPER BREAD

UMBRIAN CHEESE BREAD

BLACK PEPPER BRIOCHE

PROSCIUTTO BREAD

BLACK OLIVE BREAD

SUNFLOWER RYE

FRENCH DINNER ROLLS

CHEDDAR-CUMIN ROLLS

SOFT ROLLS

AMERICAN IN PARIS BISCUITS

HAM AND JALAPENO CORNBREAD

ROSEMARY BREADSTICKS

Rosemary Grissini" may sound like a character from a Mario Puzo novel, but in fact it refers to homemade herbed breadsticks, which are called *grissini* in Italian. Unlike any you can buy in a market or even find in most restaurants, these breadsticks are addictive—thin, crisp, and packed with the flavor of rosemary. When I made them for the Sunday "Today" show, the hostess, Maria Shriver, ate them all through the segment.

The breadsticks (pictured on the cover) are made from a pizza dough, and since they are very thin, no additional rising time is required before baking.

FLEXIBLE MENU SUGGESTIONS

The recipe is included in menus based on Pasta with Four Cheeses (page 132), Risotto Primavera (page 172), Bollito Misto (page 188), Milanese Beef Stew (page 185), One-Side Grilled Fish (page 216) with Tomato Butter (page 220), Avocado Vinaigrette (page 224), Bouillabaisse Sauce (page 228), Scampi alla Busara (page 272), and Veal Scallops Giardino (page 284). The dough can replace the Oregano Dough (page 112) for pizza.
Makes about 4½ dozen

PREPARATION: 10 MINUTES
RISING: 2 HOURS
BAKING: 15 MINUTES

SPONGE

½ cup bread flour or unbleached all-purpose
   flour
¾ teaspoon dry active yeast
⅓ cup warm (110 degrees) water

DOUGH

⅔ to ¾ cup bread flour or unbleached all-
   purpose flour
½ cup plain cake flour
Salt
2 to 3 tablespoons warm water
2 tablespoons olive oil
1 tablespoon crushed dried rosemary leaves

1. For the sponge, mix the flour, yeast, and warm water in a medium bowl until the mixture forms a thick, gluey paste. Cover the bowl tightly with plastic wrap and set it aside for 2 hours, or until the mixture triples in volume. (Can stir well, cover with plastic wrap, and refrigerate the sponge in the bowl for as long as 36 hours.)

2. For the dough, insert the metal blade in a food processor. Add ⅔ cup flour, cake flour, ¾ teaspoon salt, 2 tablespoons water, oil, and rosemary. Stir the sponge mixture and add it to the machine. Process until the mixture forms a soft shaggy ball. Process in additional water or flour by tablespoons until the ball of dough forms.

3. Rinse the inside of a zipper-lock plastic bag with warm water, add dough, press out excess air, seal, and refrigerate the dough overnight, or as long as 2 days without letting it rise in a bowl. (Or, rinse a large mixing bowl with warm water, add the dough,

Continued

cover the bowl tightly with plastic wrap, and set it aside until the dough triples in volume, about 2½ hours. Punch down, wrap, and refrigerate the dough in plastic for 2 hours before cutting breadsticks.)

4. Lightly flour a work surface. Remove dough from bag (or plastic wrap) without kneading and divide the dough into two pieces. Roll each piece of dough into a 9 × 7-inch rectangle. With the edge of a ravioli wheel (or with a knife), cut the dough lengthwise into ¼-inch-wide strips. Gently roll strips between your hands to round edges, without twisting the dough. Transfer strips to a baking sheet; repeat to cut all breadsticks.

5. Adjust oven rack to middle position. Heat oven to 400 degrees. Bake 15 to 18 minutes, or until breadsticks are crisp and lightly browned. Cool to room temperature before serving.

There are many ways to make bread dough. Those of us who learned to bake bread in the United States and Canada are most familiar with the two methods known as "ferment and dough," and "sponge and dough." It is interesting to note that the word *ferment* comes from the Latin verb *fervere,* "to boil or seethe," which vividly describes the action of yeast once it comes in contact with warm water and a small amount of flour or sugar. The term also applies to the foam of beer, which also is used for leavening.

"Ferment and dough" calls for yeast, water, and an optional small amount of flour —the ferment—to be mixed together. After the remaining ingredients are assembled, the ferment is added, and the dough is set aside to rise.

A sponge is a combination of yeast, water, and flour (and sometimes salt and sugar) that ferments or rises before it is mixed with the remaining dough ingredients; a piece of left-over dough is equivalent to a sponge.

"Sponge and dough" breads are considered to have better flavor than breads made by other methods because lactic and acetic acids, produced along with carbon dioxide during fermentation, help make dough more elastic and improve its flavor.

A third procedure calls for adding dry yeast directly to dry ingredients, without dissolving it in liquid, and since dry active yeast is date-stamped and proofing is not strictly necessary, some bakers would say that this is the most efficient and modern method of all.

All three techniques are used in these recipes. I find that adding undissolved yeast to dry ingredients or using the "ferment and dough" technique is best for breads that contain a high proportion of fat in the form of butter, cheese, or meat such as prosciutto. Since fat tends to inhibit the action of yeast, these methods help to ensure that breads of this type rise evenly and sufficiently.

For pizza or French bread-style doughs, the "sponge and dough" method has given me consistently fine results from the standpoint of producing doughs with a crisp crust, a cheesy crumb, and a slightly acidic or tangy taste.

KNEADING

Most conventional bread recipes call for kneading dough by hand to an even texture that is usually achieved within 6 to 10 minutes. Bread must be kneaded to develop gluten—the elastic structure composed of insoluble proteins in flour that permits bread dough to stretch.

Gluten also can be developed in the food processor, normally within 30 to 45 seconds after the yeast has been added. This is the fastest, most efficient, and effortless way I know to knead bread dough, which is why these recipes use the food processor. Of course, all the doughs in this chapter can be kneaded by hand.

Take care not to overprocess doughs. However, using bread flour, or unbleached all-purpose flour with protein contents specified on page 131, will help to offset this danger, since "strong" flours require substantial kneading to produce top-quality loaves.

A NOTE ON OVEN TEMPERATURE

There is a good reason why certain bread doughs are baked at moderate temperatures —about 350 degrees—and others at 400 to 450 degrees. Rich, heavy doughs, or those that contain large amounts of sugar, require moderate oven temperatures so that their final expansion (called "oven spring") can fully take place during baking. Another reason for lowering the oven temperature is to prevent the exterior of these breads from becoming too brown before the insides have completely set. Otherwise, you run the risk of gummy areas in baked bread, or in extreme cases, loaves that may collapse.

TOMATO FLATBREAD WITH TWO HERBS

Flatbreads, or focaccias, combine the best attributes of bread and pizza because they are wonderfully chewy and satisfying, yet they are adaptable to a limitless variety of flavorings and toppings.

My basic focaccia recipe was acquired during a trip to Genoa, where making this bread is something of an art. While experimenting with variations on the theme, I tried using up some sun-dried tomatoes *(pumate),* but found them to be less than spectacular when baked on top of the dough. When I pureed them into the dough, the result was this unusual and intensely flavored flatbread that is enhanced by dried herbs and flecks of ground pepper on top.

You will need oil-packed sun-dried tomatoes for the recipe, and you may wish to add the rosy-hued tomato oil.

FLEXIBLE MENU SUGGESTIONS

This bread is included in menus based on Pasta with Four Cheeses (page 132), Risotto Primavera (page 172), Milanese Asparagus Soup (page 162), Milanese Beef Stew (page 185), Penne with Broccoli and Scallops (page 206), One-Side Grilled Fish (page 216) with Orso Butter (page 221) or Whole-Grain Mustard-Chive Butter (page 277), or Sage-Rubbed Veal Chops (page 242). *Makes 8 to 10 servings*

PREPARATION: 45 MINUTES
RISING: 2½ HOURS OR OVERNIGHT
BAKING: ABOUT 20 MINUTES

3½ to 4 cups unbleached all-purpose flour
1 package dry active yeast
Salt
1¼ cups warm water
⅓ cup oil-packed sun-dried tomatoes, drained and patted dry
5 tablespoons tomato or olive oil
Flour
1½ teaspoons dried oregano
¾ teaspoons dried summer savory
Ground black pepper

1. Insert the metal blade in a dry food processor. Add 3½ cups flour, the yeast, and 1½ teaspoons salt. With the motor on, add water to the dry ingredients in a thin stream. Cut the tomatoes in half and process them into the dough until the mixture forms a smooth, moist ball. (Process in additional flour by tablespoons if dough does not form a ball.)

2. Rinse the inside of a zipper-lock plastic bag, add the dough, press out excess air, and seal. Refrigerate the dough overnight or as long as 2 days without letting it rise in a bowl. (Or, rinse a mixing bowl with warm water, add the dough, cover the bowl tightly with plastic wrap, and set it aside until the dough triples in volume, about 2 to 3 hours.)

3. Adjust oven rack to lowest position. Heat oven to 425 degrees.

4. Coat a 15 × 10-inch jelly-roll pan with 3 tablespoons oil. Remove dough from bowl or bag without kneading. On lightly floured surface, stretch dough into a rectangle large enough to fill the pan (if dough becomes

elastic, refrigerate for 30 to 40 minutes, then stretch it carefully in the pan), and drizzle the top of the dough with 1 tablespoon oil. Set dough aside to rise for 30 minutes.

5. Sprinkle the oregano, savory, and ½ teaspoon pepper over the top of the dough, then drizzle it with the remaining oil. Bake 18 to 20 minutes, or until bottom of crust is lightly colored. Cut the bread into 2-inch squares and serve it warm.

IT'S IN THE BAG

While the refrigerated rise was explained briefly in the pizza chapter, some additional information may be helpful to bread bakers. Cooks who do not have time to wait for bread dough to rise, who wish to prepare bread or pizza dough a day before baking it, and who wish to avoid messy clean-up are sure to find the "refrigerated rise" to be an especially convenient technique.

This method calls for fully kneading bread dough and immediately transferring it to a wet plastic bag (with zipper-lock closure), pressing out excess air, sealing the bag, and placing it in the refrigerator overnight.

This technique completely eliminates the conventional practice of letting dough rise in a bowl at room temperature and punching it down before it is shaped.

The refrigerated rise is a commercial bread-baking technique that I first encountered in a recipe created by Manhattan chef Larry Forgione, and it offers a superb shortcut for busy cooks.

I have found it to be an excellent technique for any bread dough, but particularly for those rich, flavored breads that often rise sluggishly in the oven. In addition, overnight refrigeration helps develop those all-important acids that give bread dough great flavor.

Dough can be kept in an airtight zipper-lock bag for as long as 3 days without any loss of flavor or texture in the baked results. This particular type of plastic bag is the key to the technique—I have not had successful results when doughs are refrigerated in mixing bowls.

Once the dough is shaped, count on approximately double the normal time for "proofing" (the final rise) if it has been refrigerated.

PARMESAN AND BLACK PEPPER BREAD

A trio of ingredients—Parmesan cheese, oregano, and black pepper—distinguishes this bread, but only Parmigiano-Reggiano cheese (see page 163) gives it a fabulous, full-blown flavor. The loaves have a lovely, rustic look that comes from wrapping the cigar-shaped cores with narrow dough strips that have been pressed into grated Parmesan. When baked, the central cores swell around the strips, while the cheese perfumes the breads and colors the crusts a rich brown.

FLEXIBLE MENU SUGGESTIONS

This bread is included in menus based on each of the Milanese-style soups (pages 156 and 162), Milanese Beef Stew (page 185), Bollito Misto (page 188), Veal Scallops Giardino (page 284), and Cognac-Marinated Beef Fillet (page 298).

It also would be good with Tomato Soup with Garlic and Basil (page 44), Lettuce, Radicchio, and Fennel Salad (page 70), Capretto with Lemon and Rosemary (page 246), and Sage-Rubbed Veal Chops (page 242). *Makes 3 loaves*

PREPARATION: 45 MINUTES
RISING: 3½ HOURS
BAKING: 20 TO 25 MINUTES

1 package dry active yeast
1 teaspoon sugar
1⅓ cups warm (110 degrees) water
6 ounces Parmesan cheese, rind removed, cut in 1-inch chunks
3½ to 4 cups bread flour or unbleached all-purpose flour
Salt
2 tablespoons olive oil or Herbed Oil (page 73)
Vegetable shortening
1½ teaspoons dried oregano
⅜ teaspoon ground black pepper
1 egg white, beaten until foamy

1. Mix the yeast with sugar and ⅔ cup of the warm water and set the mixture aside for 10 minutes.

2. In a food processor fitted with the metal blade, process the Parmesan cheese until it is grated and powdery; measure and set aside ½ cup of the grated cheese, and put the remainder aside separately.

3. Put 3½ cups flour, ¾ teaspoon salt, and the oil in the processor container. With the motor on, add the remaining ⅔ cup warm water in a thin stream. Stir yeast mixture well and pour it into the machine with the motor running. Add ½ cup of the cheese, and process until dough forms a soft, moist ball. (If dough seems loose or runny, process in additional flour, 2 tablespoons at a time, until dough holds its shape.)

4. Rinse a large mixing bowl with warm water. Without drying the bowl, add the dough, cover the bowl tightly with plastic wrap, and set it aside at room temperature until dough triples in volume, about 1½ to 2 hours. (Or, rinse the inside of a zipper-lock plastic bag, add the dough, press out excess air, seal, and refrigerate the dough overnight or as long as 2 days without letting it rise in the bowl.)

5. Coat a curved metal French bread pan or a baking sheet generously with vegetable shortening; set aside. Remove dough from the bowl (or bag) without kneading and cut it into three equal pieces. Cut off and reserve ⅓ cup of dough from each piece.

6. To shape each loaf, sprinkle 1 tablespoon of the remaining Parmesan cheese on a work surface. With a ruler nearby, roll out one large piece of dough to a 12 × 8-inch rectangle, turning to coat both sides evenly with cheese.

7. Sprinkle 1½ tablespoons of Parmesan, ½ teaspoon oregano, and ⅛ teaspoon pepper evenly over the top of the dough. Fold the dough lengthwise into thirds, to make a long, thin dough rectangle. Pinch the two long edges together tightly to form a cigar-shaped loaf.

8. For the dough strips, sprinkle the work surface with 1 teaspoon Parmesan cheese. Roll out one of the reserved ⅓-cup pieces of dough to a 12 × 3-inch rectangle. Cut it in half lengthwise to form two strips.

9. With the cheese-side facing in, attach one strip of dough to one end of the shaped loaf, then wrap it around the loaf clockwise, pinching to secure it to the opposite end. Attach the second strip where the first ended and wrap it counterclockwise to form a criss-cross or diamond pattern around the shaped loaf. Pinch dough strips at the ends to fasten them securely to the loaf. Put the loaf seam-side down in the pan, or on the baking sheet.

10. Repeat steps 6 through 9 to shape the two remaining loaves. Cover them with a dry towel and set them aside at room temperature until they double in volume, about 1½ to 2 hours (or as long as 4 hours if dough was refrigerated).

11. Adjust oven rack to lowest position. Heat oven to 425 degrees. Use a soft damp pastry brush to glaze the tops of the risen loaves with beaten egg white. Gently press 1 tablespoon cheese onto the top of each shaped loaf. Bake 20 to 25 minutes, or until golden brown. While still hot, loosen loaves from bread pan or baking sheet with a metal spatula. Cool loaves to room temperature before slicing.

UMBRIAN CHEESE BREAD

We were hungry when we arrived in Perugia, an ancient but lively town in the mountainous province of Umbria. Our first meal began with an hors d'oeuvre—small prosciutto sandwiches made from thin slices of one of the most delicious cheese breads I had ever tasted.

The next day, while tramping through the town, I spotted one of the handsome domed loaves in the window of a rather elegant bakery, and learned that it was called *torta di Pasqua*, or Easter cake, no doubt because its shape is similar to *panettone*. The following morning, at 5:45, I was in the bakery, watching the baker combine three different types of cheese and coarsely ground pepper into this rich loaf, which bakes beautifully in a soufflé dish.

Because the dough contains such an abundant amount of cheese, which inhibits the action of the yeast, I have found the texture of this bread to be best when it is made one day in advance and given a refrigerated rise. If you wish to let it rise in a bowl at room temperature, be sure that once it is shaped and set aside for the final rise, you give it enough time to triple in volume and expand at least ½ inch above the rim of the mold.

FLEXIBLE MENU SUGGESTIONS

This recipe is included in menus based on Scallion and Black Pepper Lasagne (page 144), Garlic-Rubbed Chicken (page 278), and Pork with Port Wine Sauce (page 292). Additionally, it can be substituted for Parmesan and Black Pepper Bread (page 348), or sometimes used in place of Black Pepper Brioche (page 352). *Makes 1 loaf*

PREPARATION: 30 MINUTES
RISING: OVERNIGHT PLUS 4 HOURS
BAKING: 45 TO 50 MINUTES

3 to 3½ cups bread flour or unbleached all-
   purpose flour
1 package dry active yeast
1¼ cups warm (110 degrees) water
2 ounces (four 1-inch chunks) imported
   Parmesan cheese
2 ounces (four 1-inch chunks) imported
   Romano cheese
Salt and coarsely ground black pepper
4 tablespoons unsalted butter
2 eggs
2 ounces Gruyère cheese, in ¼-inch dice (½
   cup)
Vegetable shortening or unsalted butter

1. Combine 1 cup flour with the yeast and ¾ cup warm water in a small mixing bowl. Cover with plastic wrap and set aside 2 to 3 hours, until mixture triples in volume. (Can push down, cover tightly with plastic wrap, and refrigerate the mixture overnight.)

2. In a food processor fitted with the metal blade, grate the Parmesan and Romano cheeses by processing until they are powdery; set aside. Put 2 cups flour, 1¼ teaspoons salt, ¼ teaspoon pepper, and the butter into the processor.

3. Mix 1 egg with the remaining ½ cup water, and with the machine running, add the mixture to the dough. Add the grated Parmesan and Romano cheese and process

until mixture forms a soft, shaggy ball. (Process in remaining flour by tablespoons if the dough does not form a ball.)

4. Transfer the dough to a lightly floured work surface. Press the cubes of cheese into the dough, then knead until they are evenly distributed throughout.

5. Rinse the inside of a zipper-lock plastic bag, add the dough, press out excess air, seal, and refrigerate the dough overnight or as long as 2 days without letting it rise in a bowl.

6. Coat a 2-quart soufflé dish generously with shortening or butter. Remove dough from the bag, knead it into a ball, and put it into the dish with the smoothest side up. Set the dish aside, uncovered, until the dough triples in volume, about 3 to 4 hours.

7. Adjust oven rack to lowest position. Heat oven to 350 degrees. Lightly beat the remaining egg and brush it over the top of the risen dough. Bake 45 to 50 minutes, or until the top of the bread is golden brown. Cool bread in the dish for 30 minutes before loosening it with a knife and removing it from the mold. Cool the loaf to room temperature before slicing.

BLACK PEPPER BRIOCHE

Brioche, the queen of French breads, is not just for breakfast. When the usual quantity of sugar is replaced by coarsely ground black pepper and the bread is baked in a loaf pan, this spicy brioche can be used for hors d'oeuvres, sandwiches, and as an accompaniment to salads and other savory foods.

For many cooks, the great stumbling block with brioche always has been kneading the dough, a gluey mass into which a large proportion of butter must be perfectly blended. When the bread is made in the food processor, butter can be cut thoroughly into the dry ingredients prior to adding the yeast mixture—a reversal of the usual procedure. This technique avoids the mess of adding the butter, and the dough is flawlessly kneaded in just 40 seconds.

This recipe, as well as the notion of the refrigerated rise, was inspired by Chef Larry Forgione. Be sure to allow time for a rather slow rise once the chilled dough is shaped and put in the pan.

FLEXIBLE MENU SUGGESTIONS

This bread is included in menus based on One-Side Grilled Fish (page 216) with Whole-Grain Mustard-Chive Butter (page 277) and Mushroom and Prosciutto-Stuffed Chicken Breasts (page 274). It can also be substituted for Parmesan and Black Pepper Bread (page 348) in all menus.

For elegant sandwiches, consider this with cold leftover beef fillet (page 298) or pork loin (page 211), garnished with plain mayonnaise and Mixed Plum Chutney (page 338); or, a club sandwich of cold grilled salmon (page 216) with Dill Dressing (page 79) or Fresh Herb Butter (page 219), Bibb lettuce, thinly sliced tomato, and thinly sliced boiled new potatoes; or, a club sandwich of cold, sliced Chili-Rubbed Chicken (page 278) with Jalapeño Mayonnaise (page 271), Boston lettuce, tomato, avocado, bacon, and cilantro. *Makes 1 loaf*

PREPARATION: 20 MINUTES
RISING: OVERNIGHT PLUS 4 HOURS
BAKING: 40 MINUTES

5 tablespoons milk
1 teaspoon dry active yeast
1½ tablespoons sugar
2 eggs
1⅔ to 2 cups bread flour or unbleached all-purpose flour
Salt and coarsely ground black pepper
4 ounces chilled unsalted butter, cut in 8 pieces

1 tablespoon vegetable shortening
Flour
1 egg yolk

1. Scald 4 tablespoons milk, then set it aside in a measuring cup to cool to lukewarm (110 degrees). Stir in the yeast and sugar, then lightly beat in the eggs with a fork.

2. In food processor fitted with the metal blade, combine 1⅔ cups flour, ½ teaspoon salt, 1¼ teaspoons pepper, and the butter.

Process until the butter completely disappears. With the motor on, add the yeast mixture to the dry ingredients in a steady stream, then process until the dough is thick, smooth, and weblike—but not liquid. (If the dough looks liquid or runny, process in additional flour by tablespoons until it holds its shape.)

3. Rinse the inside of a zipper-lock plastic bag, add the dough, press out excess air, seal, and refrigerate the dough overnight, or as long as 2 days without letting it rise in a bowl.

4. Generously coat a 6-cup metal loaf pan with vegetable shortening. Flour a work surface. Remove the chilled dough from the bag without kneading. Dust the dough with flour, and flatten it into a 10 × 8-inch rectangle. Brush off excess flour and fold the dough lengthwise into thirds to make a long, thin rectangle. Pinch the two long edges together tightly to form a fat cigar-shaped loaf.

5. Put dough into the pan. Cover with a lightweight cloth towel and set aside until it rises 1 inch over the rim of the pan, about 4 hours.

6. Adjust oven rack to lowest position. Heat oven to 350 degrees. Lightly beat the egg yolk and remaining tablespoon of milk together with a fork. Using a damp pastry brush, glaze the top of the risen dough with the egg-yolk mixture. Bake 40 minutes, or until loaf swells into a tall, golden-brown loaf. Cool for 10 minutes in the loaf pan, then unmold and cool to room temperature on a cake rack before slicing.

"So I think that in the eighteenth century, and at the time that poor, foolish Marie Antoinette is supposed to have said, when told that the people of Paris were rioting for bread, *'qu'ils mangent de la brioche,'* the composition of the cake must have been simply that of an enriched bread . . ."

—ELIZABETH DAVID

PROSCIUTTO BREAD

Visitors to New York's Little Italy may have encountered the savory ring-shaped prosciutto breads that are the inspiration for this recipe. Undoubtedly, similar breads are made somewhere in Italy, or these simply may be a native creation intended to use up leftover prosciutto. In any event, they are delicious.

Like bread dough that contains a large quantity of cheese, this one rises quite slowly, and is best worked into rather small loaves. In addition to using the dough for pizza (page 112), variations can include round or oval rolls similiar to French Dinner Rolls (page 360), made from 2-ounce (¼-cup) portions.

If you are making these breads without a food processor, cut the prosciutto into ⅛-inch dice before kneading it into the dough.

FLEXIBLE MENU SUGGESTIONS

Prosciutto bread, which slices neatly into wedges, is included in menus based on Pasta with Four Cheeses (page 132), Shrimp and Curry Risotto (page 166), Penne with Broccoli and Scallops (page 206), Sage-Rubbed Veal Chops (page 242), Capretto with Lemon and Rosemary (page 246), Scampi alla Busara (page 272), Herb-Rubbed Chicken (page 278), and Veal Scallops with Black Olive Gremolada (page 286). *Makes four ½-pound bread rings*

PREPARATION: 10 MINUTES
RISING: OVERNIGHT PLUS 3 HOURS
BAKING: 35 TO 40 MINUTES

¼-pound slice of prosciutto
3 to 3¼ cups bread flour or unbleached all-
    purpose flour
1 package dry active yeast
Salt and coarsely ground black pepper
3 tablespoons Herbed Oil (page 73) or olive
    oil
1 cup warm (110 degrees) water

1. Coarsely chop the prosciutto and set aside. Put 3 cups flour, the yeast, ¼ teaspoon salt, ½ teaspoon pepper, and 2 tablespoons oil in a food processor fitted with the metal blade. With the motor on, add water to the dry ingredients, processing until the dough begins to form. Add the prosciutto

and process until dough is thoroughly kneaded. (Do not overprocess—small bits of prosciutto should remain in the dough.)

2. Rinse the inside of a zipper-lock plastic bag, add the dough, press out excess air, seal, and refrigerate the dough overnight, or as long as 2 days without letting it rise in a bowl. (Or, rinse a large mixing bowl with warm water, add the dough, cover the bowl tightly with plastic wrap, and set it aside until the dough doubles in volume, about 2 to 2½ hours.)

3. Remove dough from the bag (or bowl) without kneading and cut it into four even pieces. Shape each piece of dough into a disk. Poke a hole into the center of one dough disk. With your thumb inserted in the hole, rotate the dough around your thumb

to stretch it into a 1-inch-thick, doughnut-shaped ring. Be sure that the hole in the ring is at least 5 inches in diameter since dough will shrink slightly as it rises, and swell as it bakes. Repeat to shape the three remaining dough rings.

4. Use ½ tablespoon of remaining oil to coat two baking sheets. Transfer two dough rings to each baking sheet. Cover the dough with cloth towels and set it aside to rise until the rings double in volume, about 1½ hours if dough has risen at room temperature, or as long as 3 hours if dough has been refrigerated.

5. Adjust oven rack to lowest position. Heat oven to 350 degrees. Brush tops of breads with remaining oil. Bake 35 to 45 minutes, or until dough rings are lightly browned. Can serve breads warm or at room temperature.

BLACK OLIVE BREAD

The flavor and color of this unusual bread will vary according to the type of olives used in the recipe. Standard pitted black California olives, Oil-Marinated Olives (page 63), or pitted Niçoise olives yield a dark, speckled loaf with a relatively mild flavor. Ripe black olives cured in salt or oil, which can be recognized by their shriveled skins, will produce a loaf that resembles pumpernickel, with an extremely pronounced olive flavor—take your pick.

The dough is very workable, and can be fashioned into two small breads, a single round bread, or a dozen rolls; it can even used as a base for pizza, calzone, or breadsticks.

FLEXIBLE MENU SUGGESTIONS

This bread is included in menus based on Risotto Primavera (page 172), Milanese Asparagus Soup (page 162), One-Side Grilled Fish (page 216) with Roasted Garlic and Saffron Butter (page 222) or Winter Pesto (page 227), Capretto with Lemon and Rosemary (page 246), Leg of Lamb with Niçoise Seasoning (page 248), Scampi alla Busara (page 272), Scallop and Basil-Stuffed Sole (page 265), Herb-Rubbed Chicken (page 278), or Garlic-Roasted Leg of Lamb (page 295). *Makes 2 small loaves*

PREPARATION TIME: 10 MINUTES
RISING: 6 HOURS OR OVERNIGHT
BAKING TIME: 25 TO 30 MINUTES

2 medium shallots, peeled
¼ cup olive oil
¾ teaspoon dry active yeast
½ cup warm water
1¾ to 2 cups bread flour or unbleached
   all-purpose flour
5½ ounces black pitted olives, drained
   (1⅓ cups)
Salt
1 teaspoon dried thyme leaves
Flour
Cornmeal
1 egg white

1. Mince the shallots and transfer them to a small skillet with 2 tablespoons of the oil. Sauté over low heat until softened, about 2 minutes; cool.

2. Mix yeast with ⅓ cup warm water and ¼ cup of the flour in a small bowl; set aside.

3. Coarsely chop the olives and put them in a food processor fitted with the metal blade. Add 1½ cups flour, ¾ teaspoon salt, the shallots, thyme, and the remaining warm water and 2 tablespoons oil. Add the yeast mixture and process until a soft ball of dough forms, about 30 seconds. (If dough is very sticky, add additional flour by table-spoons and process until dough is smooth and slightly sticky.)

4. Rinse a large bowl with warm water, add the dough, cover the bowl tightly with plastic wrap, and set it aside until the dough triples in volume, about 2½ hours. (Or, rinse the inside of a zipper-lock plastic bag, add the dough, press out excess air, seal, and refrigerate overnight, or as long as 2 days without letting it rise in a bowl.)

5. Lightly flour a work surface. Remove dough from the bowl (or bag) without kneading and cut dough in half. Flatten each half into a circle, gather the edge towards the center, and knead each piece of dough into a ball.

6. Sprinkle a baking sheet with 1 tablespoon cornmeal. Put each ball of dough (smooth side up) on the cornmeal. Cover the dough loosely with a cloth towel and set aside until it doubles in volume, about 1 to 1½ hours (or as long as 3 hours if dough has been refrigerated).

7. Adjust oven rack to lowest position. Heat oven to 400 degrees. Beat the egg white lightly with 1 teaspoon cold water. Brush the top of each loaf with egg white glaze and set aside for 5 minutes. Use a sharp knife or razor blade to make an **X** in the top of each ball of dough. Bake until loaves are golden brown, about 25 to 30 minutes. Cool to room temperature before slicing.

Pluck a ripe olive from a tree, pop it into your mouth, and your natural reaction will be to spit it out immediately! Raw olives are extremely bitter because of the presence of a chemical compound called *oleuropein,* which imparts a strong taste but can be removed by soaking the fruit in an alkaline solution.

SUNFLOWER RYE

It was noon on the day before Christmas, and nearly all the bakeries in Bonn, West Germany, had sold out of bread. My friend Lindy had warned me that the country completely shuts down for the three-day Christmas holiday, and that buying bread was a must, but as usual we got off to a late start. Only a few loaves remained—a crusty Bavarian beer bread, a crunchy six-grain health loaf, and an odd-looking loaf called *blumenbrot,* or "flower bread," so we bought them all.

What was this yeasty flower with cheese baked over the center of the bread and "petals" rolled in sesame, caraway, and poppy seeds? Clearly, it was meant to be a sunflower, and when I returned home, I developed my own *blumenbrot* recipe using medium rye flour (Pillsbury's), patterned after that delicious German loaf.

FLEXIBLE MENU SUGGESTIONS

This is a particularly attractive bread to accompany Sausages and Sauerkraut (page 186) or to serve with cold meats and cheese. *Makes 8 servings*

PREPARATION: 20 MINUTES
RISING: 3 TO 4 HOURS
BAKING: 30 MINUTES

1 ounce (two 1-inch chunks) Swiss or
   Gruyère cheese, chilled
1 cup medium rye flour
2¼ to 2½ cups bread flour or unbleached all-
   purpose flour
Salt
2 packages dry active yeast
2 tablespoons sugar
2 tablespoons dried minced onion
1 can (12 ounces) beer, room temperature
Flour
2 tablespoons sesame seeds
2 tablespoons caraway seeds
1 tablespoon poppy seeds

1. Shred the cheese (¼ cup) and set it aside in the refrigerator.

2. In a food processor fitted with the metal blade, combine the rye flour, 2¼ cups bread flour, 1½ teaspoons salt, the yeast, sugar, and onion. With motor on, add beer to the dry ingredients in a thin stream. Process until the mixture forms a moist, sticky ball of dough. (Add remaining ¼ cup flour by tablespoons if dough is liquid or runny.)

3. Rinse a large mixing bowl with warm water, add the dough, cover the bowl tightly with plastic wrap, and set it aside until the dough triples in volume, about 2½ hours. (Or, rinse the inside of a zipper-lock plastic bag, add the dough, press out excess air, seal, and refrigerate the dough overnight, or as long as 2 days without letting it rise in a bowl.)

4. Without kneading, transfer the dough to a generously floured surface and cut it into three even pieces. Cut each piece into five equal pieces to make a total of fifteen small pieces of dough.

5. To shape the "flower" loaf, sprinkle 1 tablespoon sesame seeds evenly over the center of a baking sheet. With floured hands, shape six pieces of the dough into smooth balls. Put one ball of dough on the center of the baking sheet. Add five balls of dough in a circle around, and just touching, the center piece.

6. Roll the remaining nine pieces of dough into balls. With moist hands, moisten and dip three dough balls into the remaining sesame seeds. Repeat to moisten and dip three balls into the caraway seeds, and the remaining three balls into the poppy seeds.

7. To make the outer ring, put balls of dough—alternating the seed coatings—in a ring around the dough balls on the baking sheet. Be sure that the outer ring of dough balls just touches the inside pieces so the bread will hold together when risen and baked. Cover the loaf with a dry towel. Set aside until it doubles in volume, about 1 to 1½ hours. (Rising time may be as long as 3 hours for refrigerated dough.)

8. Adjust oven rack to lowest position. Heat oven to 350 degrees. Sprinkle cheese shreds over the center ball of dough and the inner ring. Bake 30 minutes, until golden. Cool to room temperature. Serve by pulling bread apart.

FRENCH DINNER ROLLS

One of my friends, who entertains frequently and graciously, began making my recipe for these rolls (which are pictured in the color section) for dinner parties. She soon developed a very professional hand, and eventually her rolls looked so good, guests thought they were store-bought and did not bother to eat them. The moral of the story just may be that home-made bread can never look too homemade.

I have been making these rolls for years. They are so basic they go with almost any menu, and I am especially partial to their crackling crust and chewy crumb. This recipe was first developed for French bread, but rolls are easier to shape and handle than the long loaves. Also, I like to let the dough age a day or two in the refrigerator (in a zipper-lock bag), although the rolls are equally good if made and baked the same day.

A plant mister helps to create the all-important steam that produces a crunchy crust. Be very careful when you spray into the oven since cool water can cause the hot oven light bulb to break. Do not be concerned if the baking sheet warps slightly as it is sprayed with water, or if excess flour on the baking sheet browns. An injector-type razor blade is useful to slash the dough, since most knife blades are too dull for the task.

FLEXIBLE MENU SUGGESTIONS

French dinner rolls are included in menus based on Country Pork Terrine (page 90), Curry Noodles with Scallops and Cilantro (page 146), Sausages and Sauerkraut (page 186), Bollito Misto (page 188), One-Side Grilled Fish (page 216) with Fresh Herb Butter (page 210), Whole-Grain Mustard-Chive Butter (page 277), Winter Pesto (page 227) or Bouillabaisse Sauce (page 228), Leg of Lamb with Niçoise Seasoning (page 248), Yogurt and Spice-Marinated Leg of Lamb (page 252), Cold Chicken-Poached Lobster (page 270), Scallop and Basil-Stuffed Sole (page 265), Szechwan Pepper Ribeyes (page 288), and Garlic-Roasted Leg of Lamb (page 295). *Makes 1 dozen*

PREPARATION: 20 MINUTES
RISING: 6 HOURS
BAKING: 20 MINUTES

SPONGE

¾ *cup bread flour or all-purpose unbleached flour*
1¼ *teaspoons dry active yeast*
⅔ *cup warm water (110 degrees)*

DOUGH

1½ *to 2 cups bread flour or all-purpose unbleached flour*
1 *cup plain cake flour*
Salt
⅔ *cup warm water (110 degrees)*
Flour
1 *egg white, lightly beaten*

1. For the sponge, mix the flour, yeast, and warm water in a medium bowl until the mixture forms a thick, gluey paste. Cover the bowl tightly with plastic wrap and set it aside for 2 hours, or until the mixture triples in volume. (Can stir well, cover with plastic wrap, and refrigerate the sponge in the bowl for as long as 36 hours.)

2. For the dough, insert the metal blade in a food processor. Add 1½ cups bread flour, the cake flour, and 1½ teaspoons salt. With motor on, quickly pour the water into the dry ingredients. Stir the sponge mixture and add it to the machine. Process until the dough is smooth, very sticky, and even-textured throughout (it may not form a ball), about 45 seconds. (If dough is liquid or runny, process in bread flour by tablespoons until the dough holds its shape.)

3. Rinse a large mixing bowl with warm water, add the dough, cover the bowl tightly with plastic wrap, and set it aside until the dough triples in volume, about 2 to 2½ hours. (Or, rinse the inside of a zipper-lock plastic bag, add the dough, press out excess air, seal, and refrigerate the dough overnight, or as long as 2 days without letting it rise in the bowl.) Dough is ready to shape into rolls. (To sour the dough slightly, let it rise in the bowl, punch it down, then refrigerate the dough in a sealed zipper-lock bag overnight or as long as 2 days.)

4. Sift 1 tablespoon flour evenly over a baking sheet; set aside. Remove the dough from the bowl (or bag) without kneading and transfer it to a work surface that has been lightly dusted with bread flour. Dough will be very sticky. Working with floured hands, cut the dough into twelve even pieces (each ¼ cup or 2 ounces).

5. To make oval rolls, press each piece of dough into a flat rectangle. Brush off the excess flour and fold the dough lengthwise into thirds like a business letter. Gather the two long edges together and pinch to form a small, cigar-shaped loaf. (For round rolls, knead dough into balls, gather edge at center, and pinch). Put rolls, seam- (or pinched-) side down, on the baking sheet. Cover with a dry cloth towel and set aside until dough triples in volume, 1½ to 3 hours, depending on length of refrigeration.

6. Adjust oven rack to lowest position. Heat oven to 450 degrees. To slash the rolls, use a razor blade held at a 20-degree angle and make a 1- to 1½-inch-long cut lengthwise on oval rolls, or across the top of round rolls. Set rolls aside for 10 minutes. With a damp pastry brush, glaze rolls gently with the beaten egg white.

7. Put rolls into the oven and immediately spray with cold water from a plant mister or plastic spray gun until a cloud of steam rises from the baking sheet. Bake 10 minutes and spray again. Bake 10 to 15 minutes longer, or until nicely browned. Transfer rolls to a cake rack or basket to cool.

CHEDDAR-CUMIN ROLLS

Sharp cheddar cheese and ground cumin give these rolls just the right set of flavors to accompany Tex-Mex, Cal-Mex, or Mexi-zona foods. Since the cheese gives the rolls a high fat content, they are one of the few breads I recommend for baking and freezing.

FLEXIBLE MENU SUGGESTIONS

These rolls are included in menus based on Arizona Chicken with Corn Ragout (page 192), Chicken Enchiladas Verdes (page 197), Mesquite-Grilled Cornish Hens (page 240), Chili and Garlic-Rubbed Flank Steak (page 245), Leg of Lamb with Malay Seasoning (page 250), Yogurt and Spice-Marinated Leg of Lamb (page 252), Chili-Rubbed Chicken (page 278), and Cognac-Marinated Beef Fillet (page 298). *Makes 1 dozen*

PREPARATION: 35 MINUTES
RISING: 4½ TO 6 HOURS
BAKING: 20 MINUTES

1¼ teaspoons dry active yeast
1 teaspoon sugar
1¼ cups warm (110 degrees) water
¼ pound sharp cheddar cheese, chilled, cubed
*3¼ cups bread flour or unbleached all-
    purpose flour*
Salt
1½ teaspoons ground cumin
3 tablespoons cornmeal

1. Mix yeast, sugar, and water in a measuring cup; cover and set the mixture aside until it bubbles, about 10 minutes.

2. In a food processor fitted with the metal blade, process the cheese with ½ cup flour until it is finely ground. Add the remaining flour, 1½ teaspoons salt, and the cumin. Process to mix the ingredients thoroughly.

3. Stir the yeast mixture, and with the motor on, pour it into the dry ingredients. Process until the dough forms a shaggy mass and is slightly sticky.

4. Rinse a large mixing bowl with warm water, add the dough, cover the bowl tightly with plastic wrap, and set it aside until the dough triples in volume, usually 3 to 3½ hours. (Or, rinse the inside of a zipper-lock plastic bag, add dough, press out excess air, seal, and refrigerate the dough overnight or as long as 2 days without letting it rise in the bowl.)

5. Remove dough from bowl (or bag) without kneading. Working on a lightly floured surface, cut the dough in half. Cut each half into six even pieces. To shape each roll, flatten the dough, and fold the corners inward while turning the dough clockwise. Gather the edge toward the center, and pinch in one spot to form a tight ball of dough.

6. Sprinkle a baking sheet with the cornmeal. Put the dough balls, pinched sides down, onto the cornmeal at least 2 inches apart. Put a lightweight cloth over the rolls. Cover and let the rolls rise until they triple in volume, about 1½ to 2 hours (or up to 4 hours if dough has been refrigerated).

7. Adjust oven rack to lowest position. Heat oven to 450 degrees. Put the rolls in the oven and immediately spray them with cold water from plant mister or plastic spray gun. Bake for 20 minutes, until tops are golden. Transfer rolls to a cake rack and cool them to room temperature before serving.

> When dried and ground to a powder, the seeds of cumin, or *Cuminum cyminum,* have a distinct, pungent aroma that many people associate with Middle Eastern foods. The plant is indigenous to Egypt and was used there as a component in the mummification process as early as 5000 B.C.

SOFT ROLLS

With their soft-crusted charm, these tender, slightly sweet, old-fashioned rolls are a classic American dinner bread. The dough is a snap to handle, and the rolls are easy to make in any of the three shapes suggested below: rounds, braids, or butterflies.

FLEXIBLE MENU SUGGESTIONS

Use the rolls for sandwiches made of any leftover roasted or barbecued main-course meats. They are included in menus based on Chili- or Curry-Rubbed Chicken (pages 278 and 282), Chili and Garlic-Rubbed Flank Steak (page 245), and Hickory-Grilled Baby Back Ribs (page 259). The rolls are also good accompaniments for Duck and Sausage Gumbo (page 158). *Makes 16 to 20*

PREPARATION: 35 MINUTES
RISING: 5½ TO 6 HOURS
BAKING: 15 MINUTES

SPONGE

1 package dry active yeast
¼ cup warm (110 degrees) water
2 tablespoons sugar
⅓ cup unbleached all-purpose flour

DOUGH

3 to 3¼ cups unbleached all-purpose flour
Salt
2 tablespoons sugar
6 tablespoons melted butter
1 egg, lightly beaten
Flour
1 cup milk, scalded and cooled to lukewarm
(110 degrees)

1. For the sponge, mix the yeast, water, sugar, and flour in a medium bowl until the mixture forms a thick, gluey paste. Cover the bowl tightly with plastic wrap and set it aside for 1½ hours, or until the mixture is thick and frothy.

2. For the dough, insert the metal blade in a dry food processor. Add 3 cups flour, 1½ teaspoons salt, and sugar. Process briefly to mix the dry ingredients, then add 3 tablespoons of the butter and the sponge mixture. Beat the egg into the cooled milk. With the motor on, add the milk mixture to the dough in a thin stream. Process until dough is soft, sticky, taffylike, and thoroughly kneaded. (If dough appears to be liquid or runny, process in remaining flour by tablespoons until the dough holds its shape.)

3. Rinse a large mixing bowl with warm water, add the dough, cover the bowl tightly with plastic wrap, and set it aside until the dough triples in volume, about 2 to 2½ hours. (Or, rinse the inside of a zipper-lock plastic bag with warm water, add dough, press out excess air, seal, and refrigerate the dough overnight, or as long as 2 days without letting it rise in the bowl.)

4. Remove dough from bowl (or bag) without kneading, transfer it to a lightly floured work surface, and make round, braided rolls, or butterfly rolls as described in step 5.

5. *For round rolls:* Divide dough in half. Divide each half into eight pieces. Gather each small piece into a ball and put them on a buttered baking sheet, 1 inch apart.

For braided rolls: Divide dough in half. Divide each half into eight pieces. Cut each eighth into three small pieces; roll each piece into an 8-inch-long rope. Braid the three ropes to make a 4- to 4½-inch-long braided roll. Pinch and tuck ends under. Put rolls on a buttered baking sheet, 1 inch apart.

For butterfly rolls: Divide dough in half. Roll each half to a 15 × 7-inch rectangle; brush with melted butter. Roll up longest side tightly like a jelly roll. Cut crosswise into ten pieces (each 1½ inches wide). Press down center of each piece with back of a knife to form spiral butterfly wings. Put rolls on a buttered baking sheet, 1 inch apart.

6. Cover the shaped rolls loosely with a cloth towel and set them aside until the dough rises to slightly more than double, 1½ to 2 hours (or up to 3 hours if dough has been refrigerated).

7. Adjust oven rack to lowest position. Heat oven to 400 degrees. Brush tops of risen dough with some of the remaining melted butter. Bake 15 minutes, or until light brown. Cool on cake rack to room temperature.

AMERICAN IN PARIS BISCUITS

I once spent a month in Paris working with my friend, Joe Allen, on some new recipes for his well-known American restaurant near Les Halles. Joe wanted Paris to have real biscuits to serve with fried chicken, but the recipe called for vegetable shortening and buttermilk, two ingredients that are not easily found in France.

Fearing disaster, I substituted butter and a mixture of milk, cream, and lemon juice, and, to my surprise, baked absolutely sensational biscuits. After returning to New York, I made the biscuits twenty times trying to duplicate their texture. This recipe is very close.

FLEXIBLE MENU SUGGESTIONS

The biscuits are included in menus based on Duck and Sausage Gumbo (page 158), Arizona Chicken with Corn Ragout (page 192), Mesquite-Grilled Cornish Hens (page 240), and Jalapeño and Jack Cheese Sausages (page 256). They are also wonderful for breakfast! *Makes 13*

PREPARATION: 15 MINUTES
BAKING: 20 MINUTES

3 cups unbleached all-purpose flour
Salt
1 tablespoon sugar
1 tablespoon baking powder
¼ pound unsalted butter, cubed
½ cup whipping cream
¾ cup milk
2 tablespoons lemon juice
Flour
Additional milk
2 tablespoons melted butter

1. Put 3 cups flour, 1¾ teaspoons salt, sugar, and baking powder in the container of a food processor fitted with the metal blade. Process briefly to mix the ingredients. Add the butter and process until it completely disappears and the mixture has a sandy consistency. Transfer the contents of the food processor to a large bowl.

2. Combine cream, milk, and lemon juice in a measuring cup and stir well, then add it to the dry ingredients and mix only until the dough holds together in a sticky mass.

3. Adjust oven rack to lowest position. Heat oven to 425 degrees. Sprinkle a work surface generously with flour.

4. Turn the dough onto the work surface and dust the top of the dough with flour. Working it as little as possible, gently pat the dough into a 1-inch-thick cushion. With a 2-inch-diameter cutter, gently cut out biscuits, then press scraps together to make remaining biscuits.

5. Transfer biscuits to an ungreased baking sheet. Brush the tops with milk. Bake 20 minutes, until lightly browned. Remove biscuits from the oven and immediately brush them with melted butter. Serve warm within 30 minutes, or at room temperature.

HAM AND JALAPEÑO CORNBREAD

My passion for cornbread was rekindled one summer after attending a dinner party where Southern food was served. I had forgotten how good cornbread can be, and I immediately went to work on a recipe.

To create an especially moist bread I found that the batter required vegetable oil in addition to butter, and that plain cake flour was the key to crumbly tenderness. My friend and colleague Betsy Schultz, who is a Texan, encouraged me to add jalapeños, and I decided also to include the ham. The combination is unbeatable, although both ingredients can be omitted if you prefer plain cornbread.

FLEXIBLE MENU SUGGESTIONS

Whether it is served plain or spicy, cornbread is included in menus based on Duck and Sausage Gumbo (page 158), Arizona Chicken with Corn Ragout (page 192), Chicken Enchiladas Verdes (page 197), Mesquite-Grilled Cornish Hens (page 240), Jalapeño and Jack Cheese Sausages (page 256), and Chili-Rubbed Chicken (page 278). *Makes 8 servings*

PREPARATION: 8 MINUTES
BAKING: 20 MINUTES

¼ pound softened unsalted butter
1 medium shallot, peeled
2 fresh jalapeño peppers, seeded, cored
¼ pound boiled ham
1 egg
⅓ cup vegetable oil
1¼ cups milk
1 cup plain cake flour
¾ cup yellow cornmeal
1 tablespoon baking powder
Salt
3 tablespoons sugar

1. Adjust oven rack to lowest position. Heat oven to 400 degrees. Coat an 8-inch square glass baking dish with 2 tablespoons of the butter; set the dish aside.

2. Mince the shallot and jalapeños, and coarsely chop the ham. Melt 2 tablespoons butter in a medium skillet, add the shallot, jalapeños, and ham, and sauté until lightly browned, about 3 to 4 minutes.

3. Melt the remaining 4 tablespoons butter. Put the egg into a food processor fitted with the metal blade. With motor on, add the hot melted butter to the egg. Pulse in the oil and the milk.

4. Thoroughly mix the flour with the cornmeal, baking powder, ¼ to ½ teaspoon salt (depending on saltiness of ham), and the sugar in a large bowl. Add the sautéed ham mixture to the bowl, then stir in the egg mixture just until the dry ingredients disappear. Pour the batter into the prepared dish. Bake 20 minutes, until the top of the bread is lightly colored, and a cake tester inserted in the bread is withdrawn clean. Cool, then cut into 2-inch squares. Serve warm.

PART FIVE

DESSERTS

FETES NOIRES: CHOCOLATE DESSERTS

BEARING FRUIT: TARTS, COMFORTING DESSERTS, ICES, AND COOKIES

FETES NOIRES:
CHOCOLATE DESSERTS

Only one food in the universe inspires such rapturous praise as "food of the Gods," "divine decadence," or "sinfully rich." That food is chocolate.

Indeed, what *is* more heavenly than a silken chocolate frosting, more divinely decadent than a dense flourless fudge cake, or more sinfully tempting than a creamy, chocolate-filled truffle held unmoving on your tongue until it melts away?

I have long believed that chocolate desserts are remembered more vividly and fondly than others. Attribute it, if you will, to the stimulating properties of theobromine and caffeine, or to the fact that cocoa contains considerable amounts of phenylethylamine, a substance similar to one produced by brain cells during emotional highs. Nothing quite replaces chocolate in the affections of a dessert lover.

If left to my own devices, I would eat a chocolate dessert every night. This passion is a well-known source of amusement to friends, who marvel at my love of even the most banal chocolate candy bars. And over the years, my interest in baking, and in the intricacies of bringing the flavor of chocolate to its peak in great desserts, has led me to develop a number of recipes that I truly prize. I call these my "killer" chocolate desserts.

It is a very old food. Evidence that the Mayans and Aztecs first harvested and dried beans of the cacao tree, then roasted and milled them to make a chocolate drink, is cited in *The Discovery and Conquest of Mexico,* by Bernal Diaz del Castillo, a foot soldier in Cortez's army, who gives us a firsthand account of a meal eaten by Montezuma, the emperor of Mexico.

He was served on Cholula earthenware either red or black. While he was at his meal the men of his guard who were in the rooms near to that of Montezuma . . . they brought him fruit of all different kinds that the land produced, but he ate very little of it. From time to time they brought him, in cup-shaped vessels of pure gold, a certain drink made from cacao, and the women served this drink to him with great reverence.

Chocolate made its way to Europe after the Mexican conquest, and by 1828, Conrad van Houten of Amsterdam had invented cocoa powder. Eating chocolate was introduced in England in 1847, and by 1876, solid milk chocolate made its first appearance, invented by two Swiss—Daniel Peter and Henri Nestlé.

Chocolate has been an American favorite ever since Milton Hershey launched his chocolate bar in 1894. But the gourmet food boom of the 1970s ushered in a new era of appreciation, along with a host of European-style imported desserts, chocolates for baking and eating, and luxury candies—most notably the jewel-like, adults-only chocolate truffle.

Today, even the most diet-conscious guest will succumb to the lure of a chocolate indulgence. Which is my favorite? That is impossible to say. Each recipe has its own special quality that completes a dinner party, making it a "fête noire," an occasion made memorable, in part, by chocolate.

Ultra-Fudge Brownies produced moans of delight at a large Mexican dinner I cooked one year for a friend's birthday. The Dome Cake was the finale of several meals that consisted of new recipes gathered on my trips to Italy, and each version became successively richer, until I decided that it had to be done with chocolate—rather than plain—sponge cake. To please a colleague who adores chocolate and also loves hazelnuts, I transformed the flavors of an ice cream into the Gianduia Cheesecake.

And how can I ever forget the grin of pure delight on a friend's face when I caught him, several hours after a substantial dinner, secretly snacking on a wedge of a then-unnamed chocolate, caramel, and pecan tart. The wedge was easily equivalent to two normal pieces, and when I suggested, diplomatically, that three servings of such an outrageously rich dessert in one evening might make him ill, he looked at me and replied, "I can't resist, kid. It's too good." Then he kept on eating.

CHOCOLATE MACADAMIA TORTE

CHOCOLATE-WALNUT LINZER TORTE

Definitions—Light and Dark

Melting Methods

The Chocolate Conundrum

THE BARRY TART

CHOCOLATE TRUFFLE CAKE

GIANDUIA CHEESECAKE

GIANDUIA LACE COOKIES

DOME CAKE

15-MINUTE CHOCOLATE SPONGE CAKE

Coping with Cream

CHOCOLATE ROULADE

CHOCOLATE MADELEINES

ULTRA-FUDGE BROWNIES

ESPRESSO-BROWNIE CHUNK ICE CREAM

DOUBLE CHOCOLATE ICE CREAM

BITTERSWEET CHOCOLATE SAUCE

INSTANT HOT FUDGE SAUCE

CHOCOLATE MACADAMIA TORTE

It might be enough to say that this is a classic, flourless torte in the European style, but that would be selling it short. This rich cake has a marvelous, delicate texture yet is not overly sweet. If you have a good hand with frosting and a modicum of patience, it also can take on a rather formal, professional look.

The glaze is basically a French ganache: chocolate melted with hot cream that thickens to frosting texture. At first, the ganache is very liquid, and it must be stirred occasionally. The temptation is to hurry it along by refrigeration, but that will simply cause it to set around the edge while remaining liquid in the center.

It is best not to refrigerate the cake unless it is absolutely necessary to set the glaze; otherwise you risk ruining the springy texture of the torte layer.

FLEXIBLE MENU SUGGESTIONS

The torte is included in menus based on Capretto with Lemon and Rosemary (page 246), Leg of Lamb with Niçoise Seasoning (page 248), Halibut with Warm Vinaigrette (page 268), Veal Scallops Giardino (page 284), Garlic-Roasted Leg of Lamb (page 295), and Cognac-Marinated Beef Fillet (page 298). It is interchangeable with Chocolate Truffle Cake (page 382) and The Barry Tart (page 380). *Makes 10 to 12 servings*

PREPARATION: 45 MINUTES
COOLING: 4 HOURS
BAKING: 1 HOUR

GLAZE

12 ounces semisweet chocolate
1 cup whipping cream
4 tablespoons unsalted butter, cubed

TORTE LAYER

2 tablespoons softened butter
Unsweetened cocoa powder
½ pound shelled macadamia nuts
12 ounces semisweet chocolate
8 eggs, separated
4 ounces unsalted butter, cut in tablespoons
¾ cup sugar
½ cup sour cream
2 teaspoons vanilla extract

1. For the glaze, use a cleaver or large knife to chop the chocolate coarsely. (Or, cut chocolate into ½-inch pieces, divide it into four batches, and grind each batch in a food processor fitted with the metal blade.) Transfer the chocolate to a large, heatproof bowl.

2. Put the cream and butter in a medium saucepan and heat to simmering, stirring until the butter dissolves. Strain the hot cream mixture into chocolate in the bowl. Let stand 5 minutes. Stir until chocolate is melted, shiny, and completely smooth. Set the glaze aside uncovered at room temperature in a cool place (do *not* refrigerate or mixture will form lumps) until it thickens to frosting consistency, about 4 hours (can cover when cool and let stand at room temperature overnight).

3. For the torte layer, adjust oven rack to lowest position. Heat oven to 300 degrees. Coat the inside of a 10-inch springform pan and a 10-inch round of parchment paper with butter. Put the paper into the pan, buttered side up, and dust the entire pan with cocoa powder; refrigerate.

4. Chop the nuts coarsely; wrap and reserve ⅔ cup for garnish. Set the remaining nuts aside.

5. Use a cleaver or large knife to chop the chocolate coarsely. (Or, cut chocolate into ½-inch pieces, divide it into four batches, and grind each batch in a food processor fitted with the metal blade.) Transfer the chocolate to a large, heatproof bowl.

6. Put the egg yolks into a food processor fitted with the metal blade. Combine the butter and sugar in a medium saucepan and stir over low heat until sugar partially dissolves and mixture turns pale. With motor on, quickly pour the hot butter mixture into the egg yolks. Immediately pour the contents of the processor over the chocolate in the bowl. Let stand 5 minutes. Stir until mixture is melted and smooth. Stir in the sour cream and vanilla. Mixture will be very thick; cover with aluminum foil to keep it warm.

7. Put egg whites in a clean dry bowl. With electric beaters or with a whisk, whip whites until firm peaks form. Spoon half the chocolate mixture over the egg whites and continue whipping until three-quarters combined. Add remaining chocolate to whites and whip with beaters or whisk to combine thoroughly, then completely fold in the unwrapped chopped nuts.

8. Pour the batter into the springform pan in a spiral motion, beginning at the outside edge and working toward the center. Give the pan several quarter turns to settle the mixture. Bake 1 hour, or until a cake tester inserted into center is withdrawn clean. Transfer the pan to a cake rack and cool to room temperature. (Can cover pan with aluminum foil and set aside overnight *at room temperature; do not refrigerate.*)

9. To glaze the cake, remove the pan side and chip away the brittle chocolate dome on top of the cake layer if necessary. Invert the layer onto a cardboard cake round or serving platter. Remove and discard the parchment paper. Frost the sides and top of the layer generously with chocolate glaze. Make a decorative pattern with the glaze on top of the cake. Unwrap the ⅔ cup of reserved nuts. Put cake over wax paper and immediately press ground nuts all around the side of the cake for garnish.

10. Set cake aside in a cool place 2 hours (can let stand 6 hours without refrigerating). Or, refrigerate cake no longer than 30 minutes to set the glaze, then remove it from the refrigerator to a cool place. Serve within 6 hours.

CHOCOLATE-WALNUT LINZER TORTE

In Maida Heatter's *Book of Great Desserts,* America's queen of sweets writes that: "Basically torte or torta is a European word meaning cake, and, as many European cakes are made without flour, a torte is often defined as a cake without flour. . . . But it's all very complicated, especially as many classic torte recipes do call for flour. . . . And many classic desserts called tortes are really neither cakes nor tortes. Linzer Torte, for example, is really a tart or a European pie. . . . "

Call this particular recipe what you will; although it has the look of a streusel-topped cake and the chocolate-studded charm of a cookie, I see it as a variation on the Linzer theme. The filling requires nearly a pound of jam, so cooks who make their own have a luscious showcase (try raspberry, apricot, or peach). Low-sugar or "fruit-only" jams also can be substituted, but then the quantity of sugar in the recipe should be increased to ½ cup. The torte refrigerates and freezes perfectly.

FLEXIBLE MENU SUGGESTIONS

This tart is homey enough to offer with a mug of coffee, but it is included in menus based on Pasta with Four Cheeses (page 132), Lemon-Garlic Capellini with Mediterranean Sauce (page 150), Country-Style Risotto (page 176), Fettuccine with Chicken, Artichokes, and Dill (page 204), One-Side Grilled Fish (page 216) with Whole-Grain Mustard-Chive Butter (page 277), Soy-Marinated Chicken (page 238), Mesquite-Grilled Cornish Hens (page 240), Sage-Rubbed Veal Chops (page 242), Pork with Port Wine Sauce (page 292), and Chili- or Herb-Rubbed Chicken (pages 283 and 278). *Makes 8 servings*

PREPARATION: 40 MINUTES
BAKING: 1 HOUR 15 MINUTES

Softened unsalted butter
1¼ cups (5 ounces) shelled walnuts
¼ cup (1 ounce) blanched almonds
1¼ cups unbleached all-purpose flour
¼ pound semisweet chocolate, or chocolate chips
⅓ cup sugar
Salt
1 egg yolk
1 tablespoon water
11 tablespoons chilled unsalted butter
1½ cups raspberry, peach, or apricot jam or preserves

1. Adjust oven rack to lowest position. Heat oven to 350 degrees. Butter a 9-inch round of parchment or wax paper and the sides of a 9-inch springform pan. Put parchment in pan, buttered side up; set aside.

2. Chop and transfer the walnuts to a large bowl. Insert the metal blade in a food processor. Process the almonds with ¼ cup flour until finely ground; add to the bowl. Chop the chocolate to the texture of the nuts; add it to the bowl. Stir in the sugar, remaining flour, and 1 teaspoon salt, and mix the dry ingredients thoroughly. Measure and set aside 1¼ cups for the topping.

3. Put the egg yolk, water, and 6 tablespoons butter into the processor and pulse to mix. Add the remaining nut-chocolate mixture and pulse until the butter disappears and the mixture has the texture of moist cookie dough.

4. Transfer the dough to the springform pan and press it into the shape of a tart shell, with 1½-inch-high sides and an even bottom. Freeze 5 minutes. Bake 15 minutes. Cool 10 minutes.

5. Put the reserved dry ingredients for the topping in the processor. Add remaining 5 tablespoons butter and pulse until the mixture has a crumbly texture.

6. Fill the cool, partially baked crust with jam. Sprinkle the crumbly topping evenly over the top to cover the jam completely. Carefully press down the edge to join the top and bottom crusts. Bake 1 hour. Cool to room temperature and remove the side and bottom of the pan. Refrigerate 1 hour before slicing. (Can wrap and freeze 1 month.)

DEFINITIONS—LIGHT AND DARK

Regardless of the brand of chocolate you may select for use in a recipe, the U.S. government has standards of identity: regulations governing ingredients in the various types of chocolate that are available in supermarkets and specialty food stores.

According to the Chocolate Manufacturer's Association, each type of chocolate can be defined as follows (however, keep in mind that imported chocolate may vary from these standards):

Unsweetened chocolate: Also called baking, cooking, pure, or bitter chocolate. This is chocolate liquor, cooled and molded into blocks, to which cocoa butter may be added to adjust the fat content (normally 50 to 58 percent).

Semisweet or bittersweet chocolate: Also known as dark chocolate or extra bittersweet, there is wide variation in taste and sweetness from brand to brand. If manufactured in the U.S., this chocolate contains at least 35 percent chocolate liquor. Sugar (35 to 50 percent) and cocoa butter may be added to adjust the flavor. Chocolate chips, or morsels, are most often made from semisweet chocolate.

Sweet chocolate: Many brands are really semisweet but, as a rule, sweet chocolates contain a high percentage of sugar and flavorings and need only contain 15 percent chocolate liquor. A small amount of milk solids is also permissible.

Milk chocolate: Most commonly used for eating, milk chocolate is made by adding cocoa butter, milk solids, sweeteners, and flavorings to chocolate liquor. Milk chocolates made in the U.S. must contain a minimum of 10 percent chocolate liquor and 12 percent whole milk. The melting temperature (about 86 degrees) is lower than for dark chocolate.

Cocoa powder: The solid brown part of chocolate liquor, left after the removal of 78 to 90 percent of the cocoa butter, is called cocoa. Dutch-process cocoa is treated with an alkali (such as baking soda) and has a darker color and somewhat stronger flavor than standard cocoa.

Prior to melting chocolate it is best to chop it coarsely (with a cleaver or large knife) so that it will melt evenly. An alternate method is to cut chocolate into small squares and grind it to a beadlike consistency in the food processor, which takes less than 1 minute. Ground chocolate melts almost instantly in contact with heat.

Top-quality semisweet or bittersweet chocolate contains a high percentage of cocoa butter and will chop or grind into glossy beads. Chocolates that are lower in cocoa butter tend to become powdery.

Chocolate should be melted in an absolutely dry pan, bowl, or dish. When melted by itself, if very small amounts of liquid (even a few drops of water) are present, chocolate can seize or contract into a lumpy unworkable mess. Never melt chocolate with less than 2 tablespoons liquid.

Unsweetened and semisweet chocolates melt at body temperature, about 96 degrees. They hold their shape and may not look melted if left undisturbed; always stir to be sure. Sweet chocolates and milk chocolates melt between 86 and 96 degrees. The temperature of chocolate should never rise beyond 110 degrees, which feels hot to the touch.

Prior to melting, keep all chocolate stored in a cool (65 to 70 degrees), dry pantry or cupboard, preferably in an airtight container (like butter, it absorbs flavors and odors).

Residual heat method: This technique is frequently used in recipes that contain a considerable quantity of liquid that must be incorporated into chocolate. It is fast and efficient—the drawback is that chocolate may become overheated if the liquid is too hot.

Begin with chopped or ground chocolate placed in a heatproof bowl. Pour hot, but not simmering, liquid—cream, a custard, melted butter, or a sugar syrup—over the chocolate. Let it stand for 5 minutes, then stir until the chocolate is melted and smooth and the mixture is lump-free.

Double-boiler method: Here is the way to retain maximum control over the rate at which chocolate melts, or to handle a small quantity of chocolate (2 ounces or less). Heat 3 cups water to simmering in bottom of a double boiler or in a medium (2½-quart) saucepan. Remove saucepan from the heat. Put chopped or ground chocolate in a completely dry stainless steel mixing bowl or in the top pot of a double boiler. Put the bowl or boiler top over the pan of water, and begin working the chocolate with a rubber spatula to encourage melting. Remove chocolate from heat when it is three-quarters melted, and continue working it with the spatula until it has completely dissolved.

Microwave oven method: Chocolate need not be chopped or ground if you wish to melt it in the microwave, but for best results, do not leave it in large chunks, which can melt unevenly. With this method, melting time is about 2 to 4 minutes (in a 700-watt oven) for as much as 12 ounces of chopped or ground semisweet chocolate.

Put the prepared chocolate (plus any additional ingredients) uncovered in a microwave-safe, heatproof bowl, dish, or large cup. Microwave on medium power for 30 seconds. Work chocolate with spatula to aid melting. Microwave on medium at 15-second intervals, stirring each time and checking for the change in texture.

SAVING SEIZED CHOCOLATE
Seized chocolate (which looks separated) often can be saved by stirring in 2 tablespoons of vegetable shortening (but not butter or oil) and beating vigorously.

Determining which type of chocolate to use in a recipe is largely a question of personal choice. I specify semisweet in a majority of recipes. However, bittersweet chocolate can be substituted if a slight reduction in sweetness seems desirable.

Tasting a small piece of chocolate by letting it melt on your tongue will help you gauge how it will work in a recipe. Since each brand is made from a unique blend, expect a range in flavor. For example, you may find one brand of bittersweet to be a perfect substitute for semisweet chocolate in a recipe, while another may seem too bitter. Let the taste of each be your guide. However, unsweetened chocolate is *not* interchangeable with bittersweet or semisweet chocolate.

If you wish to conduct a comparative test to determine which brand of chocolate to use in a recipe, make a batch of the Ultra-Fudge Brownies (leaving out the nuts and chocolate chips) using each chocolate. You may find the variations in flavor to be surprising.

Cooks often say that chocolate desserts from restaurants taste different when they are made at home. The reason usually can be traced to the brand of chocolate used. If a restaurant makes chocolate desserts you particularly like, ask about the brand.

A PERSONAL SAMPLER

There are scores of chocolates on the market, each made from a secret formula or blend of beans, and each with a slightly different flavor. Every time I conduct blind tastings of domestic and imported semisweet and bittersweet chocolates, it is enlightening to see how they rate.

Here are three brands of semisweet and bittersweet chocolates that give desserts the deep, chocolaty taste I particularly prefer. These are by no means the only good brands to use. They are simply the ones with which I have had consistently good results in recipes.

Valrhona (Extra Bitter *couverture* grade) is a bittersweet blend with an acidic tang. Technically, this is a *couverture,* or coating chocolate, and is favored by top French candy makers because of its silky texture, exceedingly fine flavor, and high percentage of cocoa butter, qualities that make it a top-of-the-line chocolate that is a luxury to use in desserts. (To locate Valrhona chocolate, contact Van Rex Gourmet Foods, 530 West 25th St., New York, N.Y. 10001; 212-675-7777. Since Valrhona makes several types of semisweet and bittersweet chocolate, be sure to specify "extra bitter couverture."

Callebaut is a semisweet Belgian chocolate widely available in bulk at specialty food and gourmet stores. This is also *couverture* grade, and flavors include extra-bittersweet, bittersweet, semisweet, milk, and even gianduia chocolate that contains 30 percent hazelnuts. (Callebaut chocolate is distributed by Amazon de Choix, 58–25 52nd Ave., Woodside, N.Y. 11377; 718-507-8080. They will assist cooks in finding local sources.)

Ghirardelli "Eagle" chocolate is the brand that consistently was picked first in blind chocolate tastings that I conducted in cooking classes. The California-based company distributes a range of 4-ounce chocolate bars in supermarkets and specialty food stores. All are considered by Ghirardelli to be suitable for baking and candy making.

According to Ghirardelli, their bars contain the following percentages of cocoa butter and sugar, which will help match your selection to chocolate use: bittersweet (33% cocoa butter; 39 to 43% sugar), semisweet (32% cocoa butter; 45 to 49% sugar), sweet (32% cocoa butter; 49 to 53% sugar), and milk chocolate (33% cocoa butter; 45 to 49% sugar). For further information, contact Ghirardelli at 415-482-6970.

THE BARRY TART

The first time I made this tart as a recipe for my newspaper column I thought it was really very good. Just to be sure, I asked a close friend to taste it and give me an opinion. He dubbed it a "Hall of Fame" dessert, and then proceeded to consume the entire thing in twenty-four hours—an act that merits his name on the recipe.

This combination of chocolate, pecans, caramel, and chocolate pastry also has been a commercial success. When I was the menu consultant for Tavern on the Green restaurant in New York, I gave the recipe to the pastry chef, and it quickly became the restaurant's number-one dessert. Needless to say, I have served it at home with spectacular results.

The preparation is lengthy, since the tart must be made in advance and frozen before the topping is added. However, it keeps perfectly in the freezer for up to a month.

Should the finished tart be difficult to slice (which happens occasionally if the caramel is overcooked), the solution is to use a large knife that has been rinsed with hot running water and wiped dry.

The tart is pictured in the color section. The garnish is created by placing cardboard strips over the plate to make a triangle in the center, then sifting cocoa through a small strainer over the open area.

FLEXIBLE MENU SUGGESTIONS

This tart is included in menus based on Capretto with Lemon and Rosemary (page 246), Mushroom and Prosciutto-Stuffed Chicken Breasts (page 274), and Cognac-Marinated Beef Fillet (page 298). It is interchangeable with Chocolate Macadamia Torte (page 374) or Chocolate Truffle Cake (page 382). *Makes an 11-inch tart*

PREPARATION: 1 HOUR
BAKING: 40 TO 50 MINUTES
FREEZING: 6 HOURS TO 1 MONTH

CRUST

1¼ cups unbleached flour
¼ cup unsweetened cocoa powder
2 tablespoons powdered sugar
¼ pound frozen unsalted butter, cubed
¼ cup ice water
Flour

FILLING AND TOPPING

6 ounces semisweet chocolate
¼ cup sugar
¼ cup strong brewed coffee
¼ cup whipping cream
14 tablespoons unsalted butter
2 eggs, separated
5 ounces (1¼ cups) shelled pecans
1 cup granulated light brown sugar
Salt
6 tablespoons whipping cream
3 tablespoons dark rum

1. For the crust, combine flour, cocoa, and sugar in a dry food processor fitted with the metal blade. Process to mix the ingredients. Add the butter and process until it completely disappears and mixture takes on a sandy texture. Add the ice water and pulse until the dough begins to clump.

2. Gather dough into a flat disk and gently roll it, on a generously floured surface, into a 14-inch circle. Transfer the circle of dough to an 11-inch fluted tart pan with removable bottom. Ease the dough into the pan and fit it snugly around the bottom edge and against the sides of the pan. Trim off excess dough and freeze for 15 minutes.

3. Adjust oven rack to lowest position. Heat oven to 375 degrees. Line the dough with aluminum foil and add pie weights or rice. Bake 30 to 35 minutes. Remove weights and foil. Bake 5 to 7 minutes longer; set aside to cool.

4. For the filling, use a cleaver or large knife to chop the chocolate coarsely. (Or, cut chocolate into ½-inch pieces and grind it in a food processor fitted with the metal blade.) Set aside.

5. In a small saucepan, mix the sugar, coffee, and cream. Heat to simmering, stirring frequently. Add 6 tablespoons of the butter and stir over low heat until it melts. Put the egg yolks in a food processor fitted with the metal blade. With the motor on, quickly pour in the hot coffee cream. Add the chocolate and process until it is smooth; cover the chocolate mixture and set aside; do not refrigerate.

6. Coarsely chop the pecans. Wrap and reserve ¾ cup for the top of the tart; set the remainder aside.

7. Heat ½ cup of the brown sugar with a pinch of salt and 4 tablespoons butter in a small saucepan, stirring until sugar dissolves. Add 3 tablespoons of the cream and 1½ tablespoons rum. Heat to boiling and simmer just until the caramel turns a rich amber and thickens slightly, about 5 minutes.

8. Immediately pour the hot caramel into the tart shell, spreading it evenly over the crust with the back of a spoon. Sprinkle the pecans evenly over the caramel. Freeze the tart for 5 minutes.

9. In a clean dry bowl, whip egg whites to firm peaks with electric beaters or a whisk. Fold egg whites thoroughly into the chocolate filling. Put the filling over the caramel layer in the tart and smooth the top. Cover and freeze until it is solid, about 6 hours. (Can remove frozen tart from the pan, transfer it to a cardboard cake round, double-wrap, and freeze 1 month, together with the chopped pecans for the topping.)

10. For the caramel and nut topping, repeat step 7, using the remaining sugar, salt, butter, cream, and rum. Remove the pan ring and put the frozen tart on a sheet of oiled aluminum foil. Pour the hot caramel over the top of the tart, working quickly to spread it evenly. Immediately sprinkle the reserved pecans over the caramel.

11. Refrigerate the tart until the caramel is firm and the tart defrosts, about 2 hours (can cover loosely and refrigerate 3 days). Unless the kitchen is very hot, let the tart stand at room temperature for 30 minutes before slicing.

CHOCOLATE TRUFFLE CAKE

You could make truffles from this," someone once told me after tasting a slice of this cake, a fudgelike layer that could be put in the category of unforgettable chocolate experiences.

Real chocoholics invariably go mad for this cake, and many have said they would like to frost it with chocolate glaze rather than whipped cream! While that idea seems like overkill to me, it does offer another way to garnish the layer; if the idea tempts you, use half a recipe of the glaze for the Chocolate Macadamia Torte (page 374). My guests are often surprised that the cake is so easy to make, and because it yields so many servings, I often send them home with the leftover slices.

I do think that the frosting of slightly sweetened whipped cream helps to temper the effect of the chocolate and cover up flaws in the surface of the cake made by pleats in the aluminum foil. The cream also gives the cake a pretty look, and whipping it in the food processor makes it dense enough to pipe easily and durable enough to hold up for hours in the refrigerator.

FLEXIBLE MENU SUGGESTIONS

This cake is included in menus based on Baked Curried Beef (page 201), Sage-Rubbed Veal Chops (page 242), Veal Scallops Giardino (page 284), Garlic-Roasted Leg of Lamb (page 295), and Cognac-Marinated Beef Fillet (page 298). It also can be substituted for Chocolate Macadamia Torte (page 374) or The Barry Tart (page 380). *Makes 10 to 12 servings*

PREPARATION: 25 MINUTES
BAKING: 2 HOURS

CAKE

Softened unsalted butter
1 pound semisweet chocolate
1 cup strong brewed coffee or espresso
2 cups sugar
1 pound unsalted butter, cubed
8 eggs, lightly beaten

TOPPING

½ cup powdered sugar
2½ cups chilled whipping cream
Coffee-bean candies (optional)

1. For the cake, cut a sheet of aluminum foil large enough to line the bottom and sides of a 10-inch springform pan. Coat the foil generously with softened butter and place it in the pan, buttered side up, working neatly to avoid large folds or pleats in the foil; refrigerate the pan.

2. Adjust oven rack to lowest position. Heat oven to 250 degrees.

3. Use a cleaver or large knife to chop the chocolate coarsely. (Or, cut chocolate into ½-inch pieces, divide it into four batches, and grind each batch in a food processor fitted with the metal blade.) Transfer the chocolate to a large, heatproof bowl.

4. Mix the coffee with the sugar in a large saucepan. Stir the mixture over medium heat until sugar completely dissolves, about 4 to 5 minutes. Add butter and stir over low heat until butter is completely melted, about 10 minutes longer.

5. Pour the contents of the saucepan over chocolate in the bowl. Let stand 5 minutes. Stir gently until chocolate is melted, shiny, and completely smooth. Stir eggs thoroughly into the warm chocolate mixture—do not beat.

6. Pour the batter into the cake pan. Bake 2 hours, or until the center is just set. Transfer the pan to a cake rack to cool. Wrap and refrigerate the cake layer until thoroughly chilled, or up to 3 days. (Can freeze, remove from pan, wrap, and keep frozen up to 1 month. Defrost overnight in refrigerator.)

7. To make the topping, freeze the container and metal blade of a food processor for 5 minutes, then reassemble the machine. Put the powdered sugar and half the cream into the machine. Process for 30 seconds, then pour the remaining cream into the machine and process until the cream is thickly whipped and holds in firm peaks.

8. Invert the cake on a serving platter and carefully remove the foil; gently blot the surface dry with paper towels. Put whipped cream in a pastry bag fitted with a star (or other) tip. Pipe cream stars (or other decoration) over the top of the cake to cover the chocolate completely. Garnish with coffee-bean candies, if desired. Refrigerate until serving time (up to 4 hours).

GIANDUIA CHEESECAKE

Swiss and Italian confectioners have long made ice cream and candy in a flavor known as *gianduia* or *gianduja* (john-doo-ya), a seductive alliance of hazelnuts and chocolate that is barely known on this side of the Atlantic. What better way to become acquainted with this little taste of Europe than in a cheesecake spiked with hazelnut liqueur and wrapped in a crunchy chocolate cookie crust?

The *gianduia* flavor can easily be created from the blend of dark and light chocolates and hazelnuts suggested below. However, actual *gianduia* chocolate is also made by several European chocolate companies (notably Callebaut, see page 379), and it can be substituted in the recipe.

Two things will help prevent the top of the cheesecake from cracking. First, do not overbeat the batter. If overbeaten, the cake may soufflé too much in the oven, and then split after it sinks; gently stirring in the beaten eggs should help avoid this problem. Then, the cake should be removed from the oven when the center is just set—it will shimmer slightly—and it must be transferred *very* carefully from the oven rack to the cake rack. If possible, cool the cheesecake slowly and in a relatively warm location rather than in a cool spot.

FLEXIBLE MENU SUGGESTIONS

This cake is included in menus based on Scallion and Black Pepper Lasagne with Black Olive Pesto (page 144), Mushroom Pizzas on Prosciutto Crust (page 114), Sage-Rubbed Veal Chops (page 242), Fettuccine with Chicken, Artichokes, and Dill (page 204), Chili and Garlic-Rubbed Flank Steak (page 248), Chili-Rubbed Chicken (page 278), and Cognac-Marinated Beef Fillet (page 298). *Makes 10 servings*

PREPARATION: 30 MINUTES
BAKING: 1 HOUR 15 MINUTES

CRUST

1½ tablespoons softened butter
6 ounces chocolate wafer cookies, broken in
   pieces
2 tablespoons sugar
3 tablespoons warm melted butter

FILLING

2 cups (½ pound) shelled hazelnuts (filberts)
½ pound semisweet chocolate
¼ pound milk chocolate
2¼ pounds cream cheese, softened and cubed
1½ cups sugar
½ cup whipping cream
¼ cup Mascarpone (page 428) or sour cream
½ teaspoon vanilla extract
⅓ cup hazelnut liqueur (Frangelico)
5 eggs, lightly beaten

1. Adjust oven rack to middle position. Heat oven to 350 degrees. For the crust, coat the bottom and sides of a 9-inch springform pan with softened butter.

2. Insert the metal blade in a food processor. Process cookies with sugar to fine crumbs. With motor on, add warm melted butter to the cookie mixture. Press the crust evenly onto the bottom and sides of the pan. Refrigerate 5 minutes. Bake 5 minutes. Cool completely.

3. For the filling, spread the hazelnuts on a baking sheet and bake until skins blister, about 10 to 15 minutes. Immediately rub in cloth towel to remove skins; cool the nuts. Lower the oven temperature to 325 degrees.

4. Use a cleaver or large knife to chop the chocolates coarsely, and put them in a heatproof (or microwavable) bowl. Melt the chocolate in the microwave (see page 378) or over a double boiler (see page 378) until it is melted and smooth; set it aside.

5. Grind the hazelnuts finely; set aside. Put the cream cheese, sugar, whipping cream, Mascarpone, vanilla, and liqueur in the processor and process, pushing the cheese down onto the blades as necessary. Stop processing when the cheese changes to a batter that moves in a smooth whirlpool.

6. Stir the cheese mixture thoroughly into the warm melted chocolate, then stir in the eggs. Remove any large lumps of cheese. Stir in the ground hazelnuts.

7. Pour batter into the crust. Bake until the center is just set, about 1 hour to 75 minutes. Gently transfer the pan to a cake rack and cool to room temperature. Refrigerate 6 hours or overnight before serving. (Can wrap and refrigerate 3 days.)

Hazelnuts (or filberts) are gathered during the late summer or early fall, and, according to legend, they were named for Saint Philibert. The shelled nuts usually are roasted to remove the brittle, chestnut-brown skin that clings to the exterior of each nutmeat; however, they must be completely cool before grinding or they can turn to a paste.

GIANDUIA LACE COOKIES

Chocolate and hazelnuts make glorious butter cookies that are garnished after baking with a thin chocolate web spun with a knife or fork à la Jackson Pollock. (The cookies are pictured in the color section.) Their shortbreadlike texture helps these refrigerate and freeze perfectly.

FLEXIBLE MENU SUGGESTIONS

Serve the cookies interchangeably with Chocolate Madeleines (page 394), although they require far more work to make, and use them to accompany Double Chocolate Ice Cream (page 399).

They are included in menus based on Lemon-Garlic Capellini with Mediterranean Sauce (page 150), Country-Style Risotto (page 216), One-Side Grilled Fish (page 216) with Whole-Grain Mustard-Chive Butter (page 277), Sage-Rubbed Veal Chops (page 242), Mushroom and Prosciutto-Stuffed Chicken Breasts (page 274), Garlic-Rubbed Chicken (page 278), Veal Scallops Giardino (page 284), and Garlic-Roasted Leg of Lamb (page 295). *Makes 5 dozen*

PREPARATION: 30 MINUTES
CHILLING: 1 HOUR
BAKING: 20 MINUTES

1 cup (4 ounces) whole shelled hazelnuts
(filberts)
¼ pound semisweet chocolate
½ pound unsalted butter, cut in 16 pieces
¼ teaspoon vanilla extract
2 egg yolks
½ cup sugar
2 cups plain cake flour
2 tablespoons unsweetened cocoa powder

LACE TOPPING

¼ pound semisweet chocolate, or chocolate
chips
2 tablespoons vegetable oil

1. Adjust oven rack to lowest position. Heat oven to 375 degrees. Toast hazelnuts on a baking sheet until the skins char, about 8 to 10 minutes. Transfer them to a towel and rub vigorously to remove most of the skins; set the nuts aside to cool.

2. Use a cleaver or a large knife to cut the chocolate into ¼-inch chunks. Put the chocolate in a food processor fitted with the metal blade. Process until the chocolate is finely ground; set aside. Grind the nuts to medium texture, and set them aside with the chocolate.

3. Put butter, vanilla, egg yolks, and ¼ cup sugar in the machine and pulse until thoroughly mixed. Add the nuts, chocolate, flour, and cocoa and process until the dough begins to clump. Press the dough into a flat disk, wrap it in plastic, and refrigerate 1 hour.

4. Pinch off 1-inch pieces of dough and roll each into an even ball. Dip the top of each ball into the remaining ¼ cup sugar. Put them, sugared side up, 2 inches apart on a baking sheet, gently pressing each into a cushion shape. Bake 18 to 20 minutes. Transfer to cake rack to cool. Repeat to shape and bake all cookies.

5. For the lace topping, use a cleaver or large knife to chop the chocolate coarsely, and put it in a small heatproof or microwavable bowl. Add the oil and melt the chocolate in the microwave or over a double boiler (see page 378). Work the chocolate with a spatula until melted and thinned to consistency of unbeaten cream, heating gently if necessary.

6. Cover a baking sheet with wax paper. Put the cookies close together on the paper. Use a dinner knife to drizzle chocolate in a thin stream over the cookies, forming a chocolate lace design. Refrigerate 10 minutes. Repeat to top all cookies with chocolate lace. When chocolate is firmly set, transfer cookies to airtight storage containers. (Can store 1 week in refrigerator, or freeze up to 3 weeks.)

"White grapes are very attractive but when it comes to dessert people generally like cake with icing."

—FRAN LEBOWITZ

DOME CAKE

All over Italy, bakeries carry dome-shaped cakes filled with ice cream, whipped cream or Mascarpone, ground nuts, chocolate, or candied fruit. This type of cake is called a *zuccotto*, which translates literally as "skullcap." The hemispherical shape is made by lining a deep mixing bowl with thin overlapping sponge-cake slices which, when moistened with liqueur, retain the shape of the mold.

Most *zuccotti* are made from plain sponge cake, but I prefer to use a chocolate cake layer that is further enhanced by ground chocolate, nuts, and Mascarpone in the filling. However, plain sponge cake can be substituted, and the combinations of nuts can be varied.

The cake layer must be made a day in advance to become firm enough to split into rounds. Then the dessert needs overnight refrigeration before it is unmolded. For a dramatic presentation, dust the top with powdered sugar, slice it into wedges, and put each portion over a pool of Bittersweet Chocolate Sauce (page 400).

FLEXIBLE MENU SUGGESTIONS

Serve in menus based on Pasta with Milanese Meat Sauce (page 130), Fettuccine with Chicken, Artichokes, and Dill (page 204), Capretto with Lemon and Rosemary (page 246), Scampi alla Busara (page 272), Garlic- or Herb-Rubbed Chicken (pages 281 and 278), or Garlic-Roasted Leg of Lamb (page 295). *Makes 8 servings*

PREPARATION: 40 MINUTES
CHILLING: 12 HOURS

15-Minute Chocolate Sponge Cake (page 390)
½ cup blanched almonds
½ cup hazelnuts
3 ounces semisweet chocolate
¼ cup Cognac, brandy, or sweet Marsala
¼ cup Kirsch, Framboise, or dark rum
5½ tablespoons powdered sugar
1½ cups chilled whipping cream
½ cup Mascarpone (page 428) or whipping
  cream
Bittersweet Chocolate Sauce (page 400),
  optional

1. Make the sponge cake and set aside overnight.

2. Adjust oven rack to lowest position. Heat oven to 350 degrees. Put almonds and hazelnuts in separate cake pans. Bake until almonds are golden brown and hazelnut skins char, about 8 to 10 minutes. Set almonds aside to cool. Immediately transfer hazelnuts to a dry cloth towel and rub vigorously to remove the skins; set aside to cool.

3. Use a cleaver or large knife to chop the chocolate coarsely. (Or, cut chocolate into ½-inch pieces and grind coarsely in a food processor fitted with the metal blade.) Coarsely chop the nuts. When the nuts are completely cool, mix them with the chocolate in a large bowl; set aside.

4. Use a serrated knife to cut the sponge cake horizontally into four thin layers of equal thickness. Reassemble the layers and quarter the cake evenly (this will give you sixteen thin cake wedges). Set aside four wedges from the top or bottom of the cake layer.

5. Line a 6-cup mixing bowl with plastic wrap. Arrange overlapping cake wedges on the sides of the bowl with points facing, and slightly overlapping, the center bottom. If necessary, fill in the space at the bottom center of the bowl to be sure entire bowl is cake-lined, with no gaps or spaces. Mix the Cognac and Kirsch and sprinkle it evenly over the cake in the bowl, reserving about 1 tablespoon for the reserved cake wedges.

6. Freeze the food-processor container and blade for 5 minutes. Add ¼ cup powdered sugar and ½ cup cream to the processor. Process 30 seconds. With the motor on, add the remaining cream in a thin stream. Process to firm peaks, and mix in the Mascarpone. Fold the cream mixture into the chocolate and nuts.

7. Spoon the filling into the cake shell. Drizzle the cut sides of the remaining cake wedges with the reserved cognac mixture. Cover the filling with the cake wedges, crust-sides up, trimming as necessary. Cover the cake tightly with plastic wrap. Refrigerate overnight (can refrigerate up to 3 days).

8. To serve, remove the plastic and invert the cake onto a serving platter. Sift the remaining 1½ tablespoons powdered sugar over the top of the cake (remove excess on the platter with a pastry brush). Slice in wedges and serve immediately over chocolate sauce, if desired.

15-MINUTE CHOCOLATE SPONGE CAKE

~~~~~~~~~~

Buttery French sponge cake (called *biscuit au beurre*) has always been made in a mixer, but I believe it is possible to get a similar result more quickly using this surprisingly easy, six-step batter that can be oven-ready in just 15 minutes.

FLEXIBLE MENU SUGGESTIONS

Chocolate sponge cake is an ingredient of the Dome Cake (page 388); another chocolate cake layer may be substituted.
Makes an 8-inch cake layer

PREPARATION: 15 MINUTES
BAKING: 25 MINUTES

½ cup sugar
¾ cup (plus 1 tablespoon) plain cake flour
⅓ cup unsweetened cocoa powder
1¼ teaspoons baking powder
Salt
2 tablespoons softened butter
4 egg whites (⅔ cup)
¼ teaspoon lemon juice
2 egg yolks
½ teaspoon vanilla
¼ cup warm (170 degrees) melted unsalted butter

1. Heat the sugar and ¼ cup water to boiling in small nonreactive saucepan. Cover and simmer 5 minutes. Strain the syrup into a measuring cup; set aside to cool.

2. Sift ¾ cup of the cake flour with the cocoa, baking powder, and ⅛ teaspoon salt; set aside.

3. Adjust oven rack to middle position. Heat oven to 350 degrees. Butter an 8 × 1½-inch round cake pan; line with buttered wax or parchment paper. Dust pan with remaining flour, tap out excess; set the pan aside.

4. In a food processor fitted with the metal blade, process the egg whites with lemon juice until foamy, about 30 seconds. With the motor on, slowly pour ⅓ cup of the syrup into the egg whites and process until a soft meringue forms, about 2 minutes. Carefully remove meringue to a separate bowl or plate; cover.

5. Process the egg yolks with vanilla, melted butter, and remaining syrup until mixed. Sift the dry ingredients into the machine over the egg-yolk mixture. Add the meringue and combine by pulsing just until the ingredients are mixed into a smooth batter.

6. Pour the batter into pan in a spiral, beginning at the pan rim. Bake 25 minutes, or until cake tester inserted into center of layer is withdrawn clean. Cool for 10 minutes. Invert and put the layer upright on cake rack. Cool to room temperature. (Can double-wrap and freeze the sponge cake layer up to 3 weeks.)

PLAIN PROCESSOR SPONGE CAKE Omit cocoa from recipe. Increase cake flour to 1 cup (plus 1 tablespoon for dusting pan).

COPING WITH CREAM

Cream is one of the key ingredients that can become a recipe problem—particularly when whipped cream must hold up in a filling, a frosting, or when piped. For best results, use whipping cream (30 to 36 percent butterfat) or heavy cream (more than 37 percent butterfat) that is not ultrapasteurized.

According to the American Dairy Association, ultrapasteurized cream has been heated to 275 or 300 degrees and held for 2 to 4 seconds. Normally, pasteurized cream is heated to 145 degrees for 30 seconds, or to 161 degrees for 15 seconds—just long enough to destroy harmful bacteria.

The purpose of ultrapasteurization is to give fresh cream a 60- to 90-day supermarket shelf life. But the sterilization, plus the addition of legally permissible stabilizers and emulsifiers added to prevent the cream from separating, also sometimes cause it to whip less than successfully.

COMPENSATING FACTORS

Cream whipped in the food processor is far more dense than cream whipped with a mixer or whisk, since less air is incorporated. In a mixer, 1 cup of cream will double in volume, to produce 2 cups. However, if cream is whipped in the food processor, 1½ cups of liquid cream are required to make 2 cups when whipped.

Using the method specified in the recipes, cream often will hold up perfectly for 8 hours, or overnight, which is why I frequently prefer to use processor-whipped cream for fillings and frostings. The decrease in volume also helps to compensate for cream that is low in butterfat. Be sure to reduce the quantity of liquid cream slightly if you substitute whipping techniques in these recipes.

As a precaution before whipping cream by any method, chill the bowl and beaters, or the processor container and metal blade, in the freezer for 5 to 10 minutes. The utensils should be icy to the touch. If you are whipping cream by hand, whip cream in a bowl set into a bowl of ice.

Raising the butterfat content of cream sometimes will offset whipping problems. This is done most easily by adding 2 or 3 tablespoons of Mascarpone (see page 428) to the liquid cream. Commercially prepared crème fraîche, or even sour cream, can have the same effect, although the culture that gives these two products their slightly acidic taste also will alter the flavor of the whipped cream. Proceed cautiously, as the sourness of these products can increase with age.

CHOCOLATE ROULADE

The roulade, or flourless chocolate cake roll, became famous in the 1950s, when it was the signature dessert of the late cookbook author and teacher, Dione Lucas, who hosted the first televised cooking show.

Mrs. Lucas called this Roulade Léontine, and was often photographed holding the roll aloft on an unvarnished wooden paddle-shaped serving board of a type still sold in cookware stores (18 inches is standard). Over the past forty years her recipe has been published innumerable times, for the cake roll has an intense chocolate flavor combined with a light, melt-in-your mouth quality.

Guests always adore, and request, this dessert, which I include here in an updated version that shortcuts the original by using the food processor or the microwave to eliminate the on-the-stove melting of the chocolate. An added bonus is the dense whipped-cream filling, which helps retain the shape of the roll.

The only trick lies in manipulating the delicate chocolate layer into a spiral since it cracks easily, especially along the side. However, any unsightly fissures can be covered with a last-minute dusting of cocoa.

FLEXIBLE MENU SUGGESTIONS

The chocolate roll is surprisingly good in menus based on spicy main courses, including Arizona Chicken with Corn Ragout (page 192), Herb- or Curry-Rubbed Chicken (pages 278 and 282), or Garlic-Roasted Leg of Lamb (page 295). It is equally good following One-Side Grilled Fish (page 216) with Tomato Butter (page 220), Sage-Rubbed Veal Chops (page 242), Chili and Garlic-Rubbed Flank Steak (page 245), or Cognac-Marinated Beef Fillet (page 298). *Makes 8 servings*

PREPARATION: 20 MINUTES
BAKING: 15 MINUTES
CHILLING: 1 TO 2 HOURS

Vegetable oil
¼ cup strong brewed coffee
½ cup sugar
6 ounces semisweet chocolate
6 eggs, room temperature, separated
⅛ teaspoon cream of tartar
2 teaspoons vanilla extract
3 tablespoons powdered sugar
1¼ cups chilled whipping cream
¼ cup unsweetened cocoa powder

1. Adjust oven rack to lowest position. Heat oven to 350 degrees. Cut wax paper to fit the bottom of a 10 × 15-inch jelly-roll pan. Oil the sides and bottom of the pan, and oil the paper. Place the paper in the pan, oiled side up; set pan aside.

2. Mix the coffee and sugar in a small saucepan and stir over low heat until the sugar completely dissolves; set mixture aside to cool slightly.

3. Use a cleaver or large knife to chop the chocolate coarsely. (Or, cut chocolate into

½-inch pieces, divide it into two batches, and grind each batch in a food processor fitted with the metal blade.) Put the chocolate in a microwavable dish or bowl and melt it on medium power about 2 minutes, stirring until smooth. Whisk the coffee mixture slowly into the egg yolks, then add the mixture to the chocolate, stirring again until smooth. (Or, add the egg yolks to the processor with the ground chocolate, reheat the coffee mixture, and quickly pour it into the machine with the motor on to melt the chocolate.)

4. In a large dry bowl, use electric beaters or whisk to whip egg whites and cream of tartar to firm peaks. Add the warm chocolate mixture to the beaten egg whites and fold thoroughly, until no large streaks remain.

5. Gently spread the batter in the pan and smooth it into an even layer. Bake 15 minutes. Remove from oven. Cover the layer with a damp lightweight towel and cool to room temperature.

6. Freeze a clean processor container and blade for 5 minutes. Put vanilla, powdered sugar, and half the cream in the container. Process 30 seconds. With motor on, add the remaining cream and process until cream forms firm peaks. Refrigerate the cream for 10 minutes.

7. Put two long sheets of wax paper overlapping lengthwise on a work surface. Sift half the cocoa over the wax paper to cover the area of a 15 × 10-inch rectangle. Invert the chocolate layer over the cocoa and carefully peel off the wax paper. Sift remaining cocoa evenly over the top of the chocolate layer. Spoon the whipped cream evenly on the chocolate layer, leaving a narrow border at ends and on one long side.

8. Spread the cream into an even layer. Roll the layer lengthwise, gently lifting, and using the wax paper to help. If the layer begins to crack, unroll it slightly and coax it again with the wax paper, supporting the area that gives way with your hand.

9. Using wax paper to lift and manipulate the roll, turn it seam-side down on a serving board or platter, then trim the ends by gently cutting each diagonally. Refrigerate no longer than 4 hours. At serving time, dust the top of the roll with cocoa to cover additional cracks, if necessary. Slice crosswise to serve.

CHOCOLATE MADELEINES

Chocolate adds to the allure of these graceful shell-shaped tea cakes, which can be made in several different ways. This little recipe, which contains only one egg and includes a small amount of baking powder, yields eight to ten cookies in a trice. It is astoundingly quick to make these in the processor—in fact I would not bother to do them any other way.

A #80 French tin pan (available in cookware stores) will yield standard-size madeleines to use as dessert garnishes.

FLEXIBLE MENU SUGGESTIONS

These cookies are used in menus based on Saga and Watercress Tart (page 106), Penne with Broccoli and Scallops (page 206), and One-Side Grilled Fish (page 216) with Roasted Garlic and Saffron Butter (page 222) or Citrus Salsa (page 226).

The madeleines are wonderful with Banana Ice Cream (page 438), Double-Chocolate Ice Cream (page 399), or fresh fruit. The flat side can be cut off for stuffing the madeleines with an oval of ice cream—then drizzle the sandwich with Instant Hot Fudge Sauce (page 401). The madeleines can be substituted for Ultra-Fudge Brownies (page 395) or Gianduia Lace Cookies (page 386). *Makes 8 to 10 cookies*

PREPARATION: 10 MINUTES
BAKING: 12 MINUTES

5 tablespoons hot (170 degrees) melted butter
2 tablespoons sugar
1 ounce semisweet chocolate
1 egg
¼ teaspoon Cognac or brandy
½ teaspoon vanilla
½ teaspoon hot water
¼ cup plain cake flour
1 teaspoon unsweetened cocoa powder
¼ teaspoon baking powder
Powdered sugar, for garnish

1. Brush the cups of a #80 madeleine pan with 1 tablespoon of the melted butter; set the pan aside. Adjust oven rack to middle position. Heat oven to 325 degrees.

2. Mix the remaining melted butter with the sugar and stir over low heat until sugar dissolves slightly; set aside. Use a cleaver or large knife to cut the chocolate into ¼-inch pieces. Transfer the chocolate to a food processor fitted with the metal blade and process until it is finely ground. With the motor on, add the hot melted butter mixture, and process until chocolate is melted.

3. Mix the egg, Cognac, vanilla, and water into the chocolate. Sift the flour, cocoa, and baking powder together into the processor and pulse just until the flour disappears.

4. Fill madeleine cups two-thirds full with the batter. Bake 10 to 12 minutes, until tops are rounded and a toothpick inserted into the center is withdrawn clean. Loosen each madeline and invert the pan over a cake rack. Cool. (Can wrap and freeze up to 2 weeks.) Dust shell sides with powdered sugar before serving.

ULTRA-FUDGE BROWNIES

Chocolate nirvana is the best description for these brownies, which are like a flourless cake when served at room temperature, but become chewy-fudgy if refrigerated.

Despite the abundance of nuts and chocolate chips, these brownies have a special moistness and tang that comes from the addition of sour cream to the batter. Since that small amount of acidity helps to lift and accentuate the deep chocolate flavor, purists may even want to omit the chips or the nuts and make these *au naturel*.

FLEXIBLE MENU SUGGESTIONS

Brownies can be dusted lightly with powdered sugar or cocoa, or frosted with a thin layer of ganache (in which case I would omit chocolate chips from the recipe.) Use them as the base for a cake-and-ice-cream sundae, or make and freeze them for Espresso-Brownie Chunk Ice Cream (page 397). They are included in menus based on Saga and Watercress Tart (page 106), Mushroom Pizzas on Prosciutto Crust (page 114), Mesquite-Grilled Cornish Hens (page 240), Chili and Garlic-Rubbed Flank Steak (page 245), or Curry-Rubbed Chicken (page 278). *Makes 16 brownies*

PREPARATION: 25 MINUTES
BAKING: 50 MINUTES

¼ *pound plus 1 tablespoon softened unsalted butter*
1 *tablespoon unsweetened cocoa powder*
½ *pound semisweet or bittersweet chocolate*
¾ *cup sugar*
2 *eggs*
2 *teaspoons vanilla*
⅓ *cup sour cream*
¼ *cup unbleached all-purpose flour*
Salt
¼ *teaspoon baking powder*
½ *cup (2 ounces) shelled walnuts*
½ *cup semisweet chocolate chips (optional)*

1. Coat an 8-inch square baking dish with 1 tablespoon butter, dust with cocoa, and set it aside. Adjust oven rack to middle position. Heat oven to 300 degrees.

2. Use a cleaver or large knife to chop the chocolate coarsely; transfer to a heatproof bowl. (Or, cut chocolate into ½-inch pieces, divide it into two batches, and grind each batch in a food processor fitted with the metal blade.)

3. Combine sugar and the remaining butter in a small saucepan. Stir over low heat until sugar partially dissolves, about 5 to 6 minutes (do not let the mixture boil). Put the eggs and vanilla into a food processor fitted with the metal blade. With the motor on, quickly pour hot butter mixture into the machine. Pour the hot egg mixture over the chocolate; let stand for 5 minutes, then stir until chocolate is melted and smooth. (Or, add the eggs and vanilla to ground chocolate in the processor, and pour in the hot butter mixture to melt the chocolate.) Stir the sour cream into the melted chocolate mixture.

Continued

4. Sift the flour with ¼ teaspoon salt and the baking powder. Chop the walnuts coarsely. Stir the dry ingredients, walnuts, and chocolate chips (if using) into the chocolate mixture. The batter will be very thick. Transfer the batter to the baking dish and smooth it to make an even layer.

5. Bake until cake tester inserted into center is withdrawn clean, about 50 minutes. Cool to lukewarm and slice with a sharp knife into sixteen squares. Serve at room temperature for soft texture. Cover and refrigerate for chewy texture. (Can wrap and freeze 1 month; texture will be chewy.)

ESPRESSO-BROWNIE CHUNK ICE CREAM

How hard could it be?" I asked Betsy, my assistant. "It is only a matter of finely grinding the espresso beans, and brewing them double-strength." She shook her head, and tried to dissuade me from using brewed coffee as the base for espresso ice cream.

Little wonder that our first attempt yielded coffee sludge. But Betsy's method for getting real espresso flavor into ice cream proved to be surprisingly simple: crush espresso coffee beans (with a veal pounder or the bottom of a heavy pot), and steep them in the half-and-half and cream.

The quality and flavor of the beans is critical to the taste of the ice cream, so for best results be sure the beans are freshly roasted. If espresso roast beans seem too bitter, try a Viennese blend, or even a French roast coffee.

Frozen, diced brownies are added to the partially frozen ice cream for a razzle-dazzle brownie-studded dessert, but the ice cream is also wonderful plain.

FLEXIBLE MENU SUGGESTIONS

This dessert is included in menus based on Four-Vegetable Tart (page 100), Sausage and Artichoke Pizzas (page 108), Risotto Primavera (page 172), Pasta with Tomato-Seafood Sauce (page 124), Scallion and Goat-Cheese Agnolotti (page 142), Arizona Chicken with Corn Ragout (page 192), Chilaquiles (page 195), Mesquite-Grilled Cornish Hens (page 240), Sage-Rubbed Veal Chops (page 242), Leg of Lamb with Niçoise Seasoning (page 248), Chili and Garlic-Rubbed Flank Steak (page 245), Jalapeño and Jack Cheese Sausages (page 256), One-Side Grilled Fish (page 216) with Avocado Vinaigrette (page 224), Chili-Rubbed Chicken (page 278), Szechwan Pepper Ribeyes (page 288), and Cognac-Marinated Beef Fillet (page 298). *Makes about 1 quart*

PREPARATION: 30 MINUTES
FREEZING: ABOUT 20 MINUTES

½ pound brownies, cut in ¼-inch chunks
1 cup whole Espresso, French, or Vienna roast
*   coffee beans*
2¼ cups half-and-half
¾ cup sugar
3 egg yolks
1 cup whipping cream

1. Wrap and firmly freeze the brownie chunks.

2. Put the coffee beans on a jelly-roll pan and cover them with a dish towel. Using a veal pounder or the bottom of a heavy saucepan, press to crush the beans thoroughly. (Do not substitute ground coffee.)

3. Transfer the crushed coffee beans to a medium saucepan. Add the half-and-half and heat it to simmering. Cover and simmer 10 minutes, then set the pan aside, off heat, for 15 minutes longer. Strain the liquid through a fine sieve into another saucepan, pressing to remove all liquid from the coffee beans; discard the solids. *Continued*

4. Stir the sugar into the strained coffee liquid and heat it to simmering. Put the egg yolks in a heatproof bowl and slowly whisk in the coffee liquid (or put the egg yolks in a food processor fitted with the metal blade and process, pouring in the coffee liquid).

5. Cool the mixture slightly by stirring in the whipping cream. Set the bowl over ice or refrigerate until the custard is thoroughly chilled. (Can cover and refrigerate overnight.)

6. Transfer the custard to the canister of an ice-cream machine. Follow manufacturer's directions and churn until the ice cream is half frozen. Add frozen brownie pieces and continue churning until frozen. Serve immediately, or transfer ice cream to an airtight freezer container, seal, and keep frozen until serving time. (Can freeze for several hours.)

I first tasted "mix in" ice cream several years ago at Steve's, a store where people wait in line to choose the type of candy or cookies they want kneaded into their favorite flavor. Bringing the idea home, I added frozen chunks of homemade brownies to partially churned ice cream, but commercial cookies or candy could be added to this recipe. It is a good idea to freeze all mix-in ingredients firmly to avoid breakage or smashing during the freezing process.

DOUBLE CHOCOLATE ICE CREAM

More chocolate." That's my motto when it comes to ice cream, and this dense, silky-smooth chocolate fudge version, which contains a full three-quarters of a pound of semisweet chocolate and is studded with bits of ground chocolate, seems ideal.

FLEXIBLE MENU SUGGESTIONS

This dessert is especially compatible with Italian and Mexican-inspired menus. Consult menus based on Four-Vegetable Tart (page 100), Sausage and Artichoke Pizzas (page 108), Calzone with Prosciutto and Brie (page 116), Fettuccine with Chicken, Artichokes, and Dill (page 204), One-Side Grilled Fish (page 216) with Citrus Salsa (page 226), Mesquite-Grilled Cornish Hens (page 240), Sage-Rubbed Veal Chops (page 242), Leg of Lamb with Niçoise Seasoning (page 248), Chili and Garlic-Rubbed Flank Steak (page 245), Chili- or Garlic-Rubbed Chicken (pages 283, 281, and 278), or Cognac-Marinated Beef Fillet (page 298). *Makes 1 quart*

PREPARATION: 15 MINUTES
FREEZING: ABOUT 20 MINUTES

¾ pound semisweet chocolate
6 egg yolks
2 cups milk
1 cup sugar
1 cup cream

1. Use a cleaver or a large knife to chop the chocolate coarsely. Remove 1 cup of chocolate, chop it finely, and set it aside. Put remaining chocolate in a large, heatproof bowl. (Or, cut chocolate into ½-inch pieces, divide it into two batches, and grind each batch in a food processor fitted with the metal blade; set aside 1 cup of the ground chocolate; transfer remaining chocolate to a large, heatproof bowl.)

2. In a separate bowl, mix the egg yolks with ¼ cup of the milk; set aside. Combine sugar, cream, and 1 cup milk in a medium saucepan. Stir well and heat to simmering. Slowly whisk the hot cream mixture into the egg yolks. (Or, put egg-yolk mixture in the food processor and slowly pour in the hot cream liquid with the motor running.)

3. Immediately pour the hot custard over the ground chocolate. Let stand 5 minutes, then stir until chocolate is melted and smooth.

4. Cool the mixture slightly by gradually stirring in the remaining ¾ cup cold milk. Set the bowl over ice, or refrigerate until the custard is thoroughly chilled, about 4 hours. (Can cover and refrigerate overnight.)

5. Transfer the custard to the canister of an ice-cream machine. Stir in the reserved chopped chocolate. Follow manufacturer's directions and churn until the ice cream is frozen. Serve immediately, or transfer ice cream to an airtight freezer container, seal, and keep frozen until serving time. (Can freeze for several hours.)

BITTERSWEET CHOCOLATE SAUCE

Here is the quintessential "dark chocolate" sauce, made from bittersweet chocolate, or a blend of semisweet and unsweetened chocolates. The sugar-syrup base gives the sauce a natural sheen and does not lighten its color.

However, the syrup initially makes the sauce very thin—it should be stirred frequently as it cools. Do not refrigerate the sauce or the chocolate will solidify. If set aside at room temperature the sauce will thicken naturally; should it separate, whisk it briskly or give it a whirl in a food processor.

About ¼ cup of this sauce will completely cover the surface of a dinner plate, making it a dramatic background for chocolate desserts.

FLEXIBLE MENU SUGGESTIONS

The sauce is listed as an ingredient in the recipe for the Dome Cake (page 388). In addition, it is suggested in menus based on Arizona Chicken with Corn Ragout (page 192) and Leg of Lamb with Niçoise Seasoning (page 248). *Makes 2 cups*

COOKING: 5 MINUTES
PREPARATION: 10 MINUTES
COOLING: 2 HOURS

8 ounces bittersweet chocolate (or 6 ounces semisweet chocolate, plus 2 ounces unsweetened chocolate)
½ cup sugar
4 tablespoons lightly salted butter
1 tablespoon Cognac or brandy

1. Use a cleaver or large knife to chop the chocolate coarsely; transfer it to a heatproof bowl. (Or, cut chocolate into ¼-inch pieces, divide into two batches, and grind each batch in a food processor fitted with the metal blade. Leave chocolate in the processor.)

2. Combine sugar and 1 cup water in a small saucepan. Stir well, cover, and heat to simmering. Simmer 5 minutes, add the butter, and reheat to simmering, stirring just until butter dissolves. Cool the syrup for 5 minutes.

3. Pour the hot syrup mixture over the chocolate, let stand 5 minutes, then stir until chocolate is melted and thoroughly mixed with the liquid. (Or, with the motor on, add the hot syrup to chocolate in the machine.)

4. Sauce will be very thin. Stir in the Cognac and set the sauce aside at room temperature, stirring occasionally, until it thickens to a saucelike consistency, about 2 hours. Do not refrigerate or chocolate will solidify. Use at room temperature.

INSTANT HOT FUDGE SAUCE

Four ounces of chopped or ground semisweet chocolate can be transformed into a thick, rich hot fudge sauce just as fast as you can say Wow!

FLEXIBLE MENU SUGGESTIONS

Following a quick pass through a strainer, this sauce is ready to be ladled over Banana Ice Cream (page 438), Espresso-Brownie Chunk Ice Cream (page 397), Double Chocolate Ice Cream (page 399), or a sundae made from ice cream and Ultra-Fudge Brownies (page 395).

The sauce is included in menus based on Risotto Primavera (page 172), Mesquite-Grilled Cornish Hens (page 240), and Chili and Garlic-Rubbed Flank Steak (page 245).
Makes 1½ cups

PREPARATION: 10 MINUTES
COOKING: 5 MINUTES

¼ pound semisweet chocolate
½ cup half-and-half
2 tablespoons sugar
2 tablespoons softened unsalted butter
1 teaspoon instant espresso coffee powder
2 tablespoons Cognac or brandy
1 teaspoon vanilla extract

1. Use a cleaver or heavy knife to chop the chocolate coarsely; set aside in a heatproof bowl. (Or, cut chocolate into ¼-inch pieces and grind it in a food processor fitted with the metal blade; leave the chocolate in the processor.)

2. Mix the half-and-half, sugar, butter, and coffee in a saucepan. Heat to simmering, then stir over low heat until sugar and coffee dissolve. Pour hot liquid over the chocolate. Let stand 5 minutes, then stir until chocolate melts and makes a smooth sauce. (Or, with the motor on, add the hot liquid to chocolate in the machine.)

3. Stir in Cognac and vanilla. Can cover and keep warm 15 minutes. Strain, and sauce is ready to serve. (Can set sauce aside, covered with plastic wrap touching the top. Reheat sauce over a water bath or in the microwave.)

BEARING FRUIT:
TARTS, COMFORTING DESSERTS, ICES, AND COOKIES

The pages of my notebooks are stained with raspberry drips and apricot fingerprints, and some are dimpled by splatterings of vanilla—evidence of my journeys to the pastry mountain in search of the perfect fruit tart.

My freezer abounds with sticks of sweet butter, brown sugar in suspended animation, and a variety of nuts waiting to be ground into sweet fillings. In my cupboard, raisins mellow in a jar of rum, ever at the ready, for I live in a house that loves desserts bearing fruit.

To me, there is a soothing harmony in the arrangement of sliced bananas over pastry cream, and even greater pleasure when the two are churned into ice cream. During the summer, no Sunday meal seems complete without fresh berries, jamlike under a browned cobbler bonnet; while in winter, the perfume of an apple tart baking peacefully in the oven is remembered even after the last delicious slice has disappeared.

Where better to find what the nineteenth-century culinary sage, Isabella Beeton, has described as "poetry in the dessert" than in this collection of tarts, baked desserts, puddings, ices, ice creams, and cookies that offer a light and lyrical verse for the ending of a meal?

A NEW TWIST ON TARTS, PLUS THREE FRENCH CLASSICS

I am partial to desserts that combine fresh fruit with fine pastry. Of course, this is hardly a new idea, for fruit tarts of all descriptions have long been dinner party fare. However, those that seem freshest to me are based on a new twist or an altered notion. Consider a lemon tart set off by a warm, crisp, sugar glaze borrowed from Crème Brulée, the dramatic reduction in the quantities of sugar and custard under the rainbow-hued fruit of a Milanese *crostata,* or the transformation of croissant dough into a wonderfully thin crust for a custard-filled apple tart.

Three traditional French desserts each make a special point. The Almond Soufflé Tart bridges the gap between fruits and nuts, and between old and new as well, since it benefits from presentation on a plate powdered with caramelized almonds in combination with a dollop of sweetened whipped cream. My Peach Turnover may be a nostalgic homage to a pastry, yet rather than make it in the predictable "breakfast turnover" size, practicality demands its simplification and grand scale. And when I asked my friend Rita: "Does anyone need another recipe for a classic French fruit tart?" she replied, "yes," particularly when the tart is first-rate, and the directions for making it have been reduced to eight easy steps.

COMFORTING DESSERTS

"Stay me with flagons, comfort me with apples: for I am sick of love," sang King Solomon. Even today, a freshly baked, cinnamon- and raisin-stuffed apple, or even a warm serving of apple crisp, is a testament to the enduring charm of this most favored fruit. Still, many apple desserts, as well as cobblers, whole poached fruits, silky crème brulée, a slice of fruit bread, or puddings, are viewed as old-fashioned, nostalgia desserts that lack complexity, or are missing a modern edge. Yet their very simplicity is what makes them so welcome and cozy. Guests enjoy them because they are so familiar and effortless to eat.

Frozen soufflés and homemade ice creams and sorbets also fall into this category. Finely tuned to achieve a perfect harmony of fruit and sugar, they are colorful and refreshing. Added to their beauty is the ease of advance preparation—they can be ready to serve at exactly the right moment.

Like classic main courses, fruit desserts are always reliable when there is a question about compatibility in a menu. They have the power to revive a flagging appetite at the end of a meal, or soothe the effects of spice. At first glance they may appear to be merely a feast for the eyes, but they quickly become a sonnet for the stomach.

———————

LEMON TART BRULEE

———————

MILANESE FRUIT TART

———————

RUSTIC APPLE TART

———————

CARAMELIZED NUTS

———————

ALMOND SOUFFLE TART

———————

CLASSIC FRUIT TART

———————

PEACH TURNOVER

———————

MIXED BERRY COBBLER

———————

STRAWBERRY BREAD

———————

APPLE CRISP

———————

BAKED STUFFED APPLES

———————

CREME BRULEE

———————

The Miracle in Milan

———————

LEMON TIRAMI SU

———————

ALMOND AND LEMON-STUFFED PEARS

———————

―――――――

LEMON-PRALINE SOUFFLE GLACE

―――――――

Frozen Fruit Finesse

―――――――

PINK GRAPEFRUIT SORBET

―――――――

Embellishing Ices

―――――――

BLACK PLUM SORBET

―――――――

BANANA ICE CREAM

―――――――

POMEGRANATE GRANITA

―――――――

COCONUT-LIME TUILES

―――――――

MIXED NUT SABLES

―――――――

QUICK CUSTARD SAUCE

―――――――

CARAMEL SAUCE

―――――――

LEMON TART BRULEE

Although lemon tarts are always popular, what's fascinating and new about this dessert is its contrast in flavors and textures. The flaky, buttery pastry encloses a smooth, astringent filling, and both are set off by a crackling sugar glaze.

Provided close attention is paid to one or two technical requirements, this is an easy tart to make. Planning ahead is essential, since the brown sugar requires twenty-four hours to dehydrate so it will caramelize quickly under the broiler. Once dried, however, the sugar can be stored in an airtight container indefinitely. If you entertain frequently, you may want to keep a cup or two of prepared brown sugar on hand.

My old stove had a gas broiler that permitted me to put things very close to the flame, which made glazing the tart a snap. My new stove has a terrible below-the-oven broiler that cannot be raised close to the heat source. As a result, the tart must be frozen to prevent the filling from breaking down under the heat of the flame. If you have a good broiler or a salamander (which is ideal), you can chill the tart, rather than freeze it, as indicated in step 6. Restaurants have another solution, which sounds more outlandish than it actually is: use a blowtorch (which can be purchased in any hardware store) to caramelize the tart.

FLEXIBLE MENU SUGGESTIONS

The tart is included in menus based on Sausages and Sauerkraut (page 186), One-Side Grilled Fish (page 216) with Orso Butter (page 221), Roasted Garlic and Saffron Butter (page 222), or Bouillabaisse Sauce (page 228), Shrimp and Scallops with Chile-Peanut Sauce (page 232), Capretto with Lemon and Rosemary (page 246), Leg of Lamb with Niçoise Seasoning (page 248), Yogurt and Spice-Marinated Leg of Lamb (page 252), Scallop and Basil-Stuffed Sole (page 265), Szechwan Pepper Ribeyes (page 288), Roasted Duck with Apples and Campari (page 289), Pork with Port Wine Sauce (page 292), and Cognac-Marinated Beef Fillet (page 298). *Makes 8 servings*

DRYING: 24 TO 48 HOURS
PREPARATION: 30 MINUTES
BAKING: 40 MINUTES
CHILLING: 3 HOURS

¼ cup dark brown sugar

PASTRY

1 to 1¼ cups unbleached all-purpose flour
Salt
¼ pound frozen unsalted butter, cut in 8 pieces
¼ to ⅓ cup ice water

FILLING

Zest of 1 medium lemon
Zest of 1 small lime
¾ cup sugar
½ cup lemon juice
5 eggs
¼ pound unsalted butter, cut in 8 pieces

1. Spread brown sugar in a thin layer in a cake pan. Dry it near the pilot light in the oven for 24 hours, or set it aside at room

temperature for 48 hours, raking the sugar frequently with your fingers to remove lumps. Set aside or store in an airtight container.

2. Adjust oven rack to lowest position. Heat oven to 375 degrees.

3. For the pastry, put 1 cup flour, ½ teaspoon salt, and the butter in a food processor fitted with the metal blade. Process until butter completely disappears and mixture has a sandy consistency. Add ¼ cup ice water and pulse until the dough begins to clump. If dough is dry, add remaining water.

4. Gather dough into a flat disk and roll it, on a lightly floured surface, into a 13-inch circle. Transfer the circle of dough to a 9-inch fluted tart pan with removable bottom. Ease the dough into the pan and fit it snugly around the bottom edge and against the sides. Trim off excess dough, pierce the bottom of the dough at 2-inch intervals with a skewer, and freeze 10 minutes. (Can wrap and freeze overnight.)

5. Line the dough with aluminum foil and add pie weights or rice. Bake 35 minutes. Cool 5 minutes. Remove weights and foil. Bake 3 to 7 minutes, or until pastry is completely crisp and lightly browned. Set crust aside to cool.

6. For the filling, finely grate the lemon and lime zest into a 2-quart nonreactive saucepan. Whisk in the sugar, lemon juice, and eggs. Add the butter, and stir the mixture over very low heat until butter melts. Then, continue stirring until the mixture thickens to a puddinglike consistency. Strain it into a bowl, pressing to extract all the custard from the zest (discard the zest). Cover with plastic wrap directly touching the top of the mixture. Cool to room temperature. Spread the filling evenly in the pastry crust and freeze until filling is firm. (Can wrap and freeze up to a week.)

7. Sift the dried brown sugar to remove any lumps (if large lumps remain, crush with fingers, then sift). Sprinkle 3 generous tablespoons of the sugar over the tart in a thin, even layer.

8. To glaze the tart, adjust the broiler rack as close as possible to heat source and set the broiler on the highest setting. Put tart under the broiler, turning it constantly so sugar caramelizes evenly. Take care edge of crust does not burn. (If the edge of the crust browns too deeply, it may be necessary to remove the tart and protect the crust with narrow strips of aluminum foil.) Let tart defrost at room temperature for 1 hour before serving. (Can defrost in refrigerator for several hours, but sugar glaze may not be crisp.) If tart is not frozen it should be glazed and served immediately.

MILANESE FRUIT TART

An edible rainbow of five fruits, arrayed on a rectangular pastry crust, can have the same glamor that Italian jewelers give to precious gems: the golden glint of pineapple, the sparkling green of kiwi, the amber hue of papaya, the brilliant red of strawberries, and the deep purple of black grapes.

Fruit-topped tarts and cakes are found in many parts of northern Italy. But in Milan you can find a special tart with a wonderful cookielike crust that is sealed with jam and a dusting of cake crumbs to protect the pastry from the smallest droplets of fruit juice.

Since it would be quite difficult to halve the recipe for the pastry cream, the yield is twice as much as needed for one tart. However, the remaining cream freezes beautifully for up to one month. I often use all the cream and make a double version of this tart on a 15 × 10-inch jelly-roll pan (if doing so, only double the pastry and topping). The single recipe will also make four elegant 5 × 4-inch individual tarts (pictured on the back cover) that can be placed dramatically over a stripe of powdered sugar on a dinner plate.

The fruit may be arranged in rows, concentric rectangles, or diagonal stripes. It can be mixed, or you can opt for a simpler arrangement of one, two, or even three fruits on top of the tart—one of the most beautiful is covered with tiny wedges of crimson fresh figs.

One additional refinement is the scant amount of sugar—less than ⅓ cup—contained in the entire tart, which needs no sauce to cloud its flavor or mar its beauty.

FLEXIBLE MENU SUGGESTIONS

This tart can be served in place of the Classic Fruit Tart (page 416). It is included in menus based on Homemade Garlic Sausage with Pistachios (page 92), One-Side Grilled Fish (page 216) with Roasted Garlic and Saffron Butter (page 222), Shrimp and Curry Risotto (page 166), Penne with Broccoli and Scallops (page 206), Milanese Beef Stew (page 185), Bollito Misto (page 188), Baked Curried Beef (page 201), Sage-Rubbed Veal Chops (page 242), Capretto with Lemon and Rosemary (page 246), Scampi alla Busara (page 272), Mushroom and Prosciutto-Stuffed Chicken Breasts (page 274), or Garlic-Roasted Leg of Lamb (page 295). *Makes 4 to 8 servings*

PREPARATION: 1 HOUR
BAKING: 18 TO 20 MINUTES

PASTRY

4 ounces frozen unsalted butter, cut in 8
    pieces
1 tablespoon sugar
1 egg
½ teaspoon lemon juice
1¼ to 1⅓ cups unbleached all-purpose flour

PASTRY CREAM

3 egg yolks
¼ cup sugar
3 tablespoons flour
Salt
½ teaspoon vanilla extract
1 cup whipping cream

FRUIT TOPPING

3 tablespoons strained raspberry, red currant, or apricot jam
½ teaspoon Kirsch or Cognac
⅓ cup plain cake crumbs (use pound cake or sponge cake)
½ small pineapple, pared, cored
2 medium kiwis, peeled
1 firm medium papaya, pared, seeded
1 pint large strawberries, hulled, stem ends cut flat
8 ounces large black grapes, stem ends cut flat, seeded
Powdered sugar

1. Adjust oven rack to lowest position. Heat oven to 375 degrees.

2. For the pastry, put the butter and sugar in a food processor fitted with the metal blade. Chop the butter coarsely. Pulse in the egg and lemon juice. Add 1¼ cups flour and process until the dough begins to clump. (Pulse in additional flour by tablespoons if dough is sticky or gluey.)

3. Gather dough together and roll it between two sheets of wax paper to a 17 × 7-inch rectangle. Remove top sheet and trim dough to 16 × 5 inches (or cut dough into four 4 × 5-inch rectangles). From the trimmings, cut two long strips and two short strips, each about ¼-inch wide, to be used for the raised edge; set strips aside. (Cut extra edging strips for individual tarts.)

4. Grasp the wax paper and turn the pastry rectangle over onto a baking sheet. Gently remove wax paper (refrigerate 15 minutes if dough sticks). Moisten the perimeter of the rectangle and gently press the strips into place, pinching them neatly to form a raised edge. Pierce the dough with a skewer; freeze 10 minutes. Bake until pastry is golden, 18 to 20 minutes; set aside to cool.

5. For the pastry cream, whisk the egg yolks with the sugar, flour, ⅛ teaspoon salt, vanilla, and ¼ cup cream in a medium saucepan. Heat remaining ¾ cup cream to simmering, then whisk it into the egg mixture. Stir over low heat until the cream thickens to a puddinglike consistency, about 6 minutes. (If lumps form, put the cream in the food processor; process until smooth.) When cool, cover and refrigerate until chilled. (Can keep refrigerated up to 3 days.)

6. Heat the jam with the liqueur, then brush it over the pastry base. Sprinkle the pastry with cake crumbs; set aside for 5 minutes. Spoon half the pastry cream in dollops over the cake crumbs. Carefully spread the cream into a very thin layer. Remove and discard excess cream.

7. Cut the pineapple into 1½-inch-wide segments, then into ⅛-inch-thick slices. Slice the kiwis into ⅛-inch-thick rounds; set aside. Cut 1½-inch-wide segments of papaya into ⅛-inch-thick slices; set aside.

8. To assemble the tart, put the strawberries, hulled ends down, in a row extending slightly beyond one long edge of the pastry rectangle. Put closely overlapping pineapple slices snugly against the berries. Arrange closely overlapping kiwi slices (halve if necessary) slightly overlapping the pineapple. Put the grapes, cut ends down, along the outside long edge of tart, then fit slightly overlapping papaya slices in between the kiwis and grapes, trimming to fit as necessary. Be sure fruit completely covers the cream to make solid, even bands of color.

9. Cover the tart loosely with plastic wrap. Refrigerate for 1 hour. (Can refrigerate up to 6 hours.) At serving time, cut it crosswise into 2-inch portions. Dust each portion (as well as the plate) with powdered sugar.

RUSTIC APPLE TART

Buttery, flaky croissant dough makes sensational pastry for a big, rough-hewn, country-style apple tart that is partially baked, then filled with a thin layer of custard. Although this recipe offers bakers the challenge of handling the supple interlaced layers of butter and dough that create hundreds of paper-thin strata in the crust, the appearance of the tart makes it look effortless. Its charm lies in the slight chewiness of pastry that thickens wonderfully at the edges, remains crisp on the bottom, and supports a delicately sweet, fresh filling.

Let me say outright that making this dough is a labor of love; however, it is a joy to make and roll. Some time ago, I spent several weeks in the kitchen working to streamline the turning, or folding, procedure. Borrowing on my experience with puff pastry, I used frozen, finely chopped particles of butter as an interior coolant to keep the dough cold and workable enough to make all the turns consecutively—effectively eliminating the traditional resting time for the dough in the refrigerator.

Is this easier to make than puff pastry? I think so. The base of the dough, which contains yeast, milk, and sugar in addition to flour, water, butter, and salt—the principal components of puff pastry—is kneaded like bread. Therefore, it has a considerable amount of elasticity, it holds the butter well, and is less prone to tearing and butter-breakthroughs than is puff pastry.

Should the dough become too elastic to stretch easily, it can simply be left on the work surface for 5 to 10 minutes to relax, since the frozen butter keeps it cold. The turned dough will need a refrigerated rest before stretching it to a sheet large enough to line a jelly-roll pan. It also can be divided in half and rolled into two circular, freeform tarts if you prefer (or shaped on pizza pans).

Having the right equipment at hand will be enormously helpful. A large dry pastry brush, a ruler, a sturdy rolling pin (24 inches minimum), and a plain-edged pizza cutting wheel should be kept nearby. All-purpose unbleached flour can be substituted for the combination of flours specified in the recipe, but before making substitutions, be sure to read about Flour Facts (page 131).

FLEXIBLE MENU SUGGESTIONS

This tart is included in menus based on Bollito Misto (page 188), Leg of Lamb with Malay Seasoning (page 250), Capretto with Lemon and Rosemary (page 246), Herb-Rubbed Chicken (page 278), and Cognac-Marinated Beef Fillet (page 298). *Makes about 12 servings*

DOUGH PREPARATION: 1 HOUR
DOUGH RISING: 7 HOURS
TART PREPARATION: 45 MINUTES
TART RISING: 1 HOUR
BAKING: 25 MINUTES

SPONGE

*½ cup bread flour or unbleached all-purpose
    flour*
1½ teaspoons dry active yeast
½ cup warm (110 degrees) water

DOUGH

*1 to 1¼ cups bread flour or unbleached all-
    purpose flour*
¼ cup plain cake flour
Salt
2 tablespoons sugar
2 tablespoons vegetable shortening
1 tablespoon milk
3 tablespoons hot tap water
Flour
*6 ounces frozen unsalted butter, cut in
    12 pieces*

FILLING

1 cup apricot or raspberry jam
2 tablespoons dark rum or Cognac
*2 pounds tart green apples, peeled, cored,
    halved*
Flour
1 egg
⅓ cup sugar
½ cup whipping cream
Powdered sugar

1. For the sponge, mix the flour, yeast, and warm water in a medium bowl until the mixture forms a thick, gluey paste. Cover the bowl tightly with plastic wrap and set it aside for 2 hours. (Can stir well, cover with plastic wrap, and refrigerate the sponge in the bowl for as long as 36 hours.)

2. For the dough, insert the metal blade in a food processor. Add 1 cup bread flour, the cake flour, ½ teaspoon salt, sugar, and shortening. Mix the milk with hot water, and with the motor on, quickly pour the liquid into the dry ingredients. Stir the sponge mixture and add it to the machine. Process until the dough is smooth, sticky, and taffylike, about 1 minute. (If dough is liquid or runny, process in bread flour by tablespoons until the dough holds its shape.)

3. Rinse a large mixing bowl with warm water, add the dough, cover the bowl tightly with plastic wrap and set it aside until the dough triples in volume, about 2 to 2½ hours. Without uncovering, refrigerate the risen dough in the bowl for 1 hour. (Or, rinse the inside of a zipper-lock plastic bag, add the dough, press out excess air, seal, and refrigerate the dough overnight, or as long as 2 days without letting it rise in the bowl.)

4. Generously flour a work surface. Pull dough from the bowl (or bag) without kneading. Dust dough with flour and roll it to a 15 × 10-inch rectangle, with the short end facing you. Brush off the excess flour. Let dough rest while butter is prepared.

5. Insert the metal blade in a dry food processor. Sprinkle 1 tablespoon flour on the bottom of the container. Add the butter and sprinkle 1 tablespoon flour on top. Pulse until the butter is chopped to the consistency of small beads.

6. Scatter the chopped butter evenly over the upper two-thirds of the dough, pressing it gently into an even layer, but do not touch butter too much or it will soften. Fold the bottom third of dough over the central third like a business letter, then flip the dough up and over the top buttered third. The butter now will be completely enclosed in a dough rectangle measuring 10 × 5 inches, with the long side facing you. *Continued*

7. Generously flour the work surface and dough. Rotate the dough, so that the short end faces you, and roll it into a 15 × 10-inch rectangle. Brush off excess flour. Fold short ends of dough inward to meet at the center. Fold dough in half lengthwise, like closing a book sideways. The resulting dough rectangle will measure 10 × 3¾ inches (the long side will again be facing you).

8. Repeat step 7 twice more. If dough becomes elastic or difficult to stretch, cover it with plastic and refrigerate for 20 minutes. The final dough rectangle will measure 10 × 3¾ inches. Transfer dough to baking sheet, cover with plastic, and refrigerate 45 minutes. (Can double-wrap snugly in plastic and refrigerate 24 hours, or freeze dough up to 1 week. If necessary, defrost dough overnight in the refrigerator before proceeding with the recipe.)

9. To shape the tart, remove the dough from the refrigerator for 30 minutes. Put the jam in a small saucepan, stir in the rum, and cook over low heat until the jam liquefies. Strain (discard the solids); set aside to cool. Thinly slice the apple halves and set the slices aside.

10. On a generously floured work surface, roll out dough to a 16 × 11-inch rectangle. Ease dough rectangle into a 15 × 10-inch jelly-roll pan. Loosely wrap and refrigerate the dough in the pan for 20 minutes.

11. Unwrap and gently stretch the sides of the dough up and over the rim of the pan by about 1 inch. Brush the surface of the tart generously with jam. Arrange the apple slices, slightly overlapping, in even rows over entire surface of the dough. Trim the edge of the dough to ½ inch beyond the pan rim, then roll it inward, to form a raised border that frames, and slightly overlaps, the apple slices around the perimeter of the tart. Crimp the corners and edge of the dough to make a secure rim with no breaks or tears (the rim must hold in the liquid that will be poured onto the tart when it is partially baked). Cover the tart with a cloth towel and set aside at room temperature to rise for 1 hour.

12. Adjust oven rack to lowest position. Heat oven to 400 degrees. Mix the egg, sugar, and cream in a cup with pouring spout; set aside. Bake the tart for 15 minutes, remove it from the oven, and carefully and evenly pour the cream mixture over the apples. Return the tart to the oven and bake 20 to 25 minutes longer, or until the cream is browned and puffed and the center of the tart is set. Cool the tart to lukewarm, sprinkle it with powdered sugar, and serve immediately.

CARAMELIZED NUTS

The trick to making perfect candied nuts is to add them just as the sugar liquefies and browns, and to toss the nuts with the liquid sugar mixture over very low heat until they are completely coated.

The recipe doubles or triples beautifully, and any whole nut can be substituted for either the almonds or pecans. The mixture can be made several weeks in advance and stored in airtight containers.

FLEXIBLE MENU SUGGESTIONS

Use these to garnish Almond Soufflé Tart (page 414), serve them whole, or pack them in decorative boxes for gifts. *Makes 1 pound*

PREPARATION: 20 MINUTES
COOKING: 10 TO 15 MINUTES

1 teaspoon vegetable oil
2 tablespoons butter
½ cup sugar
¾ teaspoon salt
1 teaspoon vanilla
1 cup whole blanched almonds
1 cup shelled pecan halves

1. Coat a baking sheet with vegetable oil; wipe off excess oil and set the baking sheet aside. Melt butter in a 10-inch nonreactive skillet, add sugar and salt, and stir well. Cook over medium heat, stirring continuously with a metal spoon, until the mixture caramelizes and turns nut brown, about 10 minutes.

2. Immediately stir in vanilla, almonds, and pecans; stir only until the nuts are thoroughly coated with caramel (the mixture will be very sticky). Transfer the contents of skillet to the baking sheet; set aside to cool. Break the nuts apart, and store the mixture in an airtight container.

ALMOND SOUFFLE TART

Almonds—the familiar nut—are the sweet kernels of oblong, gray-green fruits that have been eaten since ancient times, and are relatives of nectarines, cherries, peaches, and plums.

Toasted sliced almonds, scattered on top of this tart, help to identify it and give it an attractive surface, whether it is baked in a single 9-inch fluted tart pan with removable bottom, or in four individual, fluted, 4-inch-diameter pans.

The filling consists of a flourless soufflé, which rises in the oven and then falls slightly, leaving the center wonderfully moist. Classic accompaniments for the tart would be whipped cream or custard sauce; a more restrained garnish is to decorate the plate with a geometric arrangement of powdered sugar and finely ground Caramelized Nuts (page 413).

FLEXIBLE MENU SUGGESTIONS

This tart is ideal to serve when fruit or spices are included in first or main courses, and it is included in menus based on Scallion and Black Pepper Lasagne with Black Olive Pesto (page 144), Curry Noodles with Scallops and Cilantro (page 146), Shrimp and Curry Risotto (page 166), Milanese Asparagus Soup (page 162), and One-Side Grilled Fish (page 216) with Tomato Butter (page 220), Roasted Garlic and Saffron Butter (page 222), Avocado Vinaigrette (page 224), or Citrus Salsa (page 226). It is also included with Leg of Lamb with Malay Seasoning (page 250), Yogurt and Spice-Marinated Leg of Lamb (page 252), Mushroom and Prosciutto-Stuffed Chicken Breasts (page 274), Chili-Rubbed Chicken (page 278), Pork with Port Wine Sauce (page 292), Garlic-Roasted Leg of Lamb (page 295), and Cognac-Marinated Beef Fillet (page 298). *Makes 6 to 8 servings*

PREPARATION: 20 MINUTES
BAKING: 35 TO 40 MINUTES

PASTRY

1 to 1½ cups unbleached all-purpose flour
2 tablespoons sugar
¼ pound frozen unsalted butter, cut in
   8 pieces
¼ to ⅓ cup ice water

FILLING

¾ cup (3 ounces) whole blanched almonds
¼ cup sliced almonds
⅔ cup sugar
2 eggs, separated
½ teaspoon lemon juice
¼ cup milk
Salt
Whipped cream (optional)

1. For the pastry, put 1 cup flour, sugar, and the butter in a food processor fitted with the metal blade. Process until butter completely disappears and mixture has a sandy consistency. Add ¼ cup ice water and pulse until

dough begins to clump. If dough is dry, add remaining water.

2. Gather dough into a flat disk and roll it, on a lightly floured surface, into a 13-inch circle. Transfer the circle of dough to a 9-inch fluted tart pan with removable bottom. Ease the dough into the pan and fit it snugly around the bottom edge, and against the sides. Trim off excess dough, pierce the bottom of the dough at 2-inch intervals with a skewer, and freeze 10 minutes. (Can wrap well and freeze overnight.)

3. Adjust oven rack to lowest position. Heat oven to 375 degrees. Put whole almonds and sliced almonds in separate pans and toast in oven until lightly browned, about 6 to 8 minutes; cool separately.

4. Line the dough with aluminum foil and add pie weights or rice. Bake 12 minutes. Remove rice or weights and foil and set the crust aside.

5. For the filling, put the whole almonds and sugar in the container of a food processor fitted with the metal blade, and process until finely ground. Add egg yolks, lemon juice, and milk, and process until smooth.

6. In a clean dry bowl, whip egg whites with a pinch of salt to firm peaks with electric beaters or a whisk. Fold egg whites thoroughly into the almond filling. Transfer filling to the crust and smooth the top. Sprinkle sliced almonds evenly over the filling. Bake until the top of the tart is golden, about 25 to 30 minutes. Cool to room temperature (can set aside, uncovered, 4 to 6 hours).

7. Serve the tart at room temperature (or warm it slightly in 250-degree oven) with whipped cream, custard sauce, or powdered sugar and Caramelized Nuts (page 413).

Inspired by a recipe of chef Fran Bigelow, Seattle.

CLASSIC FRUIT TART

Here is a classic French fruit tart reduced to eight easy steps. A staple in my dessert repertoire, it features a crisp *pâte brisée* that can be mixed, rolled immediately, then baked in a single tart pan (with removable bottom) or in four individual (3- to 4-inch) molds. Either way, the tart requires about 2 pounds of fruit.

This tart is slightly richer than its Italian cousin (page 408) but less intricate to make. Directions are given for bananas, but it can be crowned with any sliceable fresh fruit that does not need cooking, and glazed with red currant or apricot jam (depending on the fruit color) to prevent dehydration and discoloration.

During the summer, ripe peaches or nectarines can be slipped from their skins, thinly sliced, and arranged in concentric rings, or crosswise in rows. Strawberries (3 to 4 pints) or golden raspberries (about 2 pints) should be placed very close together to cover the pastry cream completely, with any gaps filled in. Combinations of sliced fruits also can be arranged in colorful patterns.

FLEXIBLE MENU SUGGESTIONS

This tart is included in menus based on Sausages and Sauerkraut (page 186), Penne with Broccoli and Scallops (page 206), One-Side Grilled Fish (page 216) with Roasted Garlic and Saffron Butter (page 222), Capretto with Lemon and Rosemary (page 246), Leg of Lamb with Malay Seasoning (page 250), Cold Chicken-Poached Lobster (page 270), Scallop and Basil-Stuffed Sole (page 265), Pork with Port Wine Sauce (page 292), and Garlic-Roasted Leg of Lamb (page 295). *Makes 6 to 8 servings*

PREPARATION: 30 MINUTES
CHILLING: 1 HOUR
BAKING: 40 MINUTES

PASTRY

1 to 1¼ cups unbleached all-purpose flour
Salt
¼ pound frozen unsalted butter, cut in pieces
¼ to ⅓ cup ice water

PASTRY CREAM

3 egg yolks
¼ cup sugar
¼ cup unbleached all-purpose flour
1 cup whipping cream
½ teaspoon vanilla extract
1 teaspoon Cognac, brandy, or rum

TOPPING AND GLAZE

½ cup apricot preserves
1 teaspoon Cognac or brandy
2 pounds firm ripe bananas

1. Adjust oven rack to lowest position. Heat oven to 375 degrees.

2. For the pastry, put 1 cup flour, ¼ teaspoon salt, and the butter in a food processor fitted with the metal blade. Process until butter completely disappears and mixture has a sandy consistency. Add ¼ cup ice water and pulse until the dough begins to clump. If dough is dry, add remaining water.

3. Gather dough into a flat disk and roll it, on a lightly floured surface, into a 13-inch circle. Transfer the circle of dough to a 10-inch fluted tart pan with removable bottom. Ease the dough into the pan and fit it snugly around the bottom edge and against the sides. Trim off excess dough, pierce the bottom of the dough at 2-inch intervals with a skewer, and freeze 10 minutes. (Can wrap and freeze overnight. Defrost in refrigerator before baking.)

4. Line the dough with aluminum foil and add pie weights or rice. Bake 35 minutes. Cool 5 minutes. Remove weights and foil. Bake 3 to 7 minutes, or until pastry is completely crisp and lightly browned. Set crust aside to cool.

5. For the pastry cream, whisk the egg yolks with the sugar, flour, and ¼ cup cream in a medium saucepan until smooth. Heat remaining ¾ cup cream to simmering in a small saucepan, then whisk it into the egg mixture. Stir over low heat until the cream thickens to a puddinglike consistency, about 6 minutes. (If lumps form, put the cream in the food processor; process until smooth.) Off heat, whisk in vanilla and Cognac. Cover the cream with plastic wrap touching the surface. When cool, refrigerate until chilled. (Can keep refrigerated up to 3 days.)

6. For the topping, heat the preserves with Cognac until liquid; strain and discard the solids. With a pastry brush, paint the inside of the crust lightly with jam. Fill the crust with pastry cream, smoothing the top, and refrigerate. Set the remaining preserves aside.

7. Thinly slice and arrange the bananas, overlapping and in concentric rings, beginning at edge of crust. Do not allow custard to show through the fruit. Arrange the center ring of bananas in a pinwheel to fill in any gaps.

8. Reheat and immediately brush the preserves over the bananas as a glaze. Refrigerate 1 hour. (Can refrigerate, uncovered, up to 6 hours before serving).

PEACH TURNOVER

During my first summer living on the left bank in Paris, I discovered *chaussons* filled with apples and baked in a wood-burning oven. I still can remember their slight smokiness, infused with the buttery taste of the pastry, which was my inspiration here.

This large turnover arrives warm, bronzed, and puffed at table, and is rather like a folded-over pie. It is a marvelous summer dessert, though it does require baking, and is a wonderful finish for numerous menus. Slice it crosswise into individual portions.

Flaky pastry is essential to turnovers. My choice is this rough puff-pastry dough, rolled and folded to produce numerous layers that expand slightly during baking. Rough puff pastry calls for mixing half the butter thoroughly into the dough base, and leaving the remaining half in pea-sized chunks spread throughout the mixture. The large butter pieces help the layers of dough separate during baking.

Frozen butter keeps the dough very cold and makes it possible to roll and fold (or turn) without waiting for it to relax in the refrigerator. While novice bakers should not begin here, once mastered, this dough is relatively fast and easy to make. You will need to have a large dry pastry brush, a ruler, and plastic wrap on hand.

FLEXIBLE MENU SUGGESTIONS

The turnover can be served with Quick Custard Sauce (page 443) or vanilla ice cream. It is included in menus based on Homemade Garlic Sausage with Pistachios (page 92), Pork and Vegetable Salad Orientale (page 210), Soy-Marinated Chicken (page 238), Mesquite-Grilled Cornish Hens (page 240), One-Side Grilled Fish (page 216) with Fresh Herb Butter (page 219), Shrimp and Scallops with Chile-Peanut Sauce (page 232), Cold Chicken-Poached Lobster (page 270), and Curry- or Chili-Rubbed Chicken (pages 282 and 278).
Makes 4 to 6 servings

PREPARATION: 35 MINUTES
CHILLING: 40 MINUTES
BAKING: 50 MINUTES

PASTRY

1 cup unbleached all-purpose flour
¼ cup plain cake flour
Salt
6 ounces frozen unsalted butter, cut in 12 pieces
⅓ cup ice water
Flour
Peach and Almond Filling (page 419)

GLAZE

1 egg yolk
1 teaspoon milk

1. For the pastry, put 1 cup unbleached flour, the cake flour, ⅛ teaspoon salt, and 6 tablespoons of the butter into the container of a food processor fitted with the metal blade. Process until the butter completely disappears and the mixture has a sandy con-

sistency. Add the ice water and remaining butter. Pulse only until the dough begins to clump; it will be very rough looking.

2. Gather the dough into a 6-inch square. Sprinkle a work surface and the dough generously with flour. Roll the dough to a 14 × 6-inch rectangle, with the short end facing you. Brush off excess flour. Fold the bottom third of the dough over the central third, like a business letter, then fold the top down, over the central third, brushing off excess flour. Rotate the dough 45 degrees, so the open ends face toward and away from you, and the folded edges are on the sides.

3. Roll dough again to 14 × 6 inches. Brush off excess flour; fold and rotate dough as described above, twice more. Add flour as needed to prevent dough from sticking to the work surface or the rolling pin. (If dough becomes too soft or difficult to roll, transfer it to a baking sheet and refrigerate until firm but pliable, about 15 minutes.) Leaving flour on the work surface, wrap and refrigerate dough for 20 minutes. (Or, clean the work surface, wrap and refrigerate dough overnight; remove dough from the refrigerator for 30 to 40 minutes before continuing with the recipe and reflouring the work surface.)

4. Prepare the Peach and Almond Filling. Adjust oven rack to lowest position. Heat oven to 400 degrees. Mix the egg yolk with milk for the glaze, and set it aside.

5. To shape the turnover, roll dough to a 12 × 18-inch rectangle, transfer it to a baking sheet, and brush off excess flour. Leaving a 2-inch border all around, paint the surface of the dough with the egg glaze. Sprinkle the ground almonds from the filling lengthwise on half the pastry to cover half the egg glaze. Put peaches over almond mixture. Lightly brush the border with cold water and fold the pastry snugly over the peaches. With the fluted wheel of a ravioli cutter or with a knife, cut off dough around edge to make an elongated half-moon shape.

6. Seal the cut edge by firmly pressing it with the tines of a fork. If desired, cut leaves or flowers out of the scraps, brush the bottoms of the cutouts with egg glaze, and attach them to the top of the turnover. (Can wrap and refrigerate overnight before baking.)

7. Brush the top of the turnover with egg glaze. Bake 50 minutes, or until puffed and golden brown. Serve warm.

PEACH AND ALMOND FILLING

PREPARATION: 20 MINUTES
COOKING: 5 MINUTES

¼ cup whole unblanched almonds
5 tablespoons sugar
2 pounds peaches or nectarines
¼ cup brown sugar
⅛ teaspoon cinnamon
⅛ teaspoon nutmeg
1 tablespoon Cognac or brandy

1. In a food processor, process almonds with 2 tablespoons sugar to powdery consistency; set the mixture aside.

2. Heat 3 quarts of water to simmering, add the peaches, and poach 3 to 5 minutes, until just tender at the center when pierced with a sharp knife. Drain.

3. Peel, halve, pit, and cut the peaches into ⅛-inch slices. Drain well and mix with remaining ingredients.

MIXED BERRY COBBLER

Few desserts offer the delicious simplicity of an unassuming cobbler, chock-full of berries and topped with a tender crust. The natural sweetness of strawberries, black, golden, or red raspberries, blackberries, blueberries, or boysenberries, which can be mixed as you wish, will give the cobbler its character.

Cobbler dough and biscuit dough are quite similar: very soft, moist, and sticky. Like biscuits, this dough must be handled gingerly, and rolled on a generously floured work surface with a very light hand.

The small amount of cornstarch, used as a thickener for the filling, is almost undetectable once the berries are cooked. (If the berries are very sweet, decrease the sugar to ⅓ cup.) Be sure to bake the cobbler as soon as possible after mixing the filling so that the thickener remains evenly distributed throughout the berries.

FLEXIBLE MENU SUGGESTIONS

Enhance the cobbler with Quick Custard Sauce (page 443), whipped cream, or ice cream. Since berries are best during the summer months, serve cobbler as an informal dessert in menus based on Country Pork Terrine (page 90), Penne with Broccoli and Scallops (page 206), One-Side Grilled Fish (page 216) with Roasted Garlic and Saffron Butter (page 222) or Winter Pesto (page 227), Shrimp and Scallops with Chile-Peanut Sauce (page 232), Grilled Ceviche (page 231), Mesquite-Grilled Cornish Hens (page 240), Leg of Lamb with Niçoise or Oriental Seasoning (pages 248 or 251), Hickory-Grilled Baby Back Ribs (page 259), Cold Chicken-Poached Lobster (page 270), or Herb-Rubbed Chicken (page 278).
Makes 6 to 8 servings

PREPARATION: 15 MINUTES
BAKING: 30 MINUTES

DOUGH

Zest of 1 medium lemon
3 tablespoons sugar
1½ cups plain cake flour
Salt
2 teaspoons baking powder
4 tablespoons unsalted butter, chilled, cubed
4 tablespoons vegetable shortening
⅓ cup milk

FILLING

2 pints fresh berries (for example, 1 pint blueberries, ½ pint strawberries, and ½ pint raspberries)
2 tablespoons cornstarch
1 tablespoon lemon juice
½ cup sugar
Flour

1. For the dough, grate the lemon zest into a food processor fitted with the metal blade. Add sugar, cake flour, ⅛ teaspoon salt, baking powder, butter, and vegetable shortening. Process until the butter and shortening disappear. Pulse in the milk, only until the dough begins to clump. Gather the dough into a square, wrap, and refrigerate for 20 minutes.

2. Generously butter an 8-inch square nonreactive baking dish. Adjust oven rack to lowest position. Heat oven to 350 degrees.

3. Rinse, hull, and cut the berries as necessary; drain and transfer to a mixing bowl.

4. On a floured surface, roll the dough to an 8½-inch square; leave it on the work surface. Quickly dissolve the cornstarch in 3 tablespoons cold water, stir in the lemon juice and sugar, and pour the mixture into the bowl with the berries. Mix well, then transfer the entire berry mixture to the baking dish.

5. Put the dough over the filling in the dish, and adjust the edge of the dough to completely cover and overlap the edge of the dish slightly (the dough tends to shrink during baking). Bake until crust is golden, about 30 to 35 minutes. Cool the cobbler on a cake rack until the bottom of dish is just warm. Serve warm or at room temperature by spooning from baking dish. Do not refrigerate.

STRAWBERRY BREAD

Late one spring, while on assignment to write an article on strawberries for the *New York Times,* I made my first trip to New York's largest greenmarket. Because it was early, and as usual I had left the house without breakfast, I bought a slice of strawberry bread from one of the fruit stands. That bread was so good, I decided to include the recipe in the article. After several calls upstate, I located the Hotaling's Farm Market kitchen, in Claverack, New York.

This recipe was adapted from the one given to me by Hotaling's. The recipe makes two loaves. Each bread contains nearly a pint of strawberries, and the slices are as good plain as they are beneath a scoop of vanilla ice cream.

Take special care to coat the strawberries with dry ingredients, as the recipe directs, to keep them evenly suspended in the batter—they tend to sink during baking. The breads also can be sticky and difficult to unmold. I have had best results using nonstick metal loaf pans, but I still coat them with vegetable shortening as insurance.

FLEXIBLE MENU SUGGESTIONS

Strawberry Bread makes a wonderful base for an ice-cream sundae, and is included in menus based on Curry-Rubbed Chicken (page 278) and Cognac-Marinated Beef Fillet (page 298). *Makes 2 breads*

PREPARATION: 20 MINUTES
BAKING: 60 TO 75 MINUTES

3 tablespoons vegetable shortening
1 medium orange
2 cups sugar
½ cup shelled walnut pieces
4 eggs
1⅓ cups vegetable oil
1½ pints strawberries, rinsed, hulled, drained
3 cups plain cake flour
1¼ teaspoons baking soda
Salt

1. Coat two 6-cup metal loaf pans (preferably with black finish) with vegetable shortening; set aside. Adjust oven rack to lowest position. Heat oven to 350 degrees.

2. Grate the orange zest and mix it with ½ cup sugar in a large mixing bowl. Coarsely chop the walnuts and add them to the bowl.

3. Put the eggs in a food processor fitted with the metal blade. With the motor on, add the oil to the eggs in a thin stream. Add the remaining sugar and process until mixed. Stir the egg mixture into ingredients in the bowl.

4. Quarter the strawberries, or cut them into sixths if large, and set them aside. Sift together the flour, baking soda, and 1 teaspoon salt. Add one-third of the flour mixture to the bowl, and put one-third of the strawberries on top of the flour mixture, spreading to coat them lightly with the dry

ingredients. Fold berries into the batter until smooth. Repeat to incorporate all the dry ingredients and strawberries into the batter.

5. Divide the batter between the loaf pans. Bake 1 hour to 75 minutes, or until a cake tester inserted into center of loaves is withdrawn clean. Cool 30 minutes. Loosen, then remove breads carefully from pans, as strawberries tend to make the breads stick. Cool breads on cake racks to room temperature. Serve at room temperature. (Can wrap and refrigerate up to 3 days, or freeze up to 3 weeks.)

"We may say of angling as Dr. Boteler said of strawberries: 'Doubtless God could have made a better berry, but doubtless God never did.' . . ."

—IZAAK WALTON

APPLE CRISP

Old-fashioned desserts like this one invariably add a homey, almost nostalgic, ending to a meal. For maximum effect, serve this lukewarm—when the puddles made from apple juices bubbling up through the crisp topping are still moist and sticky.

While the streusel topping makes this sufficiently sweet, you may want to add a scoop of vanilla ice cream or frozen yogurt. It is equally good with whipped cream, or unadorned.

FLEXIBLE MENU SUGGESTIONS

This dessert is included in menus based on Pasta with Four Cheeses (page 132), Smoked-Salmon Pizzas (page 110), Risotto Spinacciola (page 174), Pork and Vegetable Salad Orientale (page 210), One-Side Grilled Fish (page 216) with Tomato Butter (page 220) or Whole-Grain Mustard-Chive Butter (page 277), Sage-Rubbed Veal Chops (page 242), Hickory-Grilled Baby Back Ribs (page 259), or Garlic-Rubbed Chicken (page 278). *Makes 6 to 8 servings*

MACERATION: 12 HOURS
PREPARATION: 25 MINUTES
BAKING: 35 MINUTES

¼ *cup firmly packed raisins*
¼ *cup dark rum*
¼ *pound chilled unsalted butter, cut in 8 pieces*
1 *cup packed dark brown sugar*
¾ *teaspoon cinnamon*
¼ *teaspoon ground nutmeg*
1 *cup unbleached all-purpose flour*
4 *tablespoons softened unsalted butter*
2 *pounds tart green apples, peeled, cored, halved*
2 *tablespoons lemon juice*
¼ *cup granulated sugar*
1 *tablespoon vanilla extract*

1. Put raisins in a jar and add the rum. Cover and let stand overnight (raisins will keep in jar indefinitely).

2. Put the butter, brown sugar, cinnamon, and nutmeg in a food processor fitted with the metal blade. Pulse until the mixture has the consistency of coarse meal. Add the flour and pulse until the texture is sandy. Wrap and refrigerate for the topping.

3. Adjust oven rack to middle position. Heat oven to 375 degrees. Use 2 tablespoons of the softened butter to coat a 13 × 9 × 2-inch nonreactive dish or other shallow 3-quart heatproof baking dish.

4. Cut the apple halves into ¼-inch-thick slices. Heat the remaining butter in a large skillet. Add the apples, lemon juice, sugar, and vanilla. Cook over low heat, stirring frequently, until the liquid evaporates. Drain the raisins, reserving the rum. Stir raisins into the skillet.

5. Carefully warm the rum over a low flame, ignite, and pour over the apple mixture, shaking the pan until the flame subsides. Transfer the mixture to the baking dish and smooth it into an even layer; refrigerate for 15 minutes. Sprinkle the topping evenly over the fruit. Bake until the topping is browned and set, about 35 to 40 minutes. Cool to lukewarm before serving.

BAKED STUFFED APPLES

During the fall, when apples should be at their sweetest and best, this dessert is simplicity itself. I always use Rome Beauties for baking. According to the International Apple Institute, the Rome Beauty originated in Ohio, and was named in 1832 for the Rome township in which the first tree was planted. Today, the apples are produced (and therefore available) throughout the U.S. and Canada.

FLEXIBLE MENU SUGGESTIONS

This is a good dessert for menus based on earthy main courses such as Sausage and Artichoke Pizzas (page 108), either of the calzones (pages 116 to 119), One-Side Grilled Fish (page 216) with Orso Butter (page 221), Mushroom and Prosciutto-Stuffed Chicken Breasts (page 274), Garlic-Rubbed Chicken (page 278), or Veal Scallops with Black Olive Gremolada (page 286).

Unless there is a conflict in the menu, a small amount of Quick Custard Sauce (page 443), whipped cream, Mascarpone, or zesty crème fraîche can be served with the apples.
Makes 6 servings

PREPARATION: 20 MINUTES
BAKING: 1 HOUR 15 MINUTES

½ cup (4 ounces) firmly packed raisins
Boiling water
6 large Rome Beauty apples, rinsed, cored
½ cup (2 ounces) shelled walnut halves
⅔ cup sugar
1 teaspoon cinnamon
⅛ teaspoon nutmeg
3 slices white bread
2 tablespoons Calvados or brandy
4 tablespoons unsalted butter

1. Put the raisins in a heatproof dish, cover them with boiling water, and set them aside to plump, about 10 minutes. Using a sharp knife, cut a spiral pattern ⅛-inch deep into each apple skin, working from top to bottom. Set apples aside.

2. Coarsely chop the walnuts, transfer them to a bowl, and mix them with the sugar, cinnamon, and nutmeg. Process the bread slices to crumbs; add them to the bowl. Drain and add the raisins to the bowl, along with the Calvados or brandy. Toss well.

3. Adjust oven rack to lowest position. Heat oven to 325 degrees. Use 1 tablespoon butter to generously coat the bottom of baking dish large enough to hold apples snugly; set the dish aside.

4. Fill each apple snugly with stuffing, pushing a ½-tablespoon chunk of butter down into the top of the stuffing in each apple. Pour 1 cup water into the baking dish, and cover the dish with aluminum foil.

5. Bake 20 minutes. Remove the foil and baste apples with the liquid. Bake 50 to 55 minutes longer, basting every 15 minutes. Cool apples to lukewarm before serving (can cover and refrigerate overnight, then warm before serving).

CREME BRULEE

Perhaps it is the "fire and ice" quality of silky chilled custard resting beneath a warm sugar glaze that gives Crème Brulée its mystique and irresistible quality. Once you get it right, this is an easy dessert to make, but a good deal of frustration can be avoided by knowing what can go wrong—secrets that were revealed to me in the kitchen of New York's Le Cirque restaurant, which was the source for this recipe.

The single most important factor is finding the right dishes. Each should hold ½ cup of liquid, and be no more than ¾ inch high. I have had best results with straight-sided, rimless, scalloped, oval French porcelain baking dishes, which can be purchased from cookware stores and restaurant supply houses. These are thick enough to insulate the custard, and shallow enough to let it bake quickly into a thin, even layer. They also permit you to put the crèmes very close to the hot broiler for caramelizing, and the closer the better.

Once baked, crèmes can be refrigerated for 2 days. Before caramelizing the tops, it is important to dry the surface of each completely by blotting it gently with paper towels (do this even if it does not look moist).

When glazing, watch the tops carefully. It may be necessary to turn or rotate the dishes (I often put them on a dry jelly-roll pan for easy handling). Should the custards soften after glazing, refrigerate them for 30 minutes (the sugar will be slightly less crisp than just-glazed crèmes, however.)

FLEXIBLE MENU SUGGESTIONS

This dessert is included in menus based on Chinese Chicken Salad (page 207), Pork and Vegetable Salad Orientale (page 210), One-Side Grilled Fish (page 216) with Tomato Butter (page 220) or Winter Pesto (page 227), Mesquite-Grilled Cornish Hens (page 240), Leg of Lamb with Oriental Seasoning (page 251), Yogurt and Spice-Marinated Leg of Lamb (page 252), Skewered Lamb with Curry and Fruit (page 254), Mushroom and Prosciutto-Stuffed Chicken Breasts (page 274), Garlic-Rubbed Chicken (page 278), Szechwan Pepper Ribeyes (page 288), Pork with Port Wine Sauce (page 292), and Garlic-Roasted Leg of Lamb (page 295). *Makes 6 servings*

DRYING: 24 TO 48 HOURS
PREPARATION: 10 MINUTES
BAKING: 20 TO 40 MINUTES
CHILLING: 4 HOURS

½ cup dark brown sugar
3 cups whipping cream
6 egg yolks
½ cup granulated sugar
1 vanilla bean

1. Spread brown sugar in a thin layer in a cake pan. Dry it near the pilot light in the oven for 24 hours, or set it aside at room temperature for 48 hours, raking the sugar frequently with your fingers to remove lumps. Strain the sugar, discard lumps, and store the sugar in an airtight container until you are ready to glaze the custards. (Sugar keeps indefinitely.)

2. Adjust oven rack to lowest position. Heat oven to 350 degrees. Line a jelly-roll pan or a shallow roasting pan with a thin cloth towel. Put six shallow, ungreased, ½-cup heatproof ramekins on the towel in the pan; set aside.

3. Whisk ⅓ cup of the cream with the egg yolks in a medium, heatproof bowl, then whisk in the sugar. Heat the remaining 2⅔ cups cream in a medium saucepan just until warm—do not let it simmer—and slowly whisk it into the sugar mixture. Strain the liquid through a fine sieve. Slit open the vanilla bean and scrape the soft inside into the custard mixture.

4. Stir custard well to evenly distribute the vanilla flecks, then pour or ladle it into ramekins, stirring the custard each time. Pour ¼ inch hot tap water into jelly-roll pan, or enough to come halfway up the outside of the ramekins. Bake 20 to 25 minutes, until custard is just set. Remove custards from water bath and set aside to cool. Refrigerate 4 hours. (Can cover and refrigerate up to 48 hours. Blot top of custards with paper towel to remove condensation before glazing.)

5. At serving time, sprinkle 1 tablespoon of the dried brown sugar in an even layer on each custard. Put dishes on a dry jelly-roll pan under a hot broiler or salamander, as close as possible to heat source. Watch dishes carefully, turning as necessary, until sugar caramelizes, about 30 seconds. Serve immediately.

ORANGE CREME BRULEE Omit the vanilla bean. Strip off the zest of two medium oranges with a vegetable peeler and heat them with the cream. Cover and let the custard stand with the orange zest for 10 minutes before straining (discard the zest).

THE MIRACLE IN MILAN

My first encounter with Mascarpone (or Mascherpone) took place in an ideal location: the cheese counter at Peck, the premier food store in Milan. I had read numerous recipes that called for this ultrarich dessert cheese in several of my Italian cookbooks, and after tasting a scrumptious Tirami Su for the first time in Manuelina restaurant, in Recco on the Italian Riviera, I wanted to sample the cheese on its own. At the time, it was not yet available in this country.

After the first spoonful of what appeared —at first glance—to be crème fraîche, I realized that Mascarpone was not actually a cheese at all: it was the most marvelous concentrated sweet cream I had ever tasted.

Legend has it that this cream originated centuries ago in the town of Lodi, in Lombardy, where it still is mass-produced today. However, the finest examples of this cream are reputed to be made from cow's milk from the fertile area around Sondrio, just northeast of Lake Como.

While it is sometimes called a double cream, basically, it is a full-fat, heavy cream with the whey removed. The butterfat content hovers near 70 percent.

Mascarpone was first imported in 1979. Today, it is available across the country in plastic tubs. There is no commercially made substitute, and over the years I have experimented with homemade mixtures of heavy cream and cream cheese, or heavy cream and ricotta cheese, with disappointing results. Recently, I came up with a simple solution.

Homemade Mascarpone

Prepare the cream at least 5 hours in advance. It can be refrigerated overnight in an airtight container. *Makes about 1 pound (2 cups)*

PREPARATION: 10 MINUTES
STANDING: ABOUT 4 HOURS
CHILLING: 1 HOUR

3 cups heavy cream
2 tablespoons lemon juice

1. Let the cream stand at room temperature for 30 minutes. Stir in the lemon juice, and continue stirring until the mixture thickens to the consistency of sour cream, about 2 to 3 minutes.

2. Line a large Melitta-type plastic drip-coffee filter apparatus with a paper coffee filter, or a double thickness of damp cheesecloth. Add the thickened cream and let it stand in a cool place at room temperature until the cream thickens enough to hold its shape around the side, about 2 hours.

3. Carefully stir to bring the still-liquid cream from the center of the filter to the edge. Let the cream stand until ⅔ to ¾ cup of whey has drained and the cream is thickened to spreading consistency, about 2 hours longer. Discard the whey. The "Mascarpone" is ready to use.

LEMON TIRAMI SU

"Lift me up" is the lyrical translation for *tirami su,* the Italian version of an English trifle, flavored with espresso and chocolate. This dessert is said to have originated in Lombardy, although it is made and served throughout northern Italy. *Tirami su* became popular in New York Italian restaurants shortly after Mascarpone (see page 428) was first brought to the U.S. in 1979.

This Lemon Tirami Su is one of my favorite desserts. Dry ladyfingers (called *savoiardi,* or champagne egg biscuits) are moistened with lemon syrup, then layered with Mascarpone and lemon curd. After overnight refrigeration, the ladyfingers soften to the texture of sponge cake, and the dessert is ready to serve.

FLEXIBLE MENU SUGGESTIONS

This dessert is included in menus based on Pasta with Broccoli Raab (page 134), Agnolotti (page 142), Scallion and Black Pepper Lasagne with Black Olive Pesto (page 144), Milanese Beef Stew (page 185), Bollito Misto (page 188), One-Side Grilled Fish (page 216) with Fresh Herb Butter (page 219) or Tomato Butter (page 220), Shrimp and Scallops with Chile-Peanut Sauce (page 232), Sage-Rubbed Veal Chops (page 242), Capretto with Lemon and Rosemary (page 246), Leg of Lamb with Niçoise Seasoning (page 248), Yogurt and Spice-Marinated Leg of Lamb (page 252), Scampi alla Busara (page 272), Herb- or Curry-Rubbed Chicken (pages 278 and 282), Garlic-Roasted Leg of Lamb (page 295), or Cognac-Marinated Beef Fillet (page 298). *Makes 8 servings*

PREPARATION: 45 MINUTES
COOKING: 10 MINUTES
REFRIGERATION: OVERNIGHT

LEMON SYRUP

¼ cup sugar
1 medium lemon
3 tablespoons dark rum
2 tablespoons vodka

LEMON CURD

3 to 4 medium lemons
¾ cup sugar
2 teaspoons cornstarch
4 eggs
Salt
4 tablespoons softened butter

CREAM LAYER

3 eggs
7 tablespoons sugar
1 pound Mascarpone (page 428)
¼ cup whipping cream

ASSEMBLY

1 package (7 to 8 ounces) dry ladyfingers

1. For the syrup, mix the sugar and 1 cup water in a small nonreactive saucepan. Cover and heat to simmering, stirring several times to be sure the sugar dissolves. Cover and cook over low heat for 5 minutes. Strip off the lemon zest with a sharp knife,

Continued

add zest to the pan, cover, and set aside until the syrup cools. (Reserve lemon for other uses.) Stir in rum and vodka. Strain the syrup and discard the lemon zest.

2. For the lemon curd, finely grate the zest of two lemons into a large, heavy, nonreactive saucepan. Stir in the sugar and cornstarch. Squeeze and add ⅔ cup lemon juice, then whisk in the eggs and ⅛ teaspoon salt. Add the butter and whisk the mixture over low heat until it thickens to a puddinglike consistency, about 6 minutes. Transfer lemon curd to a heatproof bowl and cover with plastic wrap directly touching the surface; cool.

3. For the cream layer, separate the eggs. Whip the whites to soft peaks and gradually add 3 tablespoons of the sugar, whipping until the whites reach firm peaks; set aside. Whisk the Mascarpone with the egg yolks, remaining ¼ cup sugar, and cream, and continue to whisk until smooth. Fold the Mascarpone mixture thoroughly into the beaten egg whites.

4. To assemble the pudding, dip ladyfingers into the lemon syrup and use them to snugly line the bottom of an 8-cup baking or gratin dish. (Snap off pieces of ladyfingers to make them fit as necessary.) Spread half the lemon curd over the ladyfingers. Top with half the Mascarpone mixture. Repeat dipping and layering ladyfingers (reserve remainder for garnish). Spread remaining lemon curd over the ladyfingers and top with Mascarpone. Refrigerate 30 minutes.

5. Put remaining ladyfingers into a clean, dry food processor fitted with the metal blade and process to crumbs. Sprinkle crumbs over top of the pudding. Cover and refrigerate overnight.

ALMOND AND LEMON-STUFFED PEARS

Over the years, this has been one of the most successful desserts in my repertoire. The pears can be prepared in advance (making them trouble-free at serving time), and the burgundy-colored sauce adds both a perfect tart/sweet flavor and a dramatic pool of background color. A paste of ground almonds, lemon zest, and Italian macaroons *(Amaretti di Saronno),* packed into hollowed-out fruit, is such a delicious surprise that guests tend to eat these right down to their stems.

The recipe is a perfect partner for a fabulous dessert wine or Champagne, since both are compatible with every one of its ingredients, and it is particularly low in fat.

Amaretti are small, hard Italian cookies made from eggs, sugar, and bitter almonds (which are actually apricot pits). Legend has it that these macaroons were invented by Giuseppe Lazzaroni in 1718 in the small town of Saronno, near Milan, on the occasion of a papal visit. The cookies are now made in America; medium-size *amaretti* are used here.

FLEXIBLE MENU SUGGESTIONS

These pears are excellent for menus based on Country Pork Terrine (page 90), Onion and Chèvre Tart (page 104), Pasta with Tomato-Seafood Sauce (page 124), Pasta with Milanese Meat Sauce (page 130), Pasta with Broccoli Raab (page 134), Agnolotti (page 142), Milanese Asparagus Soup (page 162), Risotto Spinacciola (page 176), Milanese Beef Stew (page 185), and One-Side Grilled Fish (page 216) with Fresh Herb Butter (page 219), Orso Butter (page 221), Roasted Garlic and Saffron Butter (page 222), or Whole-Grain Mustard-Chive Butter (page 277). They also go wonderfully with Sage-Rubbed Veal Chops (page 242), Capretto with Lemon and Rosemary (page 246), Leg of Lamb with Niçoise Seasoning (page 248), Scampi alla Busara (page 272), Mushroom and Prosciutto-Stuffed Chicken Breasts (page 274), Garlic-Rubbed Chicken (page 278), Veal Scallops Giardino (page 284), and Veal Scallops with Black Olive Gremolada (page 286). *Makes 6 servings*

PREPARATION: 25 MINUTES
COOKING: 45 MINUTES
COOLING: 3 HOURS

1 bottle (3½ cups) dry red wine, preferably
  French Burgundy
1 cup port wine
⅓ cup sugar
2 strips (each 2 inches long) lemon zest
¼ teaspoon cinnamon
1 tablespoon lemon juice
6 medium Bosc or Anjou pears (2½ pounds),
  peeled, with stems left intact

FILLING

Zest of 1 small lemon
2 tablespoons sugar
¼ cup whole blanched almonds or pine nuts
3 ounces (about 14 medium) Italian
  macaroons
1 tablespoon lemon juice

Continued

1. Put the red wine, port wine, sugar, lemon zest, cinnamon, and lemon juice in a non-reactive 4-quart soup kettle or Dutch oven. Stir well and add the pears. Cover and heat to simmering. Set cover slightly ajar and poach pears at a slow simmer for 20 minutes. Test to be sure a sharp knife meets no resistance when inserted in the thickest part. If still resistant, cook 5 minutes; test again (very firm pears may poach as long as 45 minutes).

2. Carefully remove and cool pears. Strain the cooking liquid into same kettle, or into a large, nonreactive skillet. Cook uncovered over medium heat, stirring occasionally, until the liquid reduces to 1¼ cups, about 20 minutes. Refrigerate sauce until serving time. (Can wrap and refrigerate pears and sauce overnight.)

3. For the filling, grate the lemon zest and mix it with the sugar in the container of a food processor fitted with the metal blade. Add the almonds and cookies and process until the mixture is finely ground, about 30 seconds. Add the lemon juice and process until a paste forms.

4. To core and stuff pears, slice off enough of each pear bottom to make it stand evenly on a plate. Holding each pear gently in one hand, and using a small sharp knife, carefully hollow out a cone-shaped section from the bottom, removing the seeds and pith. Take care not to cut pear apart or pierce through to the outside. Pack the hollow centers firmly with the cookie paste. Cover and refrigerate the pears (up to 8 hours).

5. At serving time, pour sauce evenly over pears, allowing it to pool on each plate. Serve chilled or at room temperature.

The filling for the poached pears can be varied. Orange zest and juice may be substituted for lemon, and hazelnuts or walnuts could replace the almonds. Plain butter cookies could stand in for the dry macaroons. In contrast to a relatively dry stuffing, a creamy mixture based on Mascarpone (page 428) and a small amount of sugar, or a combination of rum-soaked raisins and sweetened ricotta cheese also would be a good choice.

LEMON-PRALINE SOUFFLE GLACE

A tart frozen lemon soufflé, layered with a surprising crunch of almond-flecked meringues, is a marvelous formal French dessert that I first tasted at Lutèce restaurant in New York. This recipe is adapted from one that was included in a *New York* magazine entertaining article.

The dessert is easier to make than it may appear, and will remain in perfect condition in the freezer for several days. It can be presented in individual (1-cup) soufflé dishes, or in a single 2-quart mold. For either presentation, be sure to make the meringue layers slightly smaller than the interior of the dishes.

For best results with the recipe, you will need to have a pastry bag with a plain tip to pipe the meringues, a small natural-bristle (not plastic) pastry brush, and a candy thermometer to verify the temperature of the sugar syrup used in the lemon soufflé base.

FLEXIBLE MENU SUGGESTIONS

Entrées with a French spirit such as Sausages and Sauerkraut (page 186), Scallop and Basil-Stuffed Sole (page 265), Leg of Lamb with Niçoise Seasoning (page 248), Mushroom and Prosciutto-Stuffed Chicken Breasts (page 274), Roasted Duck with Apples and Campari (page 289), or Cognac-Marinated Beef Fillets (page 298) are the linchpins of menus in which this soufflé is included. It provides a soothing ending for spicier menus based on Duck and Sausage Gumbo (page 158), Baked Curried Beef (page 201), Leg of Lamb with Oriental Seasoning (page 251), or Skewered Lamb with Curry and Fruit (page 254). *Makes 8 servings*

PREPARATION: 1 HOUR
BAKING: 2 HOURS
FREEZING: 24 HOURS

MERINGUE LAYERS

1½ cups (6 ounces) blanched almonds
1 cup sugar
5 egg whites

LEMON SOUFFLE

Zest of 3 medium lemons
1¾ cups sugar
⅔ cup lemon juice
1 teaspoon white corn syrup
2 eggs
8 egg yolks
1 quart chilled whipping cream
Fresh strawberries, raspberries, or candied
   lemon zest

1. Adjust oven rack to lowest position. Heat oven to 200 degrees. Line two baking sheets with parchment paper; set aside.

2. For the meringue layers, put the almonds and ¼ cup sugar in a food processor fitted with the metal blade, and process until almonds are ground; set aside. With an electric mixer or balloon whisk, whip the egg whites to soft peaks, while gradually adding the remaining ¾ cup sugar. Continue whipping until the whites are shiny and firm. Fold in the ground almonds.

3. Transfer the meringue mixture to a pastry bag fitted with a plain tip. For eight individual soufflés, pipe sixteen meringue disks, each ½ inch smaller than the inside

Continued

diameter of a 1-cup soufflé dish. For a single soufflé, pipe three disks, each ½ inch smaller than the inside diameter of a 2-quart soufflé dish. Bake until meringues are crisp and lightly colored, about 1½ to 2 hours. (Can store in airtight container for 1 week.)

4. Put a 3½-inch-tall parchment or wax-paper collar around the soufflé dish (or each dish) and secure it with tape; set aside.

5. For the soufflé, grate the lemon zest into a bowl and stir in ½ cup sugar. Squeeze, strain, and set ⅔ cup lemon juice aside.

6. Put the remaining 1¼ cups sugar, corn syrup, and 1 cup water into a medium non-reactive saucepan and heat to simmering. Stir with a metal spoon. Cover and cook 5 minutes. Uncover, and with a pastry brush dipped in cold water, clean the sides of the pan to remove sugar crystals. Boil the sugar mixture to hard-ball stage, 260 degrees.

7. While the sugar syrup cooks, beat the eggs and egg yolks with an electric mixer until pale and fluffy, 7 to 8 minutes, then beat in the zested sugar. With the mixer running, carefully pour the hot syrup into the egg mixture, and continue beating until bottom of bowl is cool. Beat in the lemon juice.

8. Whip cream to firm peaks; fold it into the cooled lemon mixture in three batches.

9. To assemble the soufflé, layer as follows: ¼ of the lemon mixture, one meringue, ¼ of the lemon mixture, another meringue, half the remaining lemon mixture, the third meringue, and the remaining lemon mixture. For small soufflés, divide the lemon mixture into thirds and layer it with two meringues in each dish. Freeze dishes overnight. To serve, remove collar from the dish(es). Garnish soufflés with fresh fruit or candied lemon zest. Serve immediately.

FROZEN FRUIT FINESSE

Sorbet is easy and relatively quick to make from a wide variety of fruits. The flavor and texture will depend on the sweetness of the fruit, the proportion of puree to sugar or sugar syrup, and the method by which it is frozen.

Fruit ice can be made by combining a puree of fruit juice and pulp with a simple syrup (sugar cooked briefly with water), or by dissolving sugar in fruit juice and churning that mixture to a creamy consistency.

The fastest way to make sorbet is to use an ice-cream freezer—some electric models accomplish this in 15 to 20 minutes, or less. An alternate method using the food processor is given in the recipes that follow. While it is substantially more time-consuming, it produces fine results for cooks who do not own ice-cream freezers.

Ideally, sorbet should be churned and eaten just at the moment it emerges from an ice-cream freezer, when the texture is smooth, silky, and just soft enough to be scooped but still hold its shape. However, I have had very good results freezing sorbet half a day in advance, packing it snugly into airtight plastic storage containers (which will prevent ice crystals from forming), and keeping it frozen until serving time.

Mixtures churned in ice-cream freezers generally remain stable if frozen overnight, while those churned in the food processor can become grainy or separate after 12 hours. As a remedy, try to reconstitute a sorbet by reprocessing for a minute or two, then freezing again—unfortunately, the procedure is not foolproof.

PINK GRAPEFRUIT SORBET

This ice has a lovely pastel color and is far less sweet than many other flavors. Since pink grapefruits are in season during the winter months, this sorbet can be a refreshing finale to substantial meals. Ruby-red grapefruit juice may be substituted.

FLEXIBLE MENU SUGGESTIONS

This recipe is included in menus based on Smoked-Salmon Pizzas (page 110), Spicy Homestyle Beef Soup (page 160), One-Side Grilled Fish (page 216) with Tomato Butter (page 220) or Bouillabaisse Sauce (page 228), Shrimp and Scallops with Chile-Peanut Sauce (page 232), Soy-Marinated Chicken (page 238), Halibut with Warm Vinaigrette (page 268), Scallop and Basil-Stuffed Sole (page 265), and Mushroom and Prosciutto-Stuffed Chicken Breasts (page 276). The exotic Coconut-Lime Tuiles (page 440) are a good match for the sorbet. *Makes 1 quart*

PREPARATION: 30 MINUTES
COOKING: 5 MINUTES
FREEZING: VARIABLE

1 quart fresh pink grapefruit juice
1 cup sugar

1. Combine grapefruit juice and sugar in a small nonreactive saucepan. Heat to simmering, stirring constantly. Cover and simmer 5 minutes. Uncover and refrigerate until chilled.

2. Pour mixture into a cake pan. Cover with plastic and freeze until half set. (Or, transfer mixture to an ice-cream maker. Follow manufacturer's directions for freezing and omit steps 3 and 4.)

3. In a food processor fitted with the metal blade, process the partially frozen sorbet mixture for 1 minute (it may be necessary to do this in two batches), then return it to the cake pan and freeze until three-quarters firm.

4. Reprocess sorbet for 1 minute. Return mixture to pan and freeze until three-quarters firm. Reprocess 2 minutes. Pack the sorbet into an airtight container and freeze until firm enough to scoop or spoon, usually 4 to 6 hours.

EMBELLISHING ICES

Those of us who eat out a great deal are accustomed to seeing ice creams and sorbets presented in pretty, formally worked-out arrangements with one, or even two sauces, cookies, miniature tarts, cake slices, or little fruit bouquets. While the results are often dazzling, these plates do require a considerable amount of advance planning, and a quick and artistic hand.

A handsome presentation for ice cream and sorbet is the standard oval, or *quenelle,* made by using a specially shaped scoop (available in many kitchen and restaurant supply stores), or by working the mixture with two large spoons (vegetable serving spoons are often a good size for this).

Icy ovals are easy to position on plates that have been set up in advance, particularly when fresh fruit has been cut and attractively arranged. Whether a salad or a dinner plate is used will depend on the number and type of added elements. Fruit compote also makes a colorful garnish, and the small amount of liquid replaces the need for a separate sauce.

While I am not fond of sauce with sorbet, certain sauces are delicious with ice cream. Depending on the strength of their flavors, combinations such as Quick Custard Sauce (page 443) and either Bittersweet Chocolate Sauce (page 400) or Caramel Sauce (page 444) can be delightful. They can be used in equal amounts, or one can dominate while the other is added as a garnish.

Perhaps the most straightforward and conventional approach is to scoop ice cream or sorbet into graceful coupe champagne or red wine glasses. (I try to avoid plopping ices into clunky cereal bowls, or trivializing them by presenting tiny portions or trendy mini-scoops.) A judicious amount of sauce should cushion ice cream or sorbet in the glass, rather than cover it.

In addition to presenting cookies, consider crushed *amaretti,* chopped chocolate-covered candies, Caramelized Nuts (see page 413), thin wedges of sponge cake (page 390), candied citrus peel, and small pieces of fresh fruit as other ice-cream and sorbet embellishments.

BLACK PLUM SORBET

Something magical happens when black Friar plums are cooked with sugar syrup, then pureed. The skins not only act as a colorant, tinting the pale flesh of the fruit a vivid orange-rose, but also disintegrate during cooking, creating tiny little flecks that give character to this delicate summer sorbet.

FLEXIBLE MENU SUGGESTIONS

The recipe is included in menus based on Onion and Chèvre Tart (page 104), Soy-Marinated Chicken (page 238), Smoked-Salmon Pizzas (page 110), Spicy Homestyle Beef Soup (page 160), One-Side Grilled Fish (page 216) with Roasted Garlic and Saffron Butter (page 222) or Bouillabaisse Sauce (page 228), Mushroom and Prosciutto-Stuffed Chicken Breasts (page 274), or Herb-Rubbed Chicken (page 278). *Makes 1 quart*

PREPARATION: 20 MINUTES
COOKING: 30 MINUTES
FREEZING: VARIABLE

1 cup sugar
2 pounds black Friar plums, pitted, quartered
2 tablespoons lemon juice
2 tablespoons plum brandy or vodka

1. Combine the sugar with 1 cup water, the plums, and the lemon juice in a medium nonreactive saucepan. Heat to simmering, stirring frequently. Simmer slowly, uncovered, until plum skins color the mixture and their flesh softens completely, about 30 minutes. Cool.

2. Puree the plum mixture with the brandy in a food processor fitted with the metal blade. Pour the mixture into a cake pan. Cover with plastic and freeze until half set. (Or, transfer mixture to an ice-cream maker. Follow manufacturer's directions for freezing and omit steps 3 and 4.)

3. Reprocess the partially frozen mixture 1 minute (it may be necesssary to do this in two batches). Return it to the pan and freeze until three-quarters firm.

4. Reprocess sorbet for 1 minute. Return mixture to pan and freeze until three-quarters firm. Reprocess 2 minutes. Pack the sorbet into an airtight container and freeze until firm enough to scoop or spoon, usually 4 to 6 hours.

BANANA ICE CREAM

To capture the intensity of fresh bananas in this ice cream, make it from very ripe fruit with dark skin and soft, fragrant interiors. One very ripe plantain, which has a strong flavor, can be substituted for a banana.

The cooked ice-cream base can be prepared and chilled in advance, but once the bananas are pureed, the ice cream should be frozen immediately to avoid discoloration.

FLEXIBLE MENU SUGGESTIONS

Banana Ice Cream is equally good with Caramel Sauce (page 444) or Instant Hot Fudge Sauce (page 401). The ice cream is included in menus based on Duck and Sausage Gumbo (page 158), Chilaquiles (page 195), Chinese Chicken Salad (page 207), One-Side Grilled Fish (page 216) with Whole-Grain Mustard-Chive Butter (page 277), Grilled Ceviche (page 231), Soy-Marinated Chicken (page 238), Leg of Lamb with Oriental Seasoning (page 251), Yogurt and Spice-Marinated Leg of Lamb (page 252), and Garlic-Rubbed Chicken (page 278). *Makes 8 servings*

PREPARATION: 15 MINUTES
COOKING: 20 MINUTES
FREEZING: ABOUT 20 MINUTES

4 egg yolks
½ cup sugar
2 cups milk
2 cups half-and-half
1 whole vanilla bean, split lengthwise
2 tablespoons dark rum
4 very ripe bananas (1¼ pounds), peeled
1 tablespoon lemon juice

1. Put egg yolks, sugar, and ½ cup milk into a large, nonreactive saucepan and whisk to mix the ingredients. In a separate saucepan, heat the remaining milk to simmering, and slowly whisk the hot milk into the egg-yolk mixture. Stir in the half-and-half and vanilla bean.

2. Put the saucepan over low heat and stir until the mixture thickens to the consistency of heavy cream and coats the back of a spoon, about 10 to 15 minutes. Strain it into a mixing bowl (discard vanilla bean). Set the bowl over ice and stir until the custard is chilled. Add the rum. (Can cover and refrigerate up to 2 days.)

3. Put the bananas and lemon juice into a food processor fitted with the metal blade, and process until pureed. With the motor on, pour 2 cups of the chilled custard slowly into the banana puree. Stir the banana mixture thoroughly into the remaining custard.

4. Immediately transfer mixture to the canister of an ice-cream maker and freeze according to manufacturer's directions. Serve immediately, or transfer ice cream to an airtight freezer container, seal, and keep frozen until serving time. (Can freeze for several hours.)

POMEGRANATE GRANITA

Eat the pomegranate, for it purges the system of envy and hatred," are words attributed to the prophet Mohammed—no small surprise since this fruit has been cultivated throughout Asia, Africa, and Europe since ancient times.

The sweet, tart, rosy red juice from pomegranate seeds freezes beautifully for this granita, which belongs to the family of European frozen desserts that includes sorbets and sherbets. However, granitas have a coarse, grainy texture that contrasts vividly with the smoothness of sorbet, and the name comes from *grano,* Italian for "kernel" or "grain."

Each spoonful of granita should contain distinct particles of flavor that dissolve slowly in your mouth, a texture that is similar to a snow cone. The mixture can be frozen in a cake pan, then chopped with the aid of a metal pastry scraper, or it can be frozen and chopped in the food processor to a slushy, granular texture.

To obtain a quart of pomegranate juice, you will need about eight large fruits, which are cut crosswise and squeezed with a citrus juicer, like an orange. Press gently so the bitter flavor of the white pith does not go into the juice, and discard the shell that remains after squeezing.

FLEXIBLE MENU SUGGESTIONS

This recipe is included in menus based on Smoked-Salmon Pizzas (page 110), One-Side Grilled Fish (page 216) with Fresh Herb Butter, Tomato Butter, Orso Butter, Whole-Grain Mustard-Chive Butter, or Winter Pesto (pages 219, 220, 221, 277, and 227); also, Sage-Rubbed Veal Chops (page 242), Halibut with Warm Vinaigrette (page 268), Mushroom and Prosciutto-Stuffed Chicken Breasts (page 274), Herb-Rubbed Chicken (page 278), Garlic-Roasted Leg of Lamb (page 295), and Cognac-Marinated Beef Fillet (page 298). *Makes 1 quart*

PREPARATION: 30 MINUTES
COOKING: 5 MINUTES
FREEZING: VARIABLE

1 quart fresh pomegranate juice
1 cup sugar
1 to 3 tablespoons lemon or grapefruit juice,
    to taste
1 tablespoon vodka

1. Strain the pomegranate juice into a non-reactive saucepan. Stir in the sugar and heat to simmering. Cover and simmer 5 minutes. Uncover and refrigerate until cool. Stir in lemon juice to taste and the vodka.

2. Pour mixture into a cake pan. Cover with plastic and freeze until half set. Insert the metal blade in a food processor. Process the partially frozen mixture in two batches for about 30 seconds. Return to the pan and freeze until it is three-quarters firm.

3. Cut the mixture into ice-cube-size pieces. Pulse to chop finely. Return the mixture to the pan and freeze, stirring frequently. The mixture will have a slushy, granular texture. Cover and freeze until the granules solidify, usually 2 to 4 hours, stirring occasionally. Spoon the granita into wine glasses or sherbet cups to serve.

COCONUT-LIME TUILES

Saddle-shaped almond cookies that are a fixture in most French restaurants have been adopted —albeit in different guises—as one of the "fancy" cookies American restaurants often serve with sorbet and ice cream. Here is an exotic version with toasted coconut and lime zest.

Tuiles are easy to make once you get the knack of spreading each spoonful of batter carefully into a circle so that the bits of coconut and lime zest are evenly distributed over the cookies, then removing the extremely thin, hot circles from their baking sheets and very quickly shaping the cookies by pressing them over the top of a rolling pin.

Since these cookies harden as they cool, it may take a batch or two to develop a method for handling them. When hot, they are extremely delicate, and nonstick baking sheets (which should still be buttered and floured) are a big help.

FLEXIBLE MENU SUGGESTIONS

Tuiles are good to serve with fresh fruit, Banana Ice Cream (page 438), or sorbets (pages 435 and 437). They are included in menus based on Four-Vegetable Tart (page 100), Duck and Sausage Gumbo (page 158), Chilaquiles (page 195), Shrimp and Scallops with Chile-Peanut Sauce (page 232), One-Side Grilled Fish (page 216) with Fresh Herb Butter (page 219), Yogurt and Spice-Marinated Leg of Lamb (page 252), Halibut with Warm Vinaigrette (page 268), and Garlic-Roasted Leg of Lamb (page 295). *Makes 4 to 5 dozen*

PREPARATION: 30 MINUTES
BAKING: 25 MINUTES

½ cup (1½ ounces) sweetened shredded
  coconut
1 medium lime
⅓ cup sugar
3 egg whites, at room temperature
Pinch salt
Pinch cream of tartar
2½ tablespoons flour
2 tablespoons whipping cream
4 tablespoons melted, cooled butter
¼ teaspoon coconut extract
1 teaspoon Cognac

1. Adjust oven rack to lowest position. Heat oven to 325 degrees. Spread the coconut on a jelly-roll pan. Bake until toasted, turning frequently, about 10 minutes; set aside.

2. Butter and flour four baking sheets (preferably nonstick); set aside. (A single baking sheet or two sheets may be used, then washed, rebuttered, and floured.)

3. Finely grate the lime zest and mix it with the sugar; set aside. (Reserve lime for other uses.)

4. Mix the egg whites with salt and cream of tartar in a medium bowl and whip them with an electric mixer or whisk until the egg whites are opaque and nearly hold their shape in soft peaks. Stir in the zested sugar, flour, cream, butter, coconut extract, Cognac, and the toasted coconut.

5. Stir the batter well and drop heaping teaspoons of it onto a baking sheet at 3-inch intervals (six cookies per sheet). Use the

back of a spoon to spread each portion of batter into thin 2-inch disks. Bake until lightly colored, 8 to 10 minutes.

6. While cookies bake, set a rolling pin on a work surface. Transfer the baking sheet from the oven to a cake rack. Working quickly, remove baked cookies one by one from the sheet by gently freeing and lifting each with a flat flexible metal spatula. Quickly press each cookie (top-side up) over the rolling pin to form the saddle shapes—they will harden immediately. (If cookies harden on the baking sheet, return it to the oven for 30 seconds or just until cookies soften, then continue removing them from the sheet.)

7. When crisp, remove shaped cookies to a cake rack. Repeat to bake and shape all the cookies, stirring batter well between each batch to prevent it from separating and thinning. Cool cookies to room temperature. Store in an airtight tin. (Can store 3 to 5 days; however, cookies may become sticky and chewy rather than crisp.)

MIXED NUT SABLES

In the culinary world, the term *sablé* has nothing to do with a fur coat. Rather, it is a French word that refers to the fine, sandlike texture of nutty butter cookies such as these. The baked "sandies" can be served plain, or partially dipped in chocolate (an optional step). Either way they are perfect partners for fresh fruit, ice cream, or sorbet.

FLEXIBLE MENU SUGGESTIONS

These cookies are included in menus based on Four-Vegetable Tart (page 100), Onion and Chèvre Tart (page 104), Country-Style Risotto (page 176), Spicy Homestyle Beef Soup (page 160), Penne with Broccoli and Scallops (page 206), Chilaquiles (page 195), One-Side Grilled Fish (page 216) with Tomato Butter or Bouillabaisse Sauce (pages 220 and 228), Soy-Marinated Chicken (page 238), and Chili-Rubbed Chicken (page 278). *Makes 5 dozen*

PREPARATION: 30 MINUTES
BAKING: 12 MINUTES

½ cup shelled walnut pieces
½ cup shelled pecans
2 cups unbleached all-purpose flour
½ pound plus 2 tablespoons butter, cut in cubes
1½ teaspoons vanilla extract
½ teaspoon lemon juice
1 egg
⅔ cup sugar

CHOCOLATE DIP (OPTIONAL)

¼ pound semisweet chocolate, cut in ½-inch chunks
2 tablespoons vegetable oil

1. Put the walnuts, pecans, and flour in a food processor. Process until the nuts are fine; set aside.

2. Put ½ pound of the butter, the vanilla, lemon juice, and egg into the processor and pulse to chop the butter coarsely. Pulse in the sugar. Add the nut mixture and pulse until the dough begins to clump.

3. Adjust oven rack to middle position. Heat oven to 350 degrees. Lightly coat a baking sheet with some of the remaining butter.

4. Put the dough into a cookie press (spirals work well). Press out cookies, 1 inch apart, on the buttered baking sheet. Bake one sheet at a time until a light ring forms around the edge of each cookie, about 10 to 12 minutes. Cool on cake rack. Repeat to use remaining butter for the baking sheets and to bake all the cookies. Cool, then transfer cookies to airtight storage containers. (Can store in refrigerator 1 week.)

5. Optional: For the chocolate dip, melt the chocolate with the oil (see page 378). Cover a baking sheet with wax paper. Dip half of each cookie into melted chocolate; shake off excess. Put cookies on wax paper. Repeat to dip all cookies, reheating chocolate as necessary. Refrigerate until chocolate sets, about 15 minutes, then store as indicated above.

QUICK CUSTARD SAUCE

Rich, silky custard sauce, known as crème anglaise, is usually made by cooking egg yolks, sugar, and half-and-half until the mixture thickens to a consistency that will lightly coat the back of a spoon.

For this quick method, the cooking begins just as soon as the simmering half-and-half and cream mixture (in which sugar has been dissolved) is added to the egg yolks. Provided the liquid is as close as possible to simmering, the sauce cooks perfectly in an instant without stirring it on the stove, and it will thicken slightly as it cools.

If you wish to make the sauce slightly less rich, substitute half-and-half for the cream, and cook the sauce on top of the stove in a nonreactive saucepan following directions for Banana Ice Cream (page 438).

To give the sauce an orange, lemon, or lime flavor, add the zest of the fruit to the hot custard, and let stand until the custard cools; then discard zest. Spirits and liqueurs such as dark rum, Grand Marnier (orange), Kirsch (cherry), Framboise (raspberry), or Frangelico (hazelnut) can be added to flavor the sauce. Additionally, coffee beans can be crushed and steeped in the half-and-half mixture, then strained and discarded before making the sauce.

FLEXIBLE MENU SUGGESTIONS

Custard sauce is always wonderful with fresh fruit such as strawberries, raspberries, or blueberries, and with pound cake or sponge cake. It also can accompany other desserts, and the recipe is included in menus based on Pasta with Milanese Meat Sauce (page 130), Pork and Vegetable Salad Orientale (page 210), One-Side Grilled Fish (page 216) with Fresh Herb Butter or Winter Pesto (pages 219 and 227), and Chili-Rubbed Chicken (page 278). The sauce can be served with Peach Turnover (page 418), Mixed Berry Cobbler (page 420), or Baked Stuffed Apples (page 425). *Makes 1½ cups*

PREPARATION: 15 MINUTES

⅓ cup sugar
1 cup half-and-half
½ cup whipping cream
7 egg yolks
1 teaspoon vanilla extract or liqueur

1. Combine sugar with half-and-half and cream in a saucepan and stir well. Heat to simmering, then cover pan and turn off heat.

2. Put the egg yolks in a food processor fitted with the metal blade. Reheat the half-and-half mixture to simmering. With the motor on, immediately add the simmering liquid to the egg yolks in a slow, thin stream. Cover the machine and let the hot mixture stand for 5 minutes.

3. Strain the contents of the processor container into a storage container or mixing bowl; set custard aside to cool. (Can cool mixture quickly by putting custard into a metal mixing bowl and placing bowl over ice. Stir custard frequently.) Stir in vanilla. Cover and refrigerate (up to 3 days).

CARAMEL SAUCE

There is something quite addictive about the flavor of caramel, and this sauce in particular—I prefer to eat it by the spoonful, straight from its container.

If you know precisely how to handle hot sugar mixtures, making caramel sauce is a snap, and the instructions in the recipe should help head off any problems. For best results, use a stainless steel or unlined copper saucepan, and be sure to rinse the side of the pan with a wet natural-bristle pastry brush (plastic bristles will melt) to prevent the formation of sugar crystals that can cause the syrup to seize.

As a rule, I do not recommend stirring sugar syrups while they cook. Metal utensils conduct heat away from the mixture, and the hot sugar mixture often will draw flavors out of wooden spoons, or absorb a woody taste. Instead, swirl the mixture gently on the stove. Until you are comfortable with caramel mixtures, a candy thermometer is indispensable for verifying the temperature of the syrup.

FLEXIBLE MENU SUGGESTIONS

Caramel Sauce is superb with Banana Ice Cream (page 438), store-bought ice creams, and plain cake. In addition, it is included in menus based on Chinese Chicken Salad (page 207), One-Side Grilled Fish (page 216) with Citrus Salsa or Whole-Grain Mustard-Chive Butter (pages 226 and 277), Grilled Ceviche (page 231), Leg of Lamb with Oriental Seasoning (page 251), and Garlic-Rubbed Chicken (page 278). *Makes 2 cups*

PREPARATION: 10 MINUTES
COOKING: 20 MINUTES

2 cups sugar
½ cup water
1 cup whipping cream

1. Combine sugar and water in a medium nonreactive saucepan and stir to mix thoroughly. Heat to simmering. Cover and simmer 5 minutes.

2. Uncover and rinse the side of the pan with a wet pastry brush to remove sugar crystals. Swirl mixture gently over medium heat until sugar turns a rich brown and registers 320 degrees on a candy thermometer, about 10 to 12 minutes.

3. Off heat, carefully and gradually whisk in cream until mixture is smooth. Cool to room temperature, stirring occasionally. Caramel will thicken as it cools, and is ready to use or to transfer to an airtight container and refrigerate. (Can refrigerate up to 2 weeks.) Serve at room temperature, or warm the sauce to pouring consistency.

TIDBITS:
HORS D'OEUVRES AND CANAPES

S ome time ago, I went through a "purist" phase when I thought it was unnecessary to serve hors d'oeuvres before dinner. The rationale was that my energies were better put into cooking the meal than fussing over tidbits, but the plain truth was that I didn't have the patience to scoop out the insides of cherry tomatoes, split and stuff pea pods, or pipe cheese dip down the center of endive leaves.

My mistake was apparent one evening, when I noticed a guest looking around—as if something were missing—within fifteen or twenty minutes after his arrival. Clearly, he was hungry. I later learned that he had not eaten lunch, and I began to feel inconsiderate for adding to his discomfort.

Just a bite of something good to nibble with a glass of wine or a drink *is* an expected and essential detail, be it as fancy as a Caviar Tartlet (page 460), or as simple as Spiced Nuts (page 447) or Oil-Marinated Olives (page 63). And whether these snacks are served hot or cold, finger foods are a practical solution.

While I never serve wedges of cheese before dinner—it is simply too fattening and filling—I do like hors d'oeuvres that are based on cheese, or on spice. Both ingredients are used abundantly in this handful of recipes. This is also the place to use a luxurious ingredient such as caviar, or a buttery loaf of Black Pepper Brioche (page 352), to good advantage, or to introduce a little-known food such as polenta (Italian cornmeal), which can be used in place of bread beneath a simple herbed cheese spread.

I try to limit the number of predinner snacks to one or two, and serve dinner within forty-five minutes to an hour after the last guests have arrived. After all, I'm giving a dinner party, not a cocktail party.

CHILI-SPICED NUTS

CURRY-SPICED NUTS

TWO-CHEESE QUESADILLAS

CHUTNEY TOASTS

POLENTA DIAMONDS

GOAT CHEESE AND CHIVE GOUGERE

Black Pepper Brioche Canapés

SMOKED-FISH RILLETTES

CHICKEN SATE WITH A TASTE OF TOKYO

WILD RICE BLINI

Taking a Chance on Caviar

CAVIAR TARTLETS

CHILI-SPICED NUTS

No matter what I serve with cocktails before a dinner party, I always pass bowls of these chili-spiced nuts or the curry version that follows. Pecans are my first choice for either recipe, since the spices tend to cling to the natural grooves in the nutmeats; walnuts are a good alternative.

FLEXIBLE MENU SUGGESTIONS

These nuts are included in a menu based on Duck and Sausage Gumbo (page 158).
Makes 1 pound

PREPARATION: 10 MINUTES
BAKING: 1 HOUR

1 pound pecans or walnuts
2 tablespoons chili powder
2 teaspoons ground cumin
¼ teaspoon garlic powder
¼ teaspoon onion powder
¼ teaspoon salt

1. Adjust oven rack to lowest position. Heat oven to 250 degrees. Heat 3 quarts water to boiling in a large soup kettle. Add nuts and boil 30 seconds. Drain.

2. In a large mixing bowl combine all spices and mix thoroughly with the hot nuts. Empty the contents of the bowl onto a baking sheet and spread the nuts into an even layer. Bake 1 hour. Cool. Nuts are ready to eat or pack into airtight storage containers. (Can freeze 1 month.)

CURRY-SPICED NUTS

Substitute the following ingredients for the spices in the recipe for Chili-Spiced Nuts. Yield, amount of nuts, and recipe instructions are all identical to the chili version.

2 tablespoons hot curry powder (page 203)
½ teaspoon onion powder
¼ teaspoon garlic powder
¼ teaspoon ground coriander
¼ teaspoon ground cardamom
¼ teaspoon salt
¼ teaspoon ground white pepper
⅛ teaspoon cinnamon
⅛ teaspoon cloves

TWO-CHEESE QUESADILLAS

Cheese-stuffed tortillas are called *quesadillas* in Mexico (*queso* means "cheese" in Spanish), but these snacks make no claim to authenticity. They are simply quick and easy to serve before a very informal meal, particularly a barbecue. Chile aficionados may want to use a whole jalapeño (page 198) instead of half, or if a fresh chile is not available, a hot-pepper Jack cheese can be substituted for the Monterey Jack. The quantity of chili powder and cumin also may be adjusted to taste.

FLEXIBLE MENU SUGGESTIONS

Consult menus based on Mesquite-Grilled Cornish Hens (page 240), Chili and Garlic-Rubbbed Flank Steak (page 245), Chili-Rubbed Chicken (page 278), and Cognac-Marinated Beef Fillet (page 298). *Makes 8 servings*

PREPARATION: 15 MINUTES
COOKING: 8 MINUTES

3 medium scallions, roots removed
½ cup packed cilantro leaves
½ jalapeño pepper, cored and seeded
¼ pound Monterey Jack cheese, chilled
¼ pound sharp cheddar cheese, chilled
½ teaspoon chili powder, or Ancho Chile
* Powder (page 194)*
¼ teaspoon ground cumin
1 package (10 ounces) flour tortillas (6-inch
* diameter)*
4 tablespoons vegetable oil

1. Slice the scallions into thin rings. Chop the cilantro, mince the jalapeño, and mix the two together; set aside. Shred and mix the cheeses together. Mix the chili powder and cumin together in a small bowl.

2. To assemble the quesadillas, put ½ cup of the mixed shredded cheeses on a tortilla, leaving a blank ½-inch border around the edge. Sprinkle 1 tablespoon scallions, 1 tea-spoon cilantro mixture, and ⅛ teaspoon of the spice mixture on top of cheese. Cover with a second tortilla.

3. Repeat to fill all tortillas. (Can put filled tortillas between sheets of wax paper, wrap in plastic, and refrigerate overnight.)

4. Heat 1 tablespoon vegetable oil in a large skillet or on a griddle. Cook the quesadillas 2 to 3 minutes per side, over medium heat, until the cheese melts and tortillas are lightly browned. Transfer quesadillas to paper toweling, blot to remove excess oil, then cut each into six wedges. Serve immediately. (Quesadillas can be kept warm between paper-towel-lined sheets of aluminum foil— do not wrap tightly—in a 200-degree oven.)

CHUTNEY TOASTS

Everyone asks my friend Lindy Grobler for this recipe, which she has served at countless dinner parties. These canapés freeze beautifully (on a plastic-wrapped cardboard round), defrost quickly, and hold up well if left out on a buffet or cocktail table. They are great to have on hand to serve with drinks or wine.

Homemade chutney (page 337 or 338) makes the most delicious toasts, although store-bought mango chutney can be substituted.

FLEXIBLE MENU SUGGESTIONS

These canapés are included in menus based on Duck and Sausage Gumbo (page 158), Curry-Rubbed Chicken (page 278), and Roasted Duck with Apples and Campari (page 289).
Makes 4 dozen

PREPARATION: 45 MINUTES
BAKING: 3 MINUTES

18 slices white bread
½ pound sharp cheddar cheese, chilled
1 cube (1-inch square) peeled onion
1 egg
1 tablespoon flour
⅛ teaspoon baking powder
4 ounces cream cheese, at room temperature, cut into chunks
½ cup fruit chutney

1. Toast the bread, remove the crusts, quarter each slice, and set it aside. Shred and set the cheese aside.

2. Mince the onion in a food processor fitted with the metal blade. Add the egg and process until mixed. Add the flour, baking powder, and cream cheese, and process until smooth. Add the shredded cheese and pulse until the mixture forms a smooth paste.

3. Spread bread squares lightly with some of the chutney liquid. Put 1 teaspoon cheese mixture on each bread square and spread it into a low mound.

4. Cut solid chunks of chutney into ½-inch pieces. Put one piece into center of each cheese mound and transfer the canapés to a baking sheet. (Can chill in refrigerator then wrap and freeze on cardboard rounds. Defrost in refrigerator before cooking.)

5. Adjust oven rack or broiler pan 4 inches from heat source. Broil until cheese mixture puffs slightly and becomes mottled-brown. Serve hot or warm.

POLENTA DIAMONDS

The Italian technique of boiling yellow cornmeal, pouring it onto an oiled surface, and cooling it to room temperature produces a lovely cornmeal "sheet" that easily can be cut into geometric shapes. Like toast points, these polenta triangles or rectangles can be grilled, sautéed with garlic and olive oil, or deep-fried to use as a garnish for meat, game, or sausage dishes.

Here, the cooled cornmeal is cut into small diamonds and spread with an herbed goat-cheese mixture. Strips of red bell pepper (or sun-dried tomato) brightly garnish hors d'oeuvres that are colorful, delicious, and different.

The easiest way to cook polenta is in the microwave; otherwise, it requires continual stirring for 20 minutes. If lumps form, simply transfer the cooked mixture to a food processor and give it a whirl. In Italian food stores, cornmeal for polenta ranges from fine to coarsely ground; I prefer to use the fine-textured meal. Cornmeal sold in supermarkets for cornbread also works perfectly. For information on goat cheese, see page 141.

FLEXIBLE MENU SUGGESTIONS

This recipe is included in a menu based on Milanese Asparagus Soup (page 162) and Capretto with Lemon and Rosemary (page 246). Polenta Diamonds can precede a majority of the Italian-inspired menus. *Makes about 70*

PREPARATION: 30 MINUTES
COOKING: ABOUT 20 MINUTES
COOLING: ABOUT 1 HOUR

POLENTA

1 tablespoon olive oil
1½ cups yellow cornmeal
Salt and ground black pepper

TOPPING

1 medium scallion, trimmed, cut in 1-inch
  lengths
½ pound cream cheese, cubed
¼ cup whipping cream
¼ pound fresh goat cheese, rind or coloring
  removed
1 tablespoon minced parsley
1 tablespoon minced fresh chives
Salt (optional)
1 red bell pepper, cored and seeded

1. Line the inside of a 15 × 10-inch jelly-roll pan with heatproof plastic wrap, brush the plastic with oil, and set the pan aside.

2. Mix the cornmeal with 6 cups of cold water, 2½ teaspoons salt, and ¼ teaspoon pepper in a microwavable 3-quart casserole. Stir well. Cover and microwave on high power for 8 to 10 minutes. Uncover and stir well. Microwave on high power for 8 to 10 minutes longer, stir once again, then microwave for 5 to 6 minutes, until the cornmeal has thickened and is thoroughly cooked. Let the mixture stand for 3 minutes. Carefully pour the hot cornmeal mixture onto the jelly-roll pan. Use a spatula to spread it into an even layer in the pan; set it aside to cool.

3. For the cheese topping, mince the scallion in a food processor fitted with the metal blade. Add the cream cheese, whipping cream, and goat cheese; process until smooth. Pulse in parsley, chives, and ⅛ teaspoon pepper. Taste and adjust the seasoning, adding salt if necessary (goat cheese should make the mixture sufficiently salty).

4. Line a clean baking sheet with plastic wrap. Invert the cooled sheet of polenta over the plastic wrap. Remove and discard the original plastic. Use paper towels to blot any excess oil off the cornmeal layer. Spread cheese mixture into an even layer over the polenta. Refrigerate 30 minutes. (Can cover and refrigerate overnight.)

5. With a wet, sharp, thin knife guided by a ruler, trim edges of the polenta so the rectangle measures 14 × 9 inches. Then, with a damp knife, cut the layer lengthwise into nine 1-inch-wide strips. Cut across the strips diagonally at 1½-inch intervals to form diamonds.

6. Cut the bell pepper into narrow julienne strips, then cut each strip crosswise into ½-inch-long segments. Garnish each cheese diamond with a strip of red pepper. Transfer diamonds to a serving platter. Serve at room temperature.

The size of polenta granules determines the texture of the cornmeal sheet from which diamonds are cut for the base of the hors d'oeuvres. However, the cooled cornmeal has a pliable, slightly rubbery consistency that makes it easy to cut. If you wish to make it crisper before adding the cheese topping, blot off any excess oil with a paper towel and dry the triangles slightly by toasting them under the broiler.

GOAT CHEESE AND CHIVE GOUGERE

A cheesy ring of golden pastry puffs, *gougère* is quintessential cocktail fare and a natural partner for wine and spirits. When made with goat cheese and chives, this pastry has an exceptionally tangy flavor. The ring presents well on a platter, a leaf-lined cheese basket, or even on a cutting board. It can be made in advance and frozen, but should always be served warm.

FLEXIBLE MENU SUGGESTIONS

This recipe is included in a menu based on Milanese Asparagus Soup (page 162). It also can be served before other menus that do not contain abundant amounts of starch or cheese. *Makes 6 to 8 servings*

PREPARATION: 20 MINUTES
BAKING: 35 MINUTES

4¼ tablespoons chilled unsalted butter, cubed
¾ cup unbleached all-purpose flour
Salt
½ pound fresh goat cheese, rind removed if
    necessary
3 eggs
2 tablespoons fresh snipped chives, or minced
    scallion green
1 egg yolk mixed with 1 teaspoon milk

1. Put butter and ¾ cup water in a large saucepan and heat to boiling. Off heat, stir in flour and ⅛ teaspoon salt. Return the pan to medium-low heat and knead the dough with a wooden spatula or spoon until it tightens and makes a light film on the bottom of the pan, about 4 to 5 minutes.

2. Transfer the hot dough to a food processor fitted with the metal blade. Add the cheese. Break eggs into measuring cup with a pouring spout. With the motor running, pour the eggs into the dough one at a time. Process until the dough is evenly mixed.

Pulse in the chives. The dough will be thick, gluey, and sticky.

3. Adjust oven rack to middle position. Heat oven to 425 degrees. Line a baking sheet with parchment paper and secure the paper to the sheet with a dab of dough at each corner; smooth the paper.

4. Draw an 8-inch circle on parchment as a guideline. Make a ring by dropping ¼-cup mounds of dough, with edges touching, over the pencil circle. There should be about fourteen mounds of dough.

5. Glaze the dough ring by dipping a finger into the egg-yolk mixture and smoothing the tops of the dough mounds. Bake 35 minutes, or until puffed and lightly browned. Remove the dough ring from the parchment with a pancake turner, taking care not to break it. Serve warm by pulling the puffs apart. (Or can cool, wrap, and freeze on cardboard round 2 weeks. Unwrap and defrost at room temperature; reheat until warm before serving.)

BLACK PEPPER BRIOCHE CANAPES

A loaf of Black Pepper Brioche (page 352) can be thinly sliced and made into sandwiches that are cut in quarters or sixths and used as open-face or sandwich-style canapés. Ideas for fillings (thinly sliced) and condiments include:

- Honey-baked ham or Genoa salami with honey mustard (available in specialty food stores).

- Prosciutto or Black Forest ham with sweet butter.

- Fresh mozzarella (page 64) sliced and dipped in Anchovy-Lemon Oil (page 63) and garnished with strips of drained dried tomatoes (page 118) or small fresh basil leaves.

- Thinly sliced imported Fontina or Gruyère cheese with ham or salami and Fresh Herb Butter (page 219).

- Herbed goat cheese (page 450).

- Herbed goat cheese beneath smoked salmon.

- Golden whitefish caviar with cream cheese.

- Cold roasted pork or smoked chicken with Mixed Plum Chutney (page 338) or mango chutney.

- Smoked Fish Rillettes (page 454) or steak tartare.

- Mortadella with Fresh Herb Butter (page 219).

- Thinly sliced avocado with Orso Butter (page 221).

SMOKED-FISH RILLETTES

A combination of fresh and smoked fish makes an interesting and delicious spread with the consistency of a soft pâté, similar to the traditional French *rillettes* made of pork. The choice of fish will influence both the flavor and color: smoked salmon and a white-fleshed fish such as scrod will give this a delicate pink color and a light taste, while sable and scrod will yield a smokier mixture. Smoked and fresh salmon also can be used together.

Green peppercorns make the rillettes very spicy. If you plan to serve this with Black Pepper Brioche, omit the peppercorns and double the chives.

FLEXIBLE MENU SUGGESTIONS

This recipe is included in menus based on Halibut with Warm Vinaigrette (page 268) and Scallop and Basil-Stuffed Sole (page 265). *Makes 8 servings*

PREPARATION: 30 MINUTES
COOKING: 5 MINUTES

1¾ pounds fresh scrod, monkfish, or salmon fillets
2 tablespoons dry white wine
½ cup ricotta cheese
1 tablespoon drained, rinsed green peppercorns
¼ pound unsalted butter, softened, cubed
2 tablespoons fresh snipped chives
Salt and ground white pepper
¾ pound smoked sable, whitefish, or salmon
French bread or Black Pepper Brioche (page 352)

1. Cut the fresh fish into 2-inch chunks and put it in the basket of a vegetable steamer. Put 2 cups of cold water and the wine in a large saucepan with a tight-fitting lid. Insert the steamer, cover, and steam until fish is cooked and just turns opaque throughout, about 4 to 5 minutes. Set the fish aside in the basket to cool, then pick it over to remove any bones; refrigerate. Simmer the steaming liquid until it reduces to ¼ cup; set aside to cool.

2. Knead the ricotta cheese in a cloth towel to remove as much of the moisture as possible, until the cheese holds together like dough; set the cheese aside. Put the peppercorns and the butter in the container of a food processor fitted with the metal blade. Process until the butter is fluffy. Add the ricotta and process until smooth.

3. With the motor on, drizzle the reduced fish liquid into the cheese mixture. Pulse in the chives, ¼ teaspoon salt, and ⅛ teaspoon pepper.

4. Remove bones, skin, and any hard crust from smoked fish, and cut the fish into chunks—there should be ½ pound of smoked fish. Add all the fish to the processor and pulse until mixture resembles shredded crabmeat; do not puree.

5. Adjust seasoning to taste slightly salty. Transfer to a 4-cup terrine, or divide it between onion-soup bowls, or other serving dishes. Cover tightly with plastic wrap and refrigerate 6 hours (or up to 2 days) to ripen. Serve chilled rillettes with toasted bread.

CHICKEN SATE WITH A TASTE OF TOKYO

The notion of blending Western mayonnaise with Oriental flavorings—soy sauce, sesame oil, sake, and ginger—comes from my friend Cynthia Ash, who created this saté for her Chicago restaurant. The chicken can be served on short skewers, or removed and passed with the sauce and toothpicks or cocktail forks alongside, so guests can help themselves. (See page 208 for information on Oriental ingredients.)

FLEXIBLE MENU SUGGESTIONS

This recipe is included in menus based on Saga and Watercress Tart (page 106) and Four-Vegetable Tart (page 100). *Makes 12 servings*

PREPARATION: 45 MINUTES
MARINATION: 2 TO 24 HOURS
COOKING: ABOUT 12 MINUTES

3 whole chicken breasts, boned, skinned, split
2 medium garlic cloves, peeled
2 medium shallots, peeled
½ cup olive or vegetable oil
Salt and ground black pepper

SAUCE

1 medium garlic clove, peeled
½-inch cube ginger, peeled
2 egg yolks
1½ teaspoons Dijon mustard
1¼ cups mild olive oil or vegetable oil
3½ tablespoons sesame oil
3½ tablespoons rice vinegar
3 tablespoons soy sauce
2 tablespoons sake
Dash hot red pepper sauce
¾ teaspoon sugar

1. Soak twelve bamboo skewers in warm water for 30 minutes; drain. Slice chicken breasts into 1-inch-wide strips, then cut them crosswise to make 1-inch cubes. Thread chicken cubes on the skewers.

2. Mince the garlic and shallots and transfer to a rectangular glass baking dish. Stir in the oil, ⅛ teaspoon salt, and ⅛ teaspoon pepper, then add the chicken skewers. Cover and refrigerate 2 to 24 hours, turning skewers occasionally.

3. For the sauce, mince the garlic and ginger in a food processor fitted with the metal blade. Add egg yolks and mustard. Process, adding the oils in a very slow stream until the mayonnaise begins to thicken, then add oil in a thin stream.

4. Add vinegar, soy sauce, sake, hot red pepper sauce, and sugar to the mayonnaise mixture and adjust the sauce to a pourable consistency by adding up to 4 tablespoons hot water, if necessary. Adjust seasoning with hot red pepper sauce; refrigerate.

5. Remove skewers from the marinade and pat the chicken dry. Grill or broil, turning the skewers once, until the chicken is just cooked through, about 8 to 10 minutes. Serve immediately. (Chicken skewers can be kept warm in a 200-degree oven.)

WILD RICE BLINI

Blini, the small Russian yeast-raised pancakes, have a wonderfully nutty taste when wild rice is pureed and added to the batter. I like to make these about the size of silver dollars and cook them in big batches on a pancake griddle.

The recipe calls for 8 ounces of caviar as a topping for more than four dozen blini. If that seems like a troublesome quantity, reduce it to 4 ounces and stir the caviar into the sour cream topping rather than using it as a garnish. Fresh salmon caviar (see page 459) is my first choice here, but the less costly golden whitefish caviar or pasteurized salmon caviar are also suitable.

If caviar will break the budget, substitute a good-quality smoked fish such as salmon or sable (smoked black cod), smoked chicken, or small chunks of top-quality ham.

FLEXIBLE MENU SUGGESTIONS

These blini are included in menus based on Halibut with Warm Vinaigrette (page 268) and Roasted Duck with Apples and Campari (page 289). *Makes about 4½ dozen*

PREPARATION: 20 MINUTES
RISING: 1 TO 1½ HOURS
COOKING: ABOUT 1 HOUR

BLINI BATTER

4 ounces (⅔ cup) wild rice
Salt
1 large scallion, trimmed, cut in 1-inch
  lengths
Up to 1 cup milk
1 package dry active yeast
1½ to 1⅔ cups unbleached all-purpose flour
3 eggs, separated
1 tablespoon sugar
⅓ cup cream
1 egg white
Hot red pepper sauce
Vegetable oil

CAVIAR AND CREAM TOPPING

¼ red bell pepper, roasted, peeled, seeded,
  minced
1 tablespoon lime or lemon juice
1 tablespoon minced chives or cilantro
1 cup sour cream
Pepper
Hot red pepper sauce
8 ounces fresh salmon or golden whitefish
  caviar

1. For the batter, heat 2¼ cups water to boiling in a large covered saucepan. Add the rice and ⅛ teaspoon salt. Cover and simmer 45 minutes, until rice is completely tender. Strain the rice cooking liquid into a 2-cup measure and add enough milk to equal 1⅓ cups; set the milk mixture and the rice aside separately.

2. Mince the scallion in a food processor fitted with the metal blade. Add the cooked rice and process until it is finely chopped.

Add the yeast, 1½ cups flour, egg yolks, sugar, and cream. With the motor on, add the warm milk mixture and process until the batter is well mixed and thick (add the remaining flour if the batter seems thin).

3. Transfer the batter to a bowl, cover it with plastic wrap, and set aside until it doubles, about 1 to 1½ hours.

4. In a clean, dry bowl, whip all 4 egg whites with an electric mixer or whisk to firm peaks. Stir the risen batter well, season it with several dashes of hot red pepper sauce, and thoroughly fold in the egg whites. The resulting batter will be thick and elastic.

5. To cook the blini, brush a griddle or frying pan with oil and heat. Spoon level tablespoons of batter onto the griddle (to make 2-inch-diameter pancakes). Cook on medium heat until tops bubble. Turn and cook 2 to 3 minutes longer, until lightly browned. Blini are ready to garnish and serve. (Can cool, transfer to aluminum foil, wrap, and refrigerate overnight.)

6. For the topping, mix the minced red pepper, lemon juice, and chives into the sour cream. Season with salt, pepper, and hot red pepper sauce to taste. Cover and refrigerate until serving time.

7. If refrigerated, heat blinis to lukewarm in a slow oven (do not overheat blinis or cream topping will begin to melt). Top each warm blini with a heaping teaspoon cream mixture, and put a heaping ½ teaspoon caviar over the cream. Serve immediately.

"Pancakes are one of the oldest and most traditional of Russian dishes, dating back before the ninth century and the advent of Christianity."

—V. V. POKHLEBKIN

TAKING A CHANCE ON CAVIAR

Caviar, one of the world's most luxurious foods, adds a particular note of festivity to a dinner party, whether it is offered in abundance, or as a modest garnish. Most commonly taken from sturgeon, salmon, or whitefish, caviar is lightly salted fish eggs.

While purchasing caviar should be a simple task, the variety of choices and the complexities of judging quality in relation to price make it a difficult subject to understand fully. In theory, you should get what you pay for. However, when it comes to caviar, that is not always the case. Price does, of course, vary greatly with the type, origin, and quality of the caviar; however, some can be surprisingly affordable.

SOME BASIC GUIDELINES

There is a traditional formula for making caviar. The eggs, called "berries," are extracted from female fish, and are carefully sieved to remove membranes. Then the berries are lightly salted—an important process that helps to determine quality. The term *malossol,* a Russian word that means "little salt," is used in the labeling of imported caviar. It also appears on domestic caviar labels (which is considered to be an affectation).

Top-quality fresh caviar should never taste salty or fishy. It should have a clean flavor and a slightly sweet aroma, and the berries should be firm, round, and lightly coated with their oil. Puckered, dimpled, or crushed berries are an indication of dehydration or improper handling.

Russian caviars are packed in 1.8-pound tins, then generally repacked in smaller jars. Because caviar deteriorates in contact with air, plan to use it within several days of purchase, and within 24 hours of opening the jar or tin. (Note that caviar cans are referred to as "tins.")

Caviar is sold fresh, pasteurized (or cooked), or "fresh frozen," depending upon the way the eggs are processed after packing. Pasteurized caviar (usually available in supermarkets) is subjected to high temperatures, and as a result the berries are quite firm, with a strong, or fishy, flavor. The quality varies from brand to brand, and artificially colored, pasteurized caviar (either black or red) should always be avoided. Frozen caviar can be identified by a firm, almost crunchy, texture.

IMPORTED STURGEON CAVIAR

Fresh, imported sturgeon caviar is generally considered to be best. There are several types, and many grades, each with a distinct flavor, berry size, and color. Most of the imported caviar currently available in the U.S. is of Russian origin, although keluga caviar is made from Chinese sturgeon roe.

The much-touted beluga refers to berries taken from beluga sturgeons from the Caspian Sea, which can weigh 1800 pounds and grow up to 14 feet long. Female belugas take 20 years to mature, making them relatively rare, and their eggs account for 10 percent of their body weight. Beluga caviar is light to dark gray in color, and the berries are the largest produced by sturgeon. Theoretically, beluga caviar that is graded 000 (according to the Russian system) should be the best quality, although this is not always guaranteed.

Osetra caviar is taken from sturgeons that mature in 12 to 15 years, and weigh about 200 to 600 pounds. Their roe is golden yellow to grayish-brown. There are four types of osetra caviar, and the "B" grade can look remarkably like beluga; generally, osetra berries are slightly smaller.

Sevruga sturgeon are most abundant because they mature in just 7 years. Their berries are gray, and can be about half the size of osetra caviar, but the eggs are intensely flavored.

AMERICAN CAVIAR

Domestic caviar is made from freshwater fish from the Great Lakes (both Canadian and American sides), Washington State, the Mississippi River, and the Tennessee Valley. The major domestic varieties are salmon, sturgeon, whitefish, and trout.

Top-quality, fresh salmon caviar is considered to be the best that America has to offer. The eggs are taken from 10- to 15-pound chum or keta salmon, and from coho or silver salmon that spawn during October and November and require 3 years to mature. Caviar is also made from the eggs of king or chinook Pacific salmon that weigh 10 to 50 pounds, mature in 5 to 7 years, and spawn in the spring. Top-quality fresh American salmon caviar can rival the best imported fresh salmon caviar, and often is an excellent choice for use in recipes.

Domestic sturgeon caviar is quite different from imported varieties, and in no way comparable. Because the production is small, this can be a difficult caviar to locate.

Whitefish and trout caviar is flash-frozen after processing; defrost it overnight in the refrigerator and use it immediately. Golden whitefish caviar, a trade name for natural (undyed) whitefish berries, is popularly priced.

CAVIAR TARTLETS

One, or even two types of caviar, plus a dab of sour cream, adds color and glamor to the tops of these bite-size, savory little cheesecakes. As an alternative to caviar, the tartlets can be garnished with small, whole shrimp that have been tossed with minced dill. A smoked-trout or other smoked-fish mousse mixture piped from a pastry bag is another good topping, or curled ribbons of smoked salmon can be put over some of the sour cream mixture used for Wild Rice Blini (page 456).

I prefer to mold the tartlets in mini-muffin tins with a nonstick coating. Four tins (each holds a dozen tartlets) will greatly speed up the work. The tins are available at cookware stores and at many hardware stores.

FLEXIBLE MENU SUGGESTIONS

The tartlets can precede menus that do not contain an abundance of cheese. *Makes 5½ dozen*

PREPARATION: 1 HOUR
BAKING: 20 MINUTES

CREAM-CHEESE PASTRY

2 to 2¼ cups unbleached all-purpose flour
Salt
½ pound frozen unsalted butter, cut in 16
  pieces
6 ounces cream cheese, cubed

FILLING

3 hard-cooked eggs, peeled and halved
¼ cup lightly packed parsley leaves
½ medium onion, peeled
¾ pound cream cheese, room temperature
2 tablespoons sour cream
3 eggs
Salt and ground black pepper
Hot red pepper sauce

TOPPING

Sour cream (optional)
8 ounces fresh salmon or golden whitefish
  caviar

1. For the pastry, put 1½ cups flour, ½ teaspoon salt, and the butter in a food processor fitted with the metal blade. Process until butter completely disappears. Add the cream cheese and another ½ cup flour; pulse until the dough begins to clump. Divide the dough into four pieces, and wrap each in plastic. Dough is ready to use or refrigerate. (Can wrap and freeze dough for 1 month.)

2. For the filling, finely chop the hard-cooked eggs and set aside. Mince the parsley and the onion, and set each aside. Put the cream cheese, sour cream, raw eggs, ½ teaspoon salt, ¼ teaspoon pepper, and several dashes of hot red pepper sauce in the container of a food processor fitted with the metal blade, and process until smooth. Mix in the chopped eggs, parsley, and onion.

3. Adjust oven rack to lowest position. Heat oven to 350 degrees.

4. On a lightly floured work surface, roll out one piece of dough to a 10-inch circle. Cut

out 3-inch rounds. Transfer the pastry rounds to cups of nonstick mini-muffin pans, pressing each neatly into a cup. Freeze 5 minutes. Save dough scraps, gently knead together, and reroll. Repeat cutting out and shaping dough rounds using all the dough.

5. Fill each pastry cup with a scant tablespoon of the cheese filling (cups should be three-quarters full). Bake until filling puffs and lightly browns, about 20 to 25 minutes. Cool 10 minutes and remove tartlets from pans. Repeat to bake all the tartlets.

6. Cool tartlets to room temperature and refrigerate them on a paper-lined baking sheet, covered with paper towels and plastic wrap, as long as overnight. (Can double-wrap and freeze up to 2 weeks. Thaw in refrigerator, warm 10 to 15 minutes in a moderate oven, then cool to room temperature.)

7. For the topping, spoon ½ teaspoon sour cream (optional) on top of each tartlet. Garnish each with a heaping ½ teaspoon caviar (or ¼ teaspoon each of two caviars, or other garnishes). Serve immediately.

"...Americans don't want to eat art; they just want to eat dinner."

—RUTH REICHL

INDEX

Seafood. *See also* Fish; Shellfish
  grilled
    about, 212–13
    avocado vinaigrette for, 224
    best fish for grilling, 216
    bouillabaisse sauce for, 228
    broiling as an alternative to grilling, 218
    ceviche, 231
    citrus salsa for, 226
    fresh herb butter for, 219
    one-sided grilled fish, 216
    orso butter, 221
    roasted garlic and saffron butter for, 222
    shrimp and scallops with chile-peanut sauce, 232
    thickness of fillets or steaks, 218
    tomato butter for, 220
    winter pesto for, 227
  salad of avocado, grapefruit, and, 58
  -tomato sauce, pasta with, 124
Seeds for greens and vegetables, sources for, 69
Serrano chile(s)
  about, 199
  -peanut sauce, shrimp and scallops with, 232
Serving styles, 18–19
Sesame dressing, for pork and vegetable salad
    orientale, 210
Sesame oil, about, 209
Sesame paste, about, 209
Shaohsing wine, about, 209
Shellfish
  cooking time and determining doneness, 218
  lobster, cold chicken-poached, 270
  mussel-tomato sauce, pasta with, 124
  to refrigerate, 218
  rinsing, 217
  scallop(s)
    about, 42
    and basil-stuffed sole, 265
    bisque, 42
    in ceviche, grilled, 231
    curry noodles with cilantro and, 146
    penne with broccoli and, 206
    and shrimp with chile-peanut sauce, 232
    -tomato sauce, pasta with, 124
  shrimp
    alla busara, 272
    in ceviche, grilled, 231
    and corn chowder, 46
    and curry risotto, 166
    mixed lettuces with ginger-lime vinaigrette and,
      68

Shellfish: shrimp *(cont.)*
    and scallops with chile-peanut sauce, 232
    -tomato sauce, pasta with, 124
Sherry vinegar
  about, 78
  -walnut vinaigrette, 78
Shoestring vegetables with whole-grain mustard,
    335
Shrimp
  alla busara, 272
  in ceviche, grilled, 231
  and corn chowder, 46
  and curry risotto, 166
  mixed lettuces with ginger-lime vinaigrette and,
    68
  and scallops with chile-peanut sauce, 232
  -tomato sauce, pasta with, 124
Sign of the Dove Restaurant, 69
Simon's hoisin sauce, 211
Smoked fish rillettes, 454
Smoked-salmon pizzas, 110
Snow pea(s)
  and bell pepper ribbons, 310
  guidelines for cooking, presenting, and saucing,
    317
Soft rolls, 364
Sole, scallop-and-basil-stuffed, 265
Sorbet
  about, 434
  black plum, 437
  pink grapefruit, 435
  presentation of, 436
Sorrel soup, cream of, 43
Soufflé
  lemon-praline, glacé, 433
  tart, almond, 414
Soup, 38–53
  about, 38–39
  curried vichyssoise, 48
  garnishes for, 53
  hearty
    about, 152–53
    asparagus soup, Milanese, 162
    beef soup, spicy homestyle, 160
    duck and sausage gumbo, 158
    Milanese minestrone, 156
  papaya-melon, 41
  scallop bisque, 42
  serving strategies for, 51
  shrimp and corn chowder, 46
  sweet potato and apple bisque, 45

PHOTOGRAPH CREDITS

Art Direction: Joel Avirom
Photography: Jerry Simpson
Stylist: Marianne Rohrlich
Food Stylist: Rick Ellis
All stores credited are located in New York City.

JACKET COVER

Dinnerware, flatware, and candlestick: Puiforcat
Linens: Anichini Linea Casa
Napkin ties: Bebe Winkler at Henri Bendel
Table accessories: Lyme Regis Ltd.

JACKET BACK

Plate: Puiforcat
Champagne flute: Lyme Regis Ltd.

FAVORING CURRY

Dinnerware and flatware: Adrien Linford
Wine glass: New Glass
Screen: Jim Dine

RUSTIC PIZZA

Pillows: Pierre Deux
Tumblers: New Glass

COLD CATCH

Chairs: Zona
Pillows and napkins: Sweet Nellie
Wine glasses: Toscany, Inc.
Candlestick: Eigen Arts
Cutlery: Keesal and Matthews

ALL THAT GLITTERS

Table surface: Sweetwater Studio,
    Ronkonkoma, NY
Vase: Incorporated Gallery
Champagne flutes: Zona
Chargers: Fitz and Floyd
Dinnerware: Rosenthal
Flatware: Christofle
Napkin: Liz Wain
Accessories: Adrien Linford

CHOCOLATE SUITE

Plate: Bloomingdale's